W9-CZJ-742

The Girl From Silicon Valley

Copyright 2015 *gloria jean Bodenmüller*

Editor *Joyce Arlene Grellmann*

Front cover oil by *gloria jean Bodenmüller*

ISBN # -13 978-1515359548 Library of Congress

The Master's Touch Publishing
www.christianbooks4children.com

Scripture is taken from the Holy Bible New International Version Copyright 1978 (Revised August 1983)

"Trust in the Lord with all your heart and lean not on your own understanding; in all your ways acknowledge Him and He will make your paths straight." Proverbs 3:5&6.

A note form the Author: i love hearing from my readers! So, please don't hesitate to write me at: gjbodenmuller@gmail.com Thank ewe and may the Lord bless ewe.

Printed in the U.S.A.

For my loving, patient husband: Fred. Our children, grandchildren, family and friends, who have played a great role in getting this book out to the public. A special thank you to Joan, who kept me on target during my early stages of vertigo. To Joe, with his gift of computer knowledge. And to my long-time, loving, patient sister-in-Christ: Joyce who did the final editing. Thank you for your love, prayers, dedication and believing in what the Lord has given me to accomplish for His glory.

"Be joyful always; pray continually; give thanks in all circumstances, for this is God's will for you in Christ Jesus." 1 Thessalonians 5:16-18.

Cover of "Our" Book

First and foremost i call it the 'cover of "Our" book,' the "Our" means; The Father, Son and the Holy Spirit helped us complete "Our" book.

i once heard two different Pastor's (including our's) say; the formative years 0-3, a child remembers most. In that period of time, they are weaned, learn to eat, drink, go potty, walk, talk and learn the basics of life, including shaping their faith. In that i refer to baby Moses and baby Samuel, who were both nurtured at their mother's breast for probably three years, according to Hebrew custom.

The picture, the Lord helped me paint for the cover of "Our" book, depicts the first 0-5 years of my life. When i thought about the cover, the Lord brought me back to this and helped me create it, just as i remember. i sit in awe at the outcome, it's amazing. As you read the story you will vision the chopping block, red wagon, buggy, clothes on the line, milk can, shack, outhouse and trailer; they will come to life, and of course the prune trees in Silicon/Santa Clara Valley. This was a bittersweet experience of my life. Enjoy!!!

About the Author

gloria jean is a gifted speaker and has written and illustrated seven Christian children's books; christianbooks4children.com . She has attended many writers groups, including Christian Writers Group at Mt. Hermon, California and she has earned a certificate in writing from Long Ridge Writers Group in Connecticut.

She and her husband Fred (Siegfried) have been married over forty-seven years and have two married sons and daughter-in-love's, and six grandchildren.

gloria jean, has led Bible Studies for over thirty years, taught Good News Clubs, Child Evangelism, served as a Deaconess, Women's Ministry President and taught Sunday School.

gloria jean is an entrepreneur, licensed Cosmetologist for over forty-five years, gardener, rancher, gourmet cook, artist, homemaker and helpmate. gloria jean and her granddaughter; Laurel, also performed with Steinway Artist; Steve Hall. She gives all glory to the Father, Son and Holy Spirit, for her many gifts.

gloria jean was born and raised in Silicon/Santa Clara Valley, and has a story to tell.

Gloria Bodenmuller

I've been friends with Gloria and her husband Fred for over 40 years, starting when we were neighbors in Redwood Estates, a small community in the Santa Cruz Mountains, about seven miles south of Los Gatos/San Jose.

Through good times and hard times she has stuck to her faith in Jesus, and always eager to share the word; she is a light in a world of darkness and salt in a tasteless world. Gloria is a ball of fire, full of an enthusiasm which is catching. Anyone meeting her for the first time can immediately feel they have a life-long friend.

When you read this book, you'll see that the trials and tribulations of her youth took off the rough edges of this diamond who has grown daily in her love for the Lord.

Gloria "walks the walk" and for 40 years I'm pleased to say their home has always been full of hospitality and laughter, all to the glory of God.

Hank Snyder
Beloved friend/newspaper reporter/brother-in-Christ

20 acres of land to roam, build tree forts, shoot guns, and ride motorcycles, four wheelers and bicycles. A kids dream come true! My brother and I were taught to work hard and play harder, and to put God first always. It wasn't always easy for me, but I am thankful my parents dragged us to church and instilled values like God, family and country. Today, I am the father of three awesome/crazy/frustratingly wonderful boys, a little girl on the way, and a husband to an amazing wife. I feel the values taught to me by my parents as a child gave me a Christ centered foundation upon which I can raise and lead my own family.

Franz Joseph Bodenmüller/ first born
Beloved son/husband/father/U.P.S. Driver/Pilot

November 7th 1979 I was the second and final child to join the Bodenmüller household! Through out my entire life I was raised in a Jesus loving Christian home. My dad is a real man and the best dad you could ever ask for! He raised my brother and I with a swift hand and demanded respect. He was very stern but yet the most loving father, listener and leader! My mother, like most mothers, is the glue that holds the family together. Her love for Jesus and her boys was unwavering! She had a lot on her plate but was always able to get things done and have food on the table, always with a smile! I have learned through my parents teachings and actions on how to live my life. I now have been blessed with a wonderful wife Lexie and two beautiful girls Laurel and Aubrey!

Jeffrey John Bodenmüller
Beloved son/husband/father/officer

> I love you and thank you for teaching me about Jesus. You have been like a mom to me. I am so glad you are in my life. I hope you know I will always be here with you in ♥. I hope that you feel better
>
> Love, Laurel

Beloved granddaughter; Laurel Shea Bodenmüller.

11/24/15

During the past four decades I have never seen Gloria without the sword of the spirit in her hand. When she comes knocking at your door — it's like one big party! Talk about a blessing. She not only has the scriptures in her hand, but colorful flowers, baked goods, hugs and lengthy conversations!

We have laughed, cried, prayed, and prayed some more. She has been a most faithful friend to me. I am so very proud for all she has accomplished in her life. She is truly a faithful servant of our Lord.

If you knew Gloria like I know Gloria, I am challenged with a paragraph. With her, I would need to write a novel! May God bless.

I love you sister

Beth Hollingsworth

Beth Hollingsworth: Beloved friend/ mother/ grandmother/legal secretary/sister-in-Christ

Encouraging One Another
HEBREWS 10:25

Mr and Mrs Bodenmuller,

Thank you so much for helping us head towards France. Thank you also for all of the lovely memories at your house over the years. Visiting you was always the most exciting part of our trips to California for us kids. I loved baking with you and hearing your stories and of course we all loved making ice cream in your old-fashioned bucket with the crank. I hope all is well with you both. Thanks again!

~Tiffany and Rayleen

It was so comfortable and enjoyable when Henry and I would visit you at your mountain home. Each time we drove over the cattle guard when entering your driveway, immediately I would experience feelings of peace. There were sensation was ons of joy and love surrounding me, which lasted until we again drove over the cattle guard as we headed for home. I use to think it because there was so much love in the Bodenmuller home. There was much love, yes, but now I know that I was feeling also, the presence of God

Eva: Beloved sister-in-Christ/homemaker/mother/grandmother.

In September 1994 I went to college to get away from Christians. One month later I got dynamically saved. One of the first persons I wanted to tell was Gloria Bodenmuller. I knew she would be happy with my having turned from darkness to light, especially since she had been one of few who had not stopped praying for me over the years.

As a new believer, being at a very liberal college was extremely challenging for me, especially since I was living in the dorms. I called Gloria almost every night, seeking fellowship, counsel, and comfort. Gloria's blood had been "Bible-ized" over the years, and so it was never too difficult for her to minister to me according to her rich Spirit-filled constitution. I once remember complaining to her, "all I have up here is Jesus!" Meaning that I had nothing else to rely on, since I was surrounded by so many ungodly students. Her response was simple and bold, "Yes, that's all you need!"

Gloria Bodenmuller lives by the Scriptures and faith alone. And she has inspired me to do the same. Thank the Lord for such a faithful servant of God!

Micky D.: husband/father/son-in-Christ

I met gloria jean in 1991, and we have been sister's in Christ ever since. I was not walking with our Lord at the time, and gloria, through our precious Jesus, brought me back to the fold lovingly. From the moment I met her, I knew she was someone I would be friends with for a long, long time. Her wonderful smile and warm personality is as attracting as a moth is to bright light at night. I am so glad we never lost touch through all the moving around I have done since we met. It has been a joy to watch her over the years, bring folks to Christ, offer a helping hand, a shoulder to cry on, and always reminding of the never failing love of our Lord and Savior, Jesus Christ, which was always first and foremost. gloria is the epitome of what a Christian should be. She walks the walk and talks the talk. She has had her share of challenges. From longtime friends and family turning their backs on her, to snake bites, to droughts, to several challenging illnesses, she has prevailed, and never, ever gave up hope, and through it all offered hope and encouragement to those around her. She is a true friend indeed who is never too busy to listen and give an encouraging word. Her passion is writing, of which she has a true gift. She has met up with many stumbling blocks, disappointments and interruptions with her writing career, but when others would have thrown in the towel, she perseveres, and goes for the gold! I know without a doubt when it is time for her to stand before our Lord and Savior, He will say, "Well done my good and faithful servant." Her family should be proud, I know I am.

Charlotte Martin: Beloved friend/ L.V.N/sister-in-Christ

In 1987 my husband and family moved to Angels Camp to start up a restaurant business. Being new to the town I was longing for a church home and meeting friends. One day, in walked a very happy, smiling and friendly young lady who welcomed us and invited me to her home for a Bible study and to also come to her hair salon (her other talent). I was thrilled. It was an answer to my prayer for meeting Christian friends and a hair appointment too!

After all these years and moving all over the world, we have managed to keep in touch. I even experienced a God wink when we both ran into each other on a beach in Maui!

Gloria has always had a passion to reach out to people with the message of having a personal relationship with Jesus and how it transforms every aspect of daily living. She has always had a desire to help others to grow by a strong commitment to Bible study and group leadership. The great commandment to love God and love others is a message that is not lost in Gloria. John 5:24, John 3:16 and James 4:8.

Now Gloria is adding her much loved talent as a writer. I am so happy for her and pray that God will use her to win even more people to Christ.

Sandra Morris: Beloved friend/wife/homemaker/grandmother/legal secretary/sister-in-Christ

In the year 1959 I was 5 years old and living in a small town called Alviso, which was much like Tijuana in those days. A family by the name of Joseph lived a few doors down. Gloria Jean was the youngest girl of 6 children, she was one of three at home at the time. Being 6 years older than me, she would become a babysitter for my brother, sisters and myself.

Who would of ever known, that 55 years later, we are still close friends and sisters-in-Christ. Every time I speak with her, I get refreshed in the Spirit. We share great memories and our Love for the Lord!

Paula Jean Guerrero
Beloved friend/ sister-in-Christ/wife/homemaker/co-owner carpet store in Campbell, California

We became friends with Gloria Jean and her husband Fred, after she invited us to Bible Study at her home in 2008. Randy had known them as his neighbor for several years before, but never very well. Through our Bible Study with Gloria Jean, we learned right away about her passion for the Lord. The more time we spent with her, during and outside of Bible Study, the more we saw her bring Jesus's teachings into every area of her life. Gloria Jean told wonderful stories as examples of God's promises, commandments, assurances, protection, love and more. Her vibrance, energy and enthusiasm is catching and inspiring. Her childlike soul is a blessing to any open heart.

Randy and Joan Shattuck/ beloved friends-in-Christ

Fred and Gloria Bodenmuller have had a great influence on our life for the good and for the Glory of God!

They were salt and light to us at a time when we were searching for God and did not know him yet as Savior and Lord in our lives.

Matthew 5:13 says...You are the salt of the earth. My bible (NAS) commentary says (salt preserves, creates thirst and cleanses).

Matthew 5:14 says...You are the light of the world. A city set on a hill cannot be hidden; v 15 "Nor does anyone light a lamp and put it under a basket, but on the lamp stand, and it gives light to all who are in the house.

V 16 let your light shine before men in such a way that they may see your good works, and glorify your Father who is in heaven.

Not only was their life as a couple something that my husband and I wanted, but as we hung out with them my desire to respect my husband became a part of our relationship as husband and wife. Ephesians 5:33.

We will always be grateful to God for the time He allowed us to spend with them for they played a huge part in leading us to Jesus. As a result, David and I became ministers of the faith.

Reverends, David and Judy Borst Lay Ministers for 30 plus years David Borst Associate Pastor Vineyard Christian Fellowship Salinas 2004-2005 Marriage Pastors, River of Life Church Patterson Ca, 2010-2012/Beloved brother & sister-in-Christ

"I am Sarah. I am the niece of Gloria; my dad is her sister. I have had a great bond, you could say we are kindred spirits. We share a very special passion: Hairdressing. My passion for hairdressing runs deep. I have been a hairdresser for 12 years now. However my passion and inquisitive spirit had me playing "hair" in Auntie Gloria's salon chair many many years before I became a professional. I would get whoever was willing to sit in the chair for me, usually my grandma, but others would begrudgingly allow me to pretend to color their hair, blow-dry and style it. I loved going into her salon on the bottom floor of her house and just sit there and take it all in. I would dream of my own space to call my own to beautify people and build relationships. My aunt, along with my mom and dad, believed in me and would tell me that I would make a great hairdresser.!

I am thankful for the role that Auntie Gloria has played in my life and how she was such an inspiration for me to follow my dreams. I love what I do and can say that she has helped me get to where I am today. " Auntie Gloria's heart for the Lord has been imprinted in my heart as well. I have many fond memories as a young child with her teaching us about the Lord in her home as well as taking us to church and teaching us in Sunday school. I am grateful for not only my parents' example of their strong faith, but my aunt's strong faith as well that has definitely influenced me! My aunt loves me & others well and that is from God! God is about people and my aunt is about people and loving them well!

Sarah Angelina Beloved niece/wife/mother/homemaker/licensed cosmetologist

My wife Denise and I have known Fred & Gloria Bodenmüller for approx. six years. During that time we have become more then friends; like family. We have shared Bible study, broken bread, spent holidays together, enjoyed many Christian activities and supported each other through physical challenges and even a tragic disaster. As I write this, Fred and Gloria have opened their home to us, as we have been evacuated from ours due to a horrific fire. "Thank you God" for Fred & Gloria's loving spirit.
It is very hard to sum up the feelings we have for them in a few paragraphs, but I can start off by saying "They will know we are Christians by our love." I believe this statement comes pretty close to what we feel for Fred & Gloria. They have both been an inspiration in our walk with the Lord. They have encouraged me to follow my calling to become a chaplain and supported my wife's and my ministry to carry the message to assisted care facilities. Their faith permeates prayer results. They are truly the backbone of what Jesus tells us in: Matt. 22:37-40 when he was asked, "What is the greatest commandment?". In short, His response was LOVE. We are looking forward to sharing this gracious love from God, with the Bodenmüllers in this life and into eternity. God Bless You both!

Your brother and sister-in-Christ,
Tom & Denise Acampora
Chaplain & First Lady
A.T.A.P. Ministries Beloved brother&sister-in-Christ/parents/ grandparents.

I first met Gloria about 9 years ago when she volunteered at her granddaughter Laurel's school, where I work. We became great friends from the start. Gloria is a kind, wonderful woman, that loves the Lord. She is a true gift from God and I am totally blessed to have her as my friend.

Cindy Rhorer/ Secretary Curtis Creek Elementary/ Beloved sister-in-Christ/wife/mother/ grandmother

My sister, Gloria Jean Bodenmüller, has labored long and hard on her book titled, "The Girl from Silicon Valley." About a year ago she gave me the first chapter of her manuscript and asked me to read through it. Now, she has asked me to write a few words about her life and also what I read in chapter one of her book.

My sister is the 4th child of six and she is 10 years older than me, yet 6 years younger than our oldest sibling. Her perspective from her position in our family is different from mine and by reading just the first chapter of her book, it has given me a new perspective of not only the valley that we grew up in and our families life, but it has also shed light on who my earthly father was and his relationship with me. I am grateful to my sister for helping me to see that I was closer to my earthly father than I actually knew and in turn this has helped me to understand more clearly that my true proximity to my heavenly Father is very close as well!

She too possesses a profound faith in the Lord Jesus and is not ashamed to tell anyone of His love for them. Even when trials come along that seem to show a distant God from an outsiders perspective, my sister seems to intuitively know that her actual proximity with our heavenly Father is within His strong and loving embrace.

From what I have read in her book it will be filled with stories of her life growing up in what would eventually be known as Silicon Valley. Even after she moves away from the valley her life is filled with highs and lows and throughout it all, her perspective continually lines up with her close proximity to her loving Heavenly Father. I look forward to reading the rest of her book and I hope it will give me further perspective in realizing that my own proximity to our God is very close indeed!

William C. Joseph: Beloved brother & brother-in-Christ, husband/father/grandfather/retired teacher

"What an amazing life Gloria has lived, and continues to live. Her testimony is not only a great reminisce of the days gone by in the fertile orchards of the San Jose area, but shares the hard times for struggling families of the time. God chose her at a young age, watched over her, loved her and taught her. Gloria's unwavering faith, service to our Lord, and love shared with all around her, has been an inspiration to me for 20 years. Gloria lives God's word without apology and shares it with other's everyday! Her ministry is sharing the Gospel of salvation through Jesus Christ. He saves, she is His vessel He uses to present the message."

Lynne Fritz Loving sister-in-Christ/homemaker/loving grandmother & aunt/retired park ranger

CONTENTS

Please note:
i have used the word "i" instead of capitalizing it as in proper English "I". The reason is although this is my autobiography, it is really not about me, but about the life the Lord has given and chosen for me. In using the small "i", i am giving Him all the glory, honor and praise.
Thank you for your understanding

Chapter One

"Lord, You have been our dwelling place throughout all generations. Before the mountains were born or You brought forth the earth and the world, from everlasting to everlasting You are God." Psalm 90: 1 & 2

My birth and beginnings in Silicon/Santa Clara Valley

It was a gorgeous, cool, autumn morning in the Sierra's, as i sat comfortably on the sofa looking out the window, relaxing from a very exhausting week. i have always been a very active person, and have been told by countless friends, "You absolutely amaze me, you have so much energy!" Believe me, today i did not measure up to that energetic person. Now, as i am getting older, my body keeps telling me to slow down. My mind seems young, and tells me to, "Go, go, go," but my body says, "No, no, no." If only our elders had shared with us the challenges of aging, perhaps we could have adjusted more easily. Then again, maybe they did tell us, and we were young and didn't listen. As cousin Erna, in Germany, once said to me, "Jung und dumb." Oh yes, "Young and dumb."

Fred, my husband of 47 plus years, sat beside me, gave me a hug, and showed his concern. He, too, sees me overdoing. i returned his hug and thanked him for his concern, then promised i would rest. Then, suddenly, as we peered out the window, we saw one of our calves grazing on the front lawn. Well, it didn't take long to have an adrenaline high, as we went rushing out the door; quickly slipping on some shoes and off we went to chase the calf out of the front lawn. So much for a quiet day! "PRAISE THE LORD, anyway!" is what Jeanette, one of my many mentors would tell me.

You see, my husband Fred (Siegfried), originally from Germany, and i, from California, were both raised much of our life in the country. So it was a dream for us to raise our two sons, Franz and Jeffrey, in the country, giving them the kind of life we knew, enjoyed and loved. Thirty-plus years ago the

1

Lord led us to our 20 acre barren yet beautiful and peaceful ranch in the Gold Country of northern California. Franz Joseph, our oldest son, celebrated his second birthday, just weeks after we moved here. Our second son, Jeffrey John, arrived three and one half years later; he's a Gold Country boy. We first lived in a trailer we borrowed from a dear man who soon would become our sons adopted grandfather. That is a story in itself, which i will share later in this book.

The trailer in which we lived reminded me so much of the one my three sisters and i were raised in, out in the country in San Jose, California. That trailer, in which we slept, was just a shell, with an outer wall, an empty space, no insulation and the inner wall. We had no closets, running water, bath, or fixtures, just an empty shell. In comparison, the trailer we were living in on the ranch, had all of the above, except no flush toilet. A pipe ran directly from the well we had drilled, to the trailer, giving us cold running water.

The trailer we lived in, when i was a child, was situated off of Tennant Avenue, which is now Silicon Valley Road. i can remember as far back as when i was three years old. A dear pastor friend once said: "Children learn most everything their first three years of life that will form their life; they learn to talk, walk, eat, and learn so many basics, the foundation for life." i believe he is correct.

One day, my sisters who were my stronghold, were off at school. My mother was sick in bed in the shack where she and my father slept and Mama prepared our meals. My alcoholic maternal grandmother also lived with us. She shared the trailer with my sisters and i, as sleeping quarters. My father came home that morning from his drinking, gambling, and only the Lord knows what else. He went to my mother and told her to get out of bed and fix him something to eat. My mother tried to tell him that she was ill, but he yanked her out of bed and beat her. Needless to say, at age three, i was very frightened. My sisters were in school, my Mom was getting beat up, and

2

my grandmother was in an alcoholic stupor. So with no family members or friends to turn to, i turned to myself. Now, these many years later, i've discovered and believe, that the Holy Spirit of God came upon me and comforted me and i grew up then - at the age of three. After that experience, i've always had the desire to do what was right.

At age sixty-four, during a book signing, a fellow author shared a story with me about how he knew the Holy Spirit came upon him at age five. As i listened, i realized that's exactly what happened to me, those many years ago. Because of that experience, i sought this God i'd never heard of before.

My sisters and brothers tell me, that from a young age, i always knew the Lord and wanted to serve Him, and do what was right. i was not raised in a Christian home - as you can imagine - yet, i always sought the Lord. Was i chosen at age three? Yes, i believe so. We are all chosen for a purpose, although some don't listen or hear His voice. The Lord loves us all and wants us to follow Him.

The first time i recall reading or seeing anything about this God i longed to know, was at a five and dime store we frequented. Every time Mama took us there i quickly ran to pick-up this wonderful children's book; "My Little Golden Book About God."

Years later, in my sixties, and speaking at a women's retreat, (W.O.W.), once again i spotted "My Little Golden Book About God" in a basket at their silent auction. i told my longtime friend, Joyce, "i have to bid on that basket because i want that little book for my own." It brought back fond memories of going to that five and dime, picking up the book, reading it, and putting it back on the shelf, because I knew we couldn't afford it. But it taught me about this God i was so hungry to know.

When i saw the little book once again, i thought perhaps that early experience was one of the reasons i began writing Christian children's books. If we can reach children and teach them at a moldable, early age -

especially about our faith - what a blessing that would be. Just think of the little ones we could reach for Jesus with these little books.

On another occasion at about age three or four, while i was with my mom, i spotted a doll buggy at the five and dime store. My mom didn't have a crib or cradle but she did have a big, old-fashioned buggy in which she raised each of us six children.

i loved that old buggy; it was neat because, as i found out in later years, when my two brothers arrived, the buggy could be pushed outside on a nice warm summer day in northern California. There, the baby could feel the rays of the warm sunshine.

i was helping my father and mother bale hay for a local farmer in San Jose off of the Monterey Highway. Mom worked very hard, helping my dad bale hay. That was long before hay balers were invented. We had no baby sitters in those days, or ever, for us children, so i helped as much as i could, mainly staying out of the way or bringing the workers water to drink. At the end of the baling day, Mom would sometimes stop at the five and dime store, there it was, that lovely doll buggy on display. It was just like the big one Mama raised us in, only smaller for a child's doll. Oh, how i wished i could have it! Mom must have been watching me, because at the end of the baling season, my dad actually gave her some money, which was very unusual for him. (Money was like a God to him.) He would often say, "Money is the root of all evil." Later, when i became a Christian and read the Bible passage for myself, i learned it says; "For the love of money is a root of all kinds evil." 1 Timothy 6:10a.

Anyway, Mom was delighted to finally receive something for her hard work. She headed directly to the five and dime and - you guessed it - purchased that doll buggy for little gloria jean. i could not contain myself. i was very quiet and thankful for this precious gift. i had never received such a gift before. Not a bike, not a stuffed toy, not even a doll to gently place in my

4

new doll buggy. The doll would arrive years later. What fun i had pushing that doll buggy around our yard, just like Mama did with the big one.

We did have a boy's bike that the four of us sisters shared. It was so big that when i learned to ride, i had to lean the bike against a set of steps in order to jump on and ride. One time, i recall my sister Frances, giving me a ride on the bike; i sat on the bar that made it a boy's bike.

She was peddling down Tennant Avenue (which is now Silicon Valley road) and kept telling me, "Keep your feet out of the spokes." Well, somehow i forgot the warning as we were going down the hill on the road: i caught my foot in the spokes. The bike did a three-sixty and landed back on its wheels, and it carried us the rest of the way down the hill and home. Not a scratch, bump or even a bruise on either of us! A miracle? Yes, i believe so, God's mighty angels protecting us? Yes. **Psalm 91:11 says; "For He will command His angels concerning you to guard you in all your ways;" Psalm 91:11a.**

We also had a red wagon that Papa would tie to his model T Ford. He'd put us in the wagon, and pull us down the road. As he drove off, we'd roll away to the sound of Mama shouting, "Bill, you're going to hurt those girls!" He just kept going. We thought it was fun. At another time, we also had a scooter to share and that was fun, too.

One morning my father arrived home from one of his gambling and drinking from the night before, driving a spanking brand new automobile. He was fascinated with machinery and automobiles in particular. i was excited as Papa drove up in that shiny cream-colored (**as he and old milker called it**) car. For my dear mother it was not so, with tears streaming down her sun parched cheeks, she said, "Why, Bill, what have you done?" You see, my dear reader, Papa rarely saved money for a 'rainy day' as he would say, but he and mom had been saving for a home to call their own. This new fancy automobile was all of their precious savings. It was a done deal, never again would they save, or have the opportunity to save, for the home Mama

5

always wanted: a place to settle securely without moving, a place to call our own. It was interesting because

my mother was raised the same way, in an alcoholic home. i believe it is a generational sin, passed from one generation to the next. Until someone steps up to the plate and says, "No, more. I will no longer follow the sins of my ancestors." Although my mother's parents were not poor, like we were, they were still plagued by alcoholic abuse.

My grandfather came from Switzerland and established businesses in San Jose: one being a saloon, (just what he needed), another was the first gravel pit in San Jose, and the last one were fields of fresh vegetables. Perhaps that's where i get my love for gardening, my grandfather, and of course from my mom, who would live with us later in life and taught me how to garden. Thus, came the origin of our children's books on gardening.

My grandparents eventually lost everything after my grandfather died at a young age from cancer. He and Grandma were both heavy drinkers, mostly homemade wine. Grandma did the bookkeeping for all the businesses, and would soon sign it over to a partner, in exchange for her favorite drink: wine. Much like Esau, in the Old Testament, selling his birthright to Jacob for some stew. **(Genesis 25:33).**

i have a lovely picture of my grandparents, taken when they were young and prosperous, probably in the early nineteen hundreds. Friends look at it and say, "What did your grandparents do for a living? They dressed and looked prosperous." After giving it some thought, i realized they were fairly wealthy in their time. But lost it all due to "lust of the flesh": alcohol, in their case. How sad.

My mom told me her maternal grandmother, also from Switzerland and a devout Catholic, taught my Mom about Jesus. She would say to my grandmother, her daughter, "Quit drinking and take care of your children." Many years later, i was telling my mother about a child in my Sunday school class who wanted to know what Jesus looked like. My mother said to me,

"Can you imagine? A child who doesn't know about Jesus?" i said, "Mom, i didn't know about Jesus when i was a child." She just stopped, stared, and didn't say another word. She didn't realize the importance of telling her children about Jesus. Oh yes, she lived the Christian life most of the time, but never told us or read the Bible, or shared, or took us to church. i loved my mom and always will. i cared for her in her later years of life. The question comes to mind, 'How many of us know Jesus and what He has done for us and don't share it?" Jesus says in **Matthew 28:18-20, "Therefore, go and make disciples of all nations, baptizing them in the name of the Father and the Son and the Holy Spirit, teaching them to obey everything I have commanded you and surely I am with you always, to the very end of the age."** Are we practicing that today in our lost world?

　　As for my father's parents, i never knew or met them, as he was in his fifties when i was born. His parents had long passed on. i do know that my grandmother was also a very devout Catholic. She and my grandfather came from Portugal. He was a whaler in the 1800s. The captain of the ship couldn't pronounce my grandfather's last name, so he called him Joseph. It wasn't until my father's funeral that i knew that our last name was not Joseph but Narcisso. They came to San Francisco and settled in San Jose on a ranch that was on Story Road. My father was their only son. His mother was instrumental in having the Church of The Five Wounds moved from Portugal to San Jose. Although my father was an only child, he and his wives had thirteen children: seven by his first wife and six by my mother. My father was thirty years older than my dear mother.

　　i want to take you back to the trailer in San Jose, where many fond memories, along with the fear of my father, originated. As i mentioned, i loved my sisters, and, being the baby of four girls, they loved and treated me well. Although they were not so kind to my sister Barbara, number two, because my father favored her. She was very attached to my mother and when my mother went to the hospital to give birth to sister number three,

Frances, Barbara missed mom so much she threw a convulsion. So my father always said she was the timid one and he sheltered her, which made my sisters, Josephine and Frances, jealous of Barbara because she got away with a lot. i am so thankful we all get along today.

Being very poor, we didn't have games and toys, so we made up games and played in the ashes from the wood burning stove, playing and imagining it was sand. Every morning we would awaken with our eyes shut tight and Mama would tell us to stay out of the ashes. But it was too much fun! We didn't listen to Mama's pleas, and we suffered the consequences. i guess she thought we had punishment enough with our eyes stuck shut each morning after playing in the ashes. An old wet wash- rag would remove the cold from our eyes and we'd be at it again.

One of the games we made up involved a large piece of cardboard from an old cardboard box we'd flattened. We drew a town on it, much like little San Jose, with streets, houses and stores. Yes, before San Jose became part of Silicon Valley, it was a one-horse town. We'd pretend that we were driving around town and shopping and doing whatever. Today, i see in the department stores the same such game, only now it's on carpet. Oh, if only we'd have marketed it! Just think, such ingenuity from children, no less.

Since we lived on a country road, on hot days, when the tar softened on that road, we'd break off pieces and chew it, imagining it was chewing gum. And we'd end up with blackened teeth and grit.

During the time we lived in the shack/trailer, my father worked for a slaughterhouse. He also milked cows by hand. This was prior to the days of most dairies having milking machines. We had electricity in the shack and trailer, but we did not have running water. That meant my father would bring water home in twenty-five gallon milk cans, so Mom and Grandma could wash clothes, cook, or do whatever else was needed with the precious water. A galvanized tub served as our once a week bath. Mom would heat the water in a big kettle that sat on top of the wood-burning stove.

On the days my father didn't bring water, he brought fresh milk from the dairy. What memories i have of those times! Mom would skim the rich cream off the top of the milk and make butter. We drank the remainder of the milk. If any was left, Mom and Grandma baked homemade bread, and from the leftover bread they made Torte, or bread pudding. That was the only sweets they ever baked. None of us ever had a cake baked by Mom or Grandma, not even for our birthdays. Although Mom thought it important to know the birthdays of each of her children, we never celebrated.

Perhaps that is the reason birthdays are so important to me today, especially for widows and others who are forgotten. In the book of James it says; **"Religion that God our Father accepts as pure and faultless is this: to look after orphans and widows in their distress..." James 1:27a.** Recently, a young mother and her three children came with their grandparents to visit us, and the four year old told me his birthday was the next week. i said, "Well, you need a birthday cake." So i quickly went in the house and made him a chocolate cake. It was as though this little boy had received a million dollars, his eyes just lit up with thankfulness. My not having a cake when i was a child, gave me the idea that i could make one for this boy. i also put together a piñata, using a large brown grocery bag, for he and his sisters to hit and collect the candy placed in the bag.

Not long after Fred and I moved to the Gold Country, the Lord brought together a special group of us Christian ladies to celebrate our birthdays. Oh, how we looked forward to those times of celebration. Sad to say, many of the ladies have gone home to be with Jesus, or moved away. i am in hopes of starting a new one; everyone needs to be treated special, especially on their birthday! **2 Corinthians 1:3-7.**

Let's go back to the shack. Our family lived there longer than any other place; we moved constantly due to my father's drinking, anger, and strife with the landlord. Behind the shack and trailer was a massive California Live Oak tree. My father would bring his alcoholic friends home for a good meal, more wine, and sleep. While they slept, he rolled them for their money. Then, the next day, he took them back to downtown San Jose. Most of them called St. James Park their home. So when they came to our home, they were delighted to be with a family. One particular time, one of my father's drinking buddies, Pea Wee, (he was small in statue) fell asleep under the mighty oak with a lit cigarette in his hand. Soon, the majestic oak was ablaze. My mother was the first to see it and woke my father, who, in anger wokePea Wee and chased him off. Poor Pea Wee went running down the road with only one shoe on, to get away from my angry father.

There were many other alcoholic buddies of my father, who had different names such as, Johnny the Greek, Cecil Bebout, Ham, Monkey Mack, and Sam the Shoemaker, to name a few. Johnny the Greek was the only one married, i believe, and he and his wife had a daughter. i think he was called 'Johnny the Greek' because he was Greek. His wife's name was Irene. The song, "Goodnight Irene" was popular at the time. My sister Barbara, who was the entertainer, had my other two sisters and i sing "Goodnight Irene" to these people when they came to visit. They were the only family of my father's wino friends. Other than that, no one else ever came to visit us, including our extended family. So, it was an honor to sing to these drunken friends of my father. We four girls were the same age as the Lennon sisters, (who were popular at the time) so we imagined we were them.

Cecil loved to hear us sing. His favorite, and popular, tune at the time was "The Old Rugged Cross". We knew it well from hearing it on the radio, but never knew what it meant. Cecil obviously did, because he would sit and listen and cry and throw money at us, which would encourage us to sing even more. He was a gentle, kind man and would often tell my father, "Yes, Bill you're a good man, you'd give me the shirt off your back, but first you would steal it from me." He knew my father well, but kept returning. Perhaps, he was lonely for family. Through his tears, which were often when he drank too much, he would tell us he was from Hoosier, Indiana. Wherever that was, we thought as youngsters, sounded good. We'd never traveled far from home, only through books.

Monkey Mac actually had a monkey that lived with him in his cabin in the Santa Cruz Mountains. i recall our father taking us to visit Monkey Mack, and his friendly monkey jumping all over his cabin. A strange sight for a child to see, a man living with a real monkey! Recently, my sister Josephine was telling me she had to fill out a form for her bank and was asked the question; " Where did you go for fun as a child?" She answered, "Monkey Mac's in the Santa Cruz Mountains." We both laughed so hard, because in those days, there wasn't much entertainment for young people, except drive-in theaters.

i remember my Aunt Mary/Mimi and her sister, our mother, loading us up in her 1949 Ford two-seater coop, with us four girls standing up behind them, and we'd drive off to the outdoor theater. Many times, they would have the older children duck down or hide, so as not to pay for their entrance. i knew, in my little child's heart, this was wrong, but what could i say or do?

Santa Clara Valley wasn't like it is today, with so much entertainment. It was country then, with mostly apricot and prune trees, dairies, hay ranches and farms; beautiful country living.

Ham was a gentle, kind man who enjoyed tossing a huge medicine ball to us girls. He was a quiet man who always wore a little white cap on his head. I recall, when there was arguing among us girls, or in our home, he would softly say, "Hush, hush." Those were comforting words. Those words were like magic to troubled children's ears, that needed comforting. Ham, like the others, except Cecil, never mentioned his last name.

Then there was Sam the Shoemaker. My father was a shoemaker at one time. i fondly remember all the tools he had for his once-upon-a-time trade. He must have met Sam as a fellow shoemaker. At times, my father would take us girls to, then small, downtown San Jose and leave us in the car while he visited Sam in his shoemaker shop. It seemed like hours; they would just talk while Sam worked on those, today- unheard-of, leather shoes. We were to remain in the car while my father visited. At times, Ham, Cecil, or one of my father's alcoholic friends, would stop at the car and hand us Three Musketeer bars or some kind of candy bar. What a treat! I recall Sam always smoked a big, fat cigar while my father puffed on his cigarettes. After their long conversation, we'd make the ten-mile drive back home, where Mom and Grandma had dinner waiting for us. Yes indeed, my father led a colorful life, with all his different friends.

Recently, Fred and i were watching a movie taken during the 1930's and it depicted life in those days. i finally realized since my father was born in 1896, the '30's were his hay day. As we watched the movie, i could relate to the language of the day, because that is how my father and his buddies spoke. What a privilege for me to know and understand different times of life.

The Lord's hand was upon my sisters and i, because we were never touched by any of these men. Most of them treated us with such kindness and pity, with which we are so grateful.

When my father worked at the slaughterhouse feeding cattle, we four girls would help him on the weekends. One time, my father was driving our Ford flatbed truck he used for feeding the stock, while we four girls sat on the back of the tailgate. We would be ready when he stopped, to throw alfalfa in the feeder troughs. At one point, my father was backing up the truck, our legs dangling over the side, and he backed right into the fence, crushing my older sister's legs. She let out a scream. He just kept backing up. Once he discovered what happened, my sister received a harsh scolding, i don't remember him showing much compassion. Perhaps that was how he was raised.

He seemed much harsher on my older sister than the rest of us siblings and never laid a hand on any of us, except her, and when he did, he was cruel. His very presence, when he walked in a room, made us fearful of him, especially when he was drinking.

Of course, none of these tragic experiences were ever mentioned or talked about because, as you see, like many others, we lived with an elephant (as it were) in the middle of our home, walked around it and never, ever mentioned it to anyone. We were to keep it all inside and deal with it somehow. i now know without my Lord and Savior it is impossible to deal with these circumstances. He says in His Word the Bible; **" Cast all your anxiety on Him, because He cares for you."** 1 Peter 5: 7

Mama not only worked hard in her circumstances, cooking on a wood burning stove, making butter and homemade bread, hauling water, and caring for her children and her mother, but in the spring and summer months she picked strawberries to earn extra income. With that income, she saved to purchase us girls a set of The Encyclopedia Britannica. Although Mama didn't have much education, she wanted to make sure her children did. Mama always did the best she could for us. With some of the little money she earned, she would buy things we needed, like vanilla for baking her torte. Since we lived ten miles from downtown San Jose, there was a store bus that came, once a week, i believe, and carried the basic essentials needed for homemakers. That's where mama would buy her meager purchases. Every so often she would give each of us girls a nickel to purchase a little something from the store bus. Oh, the joy we felt when we'd see the store bus coming up Tenant avenue! (Now, Silicon Valley road.) When it stopped in our gravel driveway, Mama went aboard first, and right behind trotted her four wide eyed daughters, tightly holding onto their nickels. There was gum and candy, and all sorts of treats. Oh, to make such a great decision. Happily we'd jump off the store bus with our treasure in our hand.

Speaking of the precious nickels, precious because we seldom had any money, once a week, fudge-sickles were offered for a nickel at school. They were those delicious creamy fudge ice-cream on a wooden stick. When i was in the second grade in school, my sister Frances would meet me after lunch to place in my little hand, that wonderful nickel so i could buy one of those fudge-sickles. Hmmm, i can taste it now: rich and creamy and chocolatey. One particular day, after receiving that precious nickel, i thanked my generous sister and quickly ran to the bathroom before making my purchase. Well, Mama always told us to put our hands under our bottoms as we sat on the commode, so as not to let our bottoms touch the commode. There were no paper commode liners in those days. Well, i did as Mama taught me and promptly dropped the coin in the toilet. Please remember we had an outhouse at home. Panicked, i flushed the toilet and away went the nickel and my promise of a fudge-sickle. i just stood there crying, then remembered i could run and tell my dear sister Frances. Maybe she could help me. When i found her on the playground and told her, she immediately gave me another nickel. i believe it was for her fudge-sickle, and she was willing to do without, for her little sister. Over the years i have observed my sister Frances (Fran, we fondly call her) and she is like our mama: she has the gift of giving. To this day, i've never seen either of them do without, because they gave and they received. The Lord blesses them for their generosity. He does the same for all generous givers. i once heard an elderly Pastor Bach say; "You cannot out-give the Lord because he has a bigger shovel."

"A generous man will himself be blessed, for he shares his food with the poor." Proverbs 22:9

Those were wonderful fun days with my sisters. They helped me forget the rough times of the arguing and fighting in our home due to my father's drinking. Praise the Lord, Mama was the loving, peaceful one who tried to be quiet and keep peace. Being raised in an alcoholic home herself, she understood the harm it caused. When things got bad, Mama would pack us girls and our grandmother in the Oldsmobile and go to stay with my aunt and uncle: Mom's only sister, Mary, and my dear Uncle Slim, who was from

Switzerland. As we drove away, Mama would say, "Your father is on the 'war path again.' This will give him some time to cool off." We would stay with my aunt and uncle for a few days and then go back home.

Uncle Slim and Aunt Mary had no children of their own and we became the children they never had. Uncle Slim would arrive home from work as a cement finisher. Being from Switzerland and shopping everyday for food as they did, he would arrive with food for dinner, that my aunt would prepare, not knowing that sometimes there would be six more hungry mouths to feed. Seems the Lord always multiplied the loaves and fish so there was always enough for all of us. **(Refer to; John 6:8-13).**

i loved going to my aunt and uncle's little farm in east San Jose; they had goats and cows that needed feeding and milking, and chickens for fresh eggs and a wonderful vegetable garden. My uncle, a big, red faced happy man, would stop at the grocery store every day after work to purchase what he wanted my aunt to prepare fresh from the butcher's counter. Then he would take the greens from the back of the store to feed his animals. We girls would go through the greens and pick out the decent apples, the bad parts were cut off, so we could eat the good part. We did the same with pears and bananas and other fruits and vegetables. This is where we girls first encountered coconut in the shell and whole pineapples, we had never had these delicacies before; we couldn't afford such amazing food. With great determination we learned to crack the hard coconut shell, and retrieve the delicious white coconut meat inside. Most times the coconut milk had dried up, leaving some mold inside the coconut on the meat. That didn't bother us, we just scraped off the mold and ate that fine delicious coconut, what a treat. We knew just how to salvage the fruit and vegetables because our papa would go out at night to all the markets when they were closed and take the greens home. i always wondered why Papa made his rounds at night, and my sweet uncle asked, and took the greens during the day. Hmmm.

15

Also, my aunt and uncle had running water, and it was hot and cold. They had a flush toilet, too. Wow! i soon discovered what those white lovely things my aunt called sheets were. At bedtime we slept under those nice, sweet smelling sheets. In our home, all we had were itchy, smelly army blankets.

On one occasion, after being at my aunt and uncle's for some time, Mama decided it was time to go home. When we reached our trailer, it was nighttime and pitch dark. As Mama pulled into the gravel driveway and shined the car lights on the trailer, we could see that the door and windows had been all boarded up. Our father was out cold in his drunken stupor in the shack. So mama drove us back to our aunt and uncle's for a few more days, until our father "cooled off."

Mama helped Papa rebuild and work on the engines of our cars, too. One time we were heading to my aunt and uncle's home, and my father had hidden the keys to our Oldsmobile. While he was sleeping after his drinking binge, Mama hot wired the car and off we went. When we came home, he asked her how she did it. She told him, "You taught me." Mom would share this story quite often with me in her later years of life and she'd say with a smile, "I showed him." Yes, that part was funny, but the pain and fear of coming home to a boarded up trailer was frightening for my sisters and i.

Mama was so simple, kind, yet wise in many ways, as i learned in later years when she came to live with us. She drove a car, truck, and whatever was necessary. She learned to drive a Model A Ford between the prune trees that were behind our shack. Mama never had a driver's license for fear of not passing the test. At one time, as we were traveling to my aunt and uncle's, darkness surrounded us and Mama turned on the Oldsmobile lights. Little did she know that one of the taillights was not working. It wasn't long before she was stopped by a San Jose police officer, who, of course, wanted to see her driver's license. She told him she would go the next day and get the license and have the taillight fixed. My father repaired the taillight, but Mama, never got her driver's license. She was a good driver, very cautious and considerate. I always wished she had her license. If it were today, I would have prayed with her and helped her to get the license.

My father handled household finances with what little we had. He even did all the shopping for the food, etc. When Mama didn't bake bread, my dad would purchase huge sackfuls of bread, cake, doughnuts, and bear claws. Many times he would keep the sweets in the trunk of the car, perhaps so we wouldn't eat all of them at once. The only trouble with that was, what he did give to us, after sitting in the trunk of the car for some time, they tasted like gasoline. But we were hungry and never complained. The bread sacks were brown and about two to three layers thick, and about three feet tall. They were the flour sacks, which held fifty pounds or more of flour. When I was a little girl, and misbehaved, my mother would take me outside with huge flour sack in hand, and me in the other, and turn me upside down in the sack. She would then go inside the house and lock the doors, with me screaming in the darkness of the flour sack and the frightening sounds of owls, and other nocturnal animals filling the country night air. Not knowing exactly why i was being punished, but i'd be good after that experience. Perhaps, she was angry at my father, and i got the punishment or she was upset about something i did. i just remember it was a very frightening experience, one I do not want to pass on to anyone.

My dad would also purchase sacks of oranges and apples for us to eat. They were so good, unlike the ones of today, with all the chemicals and spray on them. He would sometimes prepare pancakes for us in the morning for breakfast. Because there were no screens on the windows or doors, sometimes a fly would land in the batter. We'd be careful to watch and take out the added protein from our pancakes. One time i recall i had one of those juicy oranges in my desk at school and i was hungry. i guess the fly in the pancake wasn't enough. So i reached in my desk and began eating the orange as the third grade teacher spoke. Success! Finally, i was able to get a piece of

17

that delicious orange in my mouth. Of course, it gave off a wonderful fragrance and the children began saying, "I smell an orange!" i panicked and began to choke. Quickly, i remembered what Mama taught us: reach in your throat and retrieve the food. Finally, i did it. The teacher probably knew, but she never said a word. i'm so thankful for great teachers. But to this day, i do not care for oranges for fear of choking on them. Such memories we carry with food. On another occasion my father brought home chocolate pudding, that he got somewhere for free or he'd stolen. It was in the winter and pouring down rain. The Coyote Creek was just down the road from where we lived, and my father came home telling us how high the water level was due to all the rain and it was surely going to flood. When he said almost anything, he said it with such drama and overreacting. (Perhaps, that's why i'm so dramatic). We were eating the chocolate pudding as he dramatized the scene. To this day, i do not care for chocolate pudding, because it reminds me of this fearful scene.

i mentioned my father may have stolen the pudding, because he was notorious for being a thief. My father would go into a hat store with his hat on, and walk out with a new hat, without purchasing it. He taught us girls how to steal as well, which i hated, but knew i had to obey him. On the other hand, there was our sweet Mama who would wash our mouths out with soup for saying bad words. i'm thankful, we children chose our Mama's demeanor. My father would tell us time and time again, he served time in San Quentin Prison for grand theft, auto, mink stoles, etc. Whether it was true or not, i do not know. But i have always wondered.

Many times when my father was in a drunken rage, my older sisters somehow reached a phone - even though we didn't have one - to call for help. When the sheriff's arrived, my mom would tell them everything was okay and that my father was asleep. She too was in fear of what he might do to her or us.

Chapter Two

**"I know, O Lord, that a man's life is
not his own; is not for man to
direct his steps." Jeremiah 10:23**

**Life as it was in poverty, hard work.
We were thankful for food and shelter our reward.**

We lived in fear most of my childhood, fear of not knowing what my father would do when he got drunk. At three months of age, he took me from the baby buggy where i slept and, with a hatchet in-hand, he laid me on the chopping block. He threatened my mom, saying he was going to chop my head off if she didn't comply. My oldest sister, Josephine, at age six or seven, quickly grabbed me from my father, where i lay on the chopping block, ran with me in her little arms, for safety through the prune orchard.

In later years, i asked my mom about this incident and she said it was true. To verify it, i remembered coming home from the doctor after being treated for impetigo. Previously, i had never gone to the doctor or dentist. It was just unheard of in our family. As my father sped down the road from the doctor's visit, with the bill in his hand, he yelled and screamed at me over the many miles as we traveled home: "I should have chopped your head off when I had the chance!" As i said before, money was my father's god and so much more important than myself, more important even than the life of his daughter.

In comparison, the teachers in school were a blessing. They were kind, sweet, loving and willing to help even a poor child like my sisters and i. i can think of a time once when i was running out of the classroom to catch the bus home. i caught my skirt part of the dress in the classroom door. It wasn't a plain dress, it was a dress where the bottom was stitched in lengths

19

that went around my body. So when i caught the skirt of the dress in the door, i literally unraveled the skirt in a winding, circling motion. i stood in tears; not only was i showing my little slip underneath my skirt, now i might miss the bus. What would my parents say! i had no way to call them because we had no phone.

The teacher, bless her heart, sent another child to run and tell the bus driver to wait until she could mend my skirt. She did all right, using straight pins all the way around. It held nicely. Boy, did i do the jig that long drive home on the school bus. Try sitting on straight pins sometime, poking here and there and everywhere. But thanks to a kind teacher and the bus driver, i made it home safely. Well, kind of. i was red and poked on my bottom. Yes, school was a blessing to me.

There were many more blessings i would experience while being at school. i have been told by others, that i should have been a teacher, because i am so good with children. Guess it's because of the Golden Rule: **"Do to others as you would have them do to you." Luke 6:31.** And a favorite Bible verse that is quoted in some of "Our" children's books; " But Jesus called the children to Him and said, ' **Let the little children come to Me, and do not hinder them, for the kingdom of God belongs to such as these.'" Luke 18:16**

Our family would live in the shack and trailer for ten years. Today, on our ranch, when we have problems with the wells, due to broken pipes or whatever, i say, "My mama lived ten years without running water, so i can do it for a few months or however long it takes to get running water to our home."

From the shack we moved a short distance up the road, on Tenant avenue (Silicon Valley road) to a ranch. It wouldn't be long until things would change dramatically.

My husband, Fred and i, visited the ranch recently, that was my second home. The ranch house and barn have remained, but the house we lived in literally fell down. It was a stucco house; the first stucco i'd ever lived in. My new brother, the first boy, arrived shortly after we moved to the stucco house. Mama would put brother Frank in the baby buggy and set him out in the warm, California sunshine. It was my duty to sit outside and watch him. Mama warned me that chicken hawks flew overhead and would fly down and snatch my baby brother, if i didn't stay and watch him; i obeyed. Oh, i was so afraid, perhaps a chicken hawk would take my little brother if that should happen and then what Mama would do to me. Believe me i obeyed my Mama.

My father got a job on the ranch milking, clipping, and feeding cows. My three sisters and i had the job of changing water pipes. These huge pipes - they seemed really huge to us girls - had to be moved in the pastures for the dairy cows. Santa Clara Valley, which is now Silicon Valley, didn't have rainfall in the summer, or sometimes even spring, so we girls - two at one end of these forty foot long, four inches in diameter pipes - moved and reconnected them morning and night. Believe me, that was tough work for four skinny, barefoot girls, ranging in age from six to thirteen and we did it with gusto. Our father told us what he expected of us and we did it without question. We were tomboys, ran around barefoot and drank water from canteens.

As I look back today at those moments with my sisters, it brings tears of endearment to my sixty-plus-year-old eyes. i loved being with my sisters and we all felt worthwhile doing what our father told us to do. Crazy. He didn't ask with love, but he put a sense of fear in us, he demanded and expected us to do it and do it well. Yet we were not angry, but pleased to help out our family. It taught us to work hard and the result was food on the table and shelter - the shelter being a stucco house that came with my father's employment on the ranch. Besides, Mama not only had running water, but it was hot when she needed it. We actually had indoor plumbing as well and Mama had a gas stove to cook our meals on. We raised rabbits for meat - which Mama butchered - and we had fresh eggs from our chickens. We even had a calf.

Mama had a wringer washer; and as i think about it, she never had a new washer without a wringer as long as she raised our family. Perhaps you are wondering what a wringer washer is. Let me explain. She would wash the clothes in the washer and then run them through two rubber rollers to wring them out. Rinse them, run them through the wringers once again, then, she would hang them on the line to dry. Washday was a real chore, taking most of the day, on Monday.

These were probably my fondest days of my childhood because i shared them with my sisters and now younger brother. Well, i was the baby for 6 and 1/2 years, so i was somewhat jealous of the time my sisters and my mom spent with him. Today, i love my brother dearly, and am so proud of the artistic ways the Lord has blessed him, and given him a kind, loving heart like Mama.

i remember one sister, Barbara, loved catching frogs while changing the water pipes. She would have me hold the frogs and i couldn't, because they tickled and i'd let them go. Besides, i thought they gave me warts. There were also little tiny bird eggs in the pasture, which i would collect, take home, and Mama would prepare them for me. i had not yet started school, so i awaited the arrival of the school bus that would bring my sisters home. Somehow, i kept myself busy, either caring for my little brother Frank, or helping with the chickens, rabbits and now a new little dog that my sister, Barbara, named Cookie. i also found great pleasure in making mud pies, just keeping busy until i could see that big yellow school bus coming down the county road. i'd run to greet my sisters, wondering what my sister Frances had saved for me from her lunch that day.

My sisters worked in the school cafeteria while attending grammar school in order to get a free, hot meal for lunch. Frances always remembered me; awaiting her precious gift of food. Sometimes it would be celery sticks with peanut butter or carrots or my favorite: two slices of fresh, real cheese. Oh, what a wonderful treat! And to think, she remembered me! After my treat and welcome home, we'd head for the green pastures to change irrigation pipes. i also loved going to the milk house, where, after the cows were milked, the milk and the cream were poured into cool refrigerated coils. i would go in and take the fresh, cold, cream and eat it right off the coils.

There was a horse on the ranch and because we were too small to saddle it, one of the workers saddled it for my sister Josephine and i. One day, as we were both riding down the hill on the horse, the saddle slipped off. i found myself on the ground, looking into the mouth of the horse. From that day forward, i was fearful of riding horses, although I have great respect for them. Refer to: **Psalm 147:10-11.**

These wonderful days were not to last long. Summer was coming, school was out for my sisters, and my father would once again lose his job due to his drinking and arguing with the boss. We packed up whatever we could take along for the move across the Santa Clara Valley. The Model T Ford was loaded with our little belongings. The calf was hitched behind the pickup; she would walk those back roads to Los Gatos, our final destination this time. Mom packed the rest in the Oldsmobile along with us children and our grandma. She had to leave behind her beloved pedal Singer sewing machine that was her mother's, because there was no room for anything else to take along.

The ride across the valley was beautiful, the orchards of prunes, apricots and cherries were in full bloom and their fragrance permeated the fresh air. Telling you this sends chills up my spine, there was nothing like the fragrance of millions of these wonderful blossoms. Those living in Silicon Valley today can't even imagine such beauty, unless they experienced it for themselves. As John Muir said it was;   "This is one of the most fertile of the many small valleys of the coast; it's rich bottoms are filled with wheat fields and orchards and vineyards and alfalfa meadows"[1] Today, this lovely valley is taken up by freeways, homes, more freeways and more homes. As for our family we would end up off of Blossom Hill Road, named after all the gorgeous sweet smelling blossoms from the fruit trees that filled the air. Today, the valley is filled with smog, traffic, and lots of people. The home to which we moved sat in the middle of a prune orchard; a long lane surrounded by the trees was the entrance. It was probably one of the best homes we'd ever lived in. It too, had indoor plumbing with a kitchen with a Wedgewood stove where Mama could cook; we actually had a living room. Later, we would have a TV.

When we drove up to this old, beautiful farmhouse, I could hardly believe my eyes. To a child of six, it was massive: painted white, with stairs going up to the backdoor and kitchen. The front entrance was even lovelier, with stairs going into the front door, which no one would ever use, because we never had company except for the winos. In those days, we called alcoholics; winos, because all they could afford was cheap wine.

For half the year, that's how we lived, with Papa rolling the drunks and Grandma's social security check, because i don't recall Papa having a job after we moved. To a child, it didn't really matter. i had my sisters, a new baby brother, a roof over our heads, and food on the table. So i told myself, but it really did matter to constantly do without. That is what has helped me to appreciate life more today.Just recently, i had prolapse surgery at our wonderful Stanford Hospital, one of the finest hospitals in the United States. Our youngest son; Jeff drove four hours to be with his Dad and I, prior to and after the surgery. What a wonderful son we have, guess we did our homework raising him. He joined us in prayer with the doctors and anesthesiologist prior to my surgery. My dear friend, Paula, a sister-in-Christ for 50 plus years, even came to visit Fred and me at the hospital. What a blessing. The next day after the surgery, the lead surgeon of three, came to check on me, reaching his hands toward heaven, he said, " It went so well, you must have had some help." i reminded him that we had prayed with him. Yes, we had help - from the Great Physician.

Anyway, when we arrived home after my surgery, we were greeted by friends with food and love. One evening, after having a rough day due to the surgery and in pain, after finally getting into bed under the nice warm covers, i cried out to the Lord with a grateful heart, remembering my growing up years and not having much. Now, i prayed; "Thank You Father for the nice warm bed, with sheets, food on our table and a roof over our head, our faith in You, family and friends, we thank You for the simple pleasures in life and for this terrible pain." i had a blessed time sharing my faith with the doctors, nurses, and others at Stanford Hospital. As our Pastor Bill said; **" Let's pray that the seeds you have planted take root and grow." refer to Isaiah 55:10-11**

i'm sorry for the interruption, it goes with the story of being thankful in all things. Please allow me to take you back to the lovely old farmhouse in Los Gatos, Behind the old farmhouse was a huge barn where Papa put the calf; homing pigeons also came to the old barn. We knew they were homing pigeons because when food became scarce; Papa would capture the pigeons. It was our job to clean them and get them ready for cooking. Each one had a band around its leg. i'd ask what the band was for, and was told, "Shhh." They were homing pigeons and not for eating. But we were hungry.

Somehow Papa managed to bring the trailer, that we had used years before, onto the property. That trailer would house the winos when Papa brought them home. It was there we would sing for these sweet old drunks. The Lord sent His angels to protect us from any harm. My sister, Barbara, said many years later; " God had His hand on each one of us, and has protected us." She is correct. She was also the entertainer in our family, and would work up routines and songs for us four girls to perform for the winos or just our family. She was the director, pusher, and choreographer. You

25

name it. She had a great love for the stage and would prove so later in life, traveling with a friend - also named Barbara - throughout the United States, and to foreign countries, entertaining our troops in song. They called themselves "the Barbies." i will share more later about her career.

Chapter Three

The Lord Jesus Himself said:
"It is more blessed to give than receive."
Acts 20;35b

The Gift of Love. Grace shown to a Poor Child.

It was here in Los Gatos, i would finally start the first grade in school. i should have started the year prior, but my parents didn't have enough money to put shoes on my feet. The first day of school was very frightening for me, at almost seven years of age. You must remember, we never had family or friends visit, except the winos, and i'd never been around any other children except my sisters and baby brother, and I was very shy and unsure. Although i did meet cousins, aunts, and uncles at the Bar-b-que's Uncle Slim and Aunt Mary would have. But starting school was a very difficult experience, one i did not want repeated for our sons later in life. Mom took me that first day of school, met the teacher, and then she left. What was expected of me? What and when would i eat and, most important, how was i to get home? Somehow it all worked out. i got ready for the next day of school; it would be better because i would ride on the big yellow bus with my sisters.

During this time we would once again began working the crops in the valley. Since it was fall and walnuts were ready for picking, that's what we did. Picked walnuts. Have you ever picked walnuts? Little did i realize that they would leave a black stain on my little hands that wouldn't wash off no matter how hard i tried. It was our teacher's practice to check for cleanliness in those days. (Something we could use today to prevent the spread of bacteria, etc.) She would choose two children to be monitors to check for cleanliness. Well, you can imagine what these children thought when they saw my black palms. Yep, dirty. Each day, as i slowly revealed my hands to the monitors, knowing what they would say, i'd shy away with tears in my eyes, until one day my teacher Miss Enos, called me up in front of the class and then explained to the children why my palms were black. The next day, at that dreadful time, when the monitors came by, i slowly opened my black stained hands. They said, "clean!" and looked at Miss Enos for approval. Was i ever relieved! Oh, the things that have an effect on children. Miss Enos set the example, she made me feel accepted, something i did not understand. From that day forward i would always respect and love my teachers.

i was the youngest child and then my brother came along and i got less attention. So, i played sick and stayed home from school one day. Suddenly, a car drove up that long, country driveway to our house. i looked out the window and there before my very eyes was a woman dressed in her white uniform and nurses hat. With great fear and not knowing what to expect, i realized it was the school nurse getting out of the car and coming to our house. My mother said, "See, you're not sick at all and here comes the nurse. Now you're in trouble." i quickly went to the warm kitchen stove to make my face red to look like i was ill. Mom welcomed the nurse into our meager kitchen. The nurse had a long, narrow white box she held in her hands. It was tied with a beautiful pink satin ribbon. She said, "How is our little Gloria doing today?" i just stared at her. i sat down and she came over and handed me this beautiful package and said, "It is a gift from the school bus driver." i thought; 'a gift for me, not a lecture, not a thermometer to check my temperature, but a lovely gift for me.' Ever so slowly with my little girl fingers I untied the lovely pink bow, slid back the ribbon, opened the box, and much to my surprise, inside was a beautiful baby doll, the first I'd ever had. i could not contain the joy in my heart. Now, i had a doll to place in the buggy Mama had purchased for me, long ago.

The next day, i took the doll with me on the school bus to school, without saying one word to the bus driver. For those of you who know me now, believe it or not, i was very shy. But the bus driver kept looking in her rear view mirror and smiling at the joy she had brought to my heart. You see, after Christmas, the children would bring to school all the wonderful things they had received for Christmas. The school bus driver was very observant, and realizing i never brought anything new to share at school, so purchased this lovely doll just for me. She fulfilled a dream for a poor little girl, and i am sure the Lord rewarded her for her kindness and generosity. i was excited to share with the children my beloved doll. i often wonder about that dear bus driver, and would love to express my gratefulness. Perhaps, i will someday, in Heaven. Even though I was happy to have the doll, i felt terrible and never played a trick of being sick again, because I knew it was wrong. There again, as i look back, i see the working of the Holy Spirit in my life, to convict me of the wrong i had done. Down the long driveway from our house and across the street was a graveyard. My sisters, the neighbor children who lived next door to the graveyard, and I, would play hide and seek in the graveyard. i was always so frightened, because i was afraid of death. i couldn't wait to go home, away from this awful graveyard. But for my sisters, and friends, it was fun and they liked frightening each other. i was thankful we did not do this very often. Also our parents were very strict about us having any friends. Sometimes my sisters and i would sneak off while our father was asleep in his drunkenness and Mom was busy trying to keep things in order. Now, i believe that neither of them realized we were gone or where we went. Or perhaps, it was a break for our Mother.

Chapter Four

"There is a time for everything, and a season for every activity under heaven" Ecclesiastes 3:1

Surviving the floodwaters that destroyed our place of living. Coming out better with the help of The Red Cross.

School was soon out and summer was upon us. The apricot and prune trees i spoke of earlier had dropped their beautiful fragrant blossoms, and now fresh green leaves and the tiny fruit was beginning to take shape on the branches. It would not be long before the fruit was ready to be harvested. Our family would be part of that harvesting. i remember Mama taking us to the apricot cutting sheds when we were just babies, so she could cut those apricot colored delicacies: California Blechnum apricots, for dried fruit. They came in field boxes and were delivered to the cutting sheds by young high school boys, giving them an opportunity to work. The 'cots, as we called them, were cut in half. It always fascinated me how the Lord had made the mark on the 'cot as to where to cut them so they would lie face up on the wooden tray. The pits were saved and sold for use as face creams and later to help with those who had cancer. The cutting trays were about eight or ten feet long and four feet across, with wooden slats or spaces, and two-inch high sides. Inside one of the field boxes, Mama would place a baby blanket and then lay her precious bundle - one of us six children - so she could work.

When my three sisters and i were cutting 'cots, two would be at each end of the long trays, racing, as we cut, to meet the center of the tray. Because i was the youngest, it took me longer to learn how to handle the knife. i cut the 'cot along the line the Lord made, put the pit in the pit box and placed the delicate fruit on the tray. There were no child labor laws or anything of the sort, so Mama handed us a knife, when she thought we could

30

handle it, to cut the fruit. My sisters and i worked from early in the morning with only a lunch break at noon. There was no running water in the shed so we used a common bucket, or basin, to wash up. Some of the cutting sheds had as many as eight to ten employees. After lunch we started all over again, working as fast as we could, because we were paid by the field box or tray. We had a card with numbers, that the shed boy would punch each time we cut a box or tray of 'cots. At the end of a hard day's work, it was a joy counting how many trays or field boxes we had cut. Cutting cots was tedious work, but enjoyable in that i was with my beloved sisters, working, sharing and many times singing the hit songs of the day. Being with them was such a blessing, and we were the fastest cutters in the shed.

At the end of the season, we were paid, or should i say, Papa took the money. Oh, he'd give Mama enough to buy each of us a new pair of shoes, one new dress, panties, socks, and the rest of our needed clothing was purchased at the thrift store for school. Many a time, towards the end of the school year, we would put cardboard inside our shoes to keep rainwater from soaking our feet. At the beginning of the year, we wore taps. Papa, being a shoemaker, believed taps on the toes and heels of the sole of the shoe gave them longer wear. That was cool, so we thought. We girls thought tapping down the cement corridor at school was neat. The teachers didn't agree and soon stopped us from wearing taps.

There were fun times in the cutting shed when we did what we called slip pit. Those were apricots that we would just pop the pit out of and lay the whole fruit on the tray. You can imagine a shed full of young people slip-pitting 'cots. Soon cots were being shot at each other with the pits and whole apricots. The owner soon came and lined all who had been involved and washed them down with water and sent us all home. Once again, i didn't take part, for some reason i knew it was wrong, but enjoyed watching the others having fun. i was not perfect by any means - nor am i now - but once again, i felt the working of the Holy Spirit in my life at a young age. When the day ended at four or five in the afternoon, the cut apricot trays were placed one at a time staggered on a small, train like car, which sat on rails. Once it was stacked with the staggered trays, it was pushed on the rails into a sulfur box. An old coffee can filled with sulfur was placed in a hole in the ground at the entrance of the sulfur box. The sulfur in the can was lit and the door was closed. The apricots would be "sulfured" until morning. Early the next morning, they would be removed from the sulfur box and, one by one; the trays would be laid in the warm California sun, at an angle, to dry. It was a beautiful sight seeing all those lovely apricots lying out in the sun to dry. That's how dried apricots were produced. Once they were dried, it was a job taking them off the trays. Old license plates were used to scrape them off the trays. We were always happy to get that job, although it was difficult, because it paid by the hour.

After the apricot season, it was time to pick prunes, not plums as we call them today. Prunes are prunes and plums are plums. Prunes dry and shrivel up; plums just rot. The prunes grown in California were brought from France; thus, French prunes. Santa Clara Valley/ Silicon Valley was known for the prunes, and Californians were known as prune pickers. Our family was known as California prune pickers, or poor white trash. Believe me, they were not easy picking, being much smaller than plums, and the trees didn't give much shade under the hot California sun. We were up early, before the sun rose, and out in the orchard to pick the small, purple fruit. The soil had been freshly turned, leaving large clots of dirt to kneel or scoot around on, to pick the prunes that had fallen on the ground. We didn't pick prunes from the trees as we would apricots. Apricots are more delicate and need to be picked fresh from the trees; prunes are hardier. Our whole family joined in on the picking, including Grandma, who would scoot on her bottom. We knew bending would leave us with aching backs at the end of the day. This way, it was either sore at the bottom or knees. Kneepads were unheard of, besides they were too costly for our family. Soon the knees were worn out in our pants or jeans. We picked barefoot as well.

At one time, i stepped on a stem that went up into the heel of my right foot, causing me to limp as i picked the prunes and emptied full buckets into large field boxes. My parents just ignored my limping, but not my sweet sisters. In the evenings after supper, they would work in the tent-like structure where we slept, by the light of a kerosine lamp, with a needle heated with a match, trying to get the stem out of my foot. Try as they may, they were unable to get the stem out of my foot. It never got infected, i never went to a doctor; the great physician, JESUS, healed me. Praise Him! A few years ago, i noticed a lump on the upper part of that same foot. i thought maybe it was the stem from years ago. It was very painful. On one visit to my doctor, i had him check it and he said it was just a bursa sack. I was relieved it wasn't the stem from years ago.

In those days, we never went to the doctor, except for our births, and Mama waited until delivery before Papa took her to the Santa Clara County Hospital/ Valley Medical Center. Then, there was also the time i mentioned earlier, when i had impetigo. Dentists were unheard of as well. Papa would take a pair of pliers and just pull out his hurting tooth.

When i was in the first grade, all of the students were required to go to the county hospital to have our teeth checked. We were loaded on the big yellow school bus that took us to the dentist. That was the first time i went to a dentist. Prior to informing me or my parents he pulled out my molars. We never brushed our teeth until we were given toothbrushes and taught how to do so in school; apparently my molars were cavity ridden, so he made the decision to pull them. i think that hasty decision would be frowned upon today. Recently, i went to the dentist and he said i had beautiful teeth and that they were nice and clean. Our sweet dentist, Daniel Lee, is Korean and a devout Christian; he often tells me with his precious accent, "Mrs. Miller (me) have nice teeth, but Mr. Miller (Fred) he have no nice teeth." That doesn't make Fred too happy, but we both laugh and thank him for his honesty. **"A cheerful heart is good medicine, but a crushed spirit dries up the bones." Proverbs 17:22.** Like me, Fred also did not eat well as a child during W.W. II in Germany, and he did not have a father to support him, his mother and brother. Not eating well and brushing our teeth had a huge affect on our teeth and health. We are both thankful for the health and teeth we have today; neither one of us take prescription drugs or have false teeth. PRAISE BE UNTO THE LORD!!!

Today, i don't care for dentists or doctors because of these bad experiences as a child. But, i learned that it's important to take children to the dentist and doctor when they're young, and teach them not be afraid. That's exactly what we did for our two sons, and they in turn take their children to doctors and dentist as youngsters. i'm thankful the Lord blessed me with good teeth and i take better care of them today and eat healthy.

Soon prune-picking season was over and we no longer had the house in the middle of the orchard; we were living in trailers and tent-like structures. Next, were walnuts and those awful black hands, but that meant school would soon begin, i looked forward to school opening. School started as soon as the crops were in, as most of the school children were taught to work. Most were not like our family, we worked the crops for survival.

i loved shopping for the few new things i got for school and my "new" second hand clothes. We moved back to San Jose once again, on Tenant Avenue/ Silicon Valley Road. This time we moved to an elderly man's ranch. He was old, of American Indian decent, and his name was Charlie Hocker. We lived in trailers with no electricity or running water. The money we made picking prunes was soon used up and Papa was without work once again. The orchards and dairies were selling out to homes, which made Papa's work obsolete. My father's first job was working on his parents ranch in San Jose and during that time, he learned to make and repair shoes, next it was feeding and caring for livestock, milking and clipping cows, working on

34

automobiles, pruning the many trees in the orchards throughout the valley, But as all these things were taken over by the industrial revolution, his work became obsolete. Also, he was now in his 60's and too old to start a new trade or profession. **Besides all that he enjoyed his wine and drowned his memories, so he thought**. He was also a socialite, who enjoyed people and pleasure.

As for our lovely Santa Clara Valley, what was once beautiful country was rapidly changing into suburbs and city life. This was just the beginning of what was coming within a short period of time.

When we went to school, having lice was prevalent and guess who brought it to the school? My three sisters and i did, from our unclean living. Mama would work hard to get the lice and their eggs out of our hair, using a fine toothcomb and vinegar. After being a hairdresser for all these many years, sometimes it's difficult to realize my sisters and i were the carriers of this most dreaded thing, lice.

Living in the trailer was difficult without running water or electricity. We girls helped Mama wash clothes by hand. Out came the old aluminum tub that we bathed in, along with the scrub board. My sisters and i would wring out the clothes by hand, with one sister at one end of whatever we were wringing out and the other, at the opposite end. Papa fashioned a clothesline so we could hang the clothes to dry. We heated the trailers with old kerosene stoves that smelled awful when burning. Even with the smell, at night they made a pretty decoration on the ceiling from the different shaped holes on the top of the stove. Those ceiling decorations were very comforting for a small child like me. At night i would ask my mama, "Mama, where will i go when I die?" As i mentioned, dying was very frightening to me as a child, the childhood i knew and experienced. Mama would answer, "Don't worry, go to sleep." That was not comforting, but Mama didn't know the answer, either. So i would stare at the decorations on the ceiling from the kerosene stove, which brought me comfort, along with my sisters making shapes against the wall with their hands, using the reflection of the light on the stove. Soon sleep would come and i could rest.

Chapter Five

**"The Lord your God is with you,
He is mighty to save." Zephaniah 3: 17a**

**A new life. Learning about the God I always
wanted to know.**

During that time we lived on rice and canned milk for days and
weeks on end. i looked forward to going to school, where we had hot
lunches. Somehow, my father paid for mine since i was too young to work for
them like my sisters did. Charlie Hocker was an interesting man. Even at my
young age, i knew the things he believed did not seem right. He was into
astrology and reading the stars and that was very uncomfortable for me.

Because we didn't have electricity, we would walk with Charlie
about two miles from our home to friends who had a television so we could
watch television programs.

We had an outside toilet, and Papa was in the process of digging a
new hole for the toilet when he and Charlie got into an argument. So we
were thrown off his ranch and had to find elsewhere to live. Somehow we
made it through the year. Papa would sell whatever he could: iron, bent
metal, and perhaps get a job-clipping cows. As i mentioned before, my Father
was a 'Jack of all trades', and built a motorized machine attached somehow
to clippers, so he could clip around the cow's udder using electricity instead
of clipping by hand. He was an amazing man; very inventive, just too bad he
drank so much. Of course in the springtime, and the few orchards
throughout the Santa Clara Valley needed pruning. Papa was good at that.

School was out and we had a few weeks to enjoy the warm summer
days before work began once again in the orchards. This time, we moved the
trailer toward the Almaden area. After the season was over and we made our

37

trip to downtown San Jose to purchase our clothes for school, Papa found a house that we rented off of Tenant Avenue/ Silicon Valley Road, once again. For some reason we seemed to always move to this area. Perhaps, the Lord had it in mind for me to write this book and brought us back lest i forget. If so, thank You Lord.

Recently, when i went back to San Jose in search of Tenant Avenue, much to my surprise part of the road is called Silicon Valley Road and the rest is Tenant Avenue. So, i really believe the Lord has gone before me to write this book, and give it the title: "**The Girl From Silicon Valley**."

There was an ongoing battle between my parents because we moved so much. Mama fought to keep us in the same school district for stability. We attended Oak Grove Elementary School at the time. The school was across the street from a prune orchard. Years later IBM would be on that very spot.

We lived near, what Mama called, "the berry patch" off of Tenant Avenue/Silicon Valley Road. Her reason for calling it that, was, she worked hard in the strawberry patches that Japanese farmers owned. The Japanese were very good farmers and workers, whom i admired.

Mom was pregnant with my younger brother Bill. She worked hard picking strawberries during pregnancy. i wanted to help her. So at the age of nine i went to the strawberry patch to help my Mama. The owner came behind me after i picked the berries and scolded me because i had not done a good job. Perhaps, that was how she was taught and meant no harm. My being a very sensitive, people pleasing child, was very hurt with her remarks, but it taught me to take pride in what i do and do the best i can. That was the first and last time that i helped in the berry patch. My words to parents are, **"Be patient with your children and teach them diligently." 1 Corinthians 13:4 says; "Love is patient, love is kind. It does not boast, it is not proud."**

While living near the "berry patch", Mama awoke early one morning to the sound of pans floating around the house. It was raining hard and, the roof leaked and Mama set out pans to catch the rain. The floating pans meant that the water was coming into the house, and not only through the roof. We lived beside Coyote creek. The creek was flowing in the back door and going out the front. Mama stood on the bed and pulled the light string that was attached to the light bulb, and saw the water coming in. It was about a foot high. She awakened my father. The night before, he had parked the pickup on higher ground, little did we know that he could swim, none of us could. So, he swam to the truck and went to get help. We waited and waited for him as the water kept rising. We were wondering if he would ever return.

The time was around Christmas and we had never celebrated Christmas before in our home. But this year, 1955, my sisters had discovered a dump close to our home. They would go there and find little things that they would wrap in newspaper, for my brother and i for Christmas. They took a branch from a tree and, leaned it against the wall in the house; we decorated it with paper chains and they put the tiny gifts under the branch, not even realizing what and why we were celebrating. Although, in those days in school, we sang Christmas songs, not understanding what they meant. One song i remember well was; "O, Little Town of Bethlehem." i always wondered why we sang; "in thy dark street shineth the Everlasting Light," thinking we were singing something about lights shining in China (Shinith); a child's sweet innocent mind.

Our Papa proved his love and faithfulness to us, and our neighbors, for he soon arrived with the Sheriff's Department, who brought boats to retrieve us from the oncoming water. We had to leave everything behind, including the gifts my sisters had wrapped and my beloved doll. We had to escape for our lives. The water eventually went over the rooftops and destroyed everything. My sisters, grandma, mom, and i went to live with my aunt and uncle until the water receded. Papa went to live in downtown San

Jose. Soon the water receded and the Red Cross came in and gave us all new furniture, bedding, everything. We were better off than before. i even had a new gray coat. i'd never owned a coat. i wanted to see what the house was like after the flood, so we went to look. There was silt, about an inch thick, on the floors and very slippery. My mother warned me to not come in, but I was curious. i went sliding across that slippery silt floor and soiled my beautiful little coat. That's what i got for not obeying.

The date was April 2, 1956 when Papa drove the old Model T across the country roads to Santa Clara Hospital, now Valley Medical Center, where Mama gave birth to my brother William Cecil. Papa was so happy now to have two sons. He even did the laundry for Mom while she was in the hospital. That was a first. The only thing he forgot was to run the clothes through the wringer before hanging them on the line to dry. They took quite some time to dry, but at least he tried.

Mama told me in later years, after she had given birth to my oldest sister; Josephine, Papa was so thankful and proud. When he went to the hospital to visit Mama, he brought her a half-gallon of ice cream. She just looked at him and said, "Bill, what am I going to do with a half gallon of ice cream while I'm in the hospital?" He couldn't understand her ungratefulness. Please remember, my father being thirty years older than Mama, thought it was a big deal having ice cream, a frozen dessert. Besides, he loved ice cream.

From the berry patch, we moved again down the road to another shack. It was there that my oldest sister, Josephine, did not come home anymore. Each evening i would go with my mom in the car to pick up Josephine from the school bus. Several nights went by and we didn't pick-up Josephine. Night after night, i would ask Mom, "Can we go pick up Josephine, now?" Finally, Mama said, "She will not be coming home anymore." i sat there in disbelief as to what my mother told me. Tears welled in my eyes, and questions in my little heart that i was not allowed to ask. Why wasn't she coming home anymore? i was devastated, sorrowful, disappointed and hurt. As i mentioned earlier, an elephant was in the middle of our home and we were not allowed to ask why, just accept.

Sometime passed and i learned what had happened. One day, after school was out, Josephine went on the bus to my aunt and uncle's never to return home again. She was fifteen at the time. My aunt told my sister Barbara and i, years later, when she came home from shopping, Josephine was sitting at the kitchen table waiting for my aunt and uncle to arrive. My aunt, at first told her she must return home, my sister refused, saying she could not take my father's abuse any longer. So began the process of her living with my aunt and uncle. Oh, how i missed my sister. Little did i know that this would not be the first time of experiencing a broken heart from the loss of one of my dear sister's presence.

Grandma was getting older and she began hallucinating. i remember her telling me that there was ice cream on the ceiling and i didn't see it. i believe now, that she had either Alzheimer's or some form of Dementia; she probably had it for years, and it increased with age and drinking too much wine. When her social security check would come, my father would hand her a jug of wine in trade for her signature on her social security check. Mom would then hide the wine because she knew my grandmother would get drunk. Grandma would come to me and say, "Where did Mama hide the wine?" So i would tell her, not knowing Mama didn't want her to have it. And then the battle was on, between my Mom and Grandma.

The one thing i remember about my grandmother is that it seemed like every five minutes she would ask me, what time or day it was. As a result i learned to tell time at a young age. She would also hold me and sing to me in Italian. i loved my grandmother but i just couldn't get close to her, there wasn't any bonding. Which i have since learned is so important, especially with grandchildren. For me, our grandchildren are very important, and i want that special bonding with them and they with me. Relationships are most important, and many begin at a tender age.

While living in this shack, my father went on one of his drunken rampages again. My mother told me to run quickly to the neighbors and call my aunt. i remember running barefoot through the freshly plowed prune orchard with chunks of soil tearing my feet as i was trying to memorize my aunt's phone number so she could come and get us. To this day, it has helped me to memorize phone numbers; except with the cell phones now, there's no need to memorize phone numbers. Remembering numbers was good for my memory.

Another school year ended and it was time for my now two sisters and i, to work cutting apricots again. This time, my sisters took the money we earned, which made my father very angry. We moved again to a shack in the middle of a hayfield near Evergreen, California. That is still in Santa Clara/Silicon Valley. My sisters had taken the money we earned and hidden it under baby Bill's mattress in the baby buggy. They wanted to leave and have my mother leave my father, because now we had money and we could get away. My mom refused.

Grandma became very ill and it was decided that she would have to go into an old folk's home. For the first time, my aunt and uncles came to our home and there was a big fight that went on between my mom and my dad about my grandmother and the bad care that she gotten over the years. What puzzled me, is Mom did the best she could in caring for my grandmother, if they were in disagreement, why didn't they care for my grandmother. i also, believe Grandma loved being around all of us grandchildren. As she told my oldest sister, Josephine, "I need to help your mother raise you children." It was a two way street, she helped Mama with us children, and as she aged, Mama helped her. After a losing battle with my aunt and uncles, Mom, with great remorse, released grandma into my aunt's care, and Grandma was soon moved into a nursing home.

Not long after this tragic episode of losing Grandma, we moved again. So i attended two different schools while i was in the fourth grade. It was here i met a dear Catholic girl who would take me inside the church she attended as we walked home from school. We would only go in for a few moments, and she would kneel down to pray. i liked what she did, so followed her every move. i recall, as we walked past the church on our way home from school, how she would bless herself with the sign of the cross as we past the church. This intrigued me, and i questioned her as to why she did that. i now realize the Lord was planting seeds in my life, that would reap a harvest later. Another seed was, as i looked out the kitchen window from our home, i could see downtown San Jose. Above the city lights, was a lit up sign that shone brightly at night, that said; JESUS SAVES. i would stare at that lit sign and wonder; "What does that mean?"

One day while i was in school, i was called into the office. i couldn't understand why, because i was always a good student, and didn't get into any trouble. There was enough trouble at home, why would i want more? The reason for being called to the office was the principal wanted to question if i had sisters at home and their ages. i was very honest and told him i did have sisters at home. Upon arriving home, both of my sisters were gone. My father had called the truancy office to pick up my sister who refused to attend school. i believe she did not want to attend, yet another, different school.(Mom, understood why it wasn't good to keep changing schools, and that's why she fought my father so diligently to keep us in one school.) My other sister didn't want the other sister to be alone, so went with her. They were put in foster home care.

Once again, this was very traumatic for me, bringing back recent memories of my sister Josephine leaving home, at such a young age, never to return. With no one to talk it over with, i just went off by myself and cried and cried; i missed my sisters. i knew they, like Josephine, would never return home.

Within a short period of time, my parents went to court for a hearing as to where to place my sisters. My aunt and uncle attended the hearing and my uncle wept and said that he and my aunt would take them home. And so it was that my three sisters would be living with my aunt and uncle. Nothing more was said about my sisters after that episode. Years later my mother said to me, "I gave up the girls because it was better for them to live with their aunt and uncle than to live in the bad situation at home."

Since my Grandmother was no longer living with us and we didn't have her meager social security as income, we were literally starving. Across the street from our home was an onion field. My father would go out at night and steal onions and bring them back and make onion gravy. For weeks on end, we lived on onion gravy. It must have been at Thanksgiving/Christmas time, that someone came to our door with a food basket. It was meant for another family that had lived there prior to us, but my father took it anyway because we were hungry. Oh, there was such wonderful food in that food basket! As i look back, i believe it was a gift from God, meant for us.

Now that my sisters were no longer living with us, my brother Frank would be the one to tangle with Papa. One day, my father got so angry with him that he went after him with a butcher knife. i came between them, to stop Papa from harming my brother. Witnessing how he treated my mother and sisters, i knew it best to keep quiet in order not to have any harm come to me, too. This time, i knew i had to defend my innocent brother. Otherwise, i lived in constant fear of my father. We moved again. This time, we moved the trailers we had lived in, in the past, to Alviso. i recall visiting Alviso and how my father would tell us there were floods there all the time, and i thought, "Why would anybody want to live there?" i soon found out. It was cheap living.

In order to enlighten you, the reader, to what Alviso was like at that time; some years later, when we moved to the Sierra's, one of our neighbors son's visited us, and i told him i had lived in Alviso. With a surprised look he

44

told me; "I remember going to Alviso when I was in High School with the church I attended, on a mission trip, we were shocked at the poverty in Alviso at the time. And you lived there?" That statement reminded me of a verse in John 1 that says; " **Nazareth! Can anything good come from there?" Nathanael asked. John 1:46** (as he spoke of the Lord Jesus who came from Nazareth) to Philip. "**Come and see." said Philip**. For me it was 'Can anything good come from Alviso?' My response is a definite, "Yes." i was to make some wonderful friends there, and later, some would become relatives.

Somehow the trailers reappeared and we lived in them in a trailer park in Alviso. Our trailers had no bathroom facilities, so we used the showers and bathrooms on the premises, much like a campground. It was there i was to meet my dear friend Paula and her family. Her Mother, Thelma, would become my Mother's dearest friend. By the way, Thelma, to this day, lives in a lovely mobile home park in Morgan Hill, California; she is in her eighties. We still keep in contact after all these years. She is an amazing lady, born and raised on a farm in South Carolina.

Several years ago i took my mother to visit Thelma when she lived in her lovely home in Los Banos, California. Her comment to me was; "After seeing my nice home here, can you believe we lived in Alviso?" It was unlike how we all live today. Since my Father did not work much in his later years and social security deductions didn't take affect until he was almost retired, we were now living on his meager social security benefits.

Not only did it flood in Alviso, we were infested with mosquitoes and fleas. The fleas, we were told, were sand fleas. Well, they were regular fleas and they were everywhere: in our bedding, clothes, everywhere. The mosquitoes were everywhere, also. At night, just before we turned out the lights, they covered the ceilings in our trailer. Once the lights were turned off, we quickly dived under the covers so we didn't we get bitten terribly by those bloodsuckers. It was much like Tijuana, so much poverty. The infestation reminds me of the story in Exodus, when the Pharaoh wouldn't let the people go, the Egyptians were attacked by frogs, flies, locusts and so forth. Refer to: **Exodus 8-10.**

i was in the fifth grade when floodwaters flooded Alviso. Once again, as in the flood in San Jose, we witnessed the water coming full force, this time from a broken levy. My mom, my brothers and i, went to live with my aunt and uncle and my sisters for a short period of time, until the floodwaters receded. i loved being with my sisters again. It was a blessing that my teacher lived close to my aunt, so she would take me back and forth to school. The school was built on higher ground in Alviso, so it never got flooded.

Soon we were able to move back after the floodwaters receded. This time, we moved to a Mexican labor camp. What happened to the trailer my father had built was a mystery. Later it would reappear and house him when my parents separated. The long empty trailer went with us. i used it as a schoolroom to teach my brothers. We lived in a shack with no bathroom facilities so we would use the bathroom in the labor camp.

While living in the camp, a man, who was a neighbor in the trailer park, came to visit us. He drove a nice car that Mama would always comment about: the taillights reminded her of bird's wings. Perhaps, she thought those little bird wings could carry her away to a better life. Well, guess what? That is why this man came to visit. He came to see my mother, whom he liked and proposed to take her and us children away from my, mean angry father. When Mama told me, i was delighted and encouraged her to do so. Anything seemed better than living in such poverty and to just think of the peace. Mama was a very committed lady and told this man, "No." He was very kind, accepted her answer and never pursued her again. Guess she felt those little bird's wings on his car were not the answer.

Other than the owners, who were also of Mexican descent and their family, we were the only other family living in the Camp. There was a huge building on the grounds where the men ate after a hard day working in the vegetable fields harvesting the crops. The owner's wife prepared the food for these hard-working men and since the workers were from Mexico, she made homemade tortillas. My little brother Bill was favored by the owner's wife. She always gave him his fill of tortillas and whatever she prepared. Aside from being hungry, my brother Frank and i liked homemade tortillas as well, so we stood a ways off and coaxed our little brother Bill to go and get enough tortillas to fill all our bellies. He succeeded and we all ate until our tummies were full. i can just taste them now: fresh and warm and oh, so good.

i loved my little brothers and thought it was my duty to teach and care for them. The walls inside the trailer had no insulation, just plain walls, great for writing on with chalk. So i took upon myself to teach Frank and Bill as though we were in school. Bill seemed to enjoy learning, but as i think back, i believe Frank was not excited about it at all.

Bill would use the gift the Lord gave him to become a wonderful teacher and would help many young men and women to better their lives. He is well liked by his students. His daughter, Candace, would follow in his footsteps and become a good teacher as well. Frank would use his God given gift in using his hands to create and become a talented builder and contractor. He then taught his sons the trade and many other manly things, like fishing, racing and so forth.

All of us loved being outside, in the not so fresh, air. Alviso was surrounded by the sewage filtration plant, the city dump and the stinky slew. Those who lived in Alviso always said, "It's not Alviso that stinks, it's all the things surrounding it that gave off that unpleasant fragrance." This reminds me of a verse in **2 Corinthians**, which states; **"For we are to God the aroma of Christ among those who are perishing. To the one we are the smell of death; to the other, the fragrance of life..."** 2 Corinthians **2:15-16a.**

47

One day while living in the Camp, playing baseball with the boys (no other girls lived in the Camp), i went to catch a fly ball, ran, turned and tore my leg on a license plate on a parked car. Ouch, i still have the scar to prove it. No, doctors, no emergency, no stitches, but definitely the Lord's healing Hand was upon me, even in all that filth. Since we had no inside bathroom, tub, or shower for cleaning, i wonder how it never got infected. Somehow, as in years prior, we made it, and now i realize it was the Lord's healing touch. Although, for every cut or scratch we had, Mama used hydrogen peroxide, or iodine. We were thankful when Mercurochrome was invented as it didn't burn like iodine, but we still looked like we were in a battle with the orange stain it left on our skin. When we lived in the trailers off of Tennant Avenue, Mama used Clove Salve. That really worked, smelled good, didn't burn or stain.

Not long after this episode, i had another serious injury playing baseball with the neighborhood children. We were having a great game playing in a vacant lot behind the fences of the Labor Camp. i was up to bat and a good hitter (Mama, had taught me). The young boy pitched the ball, but, instead of the ball, he threw a big clod of dirt, aimed directly at my eye. He hit his target alright, and i lost complete sight in that eye and thought for sure i was blinded. i went running home, crying from the excruciating pain. Mom just washed it out with cold water and that was the end of that. i was not blind, thank the Lord, but my eye was quite swollen. There were no threats of lawsuits in those days. Besides, what would one sue for? We were all in the same poverty boat.

Yet, another baseball experience that Paula keeps reminding me of is when she was the catcher and i was at bat, and i kept telling her to stand further back. When i swung, the bat conked her on the head and knocked her out. You'd think i would have quit playing baseball, but i have more stories to tell later in this biography. Baseball is a good, fun sport, which i will play someday in heaven.

The streets in Alviso were muddy: no sidewalks, no street lights. It was there in Alviso, i met another friend, Celeste. She lived with her great grandparents who were related to the famous Chisholm Trail family. i found out later, that her great grandparents raised one of my half brothers. What a small world. From the Mexican labor camp, we moved to a shack next door to the Catholic Church. It was closer to Celeste, so we had many fun times together. Some things we got into, i had never thought of until we met later in life. What a pair. The Lord protected me in many of our adventures. There was not much to do in Alviso, so we walked the muddy streets at night, and investigated the old fish canneries of by-gone days. Alviso was once a thriving town, much like Monterey with all the fish canneries, providing lots of work for many people. The streets were named after the streets in Chicago. That is why at one time it was called "Little Chicago". There were different things that were done in the years past, for entertainment, perhaps some illegal as well. For Celeste and i, my little brothers and all the children, there was the Alviso Speedway. People from everywhere came to watch the races. My (soon to be) brother-in-law, Don Epperson, and his brothers; Jack and Bob, were local Alviso boys, and of course, were our favorites. We collected empty soda bottles that we found, traded them in for cash and would have enough to go to the races. Those were the days my friend.

Chapter Six

"... but the righteous will live by faith."
Habakuk 2:4b

My parents finally separate. There is
peace and no more turmoil.

In those days, we had Religious Relief Time, which as i understand, is still allowed today in California schools. During Religious Relief Time, the children were released to attend classes at the Catholic or Protestant church once a week during school time. From the time i was in the second grade at Oak Grove School in San Jose until this time, i had watched the Catholic Nuns in their black and white garb and the Protestant ladies neatly dressed, take the children with them. Where were they going? What were they learning? What were they doing i wondered? Somehow, in my little spirit i knew it was something special and good, and i wanted to go as well. But my parents never allowed us children to attend. Wide eyed, i stared out the classroom windows watching as the children were led by these kind teachers.

Then it happened, when i was in the sixth grade, my teacher Mrs. McCormick, announced that year, that all the children were going to Religious Relief Time. They were not allowed to remain in the room with her. My first thought was, "What shall I tell my parents?" I was so frightened. I went to my mother and asked her, "Should I become a Protestant or a Catholic?" Mom said that the Catholics were very strict. I had already thought that I would become a Protestant because I had watched the children returning from their lesson, and the Protestants always got more candy. My mother also told me to talk to my father. I had to approach him when he was not in an alcoholic state. When I finally got the courage to ask him, he took me to what looked like a black strong box. i had seen it before and always wondered what was inside. He took the key that opened it. i lifted the lid and inside were things from my Grandmother Joseph, pertaining to her involvement in the Catholic Church. Just seeing all those treasures before my very eyes, i knew she was very active in the Catholic Church. My father told me he had been very involved in the Catholic church and, much to my surprise, he had even been an alter boy. Was that why he kept this strong box, as he called it, those many years with him wherever we lived, because it held things dear to his heart? Things he knew about his faith but never shared, let alone live them.

Upon this new discovery and to please my alcoholic father, i decided i would become a Catholic. Within a year's time, i was baptized, made my first communion, and was confirmed, but i didn't understand. Back then, in the church i attended, Mass was celebrated in Latin and the sermon was in Spanish because we lived in a Spanish/Mexican speaking community. So how could i understand the Gospel? Once i was blind, but soon i would see.

Mrs. Tufts was my Godly teacher in the Catholic Church. She taught me that God is love. Every time i would see her car pull up to the Catholic Church, i quickly ran over to help her clean the church or whatever needed doing. i was in need of new shoes for school and Mrs. Tufts presented me with a brand new pair of nursing shoes. Reluctantly, i took them, to not hurt her, yet i was thirteen years old and i knew how the other students would make fun of me with those nursing shoes.

One day when i went to help Mrs. Tufts at the church, we were sorting through clothes and shoes that were donated by wealthy people for poor children. Mrs. Tufts told me, that in return for helping, i could take whatever i wanted. The Lord blessed me with thirteen pair of new shoes that day. i believe that happened because i accepted the gift she gave me of the nursing shoes.

In the summer months, i lived with my sisters and my aunt and uncle in San Jose. Their neighbors owned an apricot orchard, in which we cut cots to earn money for our school clothes. It was there, that my oldest sister, Josephine would meet her future husband, Robert. As it turned out, he was Mrs. Tufts, son and she was my Godmother. Could it be possible, my sister and Robert would marry and live in Alviso? If that were true, it would be a dream come true for me to have my sister living in Alviso as well. My dream came to reality when my sister Josephine soon married Robert, and they made their home in Alviso; she was back in my life. Then the Lord had yet another blessing for me. My sister Frances met Robert's best friend, Don. He was the racecar driver that Celeste and I would spend weekends going to Alviso speedway to watch race. Eventually, Don married my sister Frances and they moved to Alviso also; so, now i had both sisters within a two-mile radius. i now know the Lord orchestrated all of this, Praise Him!!! The Lord does work in wonderful, amazing ways. Praise Him!!!

Another reason for working in the summer cutting cots, was to pay the doctor bill for my impetigo. The doctor's office kept sending the bill for my treatment, and my father refused to pay it. Instead, each time the bill came he would rant and rave and tell me how he wished he had chopped my head off when he had the opportunity. i grew wise, and when the time for the bill would come, i would volunteer to ride my bike and pick-up the mail at the post office, in order to avoid the threats. Finally, i sat down and wrote a letter to the doctor explaining how i was going to work that summer and would pay the bill. After that letter, i never received another bill from the doctor. i was about thirteen at the time and very responsible. What i find interesting is, years later while living here in the Sierra's, i was talking to a dear friend and he mentioned this wealthy skin specialist who lived near him. He also said, the doctor had a terrible drinking problem and he wasn't a very nice man. When he told me the name of the doctor and where he was from, i knew it was the same doctor that helped me with the impetigo those many years prior, and who had forgiven my debt. Just as the Lord JESUS has forgiven our debt by dying on the cross and rising from the dead for our sins.

Refer to: **1 Corinthians 15:3-4**. i had intended to visit the doctor, and regret i never took the time to do so. Perhaps, i could have helped him in return. My hope and prayer is that he came to the saving grace of Jesus and gave Him his heart and life. That being the case, we will meet once again in heaven.

Chapter Seven

"...there is a future for the man of peace."
Psalm 37:37b

Mama is still in love with Papa.

i continued trying to please my alcoholic father by doing things that needed being done. Once again, we moved again, this time across the street from the Catholic Church into a house that actually had an indoor bathroom. There would be times when my father would not come home for days; i wondered where he might be, but enjoyed the peace and quiet. When he returned home, he would tell me about the experience of going to jail and how well he was treated. He would proudly say; "I got three square meals a day, clean clothes and they even came in and shaved my beard everyday." So that's where he was those days he was gone, in jail. Perhaps, he was too ashamed to tell me why he got arrested, so he built up the experience, making it sound like he had a great time, nothing to be ashamed about. i was too wise for this, and knew no matter what, getting arrested was not something to be proud of.

One Christmas, there was a knock at the door and there stood my sister Frances and her husband Don with our very first Christmas tree, including all the decorations and gifts to put under the tree. i was ever so thankful to them for this wonderful gift for my brothers and i. i was probably thirteen at the time, and still did not understand what we were celebrating.

i was now in the seventh grade. My teacher was Mr. Buford and he was a married man, yet he would take us young girls different places. i thought it quite strange. He took several of us young girls to Santa Cruz. i had never been to Santa Cruz. i was so excited to go to the beach and the ocean, being born and raised in and near the coast, yet i had never been to the ocean. We had a nice time, although i almost drowned when i got caught by one of those huge undertows. If it weren't for hanging on to the other girls' hands and Mr. Buford's, i probably wouldn't be writing this today. The Lord had sent His angel or angels to protect me once again.

While in the seventh grade, Mr. Buford and Mr. Hayes, the eighth grade teacher, nominated me, to give a speech for the eighth grade graduation. This was the first time i would speak publicly. Later i learned that public speaking is one of the most frightening things for most people, but not for me, because the Lord has gifted me in that way. i love, and am in my element, when i speak publicly. It is such a blessing to find the gift the Lord has given you, and then take the opportunity to use it for His glory.

Mr. Hayes gave me the confidence i needed to speak; he was very instrumental in my gift as a speaker today. As i look back, because of his demeanor, i believe Mr. Hayes was also a Christian man. For instance, during our lunch hour we would sit in the classroom, we had no cafeteria as such, and Mr. Hayes would tune in Paul Harvey on the radio. i enjoyed listening to this man's deep loving, convicting voice over the radio. Years later i learned that Paul Harvey was a very devout, patriotic, Christian man.

Yet, while eating my lunch with the other students, i was always embarrassed, because Mama didn't have wax paper to wrap my sandwich. She would use the wrapping from the bread, and i would have to save the paper and bring it back home for Mama to reuse. Talk about recycling, we did it way back when it was unheard of.

On rainy afternoons, my father would always pick me up in his little Model T pickup. i realize now, he loved me and wanted to keep me safe. But it was so embarrassing for this young teen-age girl, because he would pull up right next to the classroom door, about a half hour before school was out, and everyone would look at me because of the noises of the little Model T pickup. But that was his demonstration of love for me. Years later i learned how alcohol consumption can confuse the mind; one moment he wanted to kill me over the expenses i incurred from the doctor and the next, he wanted to bestow love upon me, by picking me up during a rainy day after school. We never talked about it, i was so fearful of his anger.

i loved sports, especially baseball and tetherball. My mother loved baseball and when she wasn't playing it with us children, she was watching the professionals on television. She even collected baseball cards when she was younger. i wish i had some of those today. It was only right that she would teach us how to play her beloved sport. She taught us as soon as we could hold a bat and throw a ball. And we were taught to throw the ball, none of this girlie stuff, "either throw it or forget it" was her motto. We always teased her that she needed more children to make a baseball team.

On sunny days my father didn't pick me up, i walked home with my Mexican-speaking friends. i learned a little bit of Spanish/Mexican, at that time. This was a first for me, to have close friends i could talk to, share and learn from each other. None of us dared to talk about our home lives. i had a new friend i mentioned before, Celeste. My father did not like Celeste and thought she was trouble. He was right, as i later discovered. As i go back to when the Lord touched me at three years of age, i knew in my spirit right from wrong. **"Listen, my son (daughter) to a father's instruction;..."** **Proverbs 4:1**. Since my father was in a lot of trouble with the law, he knew and could sense trouble.

Soon i graduated from the eighth grade at the top of my class. Although, my father never attended a graduation ceremony for any of us children, he felt it important to do something special for me for graduating from the eighth grade. As i look back, i realize his heart was beginning to soften, because he gave me my first gold wristwatch. He saved from the meager social security we lived on, in order to purchase the watch, and it was for me! i really liked the watch, and wore it with special pride, because it was a precious gift- the only one I ever received from my father. i only wish i would have known him better, but it seemed that no matter how hard i tried

56

to get to know him, there was a wall that was up and he would not allow anyone to come into his broken heart. Wonder what it was that hurt him so very much. No matter what, i, like my Mama loved my Papa. i once heard, that a parent is a parent to a child, it doesn't matter if the parent abuses the child or not, the child deep down inside, still loves that parent. The Bible says in **Psalm 27:10 "Though my father and mother forsake me the Lord will receive me."**

i began high school in the fall. i attended Buchser High School in Santa Clara, which was about twenty miles from where we lived. i came from a very small grammar school and i was going into a high school where students had graduated from junior highs that had two to three hundred students in them. So this was a very frightening experience for me. i would have nightmares about whether i could find the classes or even use the lockers, as i had never done that before.

My mother went to live with my aunt, uncle and sisters the summer previous to school that Fall, to work in the cannery. She was gone all week and i was left to care for my brothers. When Mom would come home on Sundays, i would tell her, "We need to get away from my father."

The abuse was getting worse and worse. He would accuse me of things that were not true; that i was prostituting myself, and not doing my job taking care of my brothers, just false accusations. So i told my mother that we would have to leave because i could not take the abuse anymore. Much to my surprise, my Mother finally listened, knew i was being honest; she too was tired of the abuse. As soon as the work was complete at the cannery she said we would move out from under my father's abuse.

Now that Mom had money, we were able to move. My two brothers, my mom and i found a lovely little place and applied for A and C: Aid for Needy Children. We also received a portion of my father's social security. It wasn't long after we settled in our little home that we were to experience another flood. So we had to move out and leave all our belongings behind.

Once the water receded, we moved again, this time closer to my sister Frances. i loved living closer to my sister. In the evenings, while her husband would be working on his racecar, my sister Frances and I would bake and shop and have great times together. It was then i had that special bonding i craved for, after she had left home as a young girl.

Although, we were much more at peace, not having my father living with us, another problem ensued for me. Mom had never shopped or handled household finances, so turned the job over to me. At the young age of sixteen, i learned how to handle grocery shopping, and all the other finances that came along with running a household efficiently. What seemed to be a problem in the beginning turned out to be a blessing, that would help me in the years to come, for my husband, sons, my mom and i, in managing our home.

Now that i was a teenager, boys were really special in my life and with it came parties and fun times. But God always had His protective hand on me. Although, i liked boys, i was still frightened of men due to my father's example. There were several young men who really liked and cared for me; the feeling wasn't mutual. i would date them briefly and then break it off. Sorry to say now, there were many broken hearts.

Several years ago, i made a trip to Alviso. It now has streetlights, sidewalks, and beautiful homes. The city of San Jose has taken it over. They built a big levy so the little town does not flood anymore. All the old fish canneries and the muddy streets are long gone. Things just don't remain the same.

Soon my sisters moved, one to Milpitas, and the other to Monte Vista. My mom, my brothers and i moved to San Jose, within walking distance of my aunt and uncle. Most of the orchards were gone by now, there were a few left, so we could still work cutting apricots in the summer. i would soon start my junior year at Overfelt High School in San Jose, with my, now longtime, friend, Joyce, whom i met in the apricot cutting shed years prior, when we were about eleven or twelve years of age. i began a new life at Overfelt, becoming the person that God wanted me to be, open and free. i felt like a butterfly coming out of it's cocoon, leaving the old behind. Previously, i felt dirty and unworthy because of my father's treatment. This was a new life at a new high school. i became very active with high school activities. i began writing school news for the San Jose Mercury newspaper, discovering yet another gift i never knew i had. Thanks be to the Lord.

i loved school, as always. The high school i attended was across the street from a Catholic church, which i attended occasionally, because i didn't have transportation; we depended on my aunt and my sisters. We knew we needed a car for transportation, so my first car was a 1957 Ford. The passenger door was wired together with baling wire. My brother-in-law, Don, and my sister, Fran, helped me purchase that first car for seventy-five dollars. It ran good enough to get us to the grocery store and whatever errands i had to run for my mother.

Chapter Eight

"Many waters cannot quench love;..."
Song of Soloman

Human love enters my life as never before.

i worked on Saturdays cleaning house for my Uncle Jim. He lived on North 19th Street in San Jose. He grew wonderful tomatoes, carrots, and other vegetables in that rich valley soil, on either side of his front lawn. My Uncle Joseph, who worked for the City of San Jose parks department, always shook his head upon seeing Uncle Jim's garden and home. i learned a lot about my maternal grandparents from my uncle Jim. He told me that i was much like my grandfather, a real go-getter. Uncle Jim fought in World War II, in the Pacific Theater. He came home to his wife and his two sons that he loved. i always teased Uncle Jim that he was like King Midas, in that, everything King Midas touched turned into gold. Everything Uncle Jim touched turned into olive oil. With a Swiss/Italian background, he cooked with a lot of olive oil. As a result, everything was sticky with olive oil, even the kitchen floor. Uncle Jim was the total opposite of his brother, Uncle Joe. They were like the odd couple. One was so neat and clean, and the other one...oh well! Years later, I met their cousins who lived in Switzerland. i found it amazing: these brothers were opposites just like my uncles, one neat and clean and the other. It's awe inspiring how the Lord works in our families. These cousins had never met, yet they were alike in many ways.

On the weekends i spent going to the races, watching my brother-in-law, Don and his brother, Jack Epperson, Marshal Sargent, Nick Ringo, Al Pombo, now racing at San Jose speedway. My half brother Leslie Joseph, much to my surprise, was active in the speedway as well. He owned and operated Les Joseph's Garage in downtown San Jose; is it any wonder why he too, loved the races? He was the only sibling from 'our' father's previous marriage that kept in contact with 'our' father and us half brothers and sisters. He was a dear sweet man, whom i will share more about later in this writing. At the speed-way i loved Linguisa sandwiches and watching the races, sitting in the stands with my dear sister Fran and many other friends, cheering Don, and our favorites, on to victory. San Jose speedway was across from East Ridge, down from Reed Hill View Airport.

i enjoyed my high school years; there were football games, basketball games, and all kinds of sporting events that i attended with my friend Joyce who was a cheerleader. At age sixteen we finally had a phone for the first time in our home. Not long after, my sister Josephine and her husband, Robert, purchased for me, my very own Princess phone. Oh, how i cherished having my own personal phone.

In high school, i participated in talent shows and plays and discovered who this once shy little girl was inside this body the Lord had given me. There were dances and senior balls and junior proms and i was always involved in getting them ready by doing the decorating and planning the events. i received many awards in English and writing and i was a top salesperson in my senior class for our senior class project. i felt very honored.

Many avenues that i had never pursued before came to reality. In the midst of these successes, i was failing typing, due to not having a typewriter at home to practice. So i dropped typing and took up sewing. i was not a very good seamstress, but at least passed the class. Today on my new computer (a precious gift from my Mom) i type very well, just imagine if i'd had my own typewriter while i was in high school. Wow!!!

My younger brothers were still at home with our Mom and i, (we had our sibling rivalries) although they were much younger than i, still i loved them very much. Our sister Barbara was doing very well in touring throughout the world entertaining our U.S. troops and had the opportunity to meet many famous movie stars at the time. She became very well acquainted with the cast of My Three Sons, especially with Don Grady, who played Robbie. Apparently, he had a Macao bird that needed a home, so my sister Barbara took the bird and gave it to my brothers, Frank and Bill. But of course, as children are children, our Mom was the one left caring for the bird. Mom would call Frank and Bill to come in from playing, as dinner was ready. Unknowingly, she would call saying; "Frank, come and eat Bill." Meaning, Frank and Bill, come and eat. We did not realize what she had been saying until our faithful Macao repeated her words. The bird came to a tragic end, when Mom left him out in our screened porch overnight and it died from the cool San Jose climate. We missed the bird and his crazy lingo, but didn't really understand what we had or where he came from, as we were just trying to survive on California's Aid for Needy Children and the meager Social Security check we received as minors. What an unbelievable contrast: a sister who knew the stars personally, and us, just making ends meet. We were so proud of her and her accomplishments, from a California prune picker to a starlet. Had she been making a fortune, i know she would have helped us, but her career was just beginning. She is much like my Mom, a very loving, giving person.

It was also the time for all the doctor shows on television, such as Dr. Kildare, Dr. Ben Casey and so on. My sister Barbara seemed to hit it off with Dr. Ben Casey aka Vince Edwards, when she met him in person. 'Those were the days my friend, we thought they'd never end." Life was full, fun and exciting. Barbara and her partner Barbara did very well in their career; the Lord blessed them and gifted them in their singing. They were called 'The Barbies'. My heart still bursts with pride on their accomplishments. i learned so much from both of them, as far as make-up, dress and caring for one self. i am the one who is blessed by knowing them, learning from them, and being part of their lives.

Another way i benefitted from my sister's career, was i had the opportunity of seeing some of the great artists of the day, like Barbra Streisand. She came to our little, then small, San Jose, to perform at the Civic Center downtown. During those days, there was not much of a choice where the entertainers performed. Today, San Jose has the HP Building downtown and other large buildings for performers. That was back in the 1960's when Barbra Streisand was just beginning her career. Wow, what a performance. The Barbie's also took voice lessons from the same person as Streisand. When my sister invited me to hear Barbra Streisand perform, i was delighted, me, an 18-year-old high school senior, going to hear the great Barbra Streisand. Prior to that performance i listened and watched intently to the one and only Ella Fitzgerald perform in Los Angles; what an amazing voice and such a lady. Later, my sister Barbara took me see the great Nat King Cole in one of his last performances, which was at the Circle Star Theater, in San Carlos. What a gift. When my Mama went to be with JESUS, and i was to speak at her memorial service, i searched for music my Mama loved. There it was: most of Nat King Cole's songs like the Autumn Leaves, Tenderly and many more. It was then i realized my Mama was such a romantic, that's who i take after, in my love for romance.

Sometimes i feel much closer to my brothers as we have grown older and love and respect each other's differences. My brother Frank is much like our father in many ways, his wonderful gifts with his hands to make and improve things, such as in his carpentry work (he is a licensed contractor). Because of his artistic ability, he goes beyond being a contractor; he amazes me as to what he can do with the hands God has given him. Yet, like our father he has difficulty with different things. And then i see the heart and love of our dear sweet mother in Frank. Mama always said he was one of the most difficult of us children to raise, yet toward the end of her life she said to me; "Of all my children, i did not think Frank would be the one to be here for me and he is." She was so thankful for his care and love. Frank is; a very loving, caring, giving individual and i'm proud to call him my brother. He has a married daughter Christen, who has a precious son and daughter, a married son Brent, with three very polite boys and one more son, Brian. Both sons are very gifted like Frank and his daughter is a gifted esthetician. As for Bill, he has grown so strong in his faith in JESUS CHRIST our LORD and that's where we come together in sharing our wonderful faith. He, like Frank, loves his family and grandchildren. That is one thing i believe we inherited from our mother: the love for children. Bill is very knowledgeable (the only of us six graduating from Sacramento State); he is the only one of us with a college degree. He earned a scholarship to college for his fantastic running ability. When our youngest son Jeff, was running in high school and his coach discovered Jeff's Uncle was Bill Joseph, he told Jeff; "Your Uncle Bill beat the pants off me when we were in college." It is a small world. Bill and his wife Deannie have two lovely daughters (whom i consider as my daughters, since we had none) and Bill, is very close to our son, Jeff. Their oldest daughter Sarah, and her husband Jordan are married and have a daughter and a son. Sarah followed in my footsteps and is a Cosmetologist. Their second daughter, Candace and her husband Bobby, are also married and have a son and a daughter. Both of Bill's children and their families love and serve our Lord JESUS. We are truly blessed and i am very proud of my siblings.

While still living at home, on weekends and some evenings, we played baseball with the neighbor kids. One time while we were playing ball, Joyce's brother Steve, told me he was sick and tired of having the casseroles that his, working outside the home mother, had fixed. i didn't even know what a casserole was. My mother was a stay at home mom and never fixed casseroles. After i got married and was working full time, i soon discovered what they were: one dish meals, easy to prepare after a long hard day at work.

We had a Mexican family for neighbors, who made homemade tortillas, and on Easter and Christmas, homemade tamales. Not only did we have fresh tortillas once again, but oh, the best tamales ever! The neighbor always sent a batch to our home to enjoy. Joyce and Steve's mother understood the poverty we were in and sent many meals and casseroles for us to enjoy. She would always say, "I cooked too much and I just wanted to share." But we knew better, she did it to help provide for our need.

Soon, graduation day came from high school. It was a sad day for me because i loved high school. My sisters gave me a big graduation party. There was a vacant field next to our home where we set up a dance floor and we held the graduation party. It was so much fun: no drinking, drugs or smoking, just a beautiful day and night up on the hill overlooking Santa Clara Valley (Silicon Valley now). It was during the party one of my fellow students took a liking to me, more than a liking. We dated for a while and it was getting too serious for me and i said, Adios Amigo.

So, June was over and July came and with it, apricot season. After cutting apricots, i had a real job working in the cannery. The cannery was called Wools Packing House, off of Center Road, near the Santa Clara County Fairgrounds. This job meant that i would get paid by the hour and not by piecework. The Packing House had been there for many years and employed Mama, Aunt Mary, me, and most of my siblings, at one time or another. We not only had work, but fun. The workers liked the atmosphere and the family-run business so much, they didn't want it to become union operated. Working there was like one big happy family, with special events happening that involved the workers if they so desired.

The packing house, being across from the fairgrounds also brought many memories of my younger years when Mama would take us children to the Santa Clara County Fair on Kid's day. On that day it was free and we would see all the livestock and, of course, the fruit from Santa Clara Valley, along with all the rides and all the wonders that a fair brings. We could not

65

afford to ride on any of the rides, but it was exciting just to see them. i loved the cupie dolls or anything in those booths that was offered for a price, all we would or could do, is stare with wide-eyes and great hopes of having one of those treasures.

Joyce and i both worked in the cannery. We were infatuated with the two Wool boy cousins. The one i liked finally asked me for a date, that was the only one and last one with him. i really liked him, but the feeling wasn't mutual. i started Cosmetology school with a partial scholarship and worked part time at the cannery in order to pay for my education. When Joyce left for school, she attended Sacramento State University, majoring in Physical Education. She was a teacher for forty years. How i missed her once she left, but we kept in contact during those years, and the years following.

Not long ago, i went to help her clean out her classroom after forty years of teaching. Both of us love music and while we were cleaning the room, i tuned the radio to a station that played the sixties music. Such memories! Where had the time gone? Both of us have been married now for over thirty years. She has three children and two granddaughters. And i have two grown sons and five grandchildren.

Back at the cannery, i met a nice young man who was from Purdue University. He was fascinated with me. But i really didn't care much about him, so i didn't encourage his interest in me. Soon the cannery ended, i finished cosmetology school, and Joyce was my model in San Francisco for my cosmetology test. It was quite an adventure for two country girls from Santa Clara Valley, (Silicon Valley); we stayed with Joyce's aunt who lived in San Francisco. After the day-long test, both written and physical application, Joyce and i had a lovely seafood dinner on Fisherman's wharf. That was a first for us, we felt so grown-up. Some weeks later i received a notification in the mail from the State of California with my Cosmetology license. And i have been working as a licensed Cosmetologist ever since. i will probably die with my boots on: love my profession and serving others. One of my customers recently asked me, how long i had been a cosmetologist. i replied, "You, really don't want to know."

After a long week of standing on my feet and working as a Cosmetologist, i was ready on Saturday night to go dancing. Can you imagine, not tired, raring to go. So, i joined the girls i worked with and we went different places to dance, throughout Santa Clara Valley (Silicon Valley) like; Cow town, Corral Club, and the Losers North. It was at the Losers North i met the man i would marry. The date was February 1967. i remember going home that night and telling my mom and her best friend, Thelma, "i met the man i'm going to marry." They just shook their heads in disbelief.

On the dance floor, with Fred that night, he asked me what i did for a profession. i stood there with my green tinted hair and said, "i am a cosmetologist." He just looked at me and said, "That figures." i really didn't do my hair green intentionally. You see, i had dyed it red, and then the girls in the Salon tried to bleach it blonde, and the lightest we could get was mint green. We cosmetologists did everything that the book said not to do. That's experience; that's how you learn. When my hair was red, my comedian brother Frank (great sense of humor) called me 'Big Red.' When it turned yellow in the process of getting it blonde he called me; 'Old Yeller.'

After the dance at The Loser's, in the parking lot, Fred and i exchanged addresses. i even drew a map for him to our home. Which later i discovered didn't help him. We cordially said our good nights and went our separate way.

The following morning, i received a call from Fred and i said to him, "Oh, i'm glad you woke me. i'm late for Mass." He was astonished because he'd left Germany to get away from his religious, Catholic mother and then he meets a Catholic girl that caught his interest. He wanted to come and visit me that day. We lived out in the country in East San Jose on Pleasant Acres Drive, and it wasn't easy to find. i actually had to go down the road a few miles to get him so he could follow me home driving his big red and white

Cadillac. i was fascinated with that big 'Caddie' and his long cigars, and at the same time embarrassed because of our poor home and belongings. i found out later that Fred is notorious for getting lost. He told me that one time during his lunch hour from work, he was going to meet his insurance man and he ended up at Bay Meadows racetrack. As he drove in, he thought, "Where am I? I'm at the horse races. I'm supposed to be meeting my insurance man." He'd taken the wrong turn and ended up at the Bay Meadows racetrack. i also recall a time when while traveling throughout Europe, it was in Austria - Fred was the driver, i was the navigator - and I said, "What does einbahn strasse mean?" Fred looked at me and said, "One way street." i said, "Oh, that's why all the traffic is coming at us." We were going the wrong way!

Chapter Nine

"Hatred stirs up dissension,
but love covers over all wrongs." Proverbs 10: 12

Finally, a place we can call home. A home of our very own, as never before, and one for me in heaven, too.

We began dating. Fred loved spending the weekends at my aunt and uncle's home because he was from Germany, and my uncle was from Switzerland, and they had a lot in common.

Fred was born and raised in Germany during World War II. Little did i know that someday i would be traveling to Europe to meet his family. What a blessing. Fred was nine years old when the war ended. He was also in the Hitler Youth Movement. Fred's father died during the war, from tuberculosis and a brain tumor. Fred was only three and his brother a year and a half when their Father died. Fred always felt cheated with no father image except his uncle's, and his uncle wasn't very kind to him. During the war, Fred would travel with his brother and mother by train to their grandparent's farm in southern Germany. He said that many times the train would stop because the tracks were bombed out and they had to walk or sleep wherever they could. Usually it was flea ridden, where they slept, and on the train cars, it was very dirty: infested with fleas. He witnessed many of his friends being shot and killed during the war. His dear sweet mother, without anyone's notice except Fred and his brother, housed two Jewish men during the war. If Fred's Uncle, who was involved with Hitler's movement, knew of these Jewish men in their home, he would have had them all shot and killed, including Fred, his brother and mother. Why would she do such a thing, taking these Jewish souls in their home? She knew she and her sons had to eat, and these two men could get them food, which they did, for all of them. The Lord's mighty hand was upon them. Because of

Fred's mother's faith in God, they survived. PRAISE BE UNTO THE LORD! The two men stayed with Fred and his family for several months, then, left to defend their country. The way things are going in our Country and world today, we may experience something very similar, and perhaps sooner than we think. The question is: are we willing to make the sacrifice as Fred's sweet mother did? As it says in **Matthew 6:33-34 " But seek first His kingdom and His righteousness, and all these things will be given to you as well. Therefore do not worry about tomorrow, for tomorrow will worry about itself. Each day has enough trouble of its own."** She lived her faith, trusted the Lord, but knew she must step up in faith, trust and believe the Lord would provide, but she had to do her part.

Fred and many other Europeans were so thankful when the American troops came in with food and shelter. It was the first time he'd ever seen cigarettes and gum. He remembers American planes flying over, dropping packages for the needy in Germany.

Fred became a machinist at the age of fourteen; he went to trade school. He saved up money three different times to go to Canada. He worked in Germany as a machinist, and in 1956 he finally made the trip to Canada. He told his maternal grandmother that he was going to Stuttgart. Her reply was, "I know you're really going to Canada. I'll probably never see you again. But promise me that you will say the Lord's Prayer every day of your life." He kept his promise to her, and prays that blessed prayer every day, even now. As for his grandmother, she was right, she never did see her grandson again. But he kept his promise to her, and i believe it has helped him in his faith and finally relinquishing his heart to Jesus. i also believe as with my grandparents and his, they must have prayed for their grandchildren, whether they knew them or not. My words to grandparents are: pray for your children and grandchildren. **Psalm 103:17-28** promises and with a command; **"But from everlasting to everlasting the Lord's love is with those who fear HIM, and his righteousness with their children's**

70

children.--- with those who keep His covenant and remember to obey His precepts."

When Fred first arrived in Canada, he was surprised to find it as cold as Germany was in the winter months. He flew on an old two-engine job plane, from Germany to Canada in 1956. His first job was in a bakery. Later he worked for a Russian man as a machinist. This dear man, had no children and owned a farm in the country. He and his wife took a liking to Fred and invited him to spend weekends on the farm with them. At one time, Fred went to the tool shed to get a hoe and noticed what he thought was a cat. Fred loves animals and started to pet the 'cat', as he did the owner quickly tried to warn him, too late, Fred got sprayed. It was a skunk. Skunks do not live in Germany, so this was quite a surprise to this young German immigrant.

Years later, when Fred was working as a machinist in Mountain View, California, he met a young man who worked in the machine shop who just came from Toronto, Canada. He told Fred about the business's that were now on the busy intersection in Toronto that was once owned by the Russian man where Fred had worked. He went on to tell Fred the property in that area is now worth a fortune.

When Fred came home from work that evening he shared with me this story. He went on to say, "That old Russian man and his wife loved me like a son and wanted me to stay in Toronto, They would have given me the business if i would have stayed. But i wanted to come to California. Guess, i missed out again." i believe this was not the Lord's will for Fred, then, too; we would not have met and married.

The years went by quickly and Fred and his friend Walter still wanted to come to the United States of America. The year was 1959 and they applied for a permanent visa to come in to the U.S.A. At that time they needed a sponsor to put up $8,000, and if they did not comply to the U.S.A. rules they would be deported back to Germany. Walter's uncle put the money up for both young men, and they made their way to America. Fred saw most of America through the windows of a Greyhound bus. The places he studied about while living in Germany, or the Westerns he watched at the movies as a boy in Germany, came to life as he traveled. He stopped at many places looking for work as a machinist, but his English was very poor and no one would hire him. He finally ended up in San Francisco, his dream. Eventually, he worked his way down the peninsula to Santa Clara Valley, working as a machinist.

Fred had some very interesting friends as roommates; there was Mike who fought in the Battle of the Bulge and his friend, none other than Little Jimmy Dickens. When he played his guitar and sang Western songs, Fred thought he sounded like a howling coyote, and would tell him, "You'll never make it, give it up." Years later, the same Little Jimmy Dickens made it in the Country Hall of Fame. Mike, who is of Polish descent, had some great stories to tell, with innocence and a great sense of humor. He told us stories of being in charge of the P.O.W'S in Germany and how he would give them nail files, small knives or whatever to keep them busy in their cells. As he said, showing us some of the woodwork they made for him, "They were talented, and I would tell them if you don't give the tool back to me in the evening, you cannot have it again." They did as he said; it was better than sitting in the cell staring at four walls. They really did make some lovely things from the wood he gave them to work with. Mike is spending his retirement years (at age 90+) on a farm in Buffalo, New York. His home is close to his children, we miss him and the fun times we had. We're honored to personally know someone who actually fought in the Battle of the Bulge.

i was working in East San Jose as a cosmetologist when i met Fred. He introduced me to his German friend who managed a beauty salon in Saratoga, which is an exclusive area in California. i applied for the job and it was one of the best things that had ever happened to this twenty year old girl. i got the job. It was in this Salon i learned etiquette, hospitality, respect, and honor. The owner, Jo, taught me how to run a business by applying the "Golden Rule"; **"Do unto others, as you have them do unto you."** To this day i use the "Golden Rule" in my Salon, my writing, and all areas of my life **"So in everything, do to others what you would have them do to you, or this sums up the Law and Prophets." Matthew 7:12.** Above all i learned about my new faith in JESUS. i will always be thankful to Jo, and all the ladies whose hair i did and learned so very much. Little did i know, that one day i would manage this Salon, and use the gifts the Lord had given me.

Prior to this, my mother, bless her heart, was still visiting my father who was now living in a halfway house in downtown San Jose. Yes, love is a many splendid thing, and she still loved my father regardless of how he treated her, her children and others. Mom would meet him briefly and they would have their visit and time together. At one point she said my father brought out a Bible and said; "Angie, have you ever read this? You should." That amazed me, yet it pleased my heart to know my father was reading Scripture. Although, at the time i had never read the Word for myself, sure i had heard it many times during Mass, but was never taught to read it for my own spiritual growth. For some reason, which i did not understand at the time, but now believe the Holy Spirit laid on my heart to purchase a large Family Bible and a set of the children's Bibles, with my first paycheck as a hairdresser. i still have the set of the children's Bibles, read it to our sons and now our grandchildren. i didn't realize it, at the time, but HE was working on me even then.

Now, back to my father. One of the most difficult things i had to do was refuse my father's request to come and live with us once again. He called one day while living at the halfway house and wanted to speak to me. i shall never forget the most difficult conversation i had with my father, as he begged and literally cried to let him come and live with us again. He was very lonely and made many promises i believed he couldn't keep in order to come back to us. i reminded him of his cruelty to his family and how mom had to

73

work in the berry patch while she was pregnant in order for us to live, and so on. By now, i too was crying, yet very strong in my convictions that he could no longer live with us. i experienced first hand the promises most alcoholics make, want to keep and just can't. Yet, my heart broke for him, as i wanted to say, "Yes, Papa, we love you, and do come home." i have learned over the years that i have a very strong personality, yet i am very sensitive in my emotions. As i write, read Scripture and look back, perhaps he too had read and understood the forgiveness of Jesus Christ found in the Bible and it really would have worked out, we will never know. Or maybe, he took out that black strong box, opened it up and realized what all those treasures meant to his mother and now meant to him. Hopefully, they convicted him and he gave his heart and life to Jesus. **"Train up a child in the way he should go, and when he is old he will not depart from it." Proverbs 22:6.** My grandmother Joseph, whom i never had the pleasure of meeting, did train up my father, "in the way he should go." She told my mom, "Bill, (my dad) was such a good boy when he was young. He just got mixed up with the wrong crowd." **Proverbs 1:10** says, **"My son, if sinners entice you, do not give in to them."** My hope and prayer is that i will meet my father in heaven, because of Jesus.

Not long after this episode, mom received a phone call that my father had passed away. i remember at the time the call came, i was reading a caption in the newspaper under a picture of a little dog that read; "You must forgive and forget." That was a Godsend. i immediately forgave but the forgetting is most difficult.

My father's funeral was organized and paid for by his son Leslie and his wife Ramona Joseph. It was then, while the arrangements were being made, that Leslie told us that our given last name was Narciso. That was a great surprise to our family. i also met a half-brother, George, on our drive to the cemetery. Another half-brother, William A. Joseph i met at Leslie's funeral years later.

74

Fred and i visited William A. a few years ago, i just wanted an opportunity to get to know him and ask about our grandparents that i had never met, and his relationship with our father. He lives near Sacramento and worked for the electric company, before retiring. My youngest brother, William C. also, lived in Sacramento and worked for the same electric company, at the same time. My brother said he was getting mail at work for a William A. Joseph, and knew it was not his mail. One day, he was assigned to work in the field with William A. As they worked and talked, they came to the realization they were half brothers, the same father, just different mothers. And of course twenty or more years age difference. Yes, indeed it is a small world. The company they worked for did a write-up on them and how unknowingly two half brothers met while working for the same company.

During our visit with my half-brother, he told me he regretted not attending our father's funeral. He also had sisters and, then of course, the brother who died in a motorcycle accident, he was the one who my friend, Celeste's great grandparents, helped raise. This was a loving God's hand orchestrating our lives.

Another orchestration of the Lord was at my half-brother, Leslie's, funeral. i met a man who taught math in High School. He told me he was my math teacher. i said, "No, i am sorry you must be thinking of one of my sisters." He replied, "No, i don't think so, i taught you at Buchser High School in Santa Clara." i meekly apologized, as i said, "You must be correct, i was the only sibling who attended Buchser, so it had to be me.' and added, "But i did terrible in math." He said, "No, you were one of my best students." i was shocked, because i felt i was doing so poorly, believed it and sadly passed that belief on to our sons. He went on to say; "My wife is Leslie's sister, your half-sister. Ramona, Leslie's wife asked me not to tell you who I was and to look out for your safety." A lesson i learned from this is; to be honest and encourage others in whatever they are doing, so they will not pass their doubt or disbelief on to others. i regret he did not tell me who he was early on, yet he kept his promise to Ramona. Fred never had the privilege of meeting my father; i wish he had. I believe they would have gotten along fine, both love the country, working with their hands and have many other things in common. It would have been nice for our sons to have a real blood grandfather, as well, and all of my nieces and nephews, but i guess it wasn't to be, life goes on and we make the best of it as the Lord allows. We know and understand, as we get older; **"For my thoughts are not your thoughts, neither are your ways my ways," declares the Lord. Isaiah 55:8**

Chapter Ten

Our New Home

"... He blesses the home of the righteous. Proverbs 3:33b

New family, friends, adventures of a whole new world.

While dating, Fred invited me to go with him on a camping trip to Pinecrest Lake. i accepted. i had never been camping before, other than camping when we were picking prunes. It was to our benefit that the tent and everything were set up for Fred and i, because we didn't know how to pitch a tent. In the morning, when a big dog came in licking Fred's toes, he said, "Something is licking my toes? I think it's a bear!" i looked over on the cot where he slept, and i saw this big old white dog licking his toes. We both jumped up! The old dog ran off scared.

Since we were awake, Fred decided to get-up, and get breakfast prepared. Wouldn't you know, as he was preparing breakfast, it started to rain. So the bacon and eggs were getting all wet and the rain was putting the fire out. To add more fuel, Fred was disappointed because I didn't put on my makeup and "look real pretty." My thoughts were; "We are camping and that primping wasn't necessary!" So, to please him, I put on my makeup and combed my hair and looked pretty.

Later in the day, we decided to take a boat out to do some fishing. Fred had his pole in the water and, as i sat and watched him fish, he decided to let the boat drift. Then the motor died. So, he kept pulling on the cable trying to get the motor started. It just wouldn't start, no matter how hard he tried. i asked, "May I try?" Reluctantly he said, "Aw, go ahead." On the first

77

pull the motor started and off we went! Oh, was he ever mad. Then, he couldn't catch any fish and i asked if i could fish. Then he said, "No! That's all I need now, for you to catch a fish!" As i tell this story, it reminds me of the movie, Dennis the Menace. Like Dennis, i only meant good and not harm. We all fight pride, whether Christian or not, it's a battle. **"Pride goes before destruction, a haughty spirit before a fall." Proverbs 16:18.**

Not long after, we packed up the gear and headed home; he hardly said one word to me he was so angry. He took me home and then he went home, and we didn't talk for over a week. Later, i discovered he called my sister Josephine, saying, "I miss Gloria and I really love her. What should I do?" My sister told him to go and apologize to me.

There was a knock on my apartment door, i opened it and there stood a bewildered Fred. Not only did he apologize, but he got on his knees and asked me to be his wife. i accepted. Family and friends helped with food, flowers, music, serving and our dear friend Dorothy baked the cake, (she was the one who always made us those delicious Christmas cookies) for our wedding. Another dear friend made my dress and the bridesmaids dresses. We were married on April 20,1968, at St. Joseph's Catholic church in Cupertino, just down the street from where Apple® Computer[2] sits today.

We spent our honeymoon in Klamath Falls Oregon. Fred took me there to see the falls, but we couldn't find them. He asked an elderly man in Klamath if he could direct us to the falls, the man said; "There ain't been falls here in years." After one night in that one horse small town, (it's a lovely town today) we left for California. As we were crossing the bridge over Lake Shasta we came upon Bridge Bay Resort. That is where we spent the remainder of our Honeymoon.

The song: Yellow Polka Dot Bikini was popular at the time, and i bought a yellow polka dot bikini for this special occasion. i still have it, these 40 plus years later, and believe it or not it still fits me. Oh yes, things are not where they were 40 some years ago, but Fred loves seeing me in it and that's what matters and to please the Lord matters.

The resort was a wonderful place to stay: nice guest rooms, a boat rental (Fred loved that he could start the engines on the boats), with a lovely dining room overlooking Lake Shasta. For the first time in my life i had lobster at the resort's restaurant; it was delicious and have loved lobster ever since, just wish we could afford it more often.

Since this trip or on any of our vacations, we choose a destination, we get packed, grab a map, (now i go on the computer and map it out), because we enjoy spending time together. We have come to the agreement, Fred is the driver and i am the navigator, works better that way. We have learned throughout our many years of marriage, if one spouse is good at doing the bills, taxes, or whatever needs doing, let that person take care of it without interruption from the other. Saves on lots of arguments. Yeah. "Peace in the Valley."

It is interesting, at the age of thirteen, when i lived in Alviso, i made a trip with Celeste and her church youth group to Pinecrest Lake during the winter months when there was snow on the ground. She and two or three other girls and i tobogganed for the first time in the snow. So, Pinecrest Lake holds a lot of memories for me. At the church Celeste attended, i met Pastor Algot and Jeanette Sporrong. Many years later, here in Calaveras County, i met them once again, not realizing they were the same couple i had met when I was thirteen years old. She remembered me, the shy little girl who hung out with my redheaded friend Celeste. Jeanette later became my Christian mentor. Once again i experienced the Lord's intervention. A few years ago i went on a hike around Pine Crest Lake with our granddaughter Laurel Shea's class, as an adult chaperone. i didn't know what i was getting into, until we arrived at her school, when the teacher asked if i had a backpack? i thought, 'What for, we're only going there for a picnic.' Picnic my eye, we were going to hike all the way around the lake, holy smoke what an adventure. i thought for sure i would have a heart attack, or something of the like, as we were nearing the end. Didn't want to disappoint my lovely granddaughter, so just kept going, only stopping for a break and then lunch along the way. At the end of the hike, the first thing we hit was the bathrooms, relief at last. Once we got on the school bus to take us back, there were some young mom's who asked if i was the grandmother to one of the students, which i said, "Yes." 'Wow,' they said, 'you did better than most of us with children.' Little did they know, how tired i was. i had made it around the lake, got home that evening, thinking pain tomorrow, no such thing. i must be in pretty good shape i thought. Thank the Lord.

Now let's go back to Fred and i. Our first home was an apartment in Sunnyvale, California. Next-door was a neighbor who had a beautiful garden. i am sorry to say i would always look in envy at his home and garden, hoping someday we could have a home of our own. Fred was having the same feelings in his heart because, every night after work, he would go through the newspapers looking for a home we could afford. Finally he found a home located in the Santa Cruz Mountains. When we went to look at it, i couldn't believe my eyes. It reminded me of the old shacks we lived in when i was a child. But Fred had great vision and could see what we could do to make it a home of our own. We met the owner and he told us how he had cleaned everything up on the property. As we looked around, we saw poison oak growing all around, climbing into the trees and around the house and there was garbage and junk everywhere. Even though i worked full time, my earnings were not considered for purchasing a home, as they are today. So the purchase was based on Fred's income. After we made the purchase, we saw most of the things wrong with the house and property, and dove right in to make it livable.

Another problem we had was; we had no furniture, not even a bed. The manager of the apartment where we lived, thought all the furniture we had belonged to us, but Fred in his honesty (even then) told him; "No, it was all lent to me when I moved in, after my divorce, I had nothing."

Our next move was to find a house full of furniture at a bargain price. Each evening after work, Fred once again hit the newspaper looking for bargains. He finally found one, and off we went to deal with the furniture store. When i was young, i watched my father wheel and deal with people, but Fred outdid him. The salesman was ready to just give-up, he knew he couldn't win with Fred's determination and little to offer. The end result was a house full of furniture, which included a bedroom set, two dressers, bed with box spring and mattress, dining room set with four chairs, and a living room set, couch, overstuffed chair, oak coffee table, two matching end tables and two lamps, the end tables and coffee table we still use in our home today, all for $500.00 delivered. The delivery part was made after the deal was confirmed, how could this poor salesman say, "No" after all that.

i was to witness many more deals Fred would make with salesmen, including an automobile salesman. One time after Fred made a deal for a brand new Ford pick-up truck, the salesman followed us home, sat down and visited, and after a glass of our homemade wine, told us he had made only $50.00 on the deal. That was after hours of bargaining with Fred.

My Mom was a sweetheart, not only did she help us clean our new home, she stayed and waited for the furniture to be delivered, so Fred and i could work to pay for our new furniture. It wasn't the best, yet it was all made in the United States of America, a rarity today.

Once we moved into our new home, we hauled at least 10 truckloads of garbage to the dump. The first winter it rained so hard that the roof was leaking. Our next project was to put roofing on the house. Getting rid of the poison oak was another matter. We had poison oak on our skin, continually, for at least another year. As i think back, we would sit at our dining room table having dinner and Fred would be scratching his legs like a hound. i would say, "Would you please stop scratching, it's annoying." Then i got poison oak, and totally understood how good it felt to scratch.

Fred continued to commute to Mountain View daily, as the foreman of a Machine Shop, and i continued working as a Cosmetologist in Saratoga. Although, Fred worked 1/2 a day at the machine shop and i a full day at the Beauty Salon on Saturday's, we still worked on our home during the weekends and nights after work. It took us all of 10 years to remodel our home, clear brush, poison oak, fence and so on, what a joy it was when we completed the task. i recall we had sheet rock delivered and it was stacked in our driveway (we didn't have a garage). Well, sure enough it began to rain and it was in the evening after we came home from work. There was only one thing to do so as not to lose all that sheet rock. Yes, we hand carried it all up the stairs where it was to go, over one hundred sheets of sheet rock. Let me tell you we slept soundly that night.

Fred and i hung all the sheet rock in that home as well as in the home where we are now living. At one time, when we were hanging sheet rock on the ceiling, my arms got so tired i let go; Fred's head went right through the sheet rock. We decided to quit for that night.

Another time, i decided to have a surprise birthday party for Fred. One problem, we did not have a kitchen per se, because it was torn up. Oh, i did have a faucet that came out of the wall so i could do the dishes while standing on the floor support beams. But we pulled it off, the guests were sitting on beams, boards, wherever; everyone had a great time. Fred was surprised.

On Sundays, when we lived in the apartment, Fred would golf with his ex-father-in-law at Deep Cliff Golf Course. i would attend Mass at St. Joseph's Church in Cupertino. One day i thought, 'there is something wrong with this picture.' So, i discussed it with Fred and he told me i needed to take golf lessons. i agreed, and he signed me up for golf lessons with an elderly professional gentleman. After my second or third lesson, the pro told me i was a natural and wanted to see me on the course. When i told Fred, he didn't believe me and called the pro, who confirmed what i said. The next Sunday, i was on the golf course with my new hubby and his ex father-in-law, and broke 100. Fred was amazed.

One day one of my elderly customers came in with a set of golf clubs just for me. "The Lord always provides." i still have the set, it is an antique set, most of the handles to the clubs are made out of wood; it's a great set. i really enjoyed golf, because it reminded me of playing baseball. Except baseball is free and golf is costly. Today, once in awhile, Fred and i will golf at small 9-hole courses that are under $10.00 to play. While remodeling our home in Redwood Estates we gave up golf. We developed many new friends and neighbors during the time we lived in Redwood Estates, and have fond memories of Hank and Leslie, the Trumbull's, Borden's, T's and many more. Seems most of these neighbors were on non-speaking terms prior to our moving there; the Lord used us to bring them together. For me it was so wonderful, and exciting to be able to make friends and keep them, since i had moved so much in my earlier years, and didn't have much of an opportunity to make friends. i also made a promise to myself, to invite people to our home, i was never able to, in the past, because of my father's drinking and abuse. i was to experience the gift of hospitality the Lord had given me, and now i could use it, and i do so even today. PRAISE THE LORD!!!

With all these new friends, a husband, a home, and a good profession, these things all helped fulfill my life, but there was still an emptiness i could not describe. As with childhood, i was always searching for God, i had no peace. The Lord would soon fill that void within my troubled soul, through one of His servants, Rachel. My dear customer, Rachel, would come in weekly for her hair appointment, with Bible in hand, and a soft, quiet, loving spirit. Only when i asked, did she begin to share her Christian faith with me. She recommended i listen to Dr. J. Vernon McGee over the radio. So, each morning on my way to work, i would tune in to Dr. J. Vernon

McGee and Through the Bible Radio. i also needed a Bible, so i asked Rachel which one she recommended. She suggested the Amplified Bible, saying that it would be the best for me, because it explained everything in detail. Other than the big Catholic Family Bible i had purchased, along with the Children's Bible Stories, when i received my first paycheck as a cosmetologist, this would be the first Bible i purchased and studied. Today, i still read from my old Amplified Bible, after taking a nap, it is such a treasure.

The year was 1970, and my life would change forever. There was a sign posted on a bulletin board next to the grocery store in Redwood Estates. Oh, yes the home we purchased was in Redwood Estates, California, just off Highway 17 en route to Santa Cruz. Anyway, the sign said; Bible Study and gave a phone number. i wrote down the information, and then asked Fred, as a submissive wife should, if i could attend the neighborhood Bible study. i just knew it was right to ask Fred first, guess the Lord was already at work in my stubborn heart. Fred said it would be fine as long as it wasn't a cult. The next day i called the guide for the Bible study and flat out asked her if it were such and such a cult, she assured me it wasn't. i was so excited to attend, and did so the very next week, which was great because it was held on my day off; that was a miracle. Everyone was so nice, helpful, and friendly. And i wanted to learn about this God, Dr. McGee and Rachel spoke about. We used the Good News New Testament for the Bible study, which made it simple because it referred to page so and so, along with the Scripture verse. This made it easy for me, since i was not familiar with the Bible, as far as locating Scriptures. My first lesson was 1 John, the guide for the study represented Stonecroft Ministries[3]. That lovely little book of 1 John, helped me to understand Who Jesus was and why He came, and that He wasn't just a man who performed miracles. And that i could invite Him into my heart and life, and He would save me from my sins, cleanse me from all unrighteousness, and welcome me into Heaven forever with Him. Because He paid the price on Calvary's cross for my sins, i'll live for HIM who died for me. 1 John 5: 13

says; " I write these things to you who believe in the name of the SON of GOD so that you may KNOW that you have eternal life." That verse alone settled it for me, i know for sure i am going to Heaven and have salvation, because of JESUS' sacrificial death on the cross for me and His resurrection from the grave. It would not be until several years later, i would confess JESUS as LORD of my life. Sometimes, it takes time, for some of us, to completely let go, and trust HIM with the reins to drive the wagon. For others, it's an immediate transition of not only receiving the gift of our salvation through JESUS CHRIST, but to make HIM Lord of their lives. That's not to say that sometimes i don't take the reins back, which i do on occasion. Realizing that doesn't work, and gladly giving it back to JESUS, " the Author and Finisher of my faith." Hebrews 12:2b.

After that Bible study lesson and i had accepted JESUS as my SAVIOR, i excitedly went home, and could not wait to share the Good News with Fred when he returned from work. As we sat on the couch sharing our day's adventures, i began telling him how i accepted JESUS CHRIST as my Lord, and that he could do the same, right there and then. His response was, "That's good for you, but i am not ready yet."He was not ready until 20 plus years later, when he and i were having marital problems, and i said to him you know what you must do. i asked are you ready, he replied, "Yes." And at that moment we both knelt at the foot of our bed and Fred gave his heart to JESUS. The next morning, i shared the Good News with our sons Franz and Jeffrey. Jeffrey, immediately brought out his Bible and said; "Dad, you have to read this every day."

We took my Mom to San Jose later that morning, and i saw the change in Fred when he didn't run the yield sign near our home (which he always did, angrily). i know our God changes hearts, i have witnessed this many times. PRAISE THE LORD!!! i believe the verse the Lord gave me for winning Fred to Jesus is; 1Peter 3:1-6. Also, the verse i claimed for Fred's salvation was; John 10:16. The 1Peter verse is not easy, but by the power of the Holy Spirit it is possible. **Matthew 19:26** says it all; Jesus... said, **"With man this is impossible, but with God all things are possible."**Just like the parable JESUS told in Matthew 13: 1-23 regarding the seed the farmer sowed; did not take root, and we went through many trials and tribulations, before it would completely take root, and becoming like the seed that fell on good soil. The Lord loves us and never gives up on us; we are the ones who give up. Perhaps, Fred, like me, did not make JESUS his Lord, only his Savior. The battle for Fred's soul lasted for years; we are the ones who need to "let go and let God." That saying is written on our bathroom mirror, as a reminder to me. Fred will point it out to me at times, to remind me what it really means, when i become discouraged or whatever the case may be. So, we all struggle from time to time. Just because we have made the commitment to follow JESUS, doesn't mean we won't have struggles, or we won't take back the reins from time to time. We are all diamonds "in the rough," who the Lord keeps chiseling, in order to make that perfect stone. That perfect stone will not occur until we are in Heaven with Him. So we must be patient with ourselves, not give-up and fully trust HIM. **"...being confident of this, that He who began a good work in you will carry it on to completion until the day of Christ Jesus." Philippians 1:6**

Chapter Eleven

"He is the light of the world." Matthew 5:14

Back home at last. There's no place quite like home.

Back to Redwood Estates and the lovely Santa Cruz Mountains,
(don't you just love the way i have you travel with me?) the year was 1970
and our home was livable but not complete. Fred felt it was time to take me
to Germany to meet his family. i was sooo excited, imagine me, this poor
country girl from an old shack on Tenant Avenue, now going to Europe; only
in America, the land of opportunity could this happen. Well, my concern was,
i could not speak or understand German, and not many of Fred's relatives
could speak or understand English. So, i went to the library and checked out
records, back in those days, on a Berlitz course in German. On my days off, i
would listen over and over again to the records, along with a little Berlitz
German book and study guide. i asked Fred to teach me the German
alphabet, thinking if i knew the alphabet the words would be easier to
pronounce. One of our dear neighbors, Mrs. T, who was from Estonia, and
was in WW II, could speak German, as well as her native tongue, and English.
She told me the pronunciation was difficult because we Americans end with
most of our words at the roof of our mouths and the Germans, and most
Europeans, end the words behind their teeth. That seemed reasonable to me,
and why i still have difficulty (after 40 plus years) to pronounce;
Bodenmüller. i loved visiting with Mrs. T, learning from her and listening to
the many stories she shared with me.

Her right hand was damaged from shrapnel during the war, but it
did not stop her from crocheting beautiful handiwork. She was an excellent
cook, gardener and stonewall builder. i learned a lot from her husband,
whose name was Manivault (not sure of the spelling). She told me the story

of them coming out of the store, he went out ahead of her, and she could not find him or their car, so she kept calling; "Manivault, Manivault." (Pronounced: like Money vault). They were new in America with our language and she wondered why people in the parking lot looked at her so strangely, as she kept calling; "Manivault".

They helped Fred and i, a lot, in remolding our home, giving us many helpful pointers. At one time, Mr. T came to help me plant some Pyracantha they had given us, and i told him that my mother was a wonderful gardener, and had a green thumb. He replied, " And you never paid attention to her." That's all he said, in that one profound statement, i learned to pay attention to my mother, and not only her, but others, so i could learn so many wonderful skills about life. Mr. T's words were like; **"A word aptly spoken is like apples of gold in settings of silver." Proverbs 25:11.**

The T's were both very loving, yet very European in their outspokenness. Being a new Christian, sometimes i did not understand their outspokenness, to me it seemed unkind and harsh. So, i searched the Scriptures, sure enough there it was in the Book of Proverbs. It says; **"Better is open rebuke than love that is hidden." Proverbs 27:5**. Years later i was to understand what this really meant as the Lord allowed me to meet many Europeans (including my dear husband), with the honesty, and openness they showed. As one dear Croatian friend once told me, "Most Americans are not truthful, they may say one thing to your face, in order not to hurt you, but then speak the truth behind your back."

After this lesson with our neighbor, i now appreciate honesty with love of course. In all of that, and being raised in some ways to 'say it like it is' i am learning to temper my words, yet speak with love and honesty.

Going back to my self-taught German, i took our neighbors advice and began trying to place my tongue in the proper place in order to speak German better. In the meantime we were making plans for our trip abroad, we joined the German Club in San Jose and were able to purchase round trip tickets to West Germany for $260.00, each. You must keep in mind, a dollar was worth a dollar at that time. As a matter of fact we received 3 German Marks for one American dollar, which meant our money would go much further.

Fred wanted to purchase his dream car in West Germany, a Mercedes Benz. i agreed that he should do just that, after all he worked hard and was a good provider. So, he ordered a Silver Grey Mercedes Benz from the factory in Sindelfingen, West Germany for $6,800.00. It was a beauty with burgundy leather interior; the dashboard and interior had Rosewood trim, gorgeous.

We flew from the San Francisco Airport to Frankfurt, West Germany, with one layover in Bangor, Maine. This was all so new to me, i had never flown before, except once to Southern California in a small aircraft to visit my sister, Barbara.

After landing in Frankfurt, we took a small plane to Sindelfingen to pick-up the Mercedes. We had a tour of the factory and then drove directly to Weisweil, West Germany, which is on the Swiss-German border, where Fred's Mom lived. Just thinking about that trip today, makes me wonder, how did we make a 16 hour flight, then another flight to pick-up the car, and then driving another 4 hours to meet Fred's Mom and family. Talk about tired and flight lag, but we were as the Germans say; 'dumm und jung' or dumb and young. As you may have seen, i referred to going to West Germany; this is before that horrible Berlin Wall came down, which separated the West from the East. Thankful, for President Reagan and his; " Mr. Gorbachev, take down that wall!!!![4] That's when the East and West became one Germany, once again.

Upon arriving in Weisweil, we first went to Fred's Tante Klara's home, was that ever an experience, Wow!!! First off, being raised with an outhouse that was outside, and now visiting his dear sweet Aunt's home, it was a shock being hit with that outhouse smell upon entering the house.

Fred explained to me, she did not have a flush toilet and the outhouse was in the house. O.K., as long as i didn't have to live there, visiting was fun. Tante Klara was a sweetheart, with a great sense of humor, just looking at her reminded me of Olive Oil (Popeye's gal), which brought love and laughter to my heart. For some reason Fred left me in the living room by myself closing the door behind him, then Tante Klara entered the room closing the door (that kept heat in each room) and she began speaking to me in German. i was shocked and afraid, thinking she was lecturing me, this was not the German i studied at home. What in the world was she saying? At that moment, thank the Lord, Fred walked into the room and told her i did not understand her dialect. She was so kind and apologetic. i finally, calmed down and learned to love and appreciate this dear lady, i would soon call Tante Klara.

Most of our German family was very warm and friendly; they usually greet you with a long handshake and a smile. i went a step further and gave them big warm, friendly hugs; that was a lot for me, considering i came from a family that did not hug. First of all, i loved hugging and secondly, i have always had sweaty palms, which have always embarrassed me, so i was ashamed to give them my sweaty hand and instead gave them hugs. Much to my surprise they loved the hugs and hugged back. Thus, i was sharing the 'Light of Christ'.

i later discovered the further one gets South of the Equator, the warmer and friendlier the people become. It is true, look at our own country or Europe, the warmer folks live in warm climates, like California, Arizona, Italy, Mexico etc. Perhaps, the sunshine does have an affect on how we feel.

Not long after arriving at Tante Klara's, Fred's quiet Mother, completely opposite of Tante Klara, came to welcome us. She was happy to meet me and glad we were there to spend time with she and the family. It would not be until later years, she and i would have a great relationship, as i would sit down and answer the letters she would write to us. The last time i saw her in Germany, just before our departure, she said to me; "Why is it the daughter-in-law i don't get along with, live so close, and the one i love so much and get along with lives so far away?" That touched my heart, and almost made me cry as i answered, "i do not know." With that, a final hug of aufviedersehen (i'll be seeing you), Fred, our sons and i left for America.

While in Germany, what amazed me most, is when we were to meet family for a gathering at a restaurant or wherever, they all showed up. The reason it was so amazing, is that most didn't have phones back in the 1970's, yet somehow the word got out and there they were. The restaurants in Germany are called Gasthaus's, translated guesthouse, so all were welcome, children included; which was so nice because the children could mingle with the adults as well as vice versa. We all sat at long tables as the waitress took orders. Each waitress had her own money belt around her waist, from which she made change and took orders, only to write everything down after the meal was complete. What wonderful memories the waitress had, and she remembered everything, even to the last drink. The children were subjected to the adults having wine or beer, and could have them as well at the legal age of 16. Everyone had a good time visiting and getting along, without anger, which impressed me, especially coming from a background of anger and arguing when drinking.

As with our home in Redwood Estates, where neighbors hadn't talked in years, so it was here with family. Fred and i seemed to be the peace makers the Lord had sent in each case, as family and friends made amends and loved one another. What a blessing to be part of this wonderful healing. **"Blessed are the peacemakers, for they will be called sons of God." Matthew 5:9.**

Fred's, Mother like mine, never owned a home of her own and lived in rent above a farmer's two story home, in an apartment. She rented a bedroom that adjoined her apartment for Fred and i during our visit. Fred endearingly called her; Mutti (Mother) in German. i out of respect called her

Mutti as well, as Fred called my Mom; Mother. Mutti, was surprised i would call her Mutti, with a smile and much appreciation she nodded and said, "Ahh, Mutti." She loved being called Mutti, and by me as well. It was an honor to call her Mutti. Mutti, was very gracious and hospitable to Fred and i. Truthfully, i miss that kind of respect today. My mom taught us to call our elders by their last name, such as Mr. Mrs., Miss. We were not allowed to call them by their first name unless they asked us to do so. i prefer to be called; "Oma", except by our children of course, who call me Mom.

Each morning Mutti had breakfast ready and waiting for us, which included; soft-boiled eggs, sweet butter, bread with marmalade (jam) she usually made, and a fresh cup of Melita drip coffee, made especially for each of us. That was before we had drip coffee makers in America; same principle, but each cup had to be prepared separately, and coffee freshly ground by hand in a grinder. It was good, i must admit. No sooner had she prepared breakfast, she was busy starting Mittoch Essen (Middle of the day dinner), which is Europeans big meal of the day. Fred referred to Mutti as 'Alte Zweibeln', which means 'old onion'. Not that she was an old onion, she just loved preparing onions with almost every meal. Actually, i once read of a dear lady who would have a busy day at work and was not able to get dinner started before her hubby returned from work. So she would start browning onions, when he arrived and smelled the delicious onions cooking, he'd relax and believe dinner was almost ready. It gave his wife time to really get started on the real deal. Perhaps, Mutti had the same thought, who knows, but the Lord, and Mutti. Whatever, it worked and always got our appetites going.

Mittoch essen consisted of meat, beef, pork or chicken, a mixed salad, (lettuce like we have today young and fresh), a vegetable in cream sauce and potatoes or spatzle (homemade noodles) or noodles. For dinner or Abend essen, we ate light, fresh Baurer brot (Farmer's bread) fresh cold cuts, cheese, hard boiled eggs, pickles, tomatoes, butter or mustard. Just thinking about the meal, makes me hungry. Think i'll stop and grab a bite to eat. i'm back, yum that was good, garden fresh tomato sandwich with a glass of iced coffee on this warm summer day. Must say, i miss our own veggie garden this year. Fred won't let me have a veggie garden; due to the rattlesnake bite i got while in our veggie garden last year. Will tell more about that later.

Let's see where was i? Oh yes, abend essen, or evening meal. Each person was given a small board, a knife and fork and napkin, to make your own meal. One of the cold cuts was deep smoked ham or schinken or speck. When we visited in later years, with our sons, they were very fond of the schinken or speck, they like it even today, if we can get it. It is similar to prosciutto.

Actually, eating a lighter meal later in the day, we found is much easier on the tummy, and for resting at night. But then, after Mittoch essen, most everyone took a nap; including the townspeople who owned business's, because the stores were closed from 12 noon until 2 p.m. each day, and absolutely closed on Sunday. The only thing you might find open on a Sunday was restaurants and coffee houses. It is a German tradition to have coffee and delicious (kuchen) cakes, made with real butter, whipped cream with no sugar. i loved going out for coffee and kuchen, just looking in the bakery windows was enough to make your mouth water. A favorite of ours is Schwarzwalder Kirsch Torte or Black Forest Cherry Torte.

While visiting, most Sunday afternoons after church, we would be invited to a relative or friends home for coffee and cake (kaffe und kuchen). Each lady who was invited brought a special cake and of course wanted us to try just a slice of each one. Needless to say, Fred and i came home several pounds heavier, but we were young, worked hard and would shed the pounds when we returned home. For the time being, we would enjoy these wonderful desserts.

The weekend soon arrived, and Fred's only brother Walter, his wife Rosewitha and their son Michael, drove from Lake Constance (Bodensee) area to greet and meet us; it was a great re-union. Walter spoke a little English, his wife and son spoke none.

Everything was so new to me, and i loved it all, except the language. As much as i tried to understand, it became more and more difficult for me. One day i said to Fred, " i want to go home, to America, i cannot hardly understand a word in German. i feel so lost, so out of touch." Fred said, " That's fine, i'll put you on the next flight home." i was shocked; he was going to send me home without him, how could he? Fred was very wise in saying that, because he gave me a choice: to either learn the language or, to give-up and go home. i do not give-up very easily, (as those who know me) so i decided i would learn the language. Within a short period of time, with the help of the Lord and the gift HE gave me, i learned to understand and speak German within a couple of weeks.

As i think back, my father could speak Portuguese and Spanish, (as well as English). He would listen to a Spanish station on the radio as well as Portuguese. They are very similar languages, being Latin based. Perhaps, i inherited some of that learning from my father as well. When my brothers were just little boys, he would take them to his Mexican-American friends and play music with his friends. My father played the harmonica and the accordion. Both my brothers have fond memories of these unusual times they spent with our father. Interesting, he was very gifted in music. But, my Mom, as much as she loved music, couldn't carry a tune in a bucket. Bless her, she probably sings well in the heavenly choir.

Back to Germany, now you must remember i was just a new babe in Christ, and wasn't familiar with praying or even how to pray. The Lord, of course, knew that, and helped me through this difficult time of learning two new languages, German and praying. My PRAISE goes to HIM!!! i was to learn in later years, that HE had given me the gift of understanding and speaking different languages. As a friend from Sweden, who spoke very little English, said to her Swedish friends about me; "She can Swedish." Which meant, i understood what she and her Swedish speaking friends were saying. Swedish has some words that are similar to German, but not many, so i could understand some of what they were saying. But mostly, i watched their expressions, hand motions and so forth.

Traveling throughout Europe was a wonderful experience. Fred and i just hopped into the Mercedes and off we went toward Austria. The Alps are majestic and breathtaking; a person would have to lean back and stretch their neck just to see the mightiness and grandeur of those God given mountains.

We stayed in places where we would see a sign that said; ZIMMER FREI (room free) to rent. One particular place we stayed was Innsbruck, Austria. The owners of the home invited us to join them and the towns people, to a dance. Fred and i love to dance (remember that's where we met, at a dance), we said," Yes." We enjoyed a marvelous dinner at a restaurant where we, for the first time ever, ordered Chateaubriand for two. The waiter brought us a huge platter with caviar, sautéed potatoes and vegetables, and fillet mignon; there was enough for four, but we ate and ate, and thoroughly enjoyed this lovely feast. It was one we still talk about today.

After that lovely dinner, we met our landlord and neighbors at the dance. We danced the night away and then went back to the home where we had rented the room, in hopes to get ready for a good nights sleep. The landlord would not have such a thing; we must spend time with them in their kitchen, laugh, and share stories. They served homemade Schnapps (like white lightning), none for me, but Fred, being raised with the clear intoxicating liquid, loved it. It got so that the host kept pouring more Schnapps in those shot glasses and Fred had had enough and was now tossing it under the table. We laugh today, because he wishes he had some of that, which he tossed under the table. You must understand, the kitchen table is set-up in such a way, like a booth that was set-up against a wall with a seating area; that is where Fred and i sat, so we couldn't get out. Besides, the host wanted to know and hear everything about America; few Americans entered their home at that time. And now was an opportunity to hear, first hand from Americans, what life was like in America. What a privilege to share our lives with them.

The next day, we left for Salzburg, where i would see a real castle for the first time in my life, The Hohen Salzburg Castle was nestled high on a hill overlooking the beautiful city of Salzburg, Austria. This is the city i mentioned previously, where, we driving in the wrong direction when i asked Fred what Einbahn strase meant? "One way street," he replied. "That's why the traffic is all coming at us," said i. Once we got out of that mess, we parked the car and made the long trek up to the monumental structure, the castle. It was a long tiring climb up stairs we thought would never end, to the very top of the hill, where the castle sat.

Upon arriving, i stood in wonder at the tremendous columns surrounding the castle; each was worn out differently. The reason being, the number of years it took to haul each column up to the top of the mountain and place it in its position. i just stood in amazement wondering how they did it, how long it took and thankful for the development of machinery in today's world. Also, keeping in mind the stories in the Old Testament of the Israeli people in captivity in Egypt, building those pyramids.

Our next stop was Vienna (Wien), the music capitol of the world. One thing i noticed is, we call cities and Countries in Europe something other than what they are called; such as Vienna is really Wien pronounced; 'Veen', Austria is 'Ostrich,' etc. Well, once we arrived in Vienna we could not find a place to stay overnight, not even in the hotels in this big wondrous city. Although, we did find one dimly lit room, which looked flea infested. That was not the usual for these very clean people. We finally ended up parking our car for the night in the gravel pit, and there we slept in our car. We woke early the next morning and headed toward Yugoslavia. So much for seeing the music capitol of the world: Vienna. We did walk through the streets and enjoy the beauty it represented.

Somewhere in Austria, Fred and i went into an exclusive leather shop. It was there he purchased a gorgeous leather dress for me, i still have it these 40 plus years later, and do wear it on occasion and the compliments i receive are worth the wearing. After we made the purchase of the leather dress, i got out my chart, which showed the break down of German Marks to Austrian Schillings; then i had to figure the final breakdown to the American dollar. It turned out we paid a whole $10.00 for this lovely soft leather dress. i asked Fred if we could go back and get something else, he was done shopping and ready to rest. So much for bargains, as men are concerned. Driving through Yugoslavia was another story; the poverty was very apparent, especially after being in such a prosperous country like Austria. We decided, after the experience we had in Austria in finding a place to stay for the night, it would be worse here, so traveled on to Italy. Now, you must realize traveling through Europe is not like traveling through America, (especially California or our larger states), the countries are so close together. So within in a couple of hours, sometimes less, you can drive from one Country to the next.

On our way to Italy, we decided we'd go to the famous sinking Venice. This would prove to be an experience in itself. First, we needed to park our car, because in Venice you travel by boat or walk, once you are there. The parking garage attendant quickly took the keys from Fred's hand and sped off with our new Mercedes. Fred just stood there in awe and fear. In as much as i wanted to leisurely float the canals of Venice in a gondola, we somehow ended up in a speed boat cruising at breakneck speed to the island, through the canals, and then, without a word, were dropped off at St. Marco's Square. What did all this mean, where were we, where was our car, we couldn't speak Italian, how could we translate?

We decided since we were there, we would make the best of it, took pictures, fed the pigeons, watched as a native pulled up his shirt sleeve to sell us any one of the number of watches he had on his arm. We visited the large cathedral, walked around the square and decided to eat at one of the outside restaurants. When we went to purchase more film for our camera, we realized almost everyone around us spoke English. We found that interesting, peaceful, yet disturbing to feel so lost.

Finally, we decided we had enough and boarded a large watercraft, which made many stops as it went through the canals, much like a bus on land. We showed the Captain our ticket where our car was parked, and he motioned us to board. Soon another Captain replaced him, so we ventured to ask him the same question; he motioned the direction and nodded as to when it was time to get off the boat. i am so thankful as a follower of Christ, that He is the Captain of my ship and will direct me in all my paths. And in the end, He will guide me beside the **'still waters and comfort me with His staff. And i will have nothing to fear for He will be with me.' Psalm 23; "The Lord is my Shepherd."**

What a relief it was to find our car, yet it was difficult to get out of the tight space without getting a scratch. Fred finally got us out and on our way to Verona, Italy, famous for Romeo and Juliette. It was July and the weather was very hot and humid, much like California, except for the humidity. Wasn't long, i had to go to the restroom. Fred stopped at a bar to get a beer and i could get relief. There was a sign hanging over the doorway which read Toilette, i immediately headed in that direction. The doorway took me to a door that led outside to what looked like someone's junk yard, a sign appeared over an open little room, which read; Toilette. Yeah, i had relief at last. But what i saw was like the bottom of a shower with a hole in the middle, no toilette at all. It was in the 1970's, when pantsuits were in style and that's exactly what i had on, a canary yellow pantsuit. 'Now what?' i thought, with no closure on the so-called toilette and me in a pantsuit; this may be easy for a man, but what was a women to do? When you're desperate you go for it. Being raised in the country, this reminded me of my prune picking days, and Grandma in her dress, just standing there and going. For me it was full exposure as i pulled down my pantsuit, praying no one would walk in and see me. Wow, i made it and quickly shared my story with Fred. We were out of there in a flash and off to find a place for the night to rest our weary heads.

We found a hotel, unpacked and went searching for a good place to eat. As we walked through the city the smell of pizza was in the air, perfect ... pizza in Italy. We followed our noses to a small restaurant where the employees were taking these luscious pizzas out of these huge brick ovens, which took up most of the restaurant. So we ordered one, not speaking Italian we just worked it out; they seemed to know what we wanted, and we waited in the hot, humid little restaurant. We didn't mind the heat; we were hungry and could hardly wait to bite into this Italian delicacy. Out of that huge brick oven it came, but it was folded over, much like an apple turnover. The first most delicious calzone, Fred and i ever had.

We walked around the town a bit and then headed off to our hotel for a good long sleep, after a tiring day, or so we thought. Just as we were dosing off, suddenly we heard the sound of electric saws, hammers, drills and different equipment used for construction. We were to learn, due to the extreme heat and humidity in that part of Italy, the construction workers took long naps during the day and worked late into the night when it was cool. Needless to say, we did not get much sleep. Next day, tired and weary, but young and vivacious, we drove along the coast of Italy. As we drove along the windy road we went in and out of dimly lit tunnels, each time we came out of these long tunnels, we saw different sceneries. Until, suddenly as we were coming out of one of the tunnels there below us, was the most beautiful aqua blue i'd ever laid eyes on before me. Turning to Fred in my innocent child like manner, i said, "What is that? It looks like a huge swimming pool." When we finally got near it, as we were going downward to this lovely site, we realized it was the Mediterranean Sea.

We drove up to a large, what appeared to be a, hotel directly on the beach, overlooking the Mediterranean. We inquired about a room for the night; the lady said something in Italian; we answered both in English and German, of which she spoke neither. Somehow we managed to get a room for a mere $10.00 per night. The next morning, when we came down from our room, people were sitting at tables in a dining room setting, with large bottles of water, or some sort of soda, at their tables. We didn't understand what was going on, so we walked into the village to get a cup of coffee and perhaps a roll or piece of bread or something. The smell of coffee permeated the air; we asked for one and got it all right, the strongest cup of java ever. Whoa!!! And with nothing to eat it really hit us hard.

We spent most of the day just walking through the village, it smelled like the floods i was in when i was a child, and purchased a few items. It was that damp, musty smell. After our purchases, we decided to purchase items for our lunch so we could enjoy it in our room. We had quite an assortment, including squid salad, which neither one of us could even stand looking at, let alone eat. That evening, we decided we would have dinner at the hotel in the large dining room. As we sat down to order, we were immediately served without ordering a thing. It was then we realized we were staying in a Pension, pronounced 'Pen see own.' Which meant we had our room and three meals included, all for $10.00 a day. What a deal, but we wanted to see more of Europe, so left the following day.

We drove along the magnificent Mediterranean into the French side, stopping to rest along the pebbled beaches. Unlike the beaches in California, the French had lounge chairs with umbrellas set-up on the pebble beaches, for anyone who cared to sit and enjoy the beach at no cost. This sure was a blessing, not to have to haul all the extra stuff down to the beach. As i mentioned, the beach itself consisted of large pebbles, until going into the sea where the sand began its stretch into the aqua blue water.

As we continued our journey, driving along the Southern part of France, a sweet relaxing scent wafted through the windows of our car. There before us were fields upon fields of lavender. i told Fred, " With this lovely fragrance and the French wine, no wonder the French are so relaxed." Keeping that in mind, we realized they are not as industrious as their neighboring Germans and Swiss.

We used a travel book to guide us on our trip; this was fun and exciting, because we never knew where we would end up at the end of a days journey. Being the navigator, i directed Fred along a long narrow entrance and there in the distance at the end of the road lie outstretched in the French landscape a gorgeous Chateau. Neither one of us had ever seen a Chateau let alone stay in one, but that's what the tour guide book said, listing it as a comfortable place to stay. Upon arrival we were shown to our lovely guest room, one of many in this one level mansion. Dinner was served in their huge dining room and of course the most delectable French food was on the menu. My mouth still waters for the delicious filet minion served with a béarnaise sauce, fresh vegetables, potatoes, French bread, and a bottle of excellent French red wine. At the close of every French meal a large wooden board was brought to the table displaying a variety of natural French cheese. As in German the saying is; "Kasea schleise the magen," so it must be in French as well; "Cheese closes the stomach." Sounded good to us, especially me, as i am a mouse when it comes to cheese.

When we went to our room that evening, the down comforter was turned back and a chocolate truffle greeted us on our pillow. Since we never had a guests staying in our home as a child (except for the winos), i would use this small act of kindness in our home in the years to come, along with many others i learned over the years.

Most recently, i was expecting my long time friend Joyce to spend the night, and had our grandson Steven Joseph, who was five at the time. i was preparing the room for Joyce's stay, and asked Steven if he would like to help me. Not only did he help me, when Joyce arrived, he took her by the hand and showed her all the things we did to make her stay comfortable and welcome. Including the small vase of flowers he placed on a doily we got out especially for her, a welcome note, a candle and of course the piece of chocolate on her pillow. i know Steven Joseph loved helping to make her stay enjoyable as well. He was so proud of his accomplishment and sharing it with Joyce. She too was thrilled, loved his special gift of sharing and thanked him.

One area i remember well in France, and being a new Christian, was seeing the huge walls formed in a circle, where the entertainment took place. Also, it was where many Christians were martyred for their faith. These coliseum's, were huge and awesome, yet a fearful sight for me. Another site was the aqueduct, which was built by King Agrippa. Although, i was new to my Christian faith, i had read about King Agrippa and realized i was seeing the actual history of which the Bible spoke, about a man that really existed as the Bible told of him. **(Please refer to Acts 25:1-Acts 26: 32)** Fred and i took the long walk through this aqueduct which at one time brought water to the city. Neither one of us cared much about purchasing souvenirs, although we did purchase a long wooden pipe with the name Aux in Provence engraved on its side. Fred smoked pipe in those days, so we thought of this as a fun useful gift. Our son, Jeff still has it along with all of Fred's pipes, tobacco etc. Once in awhile they will enjoy a pipe together and now they share as two grown men. Life brings many joys and fond memories. We had been traveling for a few weeks and decided it was time to head back to Germany and spend time with family and friends. Everyone was excited to have us back, and plans were made for more family re-unions and gatherings. Fred and i loved these times, but also enjoyed just walking out in the nearby lush green fields and forest that surrounded his homeland. It was amazing to me as we walked along the paths in Germany near Mutti's home, in just a few short walks we would be in Switzerland, and could see it's small villages from the distance. The villages and towns in most of Europe are nestled together exposing red tile rooftops and church steeples, surrounded by the farmers fields. Very few of the farmers actually live where their fields exist, unlike most of America where the farmers and ranchers have their homes on their land. For me the quiet walks in the countryside, gave this new Christian a time to meditate on the awesomeness of God and my new German family.

Always being interested in my family heritage, i was forever asking questions, but the one who really knew most about my Mom's side of the family was her brother, Uncle Jim. He was the one i cleaned house for, the one who loved olive oil. Like King Midas when he touched anything, it turned into gold, for Uncle Jim it was olive oil. Uncle Jim had a wealth of information about our Swiss Italian family, along with pictures, some he has given me. He told me that his father, my grandfather, came from a town in Switzerland called Biasca. i had always wanted to try and find family in that town; what better opportunity than now, since we were so close. Well, as it turned out, there was much convincing Fred on my part to make the long trip over the Gottard Pass (part of the Swiss Alps) and down into the Swiss Italian part of Switzerland.

Finally, Fred said, "Yes." So off we went along the Rhinefall into Zurich and on our way to Biasca. i was so excited, yet didn't know any family there or exactly where they lived. We were young and adventurous, not knowing where we were going, let alone how we were going to communicate once in Biasca. Going over the pass wasn't too bad, although it was a long way to the bottom of those magnificent mountains. We had two choices: to go over the pass or through the long, long tunnel which would take us through the Alps. The tunnel was shorter in distance than going over the mountains, but i did not like tunnels. So we opted for both, which made it nice, we could travel part of the way through the tunnel and then the rest of the journey, up the steep mountain pass.

Once we arrived in the lovely Canton of Ticino, Switzerland we followed the map in search of the town of Biasca. It didn't take us long to find the lovely little village which lies deep at the foot of the towering Alps of Switzerland. Most of the homes in this delightful little village were built with the rocks from the area's rivers and mountains. It made me stop and realize why my maternal grandfather went into the first gravel business he created in San Jose, years prior. With all those rocks in San Jose and the surrounding areas, it only made sense to do what he knew best to do with rocks: have a gravel business. Also, in the Gold Country where we reside, the old buildings that are still standing, were built in the same fashion, with rocks and boulders, most of them built by Italian immigrants. Today most of the homes in the Ticino area now have mortar and a white wash over them, but the base is still the same rocks and boulders without mortar.

We drove around Biasca, and decided to visit the cemetery behind the Catholic church, looking for names of deceased relatives. We were hoping someone would come by and know the Guidotti family, introduce themselves and take us to a relative. No one came, so we went into the village itself. Since we couldn't communicate and knew no one there at the time, we decided this venture was over for now.

Driving back to Germany, we stopped and stayed at the town of Kussnacht am Rigi, which is by Lake Lucerne with the breathtaking view of Rigi Mountain in the background. This would be a favorite spot for me to stay. It was so very lovely and peaceful. We stayed at a Guest haus, just outside of Kussnacht; it was a large two- story building. We had our own room, but shared a bathroom with other guests.

Well, i had to go to the bathroom once we got settled, which was down the hall from our room. Each room had a huge skeleton key to unlock the door, and there was one for the bathroom as well. Somehow i managed to lock myself in the bathroom with the key on the outside. Try as i may, i could not get out, and Fred was not coming to see what kept me so long, so i decided the only way out was to climb out the window of this two story building. Which i did, and slid down the side of the building. When i finally made it to our room, i told Fred what had happened and wondered why he didn't come and look for me. Oh well, i made it out with great determination.

Soon it was time to return to family and friends once again in Germany. This time we would take Mutti with us to visit Fred's hometown of Saulgau, to visit his only living Bodenmüller uncle, his father's brother, Uncle Josef and his lovely wife Tante Josefin. Although many of the family and friends warned me about this angry, bitter man, Uncle Josef, i was excited to meet he and his wife, partly because my maiden name was Joseph and my sister's name is Josephine. i loved them and treated them with respect and honor, they both fell in love with this young American girl. Uncle Josef even gave me a book written in German about the famous American Route 66. That was a treasure, because he loved his books and very seldom gave them away. i have kept that book as a reminder of Uncle Josef. He and Tante Fine (as we affectionately called her), loved hiking in their younger years, sharing many of their stories of hiking in the Alps, in dreams of coming to America to hike the Grand Tetons. Tante Fine, was an excellent, but frugal cook, had a lovely garden she worked in almost everyday, gorgeous flowers arrayed their small abode and a small yet plentiful vegetable garden.

Like most Germans they loved to walk, so we ventured through the country roads surrounding the village of Saulgau. Fred was so proud to show me all the sights of his childhood in this lovely village nestled in the Schwabish area of Germany. i had the privilege of seeing the school Fred attended as a child and meeting his head master teacher.

Fred also took me to the cemetery where his father lay; a huge white headstone rose above his grave, that Uncle Josef made. It was amazing. i also, met Frau Konig and her twin sons, who were Fred's school chums. Frau Konig and Mutti were good friends. She, too, was an excellent cook and was the first to show me how to make spatzle (homemade noodles). She loved to cook, as did Tante Fine; they were so thankful to have the necessary food to prepare, especially since WW II, when food was scarce. Such appreciation i thoroughly understood from my poverty-stricken childhood. i did not share with them my past, but am sure they thought i was a wealthy American, yet treated me with such love, I guess because i did not act spoiled. Perhaps, deep down they understood.

The Germans seem to have a festival for any occasion; my thoughts were just any excuse to drink their beer, which they are known for: German bier (beer). Well, while we were visiting Saulgau, the event they were celebrating was Kinderfest (child fest); it sounded good, since i love children and thought this was appropriate to celebrate with a festival for children.

A children's parade was held in the morning and then we all walked out to the grounds where the festival was held. There were rides for the children, and a big tent pitched for the beer drinking. We sat at long narrow tables as big Fraulines served us the beer they carried; i kid you not, a stein of beer on each finger and thumb, so five steins in each hand. The steins held a liter of beer, which is a little more than a quart.

As i stated before, i am not a beer drinker and cannot stand the taste, but there was nothing else except a soft drink called Sinaco. So i had a Sinaco; well, it must have been the bottom of the barrel, because i got so sick on this horrible acidy drink. After getting it all out, i decided no more Sinaco for me. Most Germans do not drink their water; i was told it is not good to drink. Only beer and drinks were being served, no food, which i could not understand. So i ordered a beer, well it took all afternoon and evening for me to finish it, which i don't think i did. But i did get to take the stein home as proof. We did get something to eat at the festival: good old fashioned German franks, with a brotchen (roll) or large pretzel. When it finally ended, or we decided to go back home, it was dark and late, but we walked, which all Germans do in small towns, so as not to harm anyone by driving and drinking alcohol.

Soon it was time to go back to Mutti's little town of Weisweil. Once again we were welcomed and felt right at home. When i say little, this town had one restaurant, one church, homes, some with huge piles of manure in front of their barns; Fred told me the farmer with the largest manure pile was considered the richest farmer in town. The town was surrounded by fields and fields of rich farmland. It was a quiet, quaint little town, but nowhere to purchase needed items, even food; which made it difficult for Mutti, because she had to walk everywhere or depend on her sisters or friends to purchase her needed items. Fred and i thought the next best thing for Mutti was a bicycle, so we purchased her a bicycle; not an ordinary one, this one actually folded in half, so she could load it in the back of someone's car if necessary. We had never seen one before, nor since. Also, Mutti had only the old Grudig radio Fred and his brother purchased for her, year's prior. We decided to buy her a television, especially for those long cold winter nights, to keep her company. She was so delighted to receive our gifts. On future visits we would purchase a vacuum, a hot water heater, and other useful items for her, we all take for granted here in America. Once again, understanding where i came from as a child helped me to appreciate and understand the comforts of modern living.

Time went quickly, and before we knew it, we were saying our aufwiedersehens (i'll be seeing you), to these wonderful people i had grown to love. We drove toward Northern Germany, toward Hamburg to take the car to the shipyard. On our way, we traveled through parts of the Black Forest, (much like the denseness of the trees here in Northern California and Oregon), the Rhine and Mosel Rivers, i especially liked, where they meet at Deutches Eche or German corner. We took a large boat along the Rhine River passing vineyards and lovely homes that stretched out across the hillsides.

The Germans are known for their rich, some sweet, white wines, such as: Zeller Schwarze Katz (Cellar Black Cat), Lieb Frauen Milch (Lovely Ladies Milk), Gewurztraminer, Blue Nun, and many others. Fred taught me the white wines in the blue bottles were from the Mosel and the dark brown bottles were the Rhine wines. We enjoyed and have many fond memories of the trip down the Rhine River.

We traveled further North of our destination: Hamburg. i had always wanted to visit Holland ever since I saw the movie about this lovely area of Europe. We briefly visited Holland, because, once again, we did not understand their native tongue of Dutch. We stopped in a restaurant for lunch prior to our departure, and the people were kind and accommodating. The one thing i noticed, probably having been partially raised on a dairy, was their butter. It was the most creamy, moist sweet butter, we've ever tasted. Probably due to the lovely thick green grass these milk cows ate. Unlike America, where most of our butter is salted, all European butter is unsalted, giving it a much better flavor.

We arrived safely in Hamburg, and somehow made all the connections to get the car off and on the ship. Of course, we loaded the inside of the car with wonderful purchases we made in Europe, thinking this was the best way to get them home safely. It was loaded down with a set of Winterlingen china from Germany (the first nice set of dishes i ever owned and still use today), fine crystal from Fred's hometown, and of course German beer for Fred. We sent it off with lots of prayers, that no one would break into the car as it went on its long voyage to San Francisco, California.

Thankful to get out of the big city of Hamburg, we hopped a train to Frankfurt, staying overnight and then leaving the next day from Frankfurt Airport to San Francisco Airport. But that was not to be. Upon inspection of the aircraft, there were problems and it was not allowed to depart until repairs were made. There we sat at the Frankfurt Airport, our luggage stored in compartments, we could at least walk around without lugging suitcases.

They had no wheels on them like today's suitcases. We had turned in all of
our German Marks and had very little American dollars in our possession;
those were the days prior to debit or credit cards. It was getting late, we
were hungry, tired and without much cash to do anything. i believe we had
been waiting for at least 10 or so hours, when two wonderful familiar faces
appeared, it was Cousins Heinz and Erna. They decided to drive for several
hours to see us off at the airport; had the plane left on time, we would have
been a long time in the air. They did not know that, and i believe the Lord
sent them as two angels to help us in time of need.

They took us to a restaurant in the airport, where we had our last
German meal together. Then they took us to one of the exclusive stores in
the airport and purchased a lovely blue and clear crystal basket-dish for me,
and a beer stein of Frankfurt, for Fred. We were so thankful, not only for
them to come at the perfect time and fill our tummies, but then they
presented us with these lovely gifts. The dish sits on a dresser in our
bedroom today, as a reminder of their kindness, love and how the Lord sent
these two angels to comfort us.

After Heinz and Erna left, we still had to wait a couple more hours
before work was complete on the aircraft. Finally, after 16 hours of waiting,
we were able to board for our flight home. What a relief. Being so very tired
we slept most of the trip; although, i do remember looking out the window
of the plane and seeing the sun come up on one side of the plane and the
moon going down on the opposite side, that was an amazing site.

As the aircraft was making it's final approach before landing, i
looked out the window seeing a very dry desolate site before my eyes, it was
home; California. I guess after being in the beauty of the luscious green grass
of Germany and the surrounding countries, i never realized how dry
California looks in the summer. We had been traveling for about 9 hours in
the air, and with the stop in Banger, Maine, it was a joy to arrive home,
yeah!!!

Chapter Twelve

"Even the sparrow has found
a home..." Psalm 84:3a

Santa Clara is changing, but so
is my life for Jesus.

Life began again for us with work and now the remodeling of our
home. Gradually, i could see the changes in my beloved Santa Clara Valley;
the once luscious orchards were quickly disappearing, the rich soil was
being replaced by homes and subdivisions. No longer would we enjoy the
smell of those beautiful fragrant blossoms from the apricot, cherry, pear, and
prune trees, that added such beauty to the valley.

But i was young and starting a new life with my husband, a new
faith, a home and many wonderful friends. Time and things seem to change
so rapidly, and we are so busy with life, most times we do not take notice.
"Isn't it funny how day by day nothing changes, but when you look back
everything is different..." C.S. Lewis.[5]

Before we knew it, the year was 1972 and i insisted it was time for
Mutti to visit us in America. She had not traveled far in her life, yet was very
excited to make the trip. We purchased her tickets in America, because it
was less expensive than purchasing them for her in Europe, the dollar was
still worth a dollar. Mutti flew out of Zurich, Switzerland, which was closer
for her than Frankfurt, Germany, to Oakland Airport.

She loved America and the people here. Mutti really loved all of my
family, particularly my Uncle Slim and Uncle Jim, because both made her feel
welcome and tried very hard to reach out to her. Although, she could not
speak English, she had no fear in speaking to anyone who had ears to listen. i
recall one time she was talking for quite awhile to the tree surgeon, who
came to cut down some of the huge Madrone trees that we had hanging over

our home. When he got up from listening to her lengthy talk, he politely told us he couldn't understand a word she had said. All too soon, it was time for Mutti to make the long trip back to her homeland of Germany. We drove her to Oakland Airport, with lots of hugs and aufwiedersehens (i'll be seeing you). With tears in my eyes, we made the drive home, upon arrival, Fred said we needed to put a new roof on our home. Being the hardworking German he is, we started immediately tearing off the roof on our home; i mean immediately upon returning home from the airport.

As i ponder his actions today, perhaps this was a way to keep his mind occupied and not having to think about his Mother being so far away. Most Germans do not show their emotions in the way most Americans do, they learn to cope in different ways. i am still learning today, how Fred copes with new ideas and life in general.

Speaking of the trees, in the previous chapter, that had to be dropped, Fred and i manned the ropes while the tree surgeon did the climbing and cutting of those monster Madrone trees. We later learned that Madrone trees have the highest b.t.u.'s; it's no wonder we kept so very warm over the cold foggy winter months.

Prior to having them cut, we experienced a big storm, with winds and lots of rain. We decided it would be safer to visit our neighbors across the street, Hank and Leslie. Off we went to their home and we were sitting at their table enjoying a fun card game, when suddenly there was a tremendous crash and the power went out. A huge limb came crashing down, from one of their fir trees, and took off the corner of their roof: the corner where we were sitting! So much for safety at the neighbors, we quickly left, being very careful as we walked home, so as not to step on the hot wire coiled in the road between our home and theirs. i believe it was the next week or so, that we had the Madrone's cut and some trimmed.

On another occasion, our next door neighbor's always had a big celebration on New Years Eve, not drinking and such, although they enjoyed

111

their homemade cherry brandy and an occasional beer. The wife taught me how to make cherry brandy, by putting cherries in a jar of 100 proof alcohol, and set it in the sun. i made some for Fred, drained the brandy and put several cherries in his lunch. He said, " The guys at work sure like those cherries you put in my lunch." So, i kept putting them in his lunch, until one day i realized they too were soaked with brandy, no wonder they liked them!

Back to New Years Eve with these folks, they were from what was Estonia, and had brought quite a few traditions with them from their homeland, as many do. One, of their traditions, was to melt hot metal, then pour it into a bucket of cold water to see what it formed; that was supposed to tell you what the New Year would bring. Being a new Christian, i was very doubtful and suspicious of this tradition, not believing this untruth.

Along with that, the husband would shoot off his rifle, like a firework, i guess. Fred thought that was neat and wanted to give it a try, the neighbor forewarned him about shooting it in the air and hitting a tree branch, especially in that mountainous, wooded area where we lived. No problem, thought Fred as he raised the gun to shoot. Suddenly, there was a great crackling noise and bang, a huge limb from one of the mighty fir trees came crashing down, almost striking Fred on the head. Needless to say, we came up with other ideas for neighborhood New Years Eve celebrations, like going from house to house for dinner, where one would have the salad then next, the main, etc. Now, that was fun and we could walk, eat together, and not endanger anyone.

One thing that comes to mind was Hank and Leslie's neighbor's dog, who stood on the roof of its owners home and barked. The bark wasn't so annoying, but as Hank would say; " It is the same tune." Now, that's annoying. We had some different types of people living in those mountains, which brought back memories of my father's friend, Monkey Mack, the one with the real monkey. Makes me wonder, did we fit in, too? Were we strange? It was also, the time of the Hippies and flower children, many of which, made their abode in 'them thar hills.' One group was the famous Doobie's[6]. i didn't realize what their name stood for until years later. The beauty of innocence or is it ignorance? Yet, being the late 1960's, early 1970's, the Lord had His mighty hand on me. Drugs were all around, commune living, hippies, flower children, and anti-establishment. Although i was Democrat at the time, i was very conservative, but it seems to me, Democrats were more conservative in those days. i was a Democrat because my Dad was, and my Mother never voted (she and my Dad felt women shouldn't vote). Today, i vote for the man/woman who is patriotic and best suits the job.

i remembered during President Kennedy's term, how he opened the store houses in America to feed the poor. Being part of that when i was living at home in dire poverty, we felt so blessed to receive commodities of flour, powdered milk and eggs, and many other foods.

Hank and Leslie were great neighbors and we enjoyed fun card games and just spending time getting to know them. One evening we were playing cards and one by one, opossums scurried through the cat door, nibbling on the cat food. Hank and Leslie didn't even flinch. i said, " There are opossums coming in your house." Leslie, just laughed and in her broken English/Japanese said, " We know, they come in 'most all time." They were cute, but i thought, strange. Memories of **Monkey Mack**, Oh my!!!!

While we were remodeling our home, Hank loved to come over and work and learned how to do things with Fred. They worked together well and got along good. He was a big help to us, in tearing the house apart and rebuilding. We were introduced to Fred Jennings; he was a good carpenter and friend. He also liked our homemade plum wine.

Just a few years ago, while living here in the beautiful foothills of Northern California, i needed to have my rings cleaned and checked. Most times i do not remove them from my fingers while i garden, and do other chores on the ranch. i wanted to make sure all the stones were intact. All of my most precious jewels i do not keep in a box, i wear them and enjoy them: my wedding ring and engagement ring, a ring Fred gave me on our 25th wedding anniversary, a Mother's ring from our sons and wives, and a lovely little ring my dear Mother presented to me while i was caring for her. As we sat at the doctor's office waiting for her appointment, she removed it from her small finger and said, "Here, you might as well have this, what do i need it for?" At first i told her no, but as i looked into her beautiful blue eyes, i knew she wanted me to have it. That was Mom's gift, giving. Around my neck is a gold chain with a lovely gold cross, and in the center of the cross is a stone that was taken from the Sepulcher, where Jesus was buried. That precious gift is from my sister Barbara. i had a diamond, one from my sister Fran, but somehow lost it. Then, finally, a lovely silver chain and cross from our precious granddaughter Laurel Shea.

Anyway, i took my rings to a jeweler in a nearby town. As i filled out the form, the gal taking my order said, "Did you live in Redwood Estates?" When i said yes and asked how did she know? She answered, "Your last name is Bodenmüller, my Dad is Fred Jennings, i remember your name from my Dad." Once again, what a small world we live in, here was Fred Jennings daughter and she remembered us, well at least by our last name. She told us her Dad had passed on. This was the same Fred, who helped my Fred and i, rebuild our home in Redwood Estates; he was an excellent carpenter and taught my Fred a lot about building. The Lord's mighty hand at work again.

Before we moved to the Sierra's, Fred asked my Fred, to work with him as his partner in construction. My Fred turned it down, along with another friend, Winnie's offer to run his machine shop in Fremont, so he and his wife could sail around the world in their sailboat, Fred was also offered a job at I.B.M. in San Jose. He turned all three down, because we were moving to the Sierra's and starting life a new, with no job opportunities for either of us. We simply moved in faith. i, in my new Christian faith in an almighty God knew would provide for us, and He did, and continues to do so today.

114

Chapter Thirteen

"I prayed for this child, and the Lord has granted me what I asked Him..." 1 Samuel 1:27

A child for me to love, care for and teach about Jesus.

The year was 1974 and time to go back to visit family in Germany. Once again our German family was glad to see us and gave us a warm welcome back home. On this trip, Fred and i would spend more time with family, although we did travel to other countries. i loved our German family and all of the European traditions, so i always enjoyed going 'home.'

Before we knew it, the year was 1976 and many changes would come in our lives. i was rear-ended in our V.W. hatchback, and ended up with neck and back injuries, that would affect me the rest of my life. Not long after the automobile accident i went to the doctor for a check-up because i was not feeling well. After his examination he said, "Congratulations." Shocked, i said "For what?" He said, " You are pregnant." What a miracle! Fred and i had been married for almost eight years and we were hoping to have a child. The baby would be born in June. i was still wearing back braces, due to the auto accident and had to wear one, that was especially made for pregnancy.

One day a dear elderly lady, from our Bible Study group, called to check on me, i told her my back was really hurting, especially now that i was carrying a child. She asked if she could pray for me, i thought, "i don't pray out loud (as i was not taught, now you can't stop me!); she was going to pray for me now, over the phone." And pray she did, a beautiful prayer using Scripture; from Isaiah 53:5b "...by His wounds we are healed." Little did i know the Lord would have me use that same Scripture years later. **Isaiah 53:5 "But He was pierced for our transgressions, He was crushed for**

our iniquities; the punishment that brought us peace was upon Him, and by His wounds we are healed." The Lord heard the prayers of this dear little lady, Grandma Botello, and He healed me.

Years later, when we were living in our home in the Sierra's, i was sitting in a lounge chair praying for relief from the same back pain once again. My prayer was; "Lord, i thought You took this pain away years ago, now it is back again, please take it away." Immediately, i felt a warmth start in the middle of my back, traveling down my legs and finally out the tips of my toes and the back pain was gone. i was so excited, jumped up and ran to tell Fred the good news of how the Lord removed my back pain. He didn't say a word, just took it all in, i guess. Years later he would personally, understand.

As i mentioned earlier, the Lord would have me use that same verse to help a friend. This is how it all took place; i was sitting in the bleachers at one of Franz's (that's our oldest son) baseball game, when Susan, who was sitting next to me, began sharing about the pain in her arm. She was a single mom who made beautiful things to sell at craft fairs to provide for she and her son, Sam. Sam was a good friend of Franz's. Anyway, she was telling me the pain was so bad she couldn't sew to make the items to sell, and that was her only source of income. i listened intently, when suddenly one of the other mother's said to me, "That's right, gloria why don't you lay your hands on her and pray for her healing?" And then she laughed, knowing i was a Christian she was poking fun of me, and my faith. That evening, i could hardly rest thinking of Susan and the comment made. The next morning the Lord directed me to go and see Susan and pray for her. My reply was, "No, not me Lord"(i was being like Jonah), but i obeyed. After dropping our sons off at school, i went to see Susan (called first to ask her if i could come). When i arrived, she was in bed suffering from the pain in her arm and very discouraged. The room she was in, was very dark and dreary. With Bible in hand and the courage of the Lord, i said; " The Lord has sent me to pray for you and i want you to know HE is the great Healer, i am just HIS servant." So i opened my Bible to **Isaiah 53:5**, laid my hand on her, read from the Bible and prayed.

The next time i saw her (within a few days), she told me the pain was gone and she was healed. i Praised the Lord, thanked her and invited her to a Bible Study. She came to the Bible Study and told us she had dedicated her son Samuel as Hannah (in the Bible) did, but never thought to give herself to the Lord. Not long after, she started coming to church and playing the organ (beautifully, by ear). She was living with a man at the time and knew it was wrong and was moving out on her own as soon as the school year ended. The Lord really blessed her life and i had the opportunity to share the love of JESUS with her.

Let's see, where was i? Oh yes, it was 1976, the year our precious son, Franz was born, and our 200 year celebration of The United States of America; that's why i decorated his room partially patriotic. It was that same year we purchased our property in the Sierra Foothills of California. We purchased it on a nice day in February, interesting i was sharing with Fred just a few days ago; we met on a rainy evening in February 1967, purchased our Sierra property in February 1976 and now we have it on the market in February 2013. Hmmmm, His Hand is upon us to remind us.

The main reason we purchased the property is because of the draught we were experiencing in the Bay Area, with the water rationing, along with the area getting too crowded, it was time to move to what we both knew growing up, peace and quiet. Santa Clara Valley was no longer the peaceful area we knew. And with the blessing of our son Franz, we wanted to raise him and his siblings (if the Lord granted us more) to be raised in the country, like we were.

There was an ad in a local 'throw away paper' about this wonderful land for sale in Calaveras County, i shared it with Fred and we made the long drive (being with child seemed longer) to see this open country. And that it

117

was; country, as we drove along Highway 4 there was nothing but rangeland for miles and miles, sometimes a ranch house sitting out in the middle of what seemed, no where. But it was God's country, peaceful and quiet. i had to go potty bad, so we stopped on the side of the road so i could relieve myself beside a big California oak tree. Fred hesitated at first, then said," Someone will see you." My desperate reply was, "Out here?" So we stopped and i took care of business. Each time we make the trek to Angels Camp, i take notice of that old oak with fond memories. You gals carrying babies in your womb understand.

Years later, after our sons had married and started their own families, Fred and i were making a return trip from visiting our friends, Bob and Sandy, who lived in Reno. That trip was long and tiring as well; it was after my injury i'd had while organizing a Women's chocolate night at church. i injured my back and left side after slipping and falling on the cement floor where the water fountain had a leaked. At the time, i thought nothing of it, until the next day, months and years afterwards, the pain is persistent. Of course traveling in a car over those mountain roads did not make it feel any better. As i mentioned before, Fred is a destination man, 'let's go and get there, no stopping.' The pain and discomfort kept getting worse as we traveled along the turns etc. Finally, i asked Fred to please stop so i could stretch and do my business. He finally pulled over on the side of the country road and i was just finishing my business, had jumped back in the car, pants still down, when a wonderful C.H.P. officer stopped to make sure everything was all right. i assured him it was all right, with tears in my eyes and a Lucille Ball whining, (we had just watched The Long, Long Trailer with our friends the night before) perhaps that had some affect on my dramatic reply. He kept questioning with great concern and even offered to lead us to the hospital; i believe he thought i was being abused. As he drew closer to the car and my window, i tried not to let him get close enough as to see my pants halfway down. He finally said, "O.k., ma'am, if you are sure you are all right, i will leave, but please take your time." Before departing, he offered to escort us to the hospital. i assured him everything was all right. He was such a caring man, and with that, he drove off.

Fred started our car and was going to leave as well, when i said; "Wait a minute, the officer said 'take your time', and i was going to do just that." As i opened the car door, pulled up my pants and walked around a bit, then said; "O.k., i'm ready now." Hey, i had a C.H.P.'s ok, what more could i ask for?

Little did i know at the time, years later our son Jeff would successfully complete the tough, strenuous C.H.P. Academy. We're so proud of him!!! Perhaps, i should have called this book: A TIME OF RELIEF! Whew!!!!

Now, back to the purchase of our Sierra property. We made it to Angels Camp and met with the realtor on that lovely day in February. When the realtor discovered we were from the Santa Cruz Mountains, he thought we wanted the kind of property we had had, there, steep hills, brush etc. Much to our dismay, he began showing us those types of parcels. We finally told him, no, we don't want mountain goat property anymore; we would like flat or slightly rolling hills. Once he took us to where our ranch now sits, we both knew this was the property for us. Not long after we purchased the property, the rains fell and we had one of the wettest winters. PRAISE THE LORD!!!

There were many others, at the same time, who were looking at this very property, so we made the decision to make an offer. Since there were cattle roaming on the land and because there was no fencing, i suggested the price be dropped, because we would need to fence the land to keep others cattle off the property. Not only did they drop the price for fencing, but, a road was cut into this bare land and a large stock pond dug. We were thrilled, knowing we wanted to raise our own beef and since this was beef country, perfect. The offer was accepted for $17,500 without access to

119

power or water; we were told that would take another ten years, at least, to have power and water.

That didn't stop Fred and i from coming every weekend to take in the refreshing air and quietness of the land. Fred was still working in Mountain View as the foreman of a machine shop and i had quit working in the Beauty Salon, due to my pregnancy and pain in my back from being rear ended in our car. Every Friday i had everything packed and ready to go when Fred arrived home, we headed for our property. We had a camper on our '72 Chevy truck, with a mattress inside for sleeping, and supplies.

Chapter Fourteen

"Many are the plans in a man's heart, but it is the Lord's purpose that prevails." Proverbs 19:21

A Special bonding with my mother-in-law (love). Because of Jesus and His Word the Bible.

It wasn't long, June arrived, and through a long, painful childbirth, our precious first son; Franz Joseph was born on June the third, 1976 at Good Samaritan Hospital in San Jose, California. **"For this child, i prayed the Lord has granted me what i asked Him." 1Samuel 1:27.** Franz was such a blessing and so easy to raise. Our German shepherd, Max, loved Franz, he was his protector; Franz could put his hand inside his mouth and Max tenderly held it in there. Baby showers were given in honor of Franz's birth. The two i remember, were from my sister Josephine and my mother, the second was by the ladies, whose hair i did in Saratoga; both blessed us with many gifts. We had lots of friends and family who came to see our precious new gift from the Lord, Franz.

Among those who came was Fred's, Mom (Mutti) from Germany. She was to only stay a month or so, so when Fred brought her home from the airport, he broke the news to me that Mutti was staying with us for nine weeks. He knew that would be difficult for me to accept, with a new baby and Mutti who could not speak English (except, good night and good morning). And to top it off, Fred's boss went to Sweden during this time and left Fred to handle the business. Oh, my! What was i to do? Agh!!!!

i was still attending Bible Study and taking Franz with me, leaving Mutti at home, because she didn't understand. One day she asked if she could attend with me, puzzled i thought "Why?" she couldn't understand. i called my friend and sister-in-the-Lord, Rachel, and explained my dilemma.

She calmly suggested i go to the Christian Book store and purchase a Bible in German for Mutti. That's exactly what i did and she came with me to Bible Study and i helped her find where we were in the Bible during the study. When we came home, i fed Franz, put him down for his nap, prepared lunch for Mutti and i, and after lunch we sat down and did our Bible lesson together. She would read from her German Bible and i from my English, what a team and what a blessing. It brings tears to my eyes as i think about this special bonding we had through the Word of God.

He, the Lord, orchestrated the whole thing. You see the Word of God is unchanging and fitting for every language. Mutti read the Word in German and i in English and we understood each other through, God's Holy Word. **"The Word of God is living and active. Sharper than any double-edged sword, it penetrates even to dividing soul and spirit, joints and marrow; it judges the thoughts and attitudes of the heart." Hebrews 4:12.** When the time came for Mutti to leave, we held each other and wept before she boarded the plane for Germany. Only a Lord like we serve could do such a remarkable bonding. Upon Mutti's departure at the airport, Fred said, "You would think it was your Mother, instead of mine." He was right.

While Mutti was here, we took her to our property in the Sierra's; she loved it. We had our 1970 Chevy truck with a metal camper shell at the time. We decided to take my mother and Mutti on a roadtrip; it was during the days when seat belts were not required. So, Fred, being the clever man that he is, decided to put two metal-based lawn chairs in the back of the truck, which also had metal flooring, but was covered by the camper shell. Our mothers, who got along wonderfully, even though each could not speak the others native tongue, they used lots of hand signals. Anyway, they sat in the back, on the lawn chairs. Fred, baby Franz in my arms, and i, sat in the cab of the truck. All went well, until Fred had to make a sudden stop and we heard a loud crash. Immediately, we thought of our mother's, and pulled over to the side of the road to check on them. They were a sight, sunglasses sideways, they were laughing uncontrollably and lying sprawled on the metal floor of the truck. A lesson learned for us: not to put metal against metal, especially when commuting. Couldn't do that today, anyway. Yet, we were thankful they were not hurt and both had a good sense of humor.

Prior to Franz's birth, Fred made it a habit after getting paid on Friday to go out after work with the guys, play pool and have his favorite drink; beer. At first i thought it all right, realizing Germans were known for enjoying their beer, but he began getting home later and later, each Friday. The drive from Mountain View to our home was quite a distance, and as more people were moving into the area, the traffic got worse and worse, which added to Fred arriving home later, as well. i became very concerned, not only his coming home late, but his drinking increased and it was not safe driving the mountainous roads, endangering others and himself. At first i became very upset, then angry.

My thought was, if he had a pool table of his own, perhaps he would come home. So i saved my tips from work and decided to buy Fred a pool table. That worked for a while, but soon he was out with the guys again, but only on Friday, after work, thank the Lord. My dear friend, Rachel, suggested i greet him with a smile and a hug when he arrived home and not a lecture. That too, worked for a while, but didn't last. We worked at our jobs all week, then, on weekends, worked on our home; on Sunday afternoon, we had lots of company and lots of beer drinking as well. i loved the company, but not all that drinking. Reminded me too much of my childhood and the horror of alcoholism. Many times, without realizing it, we marry into situations that are familiar, because we know no other way. i hoped this would not be the same as my childhood.

i was thankful for our property in the Sierra's; one thing i knew for sure, Fred loved it too, and looked forward to coming home right after work on Friday, so we could head for the hills for the peace and quiet of our property. Yeah!!! Leaving for our property every Friday evening helped with stopping the ongoing drinking problem. On the long drive to our property, we listened to Christian children's music, for our Franz. One in particular was, Marcy. As Franz got older and could understand the words, he would sing-along with his sweet child voice. i was beginning to teach him about Jesus at a very young age. Little did i realize at the time, it would have an affect on Fred, drawing him closer to the Lord. Franz believed Marcy really existed, so much so, when he and i flew to Redding to visit family, my sister Josephine met us at the airport with her daughter Barbara Jean. She is a few years older than Franz, and the minute he met her, he thought for sure she was Marcy and called her by that name. My sister just laughed after i explained who Marcy really was.

Being the ambitious sort that we are, we decided to begin working and clearing the land by hand, in hopes to raise some beef cattle after the land was fenced. We were the new pioneers of this beautiful area. Now that we had our precious son, Franz, we decided to purchase a small trailer and park it under a big Digger Pine tree. Fred built an awning that was attached to the trailer for shade from the hot California sun. On one particular occasion, we hired a man with a bulldozer, to clear the brush on the property. Baby Franz and i were inside the trailer, when the Lord nudged me to take him for a walk in his stroller. i obeyed, put Franz in his stroller and began walking down the country road, when suddenly i heard, what sounded like the dozer rushing down the hillside amongst the trees and brush. As i looked up from the road where Franz and i were, i saw the dozer coming down the hill without a driver, and Fred and the driver, running after the run-away dozer. i immediately fell on my knees and asked the Lord not to let it hit our trailer. Not only did it hit our trailer, but our truck went flying up in the air as the dozer hit it, shearing off the awning to the trailer and one of the beams came crashing into the trailer (where Franz and i had been). Without further damage, the rushing dozer came to a complete halt against the lone pine tree.

Fred and the driver, thinking Franz and i were still in the trailer, came running toward the crash. When i quickly ran with Franz in the stroller to the site, Fred grabbed me and just starting yelling, not realizing we were all right. Although, the trailer and truck were ruined, the Lord had protected Franz and i. " **For My thoughts are not your thoughts, neither are your ways my ways," declares the Lord. Isaiah 55:8.** On our drive home after that episode, we were appreciative, yet quiet, as we pondered the happenings of that weekend. We were probably in shock

Chapter Fifteen

Honor your father and your mother,
as the Lord your God has commanded, Deuteronomy 5:16

Time to move away from my beloved
now Silicon/Santa Clara Valley

It wasn't until the next day, when the shock hit me as i was on the phone the next morning with my sister Josephine, sharing what the Lord had done for us in protecting Franz and i. At a later date, Fred said, "If anything would have happened to Franz and you, i would have gotten rid of the property." This was only the beginning of all that was in store for us. But we persevered and have a lot to be thankful for, today.

In 1977, we received notification from our German family that Mutti (Fred's, Mom) was having heart problems and not doing very well. She had, had heart problems throughout her life, so this was not new for her or us. But she was requesting we come home to Germany, and of course, bring Franz to visit and spend time with her, thinking she did not have long to live. How bad her condition was, we did not know, but we knew she wanted to see us, perhaps, she used this in order to have us come and visit.

Now, that i am an 'Oma', i understand and need my grandchildren fix. Whatever the reason, Fred and i decided we would make the trip, it was almost Christmas. Christmas in Germany, what a wonderful thought, that's where most of our Christian traditions started in celebrating our Saviors birth. Now we could live them out and enjoy them first hand with our German family. i was still attending Bible study once a week, and asked the gals in the study to pray for us, as we made the long flight with our year and one-half-year-old son, Franz. They prayed and we did as well. The flight was very tiring, as we were cramped and uncomfortable, but our Franz did great.

When we landed in Switzerland, which was closer to where Mutti lived, the people seated around us on the flight, stood up and applauded our young Franz, for being such a good traveler. We were so pleased and proud; he was a good traveler and still is today. Is it any wonder he wanted to be a pilot; he loved flying.

While in Germany, we stayed with Mutti. Many family and friends came to visit and loved on our little Franz. Cousin Erika came by one evening with a Hanzel and Gretelhaus, (gingerbread house) especially made for Franz. She, her husband and three sons were so wonderful to all of us and bestowed love, gifts, meals and prayers on our behalf. Uncle Walter and Tante Rosewitha, came to see their new nephew, and us. It was a glorious time, but very cold, although the sun was shining, which the neighbors referred to as Florida, or California, sunshine. Delicious German cookies, breads, rolls, Schwarzwalder hams, stollen, Gluwien, wurst, bier and many other delicacies flowed during our stay. There were church services, welcoming the birth of Jesus, church bells ringing, singing, the lighting of Advent candles, and just rejoicing. And of course, the Christmas tree with presents, which originated in Germany. It was a most unforgettable time with family and friends, one i will always cherish in comparison to the Christmas's i had or didn't have as a child. The Lord gave me such special memories; ones i would use, to celebrate Christmas in our home. And yet, great sadness came when it was time to leave; it was such a long distance apart from family and friends.

Upon our arrival home, it was pouring down rain. A lovely sight we had not seen in years. When the weekend came, we made the trek to our property in the Sierra's, and saw the results of all that wonderful rain; ditches and streams running with water and luscious green grass coming up. We knew it would not be long and we would be living in this most welcoming sight. Since our little trailer was destroyed and no longer livable after the bulldozer hit it, we knew we needed a place to stay while we built our new home. The Lord always provides. And it was so, for there, on another neighbors property, sat a trailer, much like the one we lived in, when i was a child. Except, this one could actually have running water inside, and a toilet, although it couldn't be flushed, unless water was poured into the bowl, it also had cabinets and closets.

We asked the neighbor, who it belonged to, and, could we possibly use it? He said it belonged to someone in the Bay Area, and encouraged us to take it to our property; he wanted to get rid of it. i got the name and number of the owner, and Fred and i managed to have someone tow it to our property. It was a nice old trailer, but needed tender loving care.

Prior to the Lord leading us to this old trailer, (our future home), we met new neighbors; the Allemand's. They too, had moved to the property from the Bay Area, my hometown of San Jose, and moved a modular onto their property. Some weekends we would stay with them; they would always have a wonderful meal prepared for us when we arrived. Mrs. Allemand, (Kiyoko), was originally from Japan and her husband Jean was originally from France. They had two children, a daughter Karen and her younger brother Lawrence. For Fred and i, it was difficult at times, understanding what either parent was saying, not so with the children. The parents would have a discussion with them; laugh and the children just smiled and went their way. Fred and i would look at each other and wonder what had just transpired.

They were in need of underground wiring to bring into their home; the wire was very expensive, and difficult to find in our new area. Fred, being the very generous man that God made him, ordered the wire from an electrician friend of ours and gave it to the Allemand's. Now, they could have electricity for their home and also for using 220 where needed. Yes, i know this was a place for us to rest our weary heads, when we came to our ranch, but i was proud of Fred using the gift the Lord had given him, generosity.

We would become very close friends, family, to the Allemands, over the years. i will share much of our love for each other as my story continues. For now let me get back to the trailer we were to soon have as our home.

On Monday morning, after we arrived home, i immediately called the owner; Mr. Durran, who, later would be our sons only prospect of a grandfather image. He was a very kind, elderly Christian man, and was very happy to let us use the trailer. i invited him to come to our property to see the condition of the trailer. He accepted, and came the following weekend, and was to come every summer after that, with his camper parked by our barn. He adopted Franz, and later Jeff, taking them fishing, gold panning, teaching them to play tennis, golf, chess and so much more. Franz and Jeff loved the summer days when Mr. Durran would come. They would run down to his camper every morning with fresh bacon from our hogs, and gather fresh eggs from the chicken coop, bring them to Mr. Durran to prepare breakfast for he and them. The rest of the day was spent doing the things i mentioned above with the only Grandpa they knew, as such.

On his trip to the ranch from Sunnyvale, Mr. Durran would stop at one of the many fresh fruit and vegetable stands, and purchase tomatoes, onions and bell peppers, in order to prepare his famous recipe for all of us. He would use our beef, slice it thin and season it just right. Then he would prepare the vegetables separately, he also added hot Jalapeños (not for me). Fred and the boys loved it. He wrote the recipe down for me, and i prepare it on occasion for all of us.

Mr. Durran's father was a minister from Europe; he and his wife would take their son, Michael, (Mr.Durran), to hear some of the great Preachers of the day, like: Billy Sunday and many others. On one of their excursions to hear these great men of the Gospel, Mr. Durran heard beautiful piano music being played. When the family returned home, he shared with his parents how he too would like to learn to play the piano. They purchased him a piano; he said he'd never had one lesson, and began playing by ear. He was an excellent pianist, and would play the old piano in our game room for hours. One of his favorites was; **How Great Thou Art**, a favorite of mine as well, so much so, i have requested it to be played at my celebration of life, when that day arrives.

When Mr. Durran was in his nineties he went to live with his daughter in Paradise, California. He had moved from Sunnyvale, California and hated the heat in Paradise. I called him and told him, Fred and i were coming to visit and asked if he still played the piano, and, would he play; **How Great Thou Art**, for me? He said he would practice and play it for me when we arrived. A week later i called him again, to remind him that we were coming and had he been practicing the song on the piano. He responded; "What was it you wanted me to play, now?" i once again told him; How Great Thou Art.

The day finally arrived to visit Mr. Durran in Paradise, and hear him play that special piece of music, just for me. He was delighted to see Fred and I; he went to his room, sat at the piano and began playing without a single note in front of him. i brought the mini tape recorder and recorded his giftedness. Once he got started, he didn't know when to quit, he just kept playing, much to his delight. We were hoping he would soon complete this most beautiful piece, and mentioned several times it was time for us to leave. He just kept those 90 plus year old fingers, gliding gracefully across the keyboard. We hugged him and his daughter, said our aufweidersehens, and went on home. That was the last time we were to see him alive on earth, and we are thankful we made the trip. Our advice is; "never put off tomorrow what you can do today, there may not be a tomorrow."

Our family, one of his daughters and some close friends of Mr. Durran, came to our ranch and had a celebration of life, in honor of Mr. Durran. Along with wonderful stories of how he affected each of our lives. Our granddaughter, Laurel Shea, wrote her very own book about that day.

Perhaps, she too will be an author like her Oma, (me); that would be an honor.

Chapter Sixteen

"Where there is no revelation,
the people cast of restraint;...
Proverbs 29:18

Our second blessing, the Lord gives us another son.

Let's go back to living in the trailer on the ranch, shall we? We made the trek every weekend to our property in hopes, some day that is where we would live. Many changes were being made at Fred's work and the love for the country was growing on us. The first thing we needed to do was fence the property. As in the Bible, we decided to throw out a fleece as Gideon did. Our fleece was our Mercedes Benz, if we sold it we could use the money to put up the fencing. We had only one buyer who purchased it for the same price we paid for it brand new in Germany and this was six years later. We were delighted.

Fred and i had never put up barbed wire in the past, but were determined to learn and fenced the whole twenty acres. Only once did a friend come and help us fence the steep back five acres or so.

Our little Franz would take his nap and Fred and i would work on the fence. One particular time i heard a rattlesnake in the high grass, Fred threw the wire stretcher at the sound and caught the snake in the stretcher. After that we were very careful as to where we tread.

We did not have a phone and this bothered me, since we had our two-year-old Franz, and there were rattlesnakes and other critters to deal with in the country. So, i took my concerns to the Lord in prayer, and then called the oldest operating telephone company in California, Calaveras Telephone Company[7], our local carrier. After explaining my dilemma, i asked if someone could come and hook-up a telephone in our trailer. They promised they would be out at the end of the week. Sure enough they came throwing the lines across the field to the trailer. i asked, "Aren't the cows going to chew on the line?" They assured me they wouldn't, and then told me this was only temporary and they would return putting the wire underground. They also said, that ' this company, since it was one of the first in the State, in the past they usually strung the lines across the most useful object, that being the cattle fencing.' Was happy to hear they would put it underground, and thankful my prayer was answered.

Our neighbor, who claimed to be an atheist, said to me; "There must be something to this praying, you got your phone line and we haven't gotten ours yet." These neighbors were one of the first of us 'new pioneers' who had moved to God's beautiful country in the Sierra's. Although the man said he wasn't a Christian, he loved playing the organ. On many occasions i could hear him playing, Onward Christian Soldier. Mmmm, makes one wonder.

The construction of the shell and basement started on our new home, but from our small abode, the trailer; the home looked huge and it is big. My thought was, 'Where is my little house in the prairie?' When i went to Fred and asked him, he replied; "You saw the plans over and over again, couldn't you see how large it was going to be?" No, i didn't understand plans, and realize size. Many times i have given our large, lovely home to the Lord. And HE has used it mightily for HIS purpose and HIS glory!!!

While living in the trailer, one evening Fred said; "Everything is perfect here." i replied, "Except one thing, church; i would like to attend church." Before we had moved to the ranch, i had been checking out a church in San Andreas. i even asked my Bible Study guide before we moved, about the Covenant Church's belief. She assured me it was a good Bible teaching denomination. Fred didn't know any of this prior to my reply, so he asked where would i like to attend church. Without a doubt, i replied, "The Covenant in San Andreas." The next morning, Fred, Franz and i attended church together for the very first time since we had Franz. PRAISE THE

LORD!!! The very next day, Pastor Carl Johnson from the church came to visit us in our trailer. i shall never forget Fred's words to him; "Thank you for coming, yesterday we visited your church, today you are visiting our church 'on the hill' " pointing to our home under construction. My mind ran with Fred's statement, and once again i dedicated our home to the Lord; and have used our home ever since, to bring glory to HIM, through the countless ministries we have used to bless others, and continue to do so today. TO GOD BE THE GLORY!!! The church and our faith in JESUS, became the center of our lives as never before and will be until we are called to meet JESUS in Heaven.

When we first moved to our ranch, we had nowhere to store our furniture. A neighbor offered, for a fee, to store it for us until we could move into our new home. We didn't mind the fee, but when we went to check on our belongings, chickens, goats, dogs, cats were climbing all over the furniture. So, Fred and i decided the funds we would have used for the storage rental we could build a barn. Since we needed a barn anyway, we went right to work. Now, that Fred had building experience from our previous home, building the barn went up quite fast. It was still in the heat of one of the hottest summers we had, and i remember being on the roof of the barn pounding nails into the roofing material, and feeling something crawling down my back. No, it wasn't anything crawling; it was sweat running down my back. When we completed the work, we had our first barn celebration inviting the few neighbors who resided in Circle XX, and those who were weekenders. That was the beginning of festivities in our barn.

In the early winter months we had bon fires (barn fires) as Fred calls them with his German accent. As our sons grew into their teens and began playing instruments, Franz on the bass or guitar, and Jeff on the drums, we had some great dances and fun times in the barn, and enjoyed the bon fires. Our area had grown by that time, so we made sure we would invite the neighbors so they wouldn't complain about the noise. Although, one neighbor did complain (forgot to invite them), she called complaining about all the noise. My reply was; "Would you rather they be on the streets, getting into trouble?" She said; "Have fun, and tell the boys to keep playing."

On my 65th birthday we had a big Medicare celebration in the barn, along with a Bon Fire outdoors. Fred and i decorated the barn with all medical apparatus including walkers, facial masks, bandages, canes, medical gloves, and other medical supplies in hopes we would never use them. On another occasion we had a 50's-60's Party; Mike and Lynne were our d.j.'s. They set-up all their wonderful c.d.'s from that era and we had bales of hay to sit on and some hay on the floor to make dancing easier. Little did we know, the dust from the hay would get into the c.d.'s and player; they were kind enough not to tell us the amount of damage on their equipment. That was a lesson learned; we didn't use hay on the floor for dancing anymore. As the years went on, we would use the barn for a Live Nativity Scene, which the children from the Good News Club presented during Christmas. During the year i would have a Good News Club, Child Evangelism, for the neighborhood children. It was my hope to introduce Jesus to the children our sons befriended. i would meet the school bus at our main entrance gate and take home as many children as would come or i could get into our Mini van. One time, the bus driver Howard, got off the bus and said to me; " This is not the stop for some of these children." i explained that it was o.k. with their parents and i was having a Good News Club. He replied; "Would you like the rest of the children on the bus?" He too was a Christian, he and his wife had traveled to the Holy Land and were baptized in the Jordan River, so he understood the importance of Jesus in one's life.

i really enjoyed teaching the children Bible stories, arts and crafts and always having food and drinks for them to enjoy after our lesson. i got to know many of the children and still keep in contact with some of them today. There was one group of boys who were very poor, yet grateful for anything i taught them and would gladly eat whatever i served, whereas some of the children, who were better off, would turn their noses up at what i had to offer. These poor young boys reminded me of my humble beginnings, giving me a greater understanding and appreciation for them, and gratitude for my life today. Not only did i involve the children, but several of the neighbor ladies helped teach the lessons, and brought food and love to the children. We were not of the same church, but worked together well, knowing and believing we were bringing the Gospel to these needy children.

Chapter Seventeen

"Sons are a heritage from the Lord,
children a reward from Him." Psalm 127: 3

My mother-in-law (love), Mutti, as i fondly call her,
visits us for the last time.

The children would begin practicing during our Good News sessions in October for their Live Nativity performance in our barn. A dear friend would supply us with enough bales of alfalfa for the angels to stand on with flashlights in their small hands. The neighbor ladies helped me make costumes for the children. Fred, our wonderful sons, Franz and Jeff, rigged up a star for the three kings to follow, as the children sang, We Three Kings. Even though, according to the Bible, the kings did not arrive until Jesus was about three years old. (refer to Matthew 2:11) This was a great opportunity for the children to learn Christmas carols, something they do not learn in school today, as i did when i was a child. Since the Nativity took place in our barn in the evening, the cows would join us with their mooing, the chickens were clucking and the pigs, oinking, just as, on the night when Jesus was born, or so we like to believe. Our sons would either be taking part in the performance or playing music to accompany the angels singing. i would narrate the Christmas story from the Book of Luke. After the play was over, we would retreat to our home and have homemade cookies and hot cider for all. It was a glorious celebration; a wonderful way to welcome the birth of our Lord and Savior Jesus!!!

Let's travel back to the trailer where Fred, Franz and i resided until our home on the hill was livable. Winter soon set in, and with it cold weather, too cold to live in the trailer any longer. We moved into our unfinished home. My brother, Frank was in the carpet business at the time, and gave us big pieces of carpet to lay on the wooden floors until we could finish insulating the walls and ceiling, putting up the sheetrock and completing the interior of our home.

We were living on unemployment, the first time for Fred since he came to the United States. But the unemployment was running out and Fred had to find work, which he did, as a machinist. The pay was not much and he was treated unfairly, something he was not accustomed to, because he knew his trade very well and had always been a foreman in every shop he had worked in, in the past. So he quit, and we put an ad in the local newspaper that read: Freddie Fix It. He had so many jobs; he could hardly keep up with all the work.

i was pregnant with our Jeffrey John at the time, of course we didn't know he was a boy, we didn't have that technology in those days. Even though Fred enjoyed his work, we knew it would not be enough money to raise a second child and pay for his birth. Fred and i prayed that he would find a job, and that we would have health insurance coverage as well. The next day as Franz and i were walking into our church to help out, i was stopped by one of the members who told me the prayer group had been praying for a job for Fred the night before. With a smile i told the person, Fred had an interview that very day at the Asbestos Plant.

When Franz and i arrived home that afternoon, we found a proud father and husband wearing his new safety helmet from the plant. Yes, he had gotten the job. We also discovered a law had been recently passed in California: if someone started a new job and the wife was pregnant at the time, the health insurance had to pay for the child's birth. PRAISE THE LORD, another answer to our prayers!

What was interesting was, Fred was hired as a welder, a welder he was not, a good machinist he was indeed. But he was willing to learn, knowing he had a family to support. The other concern was the plant where Fred was to work, their machinery was shut down over the weekend for maintenance. Meaning the welders and others who worked on the machinery had to work weekends. This was difficult for me at first, because we were really enjoying attending church as a family on Sunday. Things were about to change again, and not for the best, spiritually speaking. When a burning log is removed from the fire it burns out, it is the same spiritually. When we stop attending church regularly, stop reading our Bible, not praying as much as we should, ("pray without ceasing"), like the log, we die spiritually, we become disconnected. We usually replace the void with something else, and in Fred's case, it was what he grew-up with in Germany: drinking.

At first the drinking wasn't as noticeable, but as time went on, it became worse and worse. For me, it was a horrible reminder of my growing up years. i did not want to accept the fact i was on the biggest river in the world: The Denial. But then we marry or get involved with ones we are familiar with, without realizing. To add to our difficulties, my dear sweet mother decided she wanted to live with us. She was living in a little house between my two sisters in Redding, before she made the decision to move in with us. Fred and i loved my mother. Fred had built a large room in our home especially for my mother; it was in the original plans. We kept it for her, until she decided to move in with us. i was happy to have mom live with us; her living quarters were downstairs and separate from us, giving both privacy. i learned more from my mom in the time she lived with us, then i had in all the years i was living at home. Perhaps, it was because i was older, had a child of my own and one on the way, or we had more time together without all the other difficulties and interruptions in life. Whatever the case, we enjoyed each other's company. Oh sure, there were times we would tangle, but that was the normal human spirit we allowed to take over our lives. But we soon forgave each other and walked in HIS ways not ours.

Mom taught me so much about gardening, raising and butchering chickens, raising animals and so forth. On one occasion we were butchering chickens, and we had visitors come up our driveway unexpectedly; they were from a Cult. They were preaching to us as we continued with our job. Suddenly, my Mom turned to them and said; "Can you see that we are busy? Would you like to help?" With that, they got into their car and drove away. i was so thankful for my Mom's honesty and forthright spirit. She was a fireball, a peaceful lovely lady with a lot of spirit and fun.

Mom helped me and taught me a lot about raising our sons as well, and i was grateful for her being with us to help our family and me. Mom was a good Grandma, who played baseball with our sons; they loved visiting her in her living quarters and watching baseball on television. She spent time reading, teaching and entertaining them with sports or whatever their interest. She loved and encouraged them, attended their games, school and church events with us. Mom was a great cheerleader.

Winter was coming, Fred was delighted to have a job, we were still in the process of finishing our home and it was cold. We had decided to put a fireplace in the upstairs, but realized it was not efficient heat for the upstairs where we lived, not even considering the downstairs where mom kept her abode. We knew something had to be done; we could not afford to heat our home using electricity. It wasn't long and we put in two air tight wood burning stoves, one for upstairs and one for downstairs. But this meant cutting and hauling a lot of firewood to keep the stoves going. That became our next project: during the spring, summer and fall, we would all go out and cut firewood, haul it and stack it for the winter. Being pregnant, i still kept up with everyone. Mom was a big help with the firewood and helping with Franz. While we cut wood, we were clearing our land, as well, for our cattle to graze.

Approximately five acres of our property lies on a steep hillside, which in the summer and fall months, when the grass dries, becomes very slippery; making it difficult to walk down or up, let alone drive a truck. After cutting firewood on this steep hillside, Fred carefully drove our ranch truck

140

down this steep hill to load it with firewood. While he was driving the truck and it not being a four-wheel drive, it kept slipping and sliding down the hill as he neared the pile of fresh cut wood. Watching him, gave me chills, i could not look, bowed my head and prayed for his safety.

Once we loaded the wood, Fred was unable to drive the truck back up the hill where we stacked the wood for the winter. He then went to the house (prior to cell phones) and called our towing service to tow him up the hill. When the tow truck driver arrived he told Fred to unload the wood and he could then wrench the truck up the hill. Fred said, "No, that's why I called you to tow our truck with the wood up the hill. How else would I get the wood where I need it?" The driver replied, "I can't do that, we're only supposed to tow." Fred said, "That is why we are paying for towing, the truck just happens to be loaded with wood." It wasn't long and the tow truck driver towed our truck loaded with wood up the hill. Actually, as i think back, it was very wise of Fred, yet comical.

Now that it is just Fred and i on the ranch, we still cut, split and haul firewood. We are so thankful for friends like; Don and Mary, Randy and Joan, Mike and Lynne, Rich and Deb, who give us the firewood. We are truly blessed to have such wonderful friends. We have learned to use only one wood burning stove, the one downstairs and it heats the whole house. But cutting, hauling and stacking firewood is still hard work, but we will do it as long as the Lord gives us the strength.

On the morning of November 7, 1979, right after Fred left for work i began having labor pains. Thank the Lord my mom was with me. i called Fred at work, and he immediately left for home. Construction was taking place on Highway 4, his route home, which delayed his arrival. When he finally arrived, we drove the nine rugged, bumpy, curvy miles to hospital, while Fred kept saying, "If it's a girl we will name her Christine and if's a boy, Jeffrey John." With contractions coming fast and furious i thought, just get me to the hospital, and let's have this beautiful baby.

Unlike birthing our first born, Franz, i decided to have this little one by natural childbirth. Our doctor was an interesting man, arriving late to the hospital in his sandals and carrying a purse over his shoulder. At his first glance of me, he seemed to forget who i was; he had just come in from a flying lesson. What type of flying, i often wondered. He finally got with it on the matter of my delivery, and told me very sternly,' to get on top of the pain.' i listened and did as he said.

Although Fred had taken the Lamaze class with me prior to my giving birth, he had forgotten everything during the delivery. The nurse finally gave him a pen and paper and told him to keep track of my contractions. This was just too much for Fred, so the nurse had to take over. She was a blessing and so very helpful. At 11 a.m., i had given birth to another handsome son; Jeffrey John Bodenmüller. The first words out of my mouth to Fred were, "Can we try for a girl?" How soon we forget the pain. But how i loved this precious babe i held in my arms, he reminded me soooo much of our Franz. As i held him, i promised the Lord and our Jeffrey, i would do a better job in raising him, and that i loved both our sons so very much.

i had the greatest gift anyone could give their child, a relationship with our Lord and Savior Jesus Christ. And now it was an honor to pass this baton of my faith to our sons, Franz and Jeffrey, and others. What a blessing!!! But along with the honor of sharing this gift with our sons, i had the great challenge of living it in our home. That meant as it says in **Proverbs 22:6 "Train a child in the way he should go, and when he is old he will not turn from it."** This verse took me back to **Deuteronomy 6: 6-9**, and the time when Franz and i (pregnant with Jeff) were walking down the hill to meet our neighbor, Frenchy, who was taking us to town. When we reached the bottom of the hill, and were waiting for our ride, i held Franz's little hands and began praying with him. Because in **Deuteronomy 6:7 it says, "Impress them (God's commandments) on your children. Talk**

about them when you sit at home and when you walk along the road…"
That's what we did, and were doing. With eyes closed and praying, i sensed
Franz was not in tune with me, mother's intuition, i was right. He was
looking at some kittens, who were in a nearby culvert. Franz loved animals
and wanted one of these baby kittens for his own. i told him if they were still
there when we arrived home, he could take one. When we returned, sure
enough the kittens were still there in the culvert. Franz, selected a pure black
one, picked it up and carried his prized possession up our steep driveway.
Soon his little arms tired and he said, " Mommy, can you carry the kitten for
me?" Not only was i pregnant, but had a bag of groceries in my arms to carry
as well. i replied, "Franz, put the kitten down, if it follows us, it is yours, if
not, then it is not yours." Gently, putting it down, we walked along and the
kitten followed. Once we got to our home, it was time for Franz's nap. Of
course he wanted to nap with his new friend, he fondly named Lissie cat. As i
tucked him in with his kitten, i reminded him that his Daddy was not fond of
cats and that we should pray he would let Franz keep Lissie cat. His childlike prayer was answered, when his Daddy arrived home from work, Franz
showed him his kitten, and his Daddy was very accepting of Lissie cat. As a
matter of fact, no other cat has fit the bill for our family since Lissie cat.

Yet another verse that comes to mind is from **Isaiah 53:2**, of course
this verse is speaking of Jesus, as we are to be rooted in Jesus. We must give
our children good strong roots in our faith and then give them wings to fly.
As **Isaiah 40:31b**, states: **"…They will soar on wings like eagles;…"** And i
like **Luke 14:34b "… I have longed to gather your children together, as a
hen gathers her chicks under her wings,…"** That's where the letting go
comes in for mothers; it's that letting go and letting God, take care of them.
They are only a gift that we raise in the Lord and then give back to Him. It is
a continual letting go, that begins with birth.

Speaking of birth, that's where we were, the birth of our precious
son Jeffrey John. Big brother Franz, cared, loved and watched out for him, as

Jeffrey slept in his little Moses basket. It was there beside that little basket, i prayed with Franz at the sweet age of 3 and ½, to accept Jesus into his little heart. i believe Franz knew and understood at that tender age, the meaning of Jesus coming into his heart and life. We had two new births in our home, one recently born of a human mother, the other **"Born of God."** The story of being **"Born again,"** is told in **John 3**. Not long after, our Jeffrey would also experience the second birth, of being **"Born of God."**

What a joy and blessing, not only to have one, but two sons, to raise for God's glory. Having the opportunity to raise them on the ranch was a blessing as well. The days and years just seemed to fly by, as we kept busy with all the things to do on the ranch and raising our sons. Franz and Jeffrey, like Fred and i, would be able to learn to work and care for animals, gardens etc. As they grew, i continued to listen to the Christian broadcast over the radio, and a favorite Dr. James Dobson, who suggested teaching your children to give from their earnings 10% to the Lord, 10% in savings, and the rest to spend. i began doing this just as soon as the boys were old enough to help out in our home and ranch. Little did i know, by the time they each became 16 years old, they had enough money in the bank to purchase their first automobile. Oh, it wasn't anything fancy, but it was bought and paid for by them, and it was theirs. Also, if they kept their grades up in school Fred and i agreed to pay for their insurance on their automobile, but they had to earn the money for the gas. It worked out real well. Once their work was done on the ranch, they could then work for our neighbors and earn extra money. This taught both of them good work ethics, which they both have today.

Franz's first vehicle was a 1946 Ford truck that needed lots of work. This gave he and his Dad a wonderful opportunity to bond as they worked on the truck. Fred, was very generous and put lots of time and extra money into the truck. Franz was now a senior in High School and wanted so much to drive his truck to school just once, without breaking down, and before he

144

graduated from High School. i called a dear friend, Frank, and asked if he could get it running for Franz so he could drive it to school, Frank did the job and Franz's dream came true.

Franz sold the truck just before he left for flight school in Arizona to help pay for his tuition. Prior to this, my mother suggested Franz apply for work at U.P.S., which he did; he began working for them at age 19 and was able to purchase a smaller truck for commuting. Franz is still under their employ today, thanks Mom, and thank You Lord, for Franz being a good provider. Fred and i are thankful to say we did our homework and taught both Franz and Jeffrey the importance of providing for your family, as they do today.

Jeff was able to purchase our Nissan, once he took his funds out of the bank. He totaled the Nissan and by the grace of God was saved in the accident. The car landed on its side in open graze land with one of the metal fence posts just passing between Jeff and the steering wheel. That was a miracle. PRAISE THE LORD!!!

i'm getting beyond myself and their growing up years, which were so precious for me. When Jeff was just a baby, we put him in his little stroller and let Franz push him around our ranch. At one point Franz decided it would be fun to just let the stroller go down the hill toward the barn on its own without my knowing, i looked and quickly ran after the stroller that held our tiny Jeffrey. Stopping it before it hit the barn. Boys will be boys and lots of fun!!!

i felt so blessed to breast feed Jeffrey. Although, i was to face another trial in that our neighbors purchased drop calves. The problem was, the neighbors came to their property only on the weekends, so during the week the hungry calves would lean against the fence between us, bawling. They missed their mommies and were begging for milk. Being raised on a ranch and knowing how to feed these little ones, and with great compassion in my heart for them, i mixed some dry milk in a bucket to feed them.

145

Each morning the calves would come to the fence by our kitchen window and bawl for their milk. i would grab a bucket, pour in the dry milk, mix it with water and then form my fingers like their mom's teat and feed the calves. They would rub their heads against my arms showing love and affection, as if i were their momma. It wasn't long i noticed a red familiar rash appearing on my arms, and it itched like crazy. Oh no, i had poison oak, and must have gotten it from the calves.

i immediately stopped feeding them and likewise had to stop nursing our baby Jeffrey as well. This was heart breaking for me, because i believe if a mother is able to breastfeed that is a blessing from the Lord. It is a time of bonding with our children.

The summer months were great when Mr. Durran would come with his van and park it by the barn and spend those precious times with Franz and Jeffrey. They enjoyed fishing; gold panning, baseball, horseshoes, chess and all the fun adventures boys have with their grandpas. Even though the boys called him Mr. Durran, i knew he was more than that to them and they loved and admired him. Although, he was stubborn at times, they still loved and forgave him. Just as our Lord Jesus said: **"I tell you the truth, unless you change and become like little children, you will never enter the Kingdom of Heaven..." Matthew 18:3a** Oh, to be as innocent as these little ones, always, loving and forgiving. Now that we have 5 grandchildren, and one on the way, i have the privilege of experiencing their innocence once again.

Chapter Eighteen

**"Rise in the presence of the aged,
show respect for the elderly and
revere God..." Leviticus 19:32**

**The experiences from my husband
and i of our poverty stricken past pay
off and we survive what is in store for us.**

About 2 years after Jeffrey's birth, Mutti decided she would make, what would be, her last trip to America to visit her beloved children and my mother, who was now living with us. We drove to Los Angeles to pick her up at the airport; she was not well and very frail. We drove to my sister Barbara's home in Palm Desert and stayed overnight, making it easier to drive home from there the next day. Barbara was so thrilled to have us and was very hospitable and gracious as she had been in the past. She had two huge grapefruit trees in her backyard. Mutti, who did not get very much citrus in Germany, enjoyed eating them. So Barbara, being the prune picker like me, picked a whole bunch of the grapefruit for Mutti. Since, she didn't have a gunny sack (like we had on the farm), to put them in, she got one of her king size pillowcases and loaded it with grapefruit for Mutti to take to our home. When we finally arrived home, Mutti ate so much grapefruit her lips and tongue began to swell. She came to me, and i immediately told her it was caused from too much acid from the grapefruit and the best was to stop eating them for a while.

Oh yes, on the way home from Barbara's, as we were nearing home, i decided to take a nap. When i awakened and saw those huge wind fans at Altamonte Pass i knew we were heading the wrong direction. i quickly told Fred to turn around we were going the wrong way. It was in the summer, very hot without air conditioning in our car, and we had already driven hundreds of miles; you can only imagine how we all felt when i discovered we were going the wrong way. Knew i shouldn't trust Fred's directions, when will i ever learn? Mutti asked in German what the problem was. When i told her, she gave her son 'what for' as well. Now he had to deal with three women, poor man.

My mom and Mutti got along very well and loved each other; although neither could speak the others tongue. A new baby was to arrive at brother Frank's home, and Mom's assistance was needed. Mom soon left for Redding, where my brother and family lived. This did not set well with Mutti, she missed my mom terribly, and kept asking when she would return. It wasn't long and mom returned which made Mutti extremely happy. What a blessing to have two mothers get along so well. And our sons were blessed to have two grandmothers staying with us. We had a fun time with both Grandmothers; Mutti was Oma and my mom was Grandma. We were having a hot, yet nice summer. Mr. Durran made his trek to stay with us, and he and the two mothers got along well. We had a doughboy pool where the boys learned to swim, neither of our mothers knew how to swim, but enjoyed watching the boys and us. Finances were slim, so we made short trips, to the beautiful redwoods near us, having picnics there and at the nearby lakes. We all enjoyed each other's company, so it didn't matter where we went. Reminded me of days past, when my Dad would take us on occasional Sunday drives that was such a big deal. Sometimes, we'd stop and even have ice cream.

Speaking of ice cream, we had a friend whose hair i did in trade for food; she called me one cold, snowy winter day and asked if we would like ice cream. Of course, i said, 'yes' we all loved ice cream. It seemed the freezer broke down at the market and all the ice cream had to be disposed, due to it being frost bitten. When we arrived at her home, we found the back of her pick-up truck loaded down with ice cream. Thankfully, it was in the winter and not much of the ice cream had melted. Our Lord always provides. We loaded up our big freezer with ice cream of different varieties.

Mutti, loved ice cream as well. In Germany she had no way of keeping even a quart in her small refrigerator/freezer. While she was here for her visit, i asked if she would like some ice cream, yes of course she would. Then i took her to her to the cellar, opened the freezer and presented her with whatever kind her heart desired. She was so thrilled, just like a child, upon seeing all that ice cream, she must have thought she had died and gone to Heaven. Needless to say, we had an ice cream summer. It was great!!!

Unknown to us due to failing health, age, distance, not speaking English as she traveled, this would be Oma Germany's, (as our sons called her), last trip to visit us in California. As time went on and we realized she was not coming again, this saddened our hearts. We will always be grateful for the times she came and all the wonderful things we learned from her. i for one, learned much about German cooking, cleaning and neatness. She was a mountain of strength in her Christian faith, each day she would spend time reading her little prayer books and praying fervently to the Lord. One of her nieces told me Oma's inspiration was the reason her son became a Catholic Priest. She loved the Lord Jesus and lived it out in her life. Certainly this would not be the last time we saw Oma Bodenmüller; we would make the trip a few years down the line to celebrate her eightieth birthday. That is a story and a miracle in itself.

As it happened, we received notification from Fred's brother, Walter, that plans were being made to celebrate this special occasion for their Mother. Fred and i took it to the Lord in prayer, realizing this would be a huge expense for the four of us to make the trip to Germany. Somehow, we knew our Lord would provide and he did in a miraculous, wondrous way that only HE could do.

Fred was working at the machine shop in Lodi, when he happened to step on a piece of newspaper with an ad, to travel to Europe offering a special discount. He immediately called to tell me, (which was a miracle, he very rarely called), about his find. i asked for the phone number on the ad, and then set-out to do the research by phone in those days. When he arrived home, i had all the information and we decided we could not pass up this great offer.

We were to fly on Lufthansa, the top German airlines. Once we boarded the plane we were treated like royalty. Great service, great food, smooth travel and just before we departed, we were each handed a warm washcloth drenched in refreshing Kölnish Wasser.

Our sons loved the flight and the welcome once we arrived at Oma's. We had a lovely visit; one we will always treasure in years to come. Oma and all the family were delighted we made the long trip to be there for Oma's birthday. Our sons loved being with their German cousins, Aunt and Uncle. It was truly a blessing sent by our Lord.

Now, back to Oma's departure, from her last visit with us; this time she would not travel alone, my Mom would travel with her. We drove them to the airport and they flew to Palm Desert to spend a few days with my sister Barbara. Barbara loved having them and they in turn enjoyed staying with her before Oma Germany left for Germany.

Once she left, i called and asked my Mom if she would mind staying with Barbara for a while. The weather had turned cool and winter was coming and the asbestos plant where Fred worked would close down for the winter months, due to water in the pit where the asbestos was retrieved. Without Fred's regular salary, it was already difficult living on the little he made; it would be even more difficult with one more person to support. Mom was very understanding, as was Barbara, so she stayed on with my sister. At the time Mom moved in with us, she was in her fifties and had no income. We didn't mind because she was such a big help to us, but it was difficult on the small income we had at the time.

Christmas vacation came and Franz who was in the first grade was on Christmas break. Fred was home, due to the Plant closing, when a neighbor called to say a huge oak tree had fallen across the road during the night's storm, and could Fred bring his chain saw to cut it up and remove it from the road. Fred immediately jumped into our old ranch pick-up with chain saw in hand to do the work and reap the harvest of firewood. We have always heated our homes with firewood and this was a Godsend.

As far as i was concerned, Fred didn't take his sons along with him enough, so smarty me decided Franz needed to be with his Dad. So i bundled little Franz up and took him to where his Dad was working on cutting up the tree. i then left, thinking Franz was in good hands; there were plenty neighbors who could keep a watchful eye on him. Wrong. It wasn't long before our neighbor boy Lawrence came running up the hill to tell me Franz decided to check-out his Dad's work and a huge limb from the oak came down and hit Franz on the back of the head. Fred, quickly held Franz in his arms, wrapped a towel around his head, as a neighbor drove them to the hospital. When Lawrence gave me the news i immediately fell on my knees praying to the Lord that Franz would be safe. i then called the hospital emergency room to notify them of their arrival while waiting at home with our little Jeffrey for them to come home.

Thirteen stitches later, Fred and Franz arrived home. We were told not to let Franz sleep due to the concussion he suffered. Since it was nearing Christmas day, we decided to let him open one of his very special Christmas gifts. That way it would keep him awake and not think of what had just happened. He and Jeffrey were so excited to open one gift early, unheard of in our home. The gift was a car racing set; they loved it and played for quite awhile. A few days later we made the trip to Redding to spend Christmas with family. Franz healed well; thank the Lord for His almighty healing

151

hands on him. He still has a scar on the back of his head as a constant reminder. i too learned not to try and push the boys on their Dad, it was his choice not mine. i asked Fred and the Lord to forgive me. **1 John 1:9**.

One more important blessing was since Fred was not working, we did not think we had health insurance to cover Franz's injury. But as our Lord promises in **Philippians 4:19 " And my God will meet all your needs according to His glorious riches in Christ Jesus."** The Lord provided for us, once again. We still had health insurance. PRAISE THE LORD!!!

Fred went back to work at the Plant, Mom came home, seasons came and went and it was time for our Jeffrey to begin Kindergarten. Like the experience i had with Franz, i did not want to let our sons go, especially to a public school. Even at that time, i could see the changes in the school system, and they were not for the better. It had always been my wish to home school them, but Fred said, "No." And knew i must submit to his authority in the home, that is how the Lord set it up; the man was to be the provider and the protector and woman was to be the nurturer. But that didn't mean i could not be involved with their learning at school, so i was there as room mother, serving, helping, watching, making sure our sons were not being taught what we were not in agreement. Being active in the school was not as easy at it may sound, because we lived twelve miles from town where the school was located. But i made it a priority.

i learned or did different things while in town, so as to not drive home and then back, and gas was much cheaper in those days than today. But i learned, coming from a poor family background, to be frugal and do without anything unnecessary.

At one time during their time in school, i took up sewing from a local seamstress, whose hair i did in trade for my classes and material. i really enjoyed doing that, and learned a lot, too. Later, i joined a Moms-In-Touch prayer group; meeting with Christian sisters, i would come to love, and pray with once a week for our children. Our marriage and families were blessed in the way this prayer time was set-up. It was such a blessing. It was to be the first one that was set-up in Calaveras County. Pam, who attended as well, once said, "It is amazing how the Lord is mindful of us ladies praying for our children and families."

This wonderful ministry is still going today and has been renamed Mom's In Prayer. We are thankful the Lord had us plant the seed of faith in our community for this blessed ministry.

To this day, i still feel the pain of putting Franz and Jeffrey on the bus for the first time, letting go has not been easy for me. Yet, i knew i had to, for them and my sake. Oh, the first day of school, i always took them, and usually stayed in town at least, so they wouldn't have to take the long bus ride home. Then the days i helped out in the classroom, i always stayed in town, took them out for ice cream after school and then made the drive home. Those were days we cherished as we discussed the days activities and their precious lives. As i reflect on that experience, i would not trade it for anything in this world. Relationships are most important: first, our relationship with JESUS, our spouse, our children and then family and friends.

i kept involved in their schooling, helping the teachers and being involved in their class in any way i could. i would share from God's Word, the Bible, using Holidays such as Valentine's Day, Easter, and of course Christmas. Telling the students this is what and why we celebrate these Holidays. They were always attentive and wanted to learn.

For Valentine's Day, i used **1 Corinthians 13,** the love chapter. On Easter, i would share Portuguese Easter Bread with the class. The round load of bread has an empty eggshell in the center with dough placed on it in the form of a cross. The empty shell, i would tell them, represents, the empty tomb after Jesus resurrected; the cross, for Him dying for our sins, and the bread, He is the bread of Life. Christmas was simpler, as i shared St. Nicklaus, the Christ child, and the many things we use to celebrate the birth of Christ.

Whenever i had the opportunity, i would go on field trips with the class. On one occasion Jeff's class just finished reading the Chocolate Factory. The class's field trip was to Hershey's Chocolate Factory, which was in our neighboring town of Oakdale. Jeff and i love chocolate, and were fascinated by the huge machinery that turned the chocolate. As it turned out, most of the machinery was made in Germany. We both thought this should be the place where Fred, his dad should work. It only made sense to us, since he was German and these machines were made in Germany, and Fred was a machinist. This would be a perfect job for him. Besides, just think of all the chocolate we could purchase at a good price.

When the tour of the factory was over, Jeff and i went to the employment office in Oakdale and picked up forms to take home for Fred to apply for this great job at the chocolate factory. It wasn't to be, once we arrived home and presented Fred with our great idea, he said, "No, i'm not interested." That went over like a lead balloon, nice try.

i also went on a field trip with our Franz to Big Trees State Park. This wonderful park has towering redwoods, which are some of the biggest and oldest in the world. This park is instrumental in helping form state national parks throughout the United States. The best part is that Big Trees is located right here in Calaveras County. i enjoyed the trip with Franz and his class and would make many trips to this park in the years that followed; we took friends and family to see the wonders of God's creation.

Years later, on one of these excursions, we were in the gift shop at the park when i noticed a picture on a post card of young students standing on the tree that was once a dance floor. Looking closer at the picture, i discovered one of the students was our very own Franz. How i wished I had purchased the card for memories.

Going back to our Jeffrey, he is a November baby, and the cut-off at that time for starting Kindergarten, was in October. After discussing it with his teacher, we decided to give it a try, besides he missed his brother and i thought going to the same school would be nice. Previous to starting public school, they both attended St. Patrick's pre-school a few days a week, which gave them opportunity to meet and play with other children. i did not want them to have the same frightening experience i had on my first of day of school.

i noticed Jeffrey was having a difficult time learning in Kindergarten, even trying to print his name was difficult for him. All i had to compare him with was Franz, who seemed to learn and pick-up quickly. i didn't compare our sons otherwise, the Lord created them differently, as we are all different and special. Perhaps, i thought Jeffrey was too young. The teacher noticed it also, so we decided we would pull him out until the next school year when he was a little older. In some ways it was disappointing for him, but yet he really didn't seem to mind. i was thankful to have more time with him at home.

Chapter Nineteen

**"God is our refuge and strength,
an ever-present help in trouble." Psalm 46:1**

**We sometimes marry or get involved
with what we know, or how we have
been raised.**

Life was becoming difficult, especially in our marriage. My Mom felt the tension, arguments, then she and i began having difficulties. i asked her if she would move out and stay with my brother Bill, his wife Deannie and their two daughters in Sacramento. She agreed it would be a good move for all of us. Oh, how i would miss her, but it was time for Fred and our sons to try to live as a family once again. i wrote Mom a letter while she was living with my brother to tell her how much i loved her and was sorry things didn't work out for us. She wrote back a beautiful letter (which i still treasure), saying she too was sorry and how much she loved me, too. Those words were a miracle. i only remember once, in all my years, my Mom telling me with her sweet caring voice, that she loved me, and that was when Fred and i were separated.

Occasionally, over the weekends, i would pack for Franz, Jeffrey and myself and we would visit Mom, my brother Bill and his family. That was an enjoyable time and a reprieve for me, to have time with family and get away from the problems at home. i knew i could not use this as an escape, and one day had to meet the problems head on. The boys loved being with their Grandmother, Aunt, Uncle and cousins. But i carried much of the pain and began sharing with my brother, i recall saying with tears in my eyes; " i couldn't help our father, and now i can't help my husband." Those words shocked me, little did i know that feeling was deep inside my aching heart.

156

Life went on as usual, i kept busy spending time with our sons, getting involved in school, sports, Boy Scouts, church, whatever or wherever. i just wanted to be there for them and this too was an escape from our marriage problems. i started doing hair once again, as i loved my profession and taught the boys to work for me, folding towels, cleaning the shop, and whatever else needed to be done. This taught them to earn a little income, tithe, save and have some to spend. i worked out of the bathroom my Mom used when she lived with us, but wanted a real shop/ salon. Jeffrey or Jeff, as we later would call him, talked his Dad into converting the extra bedroom downstairs for my Beauty Shop. What a blessing, i had a real salon sink, professional chair, hairdryer and cabinets for the combs and brushes. Fred, did an excellent job with all the plumbing and electrical hook-ups. i thanked he and Jeff over and over again. Yeah, a real shop in our home, a dream come true; and it was all legal, with State, County and sales licenses.

Fred continued to work at the Asbestos Plant and stopping at the local store after work for a beer, then coming home and drinking homemade wine. This continued on for some time. Yes, homemade wine. Fred had a huge cellar dug out under our home when we first built, with the intent of making wine, a place for my canning and an area large enough to hang and cut our own beef. The latter never happened, but the canning and wine did, and i was the one who found the place to purchase the grape vines. The cellar seemed natural to us, Fred was raised with one in Germany and i always heard the stories from my Mom about her parent's cellar. Little did i know, this would bring so many problems. i thank the Lord today, Fred does not want to make wine anymore, due to the temptation of having it readily available. He even let the vineyard go for a time, and had given it to the deer, wild turkeys, raccoons, or whatever critter would like the grapes. He's limited himself to two glasses of wine per day, with lunch and dinner. i am forever grateful. As **Psalm 19:7 states; "The law of the Lord is perfect, reviving the soul."** It is He, the Lord who changes hearts, minds and souls.

157

But prior, his drinking got out of control, and he became very angry. The boys and i left on several occasions seeking peace and shelter. i was in a Women's Bible Study on one occasion, while the boys were in school. i was sharing with the guide of the Bible Study, my delimna, and my concern of where we were going to stay until i could sort things out. When one of the gals, Pam said; "You and your sons, can come and stay with me. i have two sons about your sons ages and a husband that travels, and a big home." i didn't know her very well, but the offer sounded good and she was a sister-in- Christ. So, after the boys were out of school, we went home, packed most of belongings and headed for Pam's home. i was thankful for the distance from our home to town and back, as it gave me an opportunity to explain to our sons what my plans were for the time being.

Pam was very accommodating, caring, loving, generous, and a great friend to confide my situation. She never pried, but was there for me. Our boys got a long well. They were all in soccer and Boy Scouts, which was good; we all had something in common besides our faith; which of course was most important, our Christian faith. While staying there, cooking was not one of Pam's favorites. Since i loved to cook and knew the importance of sitting around the dinner table together, sharing the day's events, i was elected to prepare dinner. We had good times. Pam and i spent many hours talking and sharing. Our growing up years were similar, thus we were understanding each other better.

In the meantime i kept in contact with Fred over the phone, and he and the boys talked regularly. Many times after their soccer games, they would spend the weekend with him, which they loved. i stayed out of the way and kept working on myself. He loved having time with them and was learning to appreciate them and me more and more. Sometimes separation makes the heart grow fonder. During one of our conversations he admitted when he was alone and drinking too much wine it made him angry. He really had to take a good look at himself as well.

158

i don't recall how long we were separated, but eventually the boys and i returned home and we all began the healing process. i realize how difficult this was for all of us, especially Franz and Jeffrey, but something had to be done. Things settled down quite well, Fred was cutting back on his drinking and we seemed to be getting along better. i really wish i could say that we never separated again, but that was not the case. The last, and final time, we separated was when Franz was in his senior year in High School and Jeff was in the eighth grade. This time i meant business and went to an attorney and told him i wanted a legal separation. The attorney immediately wanted to write-up a certificate of divorce. i was adamant and told him; "No, a legal separation." Fred was served the papers at work and came home very angry thinking he was served with a divorce. i tried to explain, but he refused to listen and moved out, not willing to work things out. i let him go. Once again this was very difficult on Franz and Jeff, but i felt i had to stand my ground. Oh, how my heart ached for our sons, because i wanted everything to be all right and be together as a family. Perhaps, the reason i kept leaving and then returning and not being firm, is that is the way my Mother did it with my Dad. i realized i had to be tough, tough love if you will.

i remember going to our Pastor time and time again and asking him is there reason for us to divorce? He would say; " gloria, read 1 Corinthians 7: 10-14, especially, the believing and unbelieving partner. Fred was not a believer at the time, and he didn't want to leave. So, according to God's Holy Word, i had no reason for divorce. The next thing was for a legal separation to let Fred know i meant business.

During this time he went to A. A. and stayed sober for quite awhile. And i attended meetings for co-dependency. In time, we were able to work things out and i explained to our sons we were going to get back together as a family. They too, were tired of the ups and downs. Although years later, i remember Jeff saying to his first wife; "My parents worked it out, so can we." As much as we all dislike these times of unrest, i believe we grow stronger in

159

our faith and life in general. During the time of our healing, Fred was still having a difficult time. One night while in bed, he became very upset and angry. i sat up and all around our bed was a beautiful glowing Light. As i lay back down, thinking i was imagining the Light, i got up again and there the Light was again. i lay down and thought, "That must be the Light from the airport." But we couldn't see the airport from our bedroom. i arose again, and there it was; this magnificent Light all around our bed, only. i told Fred, and he, in his anger said; "You're crazy, go to sleep." i lay down again and said, "Everything is going to be alright." The Lord had given me a sense of peace.

Not long after that experience, while in bed one evening, Fred was having difficulty sleeping again and was in great turmoil in his soul. i sensed that he was very upset, and said to him; "You know what you must do, are you ready?" He replied; "Yes." i said, "Let's get on our knees at the foot of our bed." He did and there he cried out to the Lord and gave his heart to **JESUS**. A miracle. YES, AMEN!!!

The following morning i shared with our sons their Dad's decision. They were overjoyed, to say the least. Jeffrey was ten at the time and came running into the kitchen with his Bible in hand, and said to his Dad; "Dad, you have to read this every day." As the Bible states; **"From the lips of children and infants You have ordained praise..." Psalm 8:2a.** Praise be unto the Lord, our Jeff understood the difference the Bible makes in our lives if we read and put it into practice everyday. My prayer is that he does that every day, as all Christians should.

The transformation didn't end there, that same day, as we were taking my Mom back to San Jose, where she now lived, Fred actually slowed down at the Yield sign near our home. In the past he just ignored it or made some remark and just kept going. Many other things happened to him that glorious day. He had such peace and calm. What a blessing. The Holy Spirit was at work in his heart and life and there was evidence of His work.

Chapter Twenty

**"I will give you a new heart and put a
new spirit in you; I will remove from
you your heart of stone and give you a
heart of flesh." Ezekiel 36:26**

**Jesus is our rock and salvation. He will
get us through.**

Several months prior, friends from church told Fred, a friend of
theirs owned a Machine Shop in Lodi and wanted to hire a good tool and die
maker. He checked it out, and with his qualifications, was hired immediately.
Not long after being hired, he became the Foreman. That wasn't surprising to
us, because he was good at his profession and was a good leader. He was so
good that the Asbestos Plant would send the work to him, at the shop in
Lodi. Of course, with his new position, that meant higher wages for Fred, we
were delighted. But that didn't affect our way of life, we still taught our sons
the benefits of hard work, and not handouts. During the summer, when
school was out, Franz would go with his dad during the week and work in
the Machine Shop with him. Each day they would take their lunch, but on
Friday, they would go out and have lunch together.

When Franz began his freshman year in High School, i asked if he
wanted to buy his lunch or take it? He replied; "Mom, i will do like Dad does,
take it every day and buy it once a week." Also, that summer before his
Freshman year, he helped me can tomato sauce. We had a huge garden and
lots of delicious tomatoes. He helped me can the sauce, and i promised him i
would take him shopping and he could choose the shoes he wanted for
school that year. He was thrilled and was a big help in the canning process. It
was wonderful teaching him the importance of value, as Fred and i had
learned when we were young. Fred and i were thankful to be able to teach

Franz these valuable lessons in spending that would help him the rest of his life.

i, too, learned a lot about the gifts the Lord had given me. When Jeff was just a baby we needed a cabinet for his clothes. i found an old one at a garage sale, took it home and drew a picture, free hand, of Winnie the Pooh on the front of one of the doors. i then painted it. After i was through, i realized i could draw and paint. What a blessing. During the time Fred and i were having difficulties, a dear friend Chris, offered to teach me to paint with oils. i told her i couldn't even draw a straight line let alone paint. One day she said; " I am on my way to your home, and I'm going to give you a painting lesson." She arrived with her arms loaded with paint, brushes, canvas and an open heart. She taught me to paint scenery, i liked what i did, asked her to come back and i would do her hair in exchange for lessons. She agreed, and before long we had several ladies who joined us. All of the ladies were very precise and meticulous. Not me, just do it, was my theme. They all decided i was an 'impressionist.' Whatever that meant. i did enter my first painting in the Calaveras County Frog Jump and took a first prize. That surprised me!!!

A few years ago, i began teaching children how to paint with oil. i had not painted in a number of years, but decided since i was teaching, i should have something to enter in the Fair as well. So entered my oil painting, part of which would be the cover for this book; that painting took a first prize, as well. Guess, i haven't lost the ability yet. When Fred and i went to Mexico on vacation, i took a class in painting with oil on a piece of tile, using nothing but my fingers and fingernails. i loved it and came home and taught that class as well. i never knew the Lord had gifted me in such a way. i've learned, if you don't try you will never know. So, my words to you (dear reader): try and don't give-up.

i read about one of my favorite painters, who, like me did not have the opportunity to learn how to paint, because he too, came from a poor family. When he attended high school he took his first class in oil painting, from then on became one of the most famous living plain air artist of all time. Fred and i had the pleasure of meeting his daughter, who shared briefly about her father.

Sharing this story with you, the reader, shows how we too, can be all that the Lord intends us to be, if we just stretch a little. Look for those opportunities, don't feel sorry for yourself, be persistent, trust the Lord and go for it. The Lord will make a way for you. Sometimes it is the least way we expect, but He will guide you, if you trust Him. He has given each of us gifts, and we must use them for His glory.

i once read about a cathedral in Germany, that during the war, was struck by bombs. Inside the cathedral was a statue of Jesus that had fallen from the destruction. The stature was in good condition, except the arms, feet and hands were broken off. The congregation hired very talented people in the township to make new hands, arms and feet for the broken statue of Jesus. Much to the congregation's dismay, the artisans could not make the limbs to fit properly on the statue. Finally, the congregation said, we will erect the statue of our Lord without the limbs, because we are the hands, arms and feet of Jesus. This came home to me after i learned about these wonderful gifts the Lord bestowed upon me. i too, like all believers in Jesus ,are His feet, arms and hands and must use the gifts He has given me to glorify Him.

Yes, i can tell you about all the wonderful things He did for me during Fred and my separation; i discovered a part of me i never knew before. i recall when my brother Bill told me how he gave the answer in a Sunday school class, when asked if anyone knew of someone like the **Proverbs 31** woman? My brother's reply was; "Yes, my sister Gloria." When he told me that, my heart burst with pride. But it was not for long, because i fell flat on my face. As the Word of God says; **"Pride goes before destruction, a haughty spirit before a fall." Proverbs 16:18.** Well, i was to experience that prideful fall once again. Just when a person thinks they have it all together with the Lord, everyone and everything, the Lord shows us differently. He showed me in a way i will never forget. i am thankful for a forgiving Lord Who 'cleanses us from all unrighteousness', if we confess and repent. He puts us back on solid ground. Just think how many hospital rooms and other facilities probably would not have as many patients, if we confessed and repented of our sins and forgave, as the Lord has forgiven us. May the Lord help us to forgive and move on in that forgiveness. Those powerful words Jesus said as He hung on Calvary's Cross; **"Father, forgive them, for they do not know what they are doing." Luke 23:34.**

A very important subject i learned, during this time of separation, was submission. Oh, yes, there's that word, and it's in the Bible, of course. i remember going to our Pastor, counselors, and Godly people for advice on this subject. As the Word says in **Psalm 1: "Blessed is the man who does not walk in the counsel of the wicked..."** So i sought their counsel. Our Pastor said; "Well, the Word of God says, 'Wives submit to your husbands,...' but it also says, 'Submit to one another...' " My dear Godly woman friend and Pastor's wife said; "Yes, we women are to 'submit to our husbands' but the verse goes on to say, 'as is fitting to the Lord.' and 'Husbands love your wives and do not be harsh with them.' "She went on to say, " If the husband treated his wife with LOVE, the wife would not have a problem with submitting. You see, she went on, the verse says; 'as is fitting to the Lord.' " "Honey, she said, Would the Lord treat you unkindly?" Next, the counselor said, "If you were at a dance with your husband and an old drunk came up to you and said; 'Come and dance with me.' And your husband said, 'Go dance with him.' Would you dance with him?" i immediately said, "Of course not." The counselor said, "But you're supposed to submit to your husband, why wouldn't you in this case?" Now, i got it; "... as is fitting to the Lord." i am His child and He wants me to be treated with love and kindness.

The submission, i must admit i learned from my dear sweet Mom, who was also raised in the same manner of submitting to her husband, no matter what, taught, that you didn't question, you just did what you learned from the previous generation. Well, it was time to stop the cycle and stand-up and be the person the Lord made me to be.

After Fred and i got back together, one of my sisters said to me; "It must be hard for Fred, because you were always this sweet, submissive wife, now you take a stand." i replied; "i finally decided that the Lord made me special, too, and that i have something to say in this relationship. i am not a doormat, but a child of God. Eve was taken from Adam's side, to walk beside him and be his helpmate. She was not taken from his foot to stomped on."

Mentioning my dear Mom, she had moved to San Jose to live with her sister and brother-in-law on their small farm. The same Aunt and Uncle's farm we went to, to escape from my father, in years past. Franz and Jeff, would go with me on many occasions to spend time with Mom and our Aunt and Uncle. Each time we went to the Bay Area, it was changing more and more. i had difficulty driving around not knowing where thus and such were, even the old land marks were disappearing. My Mom, Aunt and Uncle were not happy with all the changes, either. Where there once stood a dairy or apricot orchard was now tract homes, many of them huge mansions. It always amazed me to see these huge homes with no one home, the owners had to work to pay the mortgage. Only the Lord knows how this affected the children and the rest of the family. When i see such wealth, most often i think of 'little house on the prairie' and wish for those days, saying; " Lord, are You sure i was born for such a time as this?" But i am not He, and He knows what is best for me.

Chapter Twenty-One

**Train up a child in the way he should
go, and when he is old he will not turn
from it. Proverbs 22:6**

**What I have learned as a parent.
The joy of parenting.**

Our sons, Franz and Jeff, were and are the pride of our lives. Please allow me to share, with you the reader, some insights Fred and i experienced in raising our two precious sons. They, like most siblings, had very different personalities, character and just being themselves, and how the Lord made them. As i mentioned previously, i raised them according to the Bible and the many wonderful books on child rearing by Dr. James Dobson. The first book i read that he wrote was given to me as a baby shower gift for Franz, entitled; **Dare to Discipline**[8]. At first sight of the title, i thought, what does that mean; do i dare to discipline my child? Was this man kidding? Of course i was going to discipline our child, and if the Lord blessed us with more, they too would be disciplined. i knew and believed what the Book of Proverbs said about raising children, especially **Proverbs** like: " **The rod of correction imparts wisdom, but a child left to himself disgraces his mother." Proverbs 29:14, " My son, (daughter) keep your father's commands and do not forsake your mother's teaching." Proverbs 6:20** and a favorite, **"Train a child in the way he should go, and when he is old he will not turn from it." Proverbs 22:6.** These are just a few, there are many more, i challenge you, the reader, to read these wonderful Proverbs as you are raising your children and grandchildren. All children need these instructions, as do those who are teaching them. i know in our world today, we are told not to lay a hand on the child. Well, the first Proverb doesn't' say 'hand' it says 'rod.'

i remember a story Dr. Dobson[9], i believe, wrote, in one of his books, telling of a child whose father just disciplined using the rod of reproof. After the act, the father was talking with his child and explaining things as he was putting the little one to bed. As the father was leaving the room the child said, "Daddy, please take that stick out of my room." The child had related the stick to the discipline and not his father's hand. When our sons were young, i had a wooden paddle i kept on the top of the refrigerator, which i very rarely used on them. All i had to say was, "Would you like me to get the paddle?" They would respond, "No, mommy, we'll behave." Then we had a nice talk, hugged and loved each other. i was not the perfect mother either; many times i yelled at them, only to feel bad later. i learned it is very important to apologize to our children, when we act like children. This worked for me as i followed the Lord's teaching. That is not to say, we are to let the discipline get out of hand, that's abuse. i saw far too much of that growing up. Although, the words we say can be abusive as well, and i confess at times i too was not choosing my words correctly. But then again, i asked for forgiveness. To this day, i wish i could take back some of the things i said or did or didn't do; not to excuse myself, but, i too, am human and am far from being perfect. Our God loves and forgives us, if we but repent and ask for forgiveness. Raising children is a difficult task, as they are sinners just like us. While attending church one Sunday, one of the dear older ladies said to me, "Never tell a child he or she is bad, it is the act they did, not the child." Great advice.

i had never heard of the words "terrible two's" until i was married and one of my customers told about her terrible two-year-old son. As for us, we never experienced terrible two's with our sons, instead they were "terrific two's". Please allow me to share the story about terrible twos that i witnessed with the customer who had the two year old, when i was managing the beauty salon in Saratoga. The mother of the child worked full time and therefore hired an elderly lady who was the child's sitter. One day while i was at work, the mother came to have her hair done and brought her two year old with her. The moment the child came in the door, he immediately started running around the shop picking up the spray water bottles and began spraying water everywhere. It didn't end there; he ran throughout the shop knocking things over and was just being a tyrant. The mother whose hair i was doing, said; "Oh, terrible two's, that's my son." i was so relieved as were the other customers and beauticians, when she finally left with her child. Wow!!! i thought, 'Is that what 'terrible two's' means?'

The very next day the child came in with the sitter, and i thought; 'Oh, no here we go again.' But this time it was different, the sitter told the child to sit in the reception area while she was getting her hair done and she would attend to him when she sat under the hairdryer (in those days). My thoughts were; 'Right, lady this little boy will sit until you are ready for him.' Was i ever in for a surprise, the little boy was an angel, not only did he sit where he was told, but as customers came and went, he greeted them. The customers were so impressed they told me i should hire him as the receptionist. Once the sitter's hair was washed and set, she retrieved the child, had him sit on her lap while she sat under the hairdryer, and read to him. When her hair was dry, she sat him in the reception area once again until the beautician completed her task.

Believe me, this incident affirmed my belief that there was no such thing as 'terrible two's', but there is such a thing as discipline and respect. Wonder of wonders, the sitter never laid a hand on the child. He was taught to love and respect her. i never told the mother of this event, but kept it in my heart that if and when we had children they would be well disciplined. PRAISE THE LORD they were and are to this day. As a result we never experienced the 'terrible two's, only the terrific two's'.

Our dear Pastor Carl gave a sermon on disciplining children; the part i remembered was, as he stated; "Undisciplined children are like a river with no banks." 'When there are no banks along a river, it goes wherever it chooses, as with an undisciplined child.' " Words of wisdom from a wise Biblical man.

Which reminds me when Jeff was in primary grade one his teachers said he was having problems learning and understanding. But he was such fun and well disciplined. i thought that was nice of her to say, but that didn't help his learning difficulty. We, too learned, as the years passed, the difficulty he had in learning and comprehending. He told me recently, "Mom, you don't treat someone different that has learning problems, they must learn to overcome and live with it." A very wise son we have raised. i will share with you, the reader, later, just how our son was so challenged and overcame his learning difficulty. i thank the Lord for Jeff's success, insight and wisdom.

As i mentioned before we kept our sons in church, school, scouts, and sporting activities. Both Fred and i were involved in all of these events. One year Fred, who grew -up playing soccer, coached Franz's soccer team. He drove from Lodi (an hour) after work, then on to Angels Camp to work with the team after school. Then on weekends he drove most of team to their games. He also brought some of the boy's home after practice, prior to seat belts, loading them in the back of our camper shell. He brought Jeff home also from his practice in town. One evening, a worn out Fred came home with Franz from practice, and i asked, "Where is Jeff?" i already knew, because Jeff's coach had called me. Fred said, "He's coming." Franz said, "No, Dad, i think we forgot Jeff." Sure enough, that is exactly what the coach had called to tell me. i had already arranged for Jeff to stay overnight with the coach and her son. Fred was embarrassed, yet relieved. We were thankful, Jeff's coach took him home for the night and Jeff was delighted. Oh, the joys of parenting.

Fred and i both agreed on the importance of sharing a meal together as a family, in the evening. This gave us opportunity to share events of the day and upcoming days. When our sons were in sports, dinners were more difficult to share, with practice and the distance we had to travel. Somehow we managed, because we knew of the importance of our family sharing a meal together each day. That is part of being in the family, sharing a home cooked meal.

On Sunday afternoon, after church, i would plan the meals for the whole week. If we had leftovers, i would call them "Potpourri", something i had learned from one of my customers, and it sounded better than leftovers. Sometimes, i would pick-up the boys after school and they would go grocery shopping with me. It was during these times, i was able to teach them about food buying and checking the labels, comparing prices etc. One thing i will mention here is, they were both very well behaved when we shopped. Before going into the market, i told them what i expected of them and if they behaved, sometimes there would be a treat for them. One year i told the boys they could each choose one sport for the year, because the running was wearing us out and we were not able to take the time to enjoy those special evening meals. It worked, and we all enjoyed those times together. Today, we learn how much affect those meals have on families, bonding, staying away from drugs, and other unacceptable activities. We always prayed before our meals. In the summer months, when we had more time, we shared the Word of God. Our hope and prayers is for our sons and families to carry on the tradition.

Parties, parties, parties!!! Yeah, parties were a time to celebrate those special birthdays, accomplishments, whatever, and to just have fun. Most of our son's parties we held in our home, with homemade cake, ice cream and punch. Oh yes, there was the piñata and others games. As our sons grew older we would have campouts in our backyard. My cake baking expanded to hamburgers (from our beef); homemade French fries, punch and the traditional home made cake and ice cream. The boys loved these campouts, even though there was not much sleep for them or us; since the boys were only an ear shot from our bedroom. Then, of course, there was breakfast in the morning for all these young, active boys. We were all worn-out when it was time for them to go home.

Later when Franz and Jeff were in their teens, i decided the teens at our church needed a youth group. This reminded me of my teen years of living in Alviso, much like us living in the country, there were no bowling alleys or other good youth activities. So several friends and i, with the support of the City of Alviso's counsel, started a youth group. We had dances, food and fun times. This was what these young people needed, too.

So began our Christian youth group for our sons and friends. Every weekend, for almost two years, we had fifteen to twenty teens in our home and of course they stayed overnight, so we could all attend church together on Sunday morning. i was a teen with them once again. We would go to different Christian youth events; i recall one we attended at a church in Modesto over an hour drive from our home. After the meeting, i took the youth shopping. Some of them didn't have much opportunity to go to the 'big city'. All at once, one of the girls came riding down the isle on one of the new bikes in the store, calling out to me; "Hey, Mom, look at me." i was so embarrassed, turning my head the other direction, as if i didn't know her. The clerk turned to me, and the girl, and said, " Please put the bike back." My girl politely did, and we immediately left the store. The fun didn't end there, the gals decided to push each other in the shopping cart in the parking area, and of course said, "Come on, Mom, get in we'll take you for a ride." A ride they did, and pushed me around the parking lot, much to my surprise they let me go saying, "Wheee!" Oh my, i just kept going, they running after me and finally, the cart came to a stop. We got in the car and went home, but, not without any more funny things going on, including, well i forget what it's called now, but they once again caught me unaware of their antics. A deacon in the church had a cabin in the mountains and offered it to our youth group for the weekend. Unbelievable as it may sound, we had the cabin, but not too many parents who were willing to drive the youth to and from the cabin. We finally pulled it together and the youth had a great time. Fred and i were thankful several adults did come to help supervise the weekend.

172

Some years later a couple joined us for dinner, as i was showing them around our home, i told them about a pipe breaking in our septic system and flooding the downstairs. i was thanking the Lord it was all covered by our insurance; they replaced the carpet, linoleum, base board and repaired all the damage. As i was speaking, the thought occurred to me, and i shared with them, how the Lord provided for us through this broken pipe, because after having the youth in our home those years, things were falling apart from use. The Lord blessed us by this flood, so we were able to have new carpet etc., which we couldn't otherwise afford. What a blessing. Most times, what we see as a curse turns out to be a blessing. As my dear friend, Jeanette would say to me; "Honey, you must have the rain before you receive the rainbow." Here was another rainbow from the Lord.

During the time i was serving as Youth Pastor, we teamed with another church youth group and went to Mexico on a missionary trip. Our oldest son Franz had gone on this same trip in the past and served as team leader two years in a row. i decided i would go with the team, not only because i was their leader, but i wanted to make sure our Jeff didn't get into any trouble. Not that he is a troublemaker; he just loves to have fun, much like his mom. Since we were going into a foreign country, i did not want to take any chances. Before we left, many at the church told me i would be surprised and not able to take the poverty. Once we arrived, i understood what they meant, but little did they know, i had been in such a state of poverty when i was young, and was able to have compassion especially for the children. i came prepared with bags of candy to give the children, and each day i wore a different hat, literally. Some i painted sayings on, others i decorated with flowers etc. The children knew and loved me by my silly hats. The hats were great for covering up a messy hairdo, knowing we were allowed only one shower in the week we spent in the village. i loved these little children so much, i began talking to each of them, not realizing, until one of the youth said; "Mom, you're talking to them in German." Ooops, i

173

wanted to reach them so badly because they didn't understand English, the German just came natural.

The nights were so cold; we slept in huge tents and had to sleep with our clothes on in our sleeping bags. The first night i didn't sleep much, due to the intense cold. i noticed the natives selling their tightly woven blankets and people were buying them like crazy. So, i splurged and purchased one, the best buy i made in Mexico, i slept so well and warm with that blanket covering me.

One of the translators who went on the trip with our team was the youth Pastor at our local Catholic church. He showed me the Catholic Church in town where we were ministering. i immediately went to our team leader and told him of the hole in the roof of the Catholic church, and couldn't we repair it? He said we had so many other things to take care of on this trip; perhaps next year we could repair the roof. And that is what was done on the trip the following year. The whole trip was a wonderful experience and outreach to these loving souls. The night before our departure, the Mexican families of the little church we ministered to, prepared a wonderful Mexican meal as a thank you to our team.

It was a sad departure the next day. But was i ever happy to reach the campus of the Bible College in California, so we could take our long awaited shower. We were all thankful to arrive home safely and with grateful hearts for everything the Lord blessed us with.

On another occasion i worked with several youth group leaders from churches throughout Calaveras County, to have a Christian event at the Fairgrounds. A lady from our church applied for a grant from the state tobacco board, of all things, and was given a huge grant for us to use this money for the event. The event was to bring the Gospel to the un-churched youth of the county and to teach them not to get involved with tobacco or drugs. It became so large, we ended up busing the students to the Fairgrounds, and youth from one of the other counties came as well. We had

174

Christian Rock bands, dancing, food, cold drinks and entrance for all was free. The police even joined us to keep it safe and drug free. The day before the event i was told we might have to cancel because we were unable to get insurance. That morning i had Mom's In Touch and we brought this to the Lord in prayer. He answered mightily: we were able to get insurance for a day with a very minimal fee. i don't really know all the details, but i do know many hearts and lives were touched for JESUS that night. As Fred said to me in German, after the event; "Der dumste Bauer hat die grosten kartoffel." Which means, "The dumbest farmer gets the biggest potato." i passed that on to our leader and we both laughed, it was true. We didn't know what we were doing, or the outcome, but our Lord knew.

One morning i was listening to Focus on the Family[10] as usual, and heard about "Praying at the Flagpole[11]" in schools throughout the United States. i called Focus and got all the information on how to start one at the local high school. Then i went to the school and asked for a certain student to help me get this started. The secretary pointing in the direction of the student, said, "She is right there." i had never met her before, and didn't know how i was going to connect with her, but the Lord knew and went before me. i was so excited to meet her right there in the office. Perhaps, that is why she seemed so surprised at my excitement in meeting her. She too, was a Christian and when i explained, she just took the ball and ran with it. From then on there has been "Prayer Around the Flag Pole" at Bret Hart High School. PRAISE THE LORD, it is such a blessing being where He wants us, when He wants us there, and for us to be obedient. All Praise goes to the Lord, the Maker of heaven and earth. **"...because those who are led by the Spirit of God are sons of God." Romans 8:14.**

There were many such God orchestrated events like this throughout my life, i wish i had more time and the memory to share them. But i will tell you, the reader, one thing for sure, when we are obedient and do as the Lord tells us, not only are others blessed, but we too are blessed. Our pay is out of this world.

i'd like to take you back to our sons growing up years; that seemed to go so quickly. It's like that saying; " Cleaning and Scrubbing can wait till tomorrow, for babies grow up we learn to our sorrow. So quiet down cobwebs, dust go to sleep, I'm rocking my baby and babies don't keep." There's a hand embroidered plaque in our son's old bedroom with that poem on it, as a reminder to me of days gone by; days, that i wanted to hang onto, and yet knowing in my heart i had to give our sons: "Roots and Wings." As i speak to Mom's, old and young alike, they realize how fast those days go and to cherish each and every moment. As one mother said, "We must work ourselves out of a job, while raising and letting go of our children."

Thinking back, i, like most moms, experienced our sons fear of the dark, monsters in their rooms. i would read and pray with them before bed, telling them not to fear, Jesus was with them. Oh, how i wish i would have written then "Our" first children's book; "Angels All Around Me." i have been told by many who have purchased this book, that since they read it to their children at night, their children's fears are gone. Even our granddaughter, Laurel Shea, told me when she reads it at night to her sister, they both feel safe and sleep well.

i remember walking past our son's bedroom window one evening while Franz and Jeff were little and in bed. i could hear Franz telling his little brother, "Jeff, don't be afraid, everything will be alright, go to sleep." Fear of the dark, monsters or whatever are very real to innocent children, and we must pray and seek how the Lord wants us to handle these fears.

Franz was about three and understood very well about Jesus being with him. i remember when i took him with me to see the doctor for my check-up when i was pregnant with Jeff. The doctor let Franz listen to his heartbeat with the stethoscope, and asked, " Do you hear that Franz?" Franz replied, "Yes, it's Jesus. He's in my heart." The kind Christian doctor nodded,

176

'yes' and then let Franz hear Jeffrey's heartbeat while i carried him in my tummy. Later, Jeffrey would understand, Jesus was in his heart too.

I always believed reading was very important, and the boys witnessed my reading quite a bit during their growing up years. Especially, as i sat at the kitchen table reading my Bible or doing my Bible study. A friend gave me a little sign, that hangs on the wall close to where i spend time with the Lord, that reads; "Shhh, I'm talking to God." The sign really helped when they came to talk to me while studying God's holy Word; all i would do is point to the sign. i recall reading about Suzanne Wesley[12] who had seventeen children. When she needed quiet time, she would put her apron over her head as she sat in a chair in her kitchen. Her children all knew to stay away. But, she made sure she spent time with each child every week. Her husband was a traveling minister, busy man. They raised two wonderful sons, who would help turn America back to the Lord. They were John and Charles Wesley.

Personally, i believe mothers have the toughest, most important job in the world, yet so rewarding. i know, there are many mother's who must be out in the working world. But if at all possible, i encourage mother's to be a stay-at-home Mom. The benefits are out of this world, and you will see benefits as your children grow into adults. It is such a joy and pleasure to be there for them, to watch that first step, the first words they say, the first tooth they cut. The joys, the sorrows, especially when they fall and scrape a knee and you are there to kiss it and make it all better. What a gift. Fred and i are thankful, that we set the stage for our sons when Fred said to me, "When we have children, i want you to stay home and raise them." And now we witness our son's wife's being stay-at-home Mom's. Our sons knew the importance of Mom being there for them. We pray our grandchildren will do the same when they marry and have families and just keep passing on our baton of beliefs and faith.

As the little poem mentioned, dust go away, have i ever wished that. Since we live in the country there is lots of dust. i tease my friends and say there is so much dust on our furniture it is a wonder it hasn't carried the furniture away. The dust doesn't bother me, although i like things neat and tidy and that is something else our sons learned from us, neatness. Guess it's the German in Fred and the Swiss in me, we like to be neat and organized. Consequently, our sons learned, at an early age, to help with chores in and around our home. They kept clean rooms for the most part; they were taught where the hamper was situated and the dirty clothes didn't go in it by themselves. i heard a story about a teacher who asked her students, "What begins with an 'm' and picks things up?" One little boy quickly raised his hand and said, "Mother." The teacher said, "No, magnet." Yes, it is true, when children are very young we mother's feel like 'magnets', constantly picking things up. The time comes to teach our children how to pick them up, how to fold clothes, how to wash clothes and, in our case, to hang the heavy things like jeans and shirts on the clothesline to dry. Also, we need to teach them how to prepare a meal.

While i was helping Fred work on our deck today, he asked me to get him a pentone (pencil). He chuckled as he said pentone and remarked, "That's what Franz called it when he was little." With that comment, i began to think of the different words our sons used for certain things such as, pentone for pencil. Jeff called a chipmunk a chickmunk, Franz said exdercise instead of exercise and slopbo was chocolate. We had these huge banana slugs when we lived in the Santa Cruz Mountains that my mom taught Franz to call beesho bugs. When Franz was little, every insect became a beesho bug. Franz also called Jeffrey, 'fluffy'. There weren't too many different words that i recall, but the ones they said were special. Which is amazing, because with Fred's accent, it's a wonder they didn't say some of the words he mispronounced with his German accent. Which reminds me, when Arnold Schwarzenegger[13] was running for governor of California, he would leave campaign messages on our phone. Friends would hear the recorded message and think it was Fred. If you ever hear Schwarzenegger, you will know what Fred sounds like, even after fifty plus years of living in America.

The 'th' sound is very difficult for most German speaking people, because it is not in their pronunciation. As in thread, the 'h' is silent, thus; tread. When Franz was born on June third, Fred would ask; "Why was our son born on the tird? With the 'th' missing you can imagine why it bothered him, he just couldn't pronounce the 'th'. As the years go by, he's getting better at saying third.

We taught our sons early on how to use a spoon and a fork. And they were to eat whatever was placed in front of them, without complaint. When Jeff was small enough and in his high chair, he didn't care much for peas, but he like to play ball. So without thinking of the outcome, i told him the peas were balls. He immediately picked one up and threw it across the room saying; "Ball, ball." We couldn't hold back our laughter. After correcting him, he ate the peas or ball, balls as he called them. To this day, they both eat what is served and clean their plates. i must say, they behaved well at home, but even better when we visited others. We are and were, very proud of them. **Proverbs 29:15 says; "The rod of correction imparts wisdom, but a child left to himself disgraces his mother."** Oh, my.

Chapter Twenty-Two

"The earth is the Lord's
and everything in it, …" Psalm 24:1a

Travels abound with our little family.
Places and people we'd never seen before,
the many wonders of the Lord.

Family trips were always fun, but work, getting things ready for our destination. Our trips were usually camping, which took time and preparation. For our first camping trips we started out small, and i do mean small, in our Ford Ranger, and later in our Ford Courier truck. Fred made a bench in the back of the truck (prior to seat belts) for the boys to sit on and for storage under the bench. We took Franz's Boy Scout dome tent that slept four uncomfortably. When we awakened in the morning after sleeping in the tent, we came out looking like pretzels. But that didn't stop us; we were adventurous, driving to the Grand Tetons and Yellowstone seeing the natural wonders that the Lord created for us to enjoy. One time, when we were camping in the Grand Tetons, we woke-up to snow on the ground and this was during the summer months. Of course Fred was the one who had to get-up and out of our pretzel tent to start the nice warm campfire. Soon the boys and i were up and collecting more wood to keep us warm.

i believe we both had enough of this cold pretzel business, and since Fred had a good stable income, we decided to purchase a motor home. Actually, the way it all happened was, we went to Reno to see a show with two other couples. That was an excursion in itself. We rode up with one of the couples, who was looking for a motor home, so we stopped and checked some out, on the way to Reno. Once we arrived in Reno, got set-up in our rooms, met the other couple, then went out for dinner before the show. One of our friends, Gerry, had a great sense of humor, so much so that as we

180

passed one of the comics who was performing, i turned and said to Gerry, "You should be on the stage, instead of the comic." At dinner he began to tell all of us about the room they were staying in. His wife had booked the trip for us, he not knowing we all had the same type of room. Kinky, as he called it with a round bed, with mirrors on the ceiling, kinky was right. But the fun was just beginning. We went in to see the Show and out came the Chorus girls; topless. All three of us ladies were so embarrassed, we had no idea what we were in for, and finally i turned to Fred and we all got up and walked out.

On the trip home the couple we drove up with, wanted to stop once again to look at motor homes. We did, that is, when we came home with a lovely used motor home. We always wondered how that worked; they were looking for a motor home, didn't purchase one, but we did. Interesting, a few years prior with the same couple, they were checking out fiberglass swimming pools, (which we always thought would be nice, since we lived in hot dry country). We ended up purchasing one, they didn't. Needless to say, both the pool and motor home were great investments for our family. Not only did we enjoy the swimming pool and motor home, we traveled many places with our new home; even on one of our anniversaries we celebrated with dinner in our motor home.

i told our sons, as soon as Dad gets home from work, we will put the dinner i prepared in the motor home and drive out to Lake Tulloch. There we will park our motor home, which had a huge bay window, overlooking the lake as we enjoyed dinner by candlelight. Fred was amazed and our sons loved the idea. What fun!!!

As a matter of fact during the winter, spring and fall seasons, Fred and i always eat dinner by candlelight. This is something i learned from our Swedish friends many years ago. Try it some time, it is very relaxing and you learn to slow down and enjoy the meal. Not long ago, while visiting our son, wife and daughters, the youngest said, "Oma, you should have brought your candles, we could light them and put them on our dinner table." Once we arrived home, i purchased two candle- holders and candles for her and her family to use at dinnertime. This was yet another wonderful tradition to pass on to our children.

As i am writing about our travels, the thought just occurred to me about our Franz, now driving, taking his brother to school and me being left at home alone with no vehicle. The following happened one morning, right after Fred left for work; little did i know that the S.W.A.T. Team had stopped Fred. It was around five a.m. that i received a very anxious call from a friend telling me of a prisoner on the loose in our area. After our conversation i prayed, awakened the boys for school. While they were having breakfast i told them of the phone call i had received. After breakfast they took me in our bedroom, retrieved a handgun their dad had purchased for me, and began explaining to me how to use it. They turned to me and said, "Mom, you're not paying attention." It was true, the whole time i was staring at my Bible sitting on my nightstand. i then told them, "Franz and Jeff, i am glad you are so concerned about my safety, but if that man does come here, i will probably pick-up my Bible and start telling him about Jesus."

Just recently a friend sent me a message and picture on Facebook, with an elderly lady holding a pistol in her hand. Under the caption was written; " The officers are on their way, in the meantime let's talk about Jesus." Apparently, she was holding a criminal at bay and wanted to share the Gospel with him: my sentiments exactly.

As for the prisoner who broke out of jail in our area, he was captured only after he shot and killed the police dog (German Shepherd), and he was put back in jail. As for me, i had Bible Study on that day, and met with the gals as usual and we prayed for this escaped convict, they warned me to be careful. i have learned to trust the Lord in this situation and am still learning to trust Him, even as i write.

Back to traveling, love keeping you on your toes with my adventures. On one of our trips we drove through Northern California, Oregon, Washington and on to Canada. Our destination was Lake Louise, then down into Idaho, across Washington, down to Oregon and home. That was an amazing trip. Each night we stayed in a different campground, and didn't come out looking like pretzels in the morning. This was living at it's best.

But we had one problem, the boys bikes were tied down to the top of the motor home and they wanted to take their bikes down to ride, once we settled in the campground. Fred, like most of our men folk, has a one-track mind; in this case his destination was Canada. So each time i mentioned the boys wanted their bikes, his reply was; "We're going to Canada." i thought, 'So.' Not Fred, this was too disturbing, too much trouble. Finally, when we reached a campground in Washington, i climbed on top of the motor home to retrieve the bikes. Fred's response was, "What are you doing? We're going to Canada." "Not a problem," i said handing the bikes to our sons. The boys were overjoyed, after sitting for so many hours, yeah, fun to ride our bikes. Fred, saw the importance of enjoying our trip, and was glad we took the boys bikes down.

i know, you see the strong will i have, and yes you are correct. i am a leader, encourager, and like a fire out of control, can be a detriment. But if that fire is well contained it can work wonders. The only way the fire in me can be controlled is by the Holy Spirit's direction and Fred tempering the fire. i am so thankful for the Holy Spirit's leading, but must admit i get so excited i am like the out of control fire if i do not seek the Holy Spirit's leading. Fred helps with that directing as well, thank the Lord. i have learned that i am emotionally very strong, yet sensitive.

Fred, finally relaxed and we enjoyed the rest of our trip. It was interesting as we traveled, almost every campground we stayed in, there was a train running past the campground. This happened especially at night, or so it seemed, needless to say it was quieter at our home than on this; 'train running' trip.

There was so much of God's creation to see on this trip. And, you the reader, if you have never taken this trip, i encourage you to do so. We drove up Highway 5 to Redding and then went West toward the Trinity Alps, alongside was the Trinity River, then onto Highway 1 North along the Redwood Coast, into the sand dunes of Oregon, then into the great state of Washington, taking in the beauty of the lovely Columbia River and then into Canada. We were going to take the ferry across to Vancouver, B.C., but it was too expensive to put the motor home on the ferry. We decided to go through Hells Canyon and then on to magnificent Lake Louise. Finally arriving at Lake Louise, it was a wonder in itself and well worth the trip. There it sat in such stillness surrounded by those majestic mountains. What an awesome sight to behold. It was summer and there was snow on the peaks of the mountain with part of a glacier going into this body of clear icy cold water.

But the quietness didn't last long. When we got ready to lie down in sleep after our long journey, we could hear the rumbling of a train going by. And this campground was in a secluded forest in the wilderness of Canada. We all laughed as we finally went off to sleep.

The next day we left for our return trip home, this time going south into beautiful green Idaho. The many ranches we passed were well kept with horses, cows and other livestock meandering through the green grass. In some parts there was still some snow on the ground from the previous snowfall. Of course all of us loved this part of the trip, reminding us of home and the country life, except it was green, where in California everything was golden or brown, it was summer. From Idaho, we traveled East again toward the state of Washington. There was a sign that said, Lake Moses so many miles East. i had never thought of Washington being this hot and dry, like a desert. We kept driving through nothing but a dry desolate land, finally arriving at Lake Moses. We stopped at the campground in Lake Moses, to camp for the night. There really was a lake, which we were very thankful to see and took paddleboats out on Lake Moses. i have a picture of the boys riding along in their paddle boat with Jeff laughing and Franz sticking his tongue out at us, as Fred and i once again, paddled around in circles. Boating just isn't our thing, i guess.

Upon leaving the next day, anxious to start our decent home, i looked back at that lake, sitting out in the middle of the desert, and realizing why it was named; Moses Lake. It reminded me of Moses from the Old Testament, trudging through the desert when he was escaping Pharaoh and Egypt. Know how he must of felt finding water and shelter from the heat of the desert, and he was on foot.

We arrived late in the day in Seattle. We visited the Space Needle and then stopped to see the Boeing Aircraft Center and Museum. This was fascinating for both Franz and Jeff, especially Franz, because it was his dream to be a pilot. It was an amazing site to behold.

The Lord kept us safe in our travels until we were going through Seattle. The traffic was very heavy and then we came to a sudden stop. A man on a motorcycle was directly in front of us, Fred hit the brakes and so did the man on the cycle. But he slid on his bike, almost landing directly under our motor home. i applaud Fred for his quick reaction and thinking. We thanked the Lord as we continued our trip home to California, recalling the many times the Lord had sent His angels to protect us, and of the times we don't even know about.

We took many trips in our motor home. One of our favorites was to Cottage Grove Oregon. We came across this lovely little town South of Portland, found a free campground that was set-up by the Army Core of Engineers. It was very clean and well maintained. A small creek ran through the campground, where our sons discovered fresh water clams. One evening we had steamed fresh water clams for dinner, along with Franz's famous blackberry cobbler cooked over our campfire. Those were the days my

185

friend, i thought they would never end; such a wonderful family time.

In the mornings we would ride our bikes to pick the many varieties of blackberries that were in the campground. Later in the day we would walk to what Fred called "Whistling Dixie." There it was, a huge dam, as the wind went through the opening of the huge pipes of the dam, it whistled. Thus "Whistling Dixie."

Sometimes, we would drive over to the dam itself and swim in the warm water. There weren't very many people who had made the discovery of this beautiful setting and dam, so it was peaceful and quiet.

We took our German shepherd pup with us on one of the trips and would take him each time there after. He too, loved running and playing in the quiet campground and surrounding area.

Speaking of dogs, when i was a child we had only two dogs, the first was a big black Labrador that my father named; Nigger. You, the reader, must understand this was not derogatory at the time. Even in the Bible we read about outstanding Christians who amongst them were; **"Barnabas, Simeon called Nigger, Lucius of Cyrene...and Saul" Acts 13:1b**. The Wycliffe Bible Commentary 1972 edition states; Nigger was a Latin word meaning black, here used as a nickname. It apparently describes the dark complexion of Simeon and suggests that he was of African origin.

My father was not far off, when he named this gentle lab, Nigger. i loved him, and being small as i was, he let me ride him like a horse. What fun i had with Nigger. This is when we lived on Tenant Avenue in San Jose, out in the country with a train that ran the tracks, off of Monterey Highway, not far from our shack. We would have what my parents referred to as bums, who would literally bum a free ride off the train. Keep in mind this was in the 1940's just after WW II, when jobs were scarce, as was travel, and this was the way most men without work got around hitching rides on freight cars.

One fine day i was playing in the front of our shack with my beloved Nigger, when a tall black complexioned man appeared on our gravel

186

driveway. My mother came out to meet him, as she did our faithful Nigger approached the man, protecting us, i am sure. Mom kept calling our lab to come, she called him by the name my Dad had given him: Nigger. Then, Mom realized what she was saying, stopped and apologized to the man, saying that was our dog's name and she didn't mean to offend him. The tall black complexioned man politely said, "Ma'am, i knows i'm a nigger, i just wonder if i could chop some wood for you for something to eat?" Apparently, the man had just jumped off the train and headed our way looking for food and work. Mom, being the kind, loving, generous person she was, of course gave him wood to chop to use for her cook stove and prepared a meal, from our meager supply. The kind man chopped the wood, ate and thanked my Mom and went on his way. We never saw him again. That was my first encounter with a black complexioned man.

The other dog we had was a small shorthaired terrier; i believe my sister Barbara named, Cooky. Although, Mom had never baked us cookies when were growing up, somehow she came up with this name, and being the entertainer, she made up a song to go with his name. The song was called Cooky the Dog, and was sung to the tune of Smokey the Bear. Whatever happened to Cooky, i really don't recall. We moved so much i believe we just left him behind in our previous house. Leaving pets behind was not uncommon for my father, he could barely put enough food on the table for us, let a lone a critter. Obviously, we never took one to the vet, and we ourselves never went to the doctor.

In my later years of life, it is still difficult for me to understand why animals are taken to the vet. Living as poorly as we did and living out in the country, it was just unheard of to take a critter to the vet. Up to this time, the only time i recall seeing a vet was on my Uncle Slims ranch, when one of his cows was having difficulty calving. Other than that, farmers and ranchers just dealt with the problems that occurred with their animals as best they could. Things such as one of the cows swallowing a piece of bailing wire that was wrapped around the hay, the farmer would put a huge magnet in the cow's mouth and try to get the wire out. Perhaps, that is why today hay is bailed with a plastic rope of some sort. Even with rope, one must be careful when feeding, so the animal doesn't ingest the rope.

When i was thirteen my father decided he liked cats, so he had a couple of cats that he would allow in our shack or trailer, whichever we lived in at the time. That is when we lived in Alviso. i believe between the filth from the floods, infestation of fleas and the cats and our unclean living, is how i contacted the impetigo i spoke of earlier in this book.

Later when i read and studied God's Word, the Bible, i learned the Lord gave man dominion over the animals. As it states in **Genesis 2:19 "Now the Lord God had formed out of the ground all the beasts of the field and the birds of the air. He brought them to the man to what he would name them, and whatever the man called each living creature, that was its name."** Wow, what an awesome privilege the Lord gave man to name the creatures of the earth.

Now, back to the motor home. It was a wonderful blessing for our German shepherd, and us all, too. i began to realize that pets are part of the family and since the Lord gave us dominion over them, we must care for them. Now it hurts me to see, dogs especially, or any critter left alone, while the owner's work or travel. We took the motor home many places; one was to the air show. Since both of our sons were fascinated with planes and of course Franz's dream was to become a pilot, we took them to several air shows. The United States Air Force, the Navy or other armed services performed most of the shows we attended back then. It was an exciting event, seeing and walking in and through most of the planes that would fly that day, or were on display. We realized the importance of our God given right to be Americans, and how our men and women served us, and so many others during time of war and peace. My mom was very patriotic and taught us children to be the same and to honor our troops and Country as well. Fred and i have carried on that tradition, in that we always have an American flag waving at the entrance of our ranch and one outside our home.

There was a pilot our sons and i particularly enjoyed at the air shows we attended; she would fly high in the sky doing her stunts. Then came her grand finale, the song, Proud to Be An American[14], came over the loud speakers and she would have red, white and blue vapor coming out of the tail pipes of the aircraft. If that didn't make us proud, i don't know what would.

Recently, our son, Jeff, took his wife Lexie, and our granddaughters, Laurel Shea and Aubrey Joy, to one of these air shows. Jeff sent us a text message with a picture of this woman pilot with the words, " I stood in line thirty years ago to get her autograph. Today I stood in line to have her picture taken with my daughters and I." Prior to this, Laurel Shea sent a message stating how she, her sister and Dad had their pictures taken with this lady, without telling me who she was; i asked and was right.

It is such a joy to know our son and daughter-in-law are passing on to our grandchildren some of the fun things we did with our sons. They are making such fond memories and supporting our Country by being good citizens.

Speaking of being proud of our Country, when Franz was in grade school, two major events took place in our great Nation. One was the explosion of the Challenger Space Shuttle on January 28, 1986, killing all seven aboard, one of which was the first teacher to travel in space. Franz, loving air or space travel of any sort, was devastated when he heard and saw the results of the Challenger. It was a sad day for our Nation.

The other tragedy was the shooting of President Ronald Reagan[15] and three others. President Reagan was in his seventies at the time of the shooting, and the doctors said if he were not in such good health, and physical shape, he probably would not have survived. That thought brings me back to how active he was on his ranch in California. My seventy-eight-year-old husband is very active on our ranch and i believe the life we live on these ranches has contributed to our good health and physical condition.

Getting back to this wonderful President and former Governor of California, after getting shot he quipped to his wife; Nancy, " I forgot to duck." And as he was going into surgery to remove the bullet, he lifted his oxygen mask and jokingly said to the doctors and nurses, "I hope you're all Republicans."[16] These quotes were found on Wikipedia. He too, was a Christian and i'm sure had no fear of dying. Franz was in Kindergarten when President Reagan was shot. He came home, and in his child like manner said; "Mom, can we write a letter to President Reagan?" Of course i said, "Yes." Franz could not write yet, so he dictated to me what i should write. i sent the letter off to the White House addressed to President Reagan, and life went on as usual. Then one day, a letter came in the mail addressed to Franz Bodenmüller, the return address was The Office of the President of the United States of America, Washington, D.C.

i handed Franz his letter, he opened it, and asked me to read it. There was a personal note for Franz and signed by The President of the United States of America; Ronald Reagan. What an honor, and to think our President took the time and was mindful of a little boy who lived on a ranch outside of the small town of Angels Camp, California.

i kept the letter in my hope chest, amongst other treasures. Recently, i came across this lovely letter from our former President and presented it to Franz. It is something he will treasure the rest of life. i learned the importance of taking time with your child, listening to what is important to them, and to act on the idea. Perhaps if you do, your child will receive a note in the mail from someone who means a lot to them as well. We never know unless we try.

Whoops, got side tracked again, was sharing our experiences with the motor home. The last big trip we took with it was when Fred's cousins came to visit us from Germany. They rented a motor home here, and had mapped out a trip to see the many rock formations in the Western part of the United States. Like most foreigners they knew more about our Country than most of us Americans. To our shame and dismay, they knew more about where they were going then we.

The first thing on their agenda was to see the ocean and Southern California. The draw was a television program that was aired during this time, (even in Germany) which took place on the beach near Malibu, California. They loved the ocean, beach and the surrounding cities along the Coast of California. The next day they wanted to visit Universal Studios. Our cousin even offered to pay the entrance fee, if Fred would drive us all there in our motor home through the Los Angles traffic. Fred took him up on his offer, and he drove us to Universal Studios.

The next day we were leaving for Palm Desert and the Grand Canyon, but they wanted to go to the ocean one last time before departing. That is when we almost lost Fred. We were all wading or swimming out in the cool Pacific, when suddenly this monster like figure came out of the sea. It was covered with green seaweed, why it was Fred, Yikes!!! He had gone out a little too far and got caught by one of the huge waves and was tossed to and fro in the ocean. None of us saw him in such danger. Somehow, (by God's grace), he was able to free himself of the breaker and come to shore.

i had a similar experience twice in my life. The very first time i had been to the ocean, i went with my seventh grade teacher and several other girls. i thought at the time, it was strange for our teacher, a married man, at that, to take us girls to the ocean. We all held hands as he took us out to the huge waves. i was terrified of water, not knowing how to swim and then being in so many floods as well. i let go of his hand and kept going around and around in that huge wave, he finally pulled me out.

The next time, was in Hawaii with Fred and our sons. We would go out into the waves and body surf onto the beach. The trick is to go out far enough behind the breakers. Well, i guess this one time i did not go out far

191

enough, and sure enough got caught in the wave, tossing me 'round and 'round. Fred realized what was happening and quickly grabbed me, removing the top of my swimsuit. And i, catching my breath said; "Where is my earring?" Can you imagine? Here i almost drowned and i was asking for my earring! It finally dawned on me the danger i was in; needless to say, i never have gone body surfing again. Water and i just don't mix, guess it's the floods i experienced when i was younger.

As we drove through Palm Desert in our motor homes, our German cousins were very impressed with the desert and the cactus. One cactus that fascinated them was the Cholla cactus. It is a very interesting cactus, once it gets into your skin or clothing, it is very difficult to remove because it has long needle like stickers that seem to jump on you once you come near them. We even saw rattlesnake skins coiled in the cactus itself.

Well, the younger cousin, sixteen or so at the time, decided to get a much closer look at the Cholla cactus, and it seemed to jump on him and digging deep into his naked legs and lower torso. His father was not very happy with him for getting into this predicament, so the son decided to ride in our motor home, away from his very upset father. Before doing so, Fred had to take a pair of pliers in order to pull the dreadful stickers out of his skin. In the end it was painful, yet we all laughed seeing what one of God's creations can do to a human, animal or reptile.

We drove on through the many natural beauties of the Arizona desert before reaching one of the most wonderful sights in God's great creation. As we stepped out of our motor homes, the most unspeakable, overwhelming site was before our very eyes. My first thought was; 'If man does not believe in our Creator God once he sees this, how can he deny Him?' Yes, my friend it was none other than the magnificent, awesome, colorful Grand Canyon.

To take a photo of what we saw was impossible. It's depth, width, colors, rock formations, river far below were too much for the naked eye to capture, let a lone a camera lens.

We stayed at the Grand Canyon overnight, leaving the next morning for Lake Havasu. Part of the London Bridge had been transported and set-up over Lake Havasu, and the cousins wanted to see the bridge. Fred could care less, he had seen the bridge when it was in England, and couldn't imagine only part of it here in America. We went on to see the Bridge.

Summers in Arizona are hot, and Lake Havasu was no exception. We parked our motor homes and headed for the lake for a swim, but even the lake was hot. We were thankful to be leaving the next day, the cousins would travel further north and we would head south toward Zion and Blythe National Parks. The cousins would meet us later in the month, back at our home in California.

Both Zion and Blythe have their own beauties to enjoy; personally i was more impressed with Blythe. It reminded me of tremendous cathedrals overlooking the red clay structures of the canyons far below. These majestic cathedral-like rock formations were throughout the landscape; a wondrous sight to behold. From there we went south once again arriving in Las Vegas, at night. Once we parked our motor home in the parking lot of one of the large Casinos, we went to have a nice dinner instead of the usual camp food.

Being from the country, our sons were not exposed to the city, especially at night, so you can imagine the wonder in their eyes as they saw all the lights of Las Vegas. Jeff, our adventurous one, was more impressed than our Franz. Jeff, was so excited he didn't want to leave, he just wanted to see everything. For him it must have been like a huge circus or carnival all lit up. For the rest of us, we wanted to have dinner, get some rest, wait for the sun to rise and leave this bustling metropolis. And that is just what we did the following day. This time we headed for Mount Whitney, which the cousins told us was the highest contiguous summit in the United States. That it is, and we realized just that, as we were driving our motor home to the summit.

Upon arriving at the summit of Mount Whitney, we told the ranger what a steep climb it was for us especially in our motor home. The ranger just stared at us in amazement and said, " You, drove your motor home up here?" he went on, " Motor homes are not allowed to drive up to the summit because it is too steep." We just looked at each other, wondering how we were going to drive back down. We then realized as we drove up, as the road got steeper and steeper, we noticed we could almost see the rear end of our motor home on each narrow turn.

We hiked a bit and enjoyed the fresh mountain air before we made the treacherous descent down the narrow winding road. Oh, yes, we prayed and the Lord got us down safely. We look back and tell the story to our friends, with laughter. Believe me we were not laughing at the time

We returned home, and the cousins followed a week or so later, in time for Fred's birthday in July. They stayed with us another week or so and then made their jaunt back to Germany. So far, they have not come back to visit. But when Franz graduated from High School the following year, they sent him a round trip ticket to visit them in Germany.

i decided to join Franz on that trip, making my last trip so far, to Europe. i will share more later, about that wonderful, amazing trip, and the blessing it was for all of us.

Santa Clara Valley/ Silicon Valley

**From right to left; my sister's Barbara, Josephine, me (gloria jean)
our beloved dog, my sister Frances.**

My sister's and i in front of trailer, off Tennant Avenue/Silicon Valley Road

Grandma Guidotti, hanging my diapers. Near shack off Tennant Avenue/Silicon Valley Road.

Ranch still standing today, where our father worked and we changed irrigation pipes.

Me, proudly riding a tricycle in front of the shack, Tennant Avenue/Silicon Valley Road

Part of the ranch where we worked, father milked cows and we
changed irrigation pipes.

The Four beauties, left to right; me, Frances, Barbara and Josephine.
Taken in front of our Uncle Slim and Aunt Mary's home in San Jose.

A rare occasion downtown San Jose. Grandma Guidotti, Mama and her daughters.

My brother's, William and Frank. Taken in front of our shack in Alviso, California.

Mama's pride and joy; her six children. From top left; Frances, me, Barbara and Josephine. Bottom left to right; Frank and William.

Our precious Mother; Angelina Myrtle Guidotti Joseph.

Our father; William Asa Joseph

Left to right; Josephine, Barbara, Frances and me.

Grandpa and Grandma Guidotti. Bringing their Swiss farming heritage to Santa Clara Valley/ Silicon Valley.

Great-Grandma Risi, from Switzerland and my Mom.

Family. Left to right; Barbara, William, me, Frances, Joseph, Frank. Bottom row,
Mom and Aunt Mary, (her sister). Mom's 80th. Birthday celebration.

Family, precious in-laws. Left to right; Robert, Donald, Deannie, Helen and Fred.
Mom and Aunt Mary.

The Bodenmüller clan. Right to left; Franz, Jennifer, Laurel, Papa, Kasey, Oma, Jeffrey, Lexie. Bottom row; Steven, Ryan and Aubrey.

Our loving granddaughter; Laurel Shea and Oma.

Papa (Fred) and Aubrey Joy.

Papa (Fred) and Steven Joseph.

.

Our grandson's; Ryan, Kasey, me, (Oma), Steven, and Papa (Fred).

The original Bodenmüller clan. Me, Fred, Jeffrey and Franz.

The results of the rattlesnake bite. Will i ever be able to write again?

The Lord's answer, thankful to all who contributed to my attending this conference.

Where it all began; Santa Clara Valley/ Silicon Valley.

The apricot tree the Lord provided across the street from our new home, in Valley Springs, where apricots rarely do well.

When i was unable to make the trip to San Jose during apricot harvest, i went to pick-up our mail and there it was, in plain sight. Why hadn't i seen it before? The Lord provided an apricot tree directly across the street from our new home, years prior. A miracle, a blessing, a picture of fresh cut apricots for "Our" book. PRAISE THE LORD!!!

Mr. Ed Rose and i on his apricot farm off of Mt. Hamilton Road. Notice the buckets used for picking the fruit.

Mr. Ed Rose and 100 year old Mother, cutting apricots. Notice the original trays in the background, before putting in the sulfur box.

One in the same; Silicon Valley Road and Tennant Avenue, where it all began for;
"The Girl From Silicon Valley"

The Author; gloria jean with her hubby; Fred (Siegfried)

gloria jean and her dear friend and sister-in-Christ; Joyce: Editor.

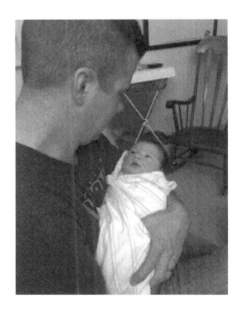

Franz holding Fred and gloria jean's newest granddaughter, Hope

Chapter Twenty-Three

"A Friend Loveth At All Times." Proverbs 17:17

The importance of friends and friendships.
Sometimes friends are closer than family.

Friends and friendship has always been so very important to me. Perhaps, it is because in my younger years we moved so much. i was just thinking, the place i lived longest or called home before marrying Fred, was Alviso, California. We lived there for six and half years, but moved seven times during those years.

Interesting my sister Barbara told me once, " You are one of six of us, and yet you are like an only child. Because, us three sisters were closer to you in age, then left home at a young age, and there you were with two much younger brothers than yourself." Great insight, i believe she is correct and that's the reason why i have so many, and am somewhat closer to my, friends than my siblings.

One of my dearest friends i mentioned before, and still keep in contact with today, is Paula. She's the one i knocked out playing baseball, when i was up to bat and she was the catcher. We have been friends over fifty years, a blessing and a miracle. The other dear long time friend is Joyce, the one i met while cutting apricots. Our friendship has been a blessing over these fifty plus years. Both of them are now sisters-in- Christ. Other than those two, most of the friends i have, are the ones we gained here in Calaveras County. Living here, these thirty plus years, has made the difference in making and keeping friends.

One of my dearest, and precious, friends was Ruth and her husband John. She reminded me of Dale Evans as she rode around in her pink jeep. i don't recall just how we met, but we were friends for quite a number of years, until the Lord took her home.

Ruth was also a customer, whose hair i did for years, until she moved to Carson City, Nevada. i would like to take a few moments and share with you what her friendship meant to me (us), and how the Lord used her in our lives, and of her coming to the saving grace of Jesus.

Ruth belonged to a group of women in the area, who raised cattle, and i would constantly ask her to join our Women's Bible Study, which began in our home. Finally, one day she decided to come to Bible Study, and after that time, she never missed until she moved. One day as she was leaving her home to attend Bible Study, her husband said, " I think you like this Bible Study more than the cattle women's group." Yes, she was hooked on the Lord Jesus, and her husband knew it and was pleased. And i was the benefactor who witnessed the spiritual growth in Ruth's life; she was seventy-nine when she came to know Him as her personal Lord and Savior. Her children gave me the nick name of "Glory Hallelujah!!!" And i loved it.

John and Ruth had moved to Calaveras County years before we did, and purchased their land from a man who was a squatter and his American Indian wife. i loved visiting with John and Ruth on their ranch, and listening to the stories of days gone by; what a privilege it was, just to sit and listen, as we sipped "Cowboy Coffee". John worked the small plot of land and with careful planning, and was able to raise his own hay to feed his cattle. They had an amazing spring, which supplied water for their home and the ranch. Behind their small abode, sat a large wooden tank that held their water supply and an old windmill that pumped the water into the tank. The water was sweet to the palate, clear and smooth when you swallowed it. Their spring held up, never went dry and they never had to drill for a well. The squatter's, must have known what they were doing when he and his wife chose this piece of land to farm. Without water the land would be worthless.

John had a very bad heart condition, but that didn't stop him from working his ranch. As his condition worsened, he spent time in the hospital. Upon one of his bouts, he returned home and the Lord directed me to visit he and Ruth. The verses the Lord gave me to share with John, were from **1Corinthians 5: 1-4,** where it talks about **"this tent" (our bodies), "we groan and are burdened, ..."** **"awaiting our heavenly dwelling,..."**

i brought my Bible and was sharing this verse with John. He was a quiet man, and with much discernment and trust, began to tell me about his boyhood and how his mother would have him hitch the team every Sunday morning and get it ready for church. i listened intently, then asked if i could pray with him, which i did. Not long after, he was taken, once again, to the hospital, never to return to his lovely ranch. i was thankful i listened to the Lord's direction and had that time with John and Ruth. From this special time with them, the Lord gave me yet another ministry in which to serve Him, which was either singing or doing the eulogy at a loved one's service. Helping serve at John's memorial opened the door for me to use the ministry of speaking, which the Lord had given me. Praise Him!!!

Before John's passing, Ruth and i were discussing the Bible and she told me she wanted a Cadillac, and would the Lord give her one? i told her there is a verse in the Book of Psalms that says; **"Delight yourself in the Lord and He will give you the desires of your heart." Psalm 37:4.** She said, "O.K., i want a Cadillac." We both smiled and went our way.

Not long after this episode, John and Ruth's grandson purchased their ranch and she asked Fred, who was like a son to them, if he would go with them to purchase a new car. Fred went and they paid cash for a brand new car, not a Cadillac, but equivalent to a Caddie. Whether this was the Lord's answer i do not know, but Ruth was delighted to have a beautiful new automobile.

One afternoon, as i was finishing up Ruth's hair, a dreadful call came from the I.R.S. At that time Fred was a self-employed machinist and paid his taxes quarterly, so the call from the I.R.S, was to inform us they had received our check, but it was over two thousand dollars short. They instructed us to send the balance within a short period of time, plus interest and penalty.

When i returned to my work on Ruth's hair, she sensed something was amiss. Whether it was my unusual quietness or perhaps the shock on my face, she picked up on it and asked what was wrong. i told her and explained we did not have the money to pay the amount due, and how could such a mistake happen. Without hesitation, Ruth offered to give us the money we needed, and we could pay her back whenever, without interest. i was pleased, but shocked, again, that a dear one like Ruth would make such an offer.

i graciously thanked her and said, "First, i must find the canceled check we sent the I.R.S., and thanked her for her offer, but said, "Fred will not accept your offer." She said, "When is he coming home from work?" Fred being the punctual man he is, i responded, "Any time soon." She added, "Then i will wait and ask him myself."

She stayed a short while waiting for him, and then immediately went out and met him as he was getting out of his truck, explaining to him what had transpired, and added, "You are like a son to me, do not refuse my offer." He was floored, and said, "O.K." i too was amazed that he would accept her offer.

i found the check, the bank had cashed it for $24.00 instead of $2,400.00. i then called the I.R.S. to make the payment and they dropped all charges and penalties because we offered to pay cash, from the money Ruth lent us. Not long after, with thankful hearts and hard work, we repaid Ruth. We all witnessed our Lord's hand in all of this and working for the good for all concerned. **"And we know that in all things God works for the good of those who love Him, who have been called according to His purpose." Romans 8:28.** What a beautiful witness for us and especially for Ruth, the Lord's hand at work.

Not long after John died, Ruth decided to move to Carson City, Nevada. Oh, how i missed her, but yet thought this would be a nice get away for our family. Each year in October, nearing Ruth's birthday, and before the first snowfall, we made our trek over one of the most scenic highways in America, beautiful Kit Carson Pass or Highway 88 into Nevada. Autumn is one of the best times to go over the pass with the radiant beauty and variety of the oranges, yellows, greens, and browns of the Autumn foliage. As we traveled further up the mountain pass, there was the white with a touch of dark on the glorious Aspens, adorned by the cloudless blue sky. i would thank the Lord for all the wonders He created just for us to enjoy, along with the thoughts of those who made this pass many years prior. Thinking of all the hardships they experienced, including wild animals, lack of food, bitter cold and even death. i often wonder how we can complain so much after all they went through, in order to have a better life for them and us.

On one of our annual trips to visit Ruth, we had quite and experience, that i am sure none of us will forget. Fred, Franz, Jeff and i, arrived on a Saturday morning, staying overnight, and i wanted all of us, to attend church with Ruth the next day. Once again, not listening to the wise words of my husband, in that, a storm was coming, we did not have snow tires or chains and it would be best for us to leave early Sunday morning. i insisted we stay and attend church. Fred reluctantly gave in to my pleas, (not please, but pleas). When will i ever learn?

After church, we made our return trip over the pass, when snow began to drift lightly on the windy mountain curves ahead of us. The snow became heavier and heavier, we could hardly see the road in front of us. Fred decided we should turn back to Carson and purchase chains for the car, so we could make it back home over the pass. As he watched for traffic to clear and a place to turn the car in the opposite direction, he lost control of the wheel due to the snow and no traction. All i remember is embracing our sons and praying, somehow the Lord would send His angels and get us out of this mess. The car went up a rocky embankment, and as we peered down across the treacherous road, there lie a deep canyon. What seemed like forever was probably only minutes, as the car came back down on the roadway going back toward Carson. There was no oncoming traffic as we crossed the road; what a God send. Now, we needed to get down off the mountain, and to Carson. The road was now covered with snow, three to four inches deep. Fred tried following in the path of the traffic ahead of us, and, soon, when that ceased, we were in the hands of the Lord. i mean that, because Fred said, " I have no control of the wheel and our car." i quickly laid my hands on his over the steering wheel and prayed the Lord would get us down to safety.

We arrived safely in Carson and went directly to the store to purchase the needed snow chains. There was only one set left and they were cables, but they fit our car, another blessing. Fred put them on and they took us safely back over the mountain pass. Once again, i learned to listen to my husband, what a lesson. i'm still learning.

Months later, Fred noticed the tires on our car were wearing at a fast uneven rate. i took the car in for new tires. As the serviceman put the car on the overhead rack, he said, "Ma'am, where have you been with this car?" He went on, " Wherever it was, it's a miracle anyone came out of this alive." He showed me the underneath of the car, explaining why he made such a frightening statement. i told him what had happened, his words were confirmation. But my words to him were a witness of how a Mighty God is mindful of each one of us. **And even the very hairs of your head are all numbered." Matthew 10:30.**

That was the last trip we made as a family over the pass. But on another occasion, our Circle XX Bible Study group, which Ruth had been a part of, decided we'd carpool to see Ruth. The drive was gorgeous, as usual. Ruth, being the careful person she was, locked up her home and went with all of us to the Casino for lunch. Upon returning to her home, she realized she had locked the keys to her home in the house. There was only one alternative and that was the small doggie door for someone to crawl through, and open the door to her home. i was the smallest in size, and without hesitation, all eyes turned on me. My Mom, who was with us, wasted

225

no time and took a picture of the event. Once i crawled through the doggie door, and got inside the kitchen, i looked out the window, just waving to all the ladies. Yes, of course, i opened the door to let them in.

Sometime after that trip, i received a brief letter from Ruth; she was not doing well, lots of pain in her abdomen. It wasn't long before a friend and i made the drive to say our last good-bye's, to a wonderful friend. Yes, cancer had taken her life at the age of eighty.

i was thankful, the summer before her eightieth birthday, her family had a lovely birthday celebration for Ruth at a beautiful park in Nevada. My brother and his family were also in the area at the same time, so we made plans to meet with them. Our combined children, with my Mom, and all of us, made some great family memories. The Lord is so good; it's those unplanned meetings that make life so special.

Being a Cosmetologist has given me the honor of meeting and making many wonderful friends. The one who comes to mind is Grandma (that's what i called her). She was one hundred and three, when she died. She lived in a cement house not far from our home; the story, she told me of the cement house, was a delight to hear from her sweet lips. It seemed her husband, who had long since passed, lived in Sonora before their marriage, and his home was lost to a fire. He moved to Calaveras County, where he built another home that burned to the ground as well. So he decided the next one, he would build with cement, so a fire couldn't destroy it. Problem was, there was no cement to be found in the area, so he purchased cement from Germany, (prior to the Panama Canal), meaning it went around the Horn of South America. Some years later, after he built his cement home, cement was discovered just a few miles down the road from their home. Later it became the cement plant. Their home and barn were also used as a way station, back in the eighteen hundreds. Stories like this always fascinated me.

Grandma loved our sons, and when Jeff was young, i would take him with me to do Grandma's hair. She didn't drive, so this was convenient for her. As bonus to us, she always served us a homemade meal. One of Jeff's favorites was her pomegranate jelly; she'd let him eat a small jar if he wished. Of course Jeff loved going with me and having his fill of pomegranate jelly.

Grandma lived on the ranch for quite a number of years, and her family faithfully visited and brought her the things she needed. The day came when she had to go into a convalescent home. i went to the home and asked if i could do her hair, and was offered the job to do all the clients hair who resided in the home, if i so desired. i told the owner, i would go home and pray and talk it over with my husband. After much prayer and discussion, we decided i could work one day a week since i was already working in our Shop at home. This opened yet another door for me to serve others with the love of Christ.

The owner of the home was very kind and generous and gave me my own shop, with equipment and anything i needed, and to top it off, she did not charge me rent. She even offered meals, and our sons could come after school and wait until i finished work. It was amazing.

One afternoon i went to visit Grandma in the home and she told me she was cold. A dear customer from the shop at home, hand crocheted a gorgeous afghan for me that i kept in our car. i immediately went and got the afghan and placed it over Grandma's legs. She thanked me and said, "Now, I must give you something in return." i told her that was not necessary. She insisted saying, "I was taught, when someone gives you a gift you must give them one in return." She reached in her meager belongings and presented me with a lovely brooch. i was so touched and pleased and have kept the gift as a constant reminder of her kind words, and try to practice what she has taught me: to give when you receive. Once again, i learned a lesson in giving. **"...remembering the words the Lord Jesus Himself said: 'It is more blessed to give than to receive.' "** Acts 20:35c.

As i had mentioned earlier, the Lord had given me a new ministry; speaking at funerals or celebrations of one's life. One such one i will always remember, and wish to share with you, the reader, are the workings of the Holy Spirit. My Mom and i went with a dear friend to visit her husband who was in a rehabilitation center. Our friend asked if i would bring my scissors and cut her husband's hair, which i did, and i knew as i was cutting it, this would be the last haircut he received on earth. Within a couple of weeks his wife called us, to tell of his death. We drove to her home to comfort her and give our condolences. She asked Fred if he would be a pallbearer, which he agreed. Later, asking me, as we were leaving, "What is a Polar Bear?" i explained, and his reply was, "He was a big man, i can't carry his casket." i explained further. i thought Fred understood, but when the day of the service arrived, well, he still wasn't quite sure exactly what was expected of him.

Never the less our friend and i went for a walk when we were visiting, and she turned to me and asked if i would do her husbands eulogy. Of course without hesitation i agreed, but wanted to know more about him. She was thankful and knew she could count on me. So we sat down, i took notes about her husband who fought in WW II, in the German army, noting he had seen Hitler during his time of service. His life was very interesting and I was hearing it from the German side, instead of the American side.

On the day of his service, we arrived at the funeral home, the pallbearers were directed to place the casket in the hearse. That's when Fred once again turned to me and said, " I can't lift that thing with him in it, into the hearse." i pointed to the other five men who would assist him, he was relieved. We were then handed signs to place on our cars that said "Funeral Procession," but Fred refused. So, i asked him to please put on our headlights and follow the procession. Once again he refused. We proceeded to follow, but it was not soon enough, because we lost the procession. We didn't know where the church was or where the service was to take place, and the wife of the deceased told me to arrive early, as the Priest, (whom i'd never met), wanted to speak briefly with me. Looking up and across the road where the Police officer was holding traffic for the procession, (not us), he had let the procession go by and we were held back, oops. We saw a caravan of cars going up a steep hill. i quickly told Fred, step on it, and follow that caravan. We arrived at the church just as the pallbearers were removing the casket to take it into the church. i told Fred to go ahead and get out and help, i'd find a parking place.

After finding a spot to park, i grabbed my Bible and ran to the church. By this time, everyone was seated in the church and as i entered you could hear a pin drop, and there i was, trying to move quickly, yet quietly, into a pew without being noticed, right. All heads, so it seemed, turned in my direction. i found a seat not next to Fred, as i usually did, he was seated in the front of the church with the family and other ushers.

The Priest went to the pulpit and gave the invocation. Then, looking directly at me, said; "Now, Mrs. Bodenmüller is going to share with you about the deceased." I was shocked that he would even know who i was, or where i was seated. That had to be the beginning of the working of the Holy Spirit, because after that everything was so amazing!!!

i approached the front of the church to share the eulogy. Now, all eyes were on me, and every word i spoke. After sharing, i then said to the congregation, "i am going to sing a song and those of you who know it, please join in." Without words or music in front of me, i sang the Lord's Prayer, a Capella. Because the deceased, his wife and family, and most present were of German decent, i presented it in German. Well, no one joined in; they all just stared in utter amazement. i knew the Holy Spirit was ever present within me that day, as i sang, not missing a beat. The Holy Spirit is always with us as believers, but this time i was not grieving Him by doing as He asked me. i spoke and sang with such power and confidence, it could only be from Him.

When i completed the song, my dear surprised husband, Fred, seated at the front of the church, was the only one who stood up and applauded. i nodded my gratefulness to him, and quietly took my seat near the center of the church.

Once we reached the cemetery, the widow of the deceased said to me, "You, never cease to amaze me." She had no idea i was going to sing the Lord's Prayer in German. Her sweet son-in-law approached me and said, " My sister sings opera and you have done much better than she, today, and in German." His wife added, "Yes, she did, but she had a good teacher, Fred." i told them," Fred had no idea what i was doing and i had taken the words from a German Bible a friend had given us, and with Bible in hand would go out on our deck and sing unto the Lord." They were absolutely amazed.

After the burial, we went to a friend's home to share in food and drink. The widow used real silverware, dinnerware and cloth napkins, something i believe she did in honor of her late husband. i offered to say the blessing before we ate, and when i finished, a bell jingled from a wind chime. That reminded me of the angel getting his wings in the movie, It's A Wonderful Life[17]. So ended a remarkable day, a day i shall not forget how the Holy Spirit led and guided me. Oh, how i wish i could live each and every day in such a manner.

Kiyoko, was another dear friend, born and raised in Japan. She and her husband Jean', who was born and raised in France, were the family Fred, Franz and i would stay with, after our little camp trailer was hit by the dozer (shared earlier). After Jean' died, Kiyoko and her son Lawrence, moved to Copperopolis. Little known to her or i, she would live right next door to a very dear Christian friend of mine: Dorothy and her elderly mother. But this was all in the Lord's plan, because it was Dorothy, who would take Kiyoko to church and eventually, lead her into the saving grace of Jesus Christ. i had been and was planting seeds of faith for years, but the Lord would use Dorothy to bring her into the 'fold'.

Kiyoko was very kind hearted and generous. Once she became a believer, she told me her family in Japan disowned her. This broke her sweet gentle spirit and heart, and many times she would tell me with her lovely accent; "I think, i go back to believing like family, easier, and family care about me, then." i would re-assure her that we and all born again believers were her family now, and that we loved and cared about her.

i so wish i could have been there for her, during her last days on earth, it was difficult making contact with her for reasons i'd rather not say. Besides we had our hands full, caring for our sweet granddaughter; Laurel Shea. But, thank the Lord, Kiyoko's church family and her sweet daughter and grandchildren were there for her.

At one point, she shared with me, while she was in Japan during WW II, and how her grandfather would tell her to go to the American missionaries. He would say, " Go to them and learn of their American God, Jesus." Her grandfather would literally sneak her off, to learn of this American God, Jesus. She added that during this time, due to the bombs, the war and filth, she lost sight in both of her eyes and wore rags wrapped around her head and across her little eyes for almost a year. Then one day, the rags were to be removed. Her grandfather reminded her that the American God, Jesus would heal her. As the rags were removed from this little girl's eyes, she began to see and remembered what her grandfather had told her, she gained full eyesight. A seed was planted and i believe this experience helped her, even more, to invite Jesus Christ into her heart and life.

Fred and I were grateful we were there as she experienced, first the sudden death of her husband, and then later, her beloved son Lawrence. Lawrence had just graduated from High School with honors and was accepted in the United States Navy, in computer technology. He was a very intelligent young man. It was the summer just after his graduation, when we received the call early in the morning from our dear Kiyoko, that Lawrence

231

met death's door after being thrown as a passenger from the back of a motorcycle.

We were all devastated, he was like a nephew to us and a big brother to our sons. We all handle death and illness differently. Fred immediately got sick to his stomach and i just broke down in tears. How do young boys handle it? Franz and Jeff were quiet, not understanding, and deep sorrow welled in their young hearts.

Our Circle XX Women's Bible study group helped prepare the food for the celebration of Lawrence's life. As a result of serving, one of the ladies began attending church on a regular basis. The High School Lawrence had graduated from just a few months prior, sent a bus loaded with students, from throughout the county, to his service. The service was held in the old church in Copperopolis on a hot summer day, with no air conditioning.

When the minister got up to speak, he began with, 'we never know what tomorrow will hold' and told of a man we knew well, who had gone for a walk that morning, and didn't return home. When his wife asked others to help find him, he was found and had perished while on his walk. When the Pastor mentioned his name, Franz just stared at me in utter shock. Here, he had just lost a dear friend, and now this announcement, of another dear friend, who had, at one time taken our sons and i flying over our county in his plane. Now, he too was gone. He was a devout Christian, which gave us peace, because he was in the presence of Jesus. **We are confident, I say, and would prefer to be away from the body and at home with the Lord." 2 Corinthians 5:8.**

Whatever was said or done after that shocking news, i do not remember. i just know my dear sweet Kiyoko, without a tear in her almond shaped eyes, greeted each and every person who attended her beloved son's service. The months that followed she would shed many tears for her son, and would call me and say in her lovely accent; " I cry today, miss Lawrence." i would tell her, that it was o.k. for her to cry for the loss of her son. The

232

Japanese are much like the Germans, in that they are very proud, yet humble. A Japanese neighbor would tell Fred, "We get 'long good Fred, because we fight in war together. We, speak same, same, with monotone." She and Fred would agree and laugh.

At the reception after the service, a young man with a cast on his arm, went passed Kiyoko and i. She turned to me and said in her broken English, "He do fine, he only have broken arm." i immediately responded, " Kiyoko, do you mean that he, is the young man who drove the motorcycle your son was riding with, when the accident occurred?" She nodded, 'yes', and did not show or have, any bitterness or anger, toward him. That, my friend, is the working of the Holy Spirit. She was a true believer in Christ.

Kiyoko and i remained friends for years after the death of her precious son, and i kept in contact with her daughter and grandchildren. Kiyoko, did not have much, but was a very giving loving soul. She no longer had her driver's license, so i would take her shopping, but not without her always taking me out for lunch, and then showering me with little gifts of love as we shopped. Many a time, unknowingly, i would give her the exact gift she was giving me, showing our love for one another. i miss her and our special times together.

Several years after her son's death, she got cancer. On one of our shopping trips, she stepped out of our car and lit up a cigarette. i took her aside and with deep love in my eyes and compassion in my heart, told her i would not continue to pray for her healing of cancer, if she did not stop smoking. She was not very happy with me, but never smoked around me again. Being around addicted people, i understood the power an addition can have on a person, and it is only through our faith in Jesus, that can break the bondage. i continued to pray and love my Kiyoko.

Later, when our Jeffrey and Laurel Shea came to live with us, and helping Jeff care for Laurel, (our granddaughter), i was not able to visit Kiyoko as much as i liked. Many times i tried calling her, but could never get through. The last time i saw and spoke with her, i just stopped by her home on my return trip from Sonora. She was frail, weak and very ill; her daughter was caring for her. After that visit, her daughter Karen called to say her mother was so thankful I had come by to visit her.

Within a few months, Karen called and told me her mother had died and she was going to have a small burial of Kiyoko's remains at the little pioneer cemetery in Copperopolis, and would i come. Without question or hesitation, i went to the cemetery, meeting just several of her dear friends, daughter and children. Her daughter asked me to dig the small area to place the urn, and help set Kiyoko's remains in the ground. With tears in my eyes, i reluctantly did as she asked. Later, we had a celebration of life at the little church Kiyoko attended, and where we had celebrated her son's life. As difficult as it was, i felt privileged, once again, to speak on my dear friend and sister-in-Christ's; Kiyoko's behalf.

There were many new friends i would meet through Kiyoko; one was Suzanne. Oh, how i loved this precious gal, she was much younger than us group of gals, but the stories she could tell were amazing. i remember when she invited Jesus into her heart and was baptized in the lake, along with many others, who the Lord directed me to share Jesus. She loved animals, and when she came to have her hair done, she would bring special gifts and treats to our German shepherd and Yorkie. Suzanne had a big loving heart, but she had some sort of illness we never discussed. i just loved her for who she was, in her sweet and tender heart.

During this time, Jeff was living in Arizona and working for the airlines, so Fred and i could fly, stand-by. We decided we'd fly to visit Fred's oldest and dearest friend, Mike, who lived in Buffalo, New York. This would be my first trip back to the Eastern part of the United States to visit. i had called to check on Suzanne, before our departure, she did not sound well, and i told her she should go to the doctor. We flew into Pennsylvania, rented a car, and drove to Buffalo, New York. The East coast is so much like Europe,

234

in that the states are smaller and it doesn't take much time to go from one state to the next; it was just like Europe, going from one Country to the next. The scenery reminded us a lot of Europe as well, it was summer, the grass and trees were so green and flourishing. i was especially thrilled upon seeing a part of the United States i'd never seen before. As i said, it reminded me of Europe, but this was America. After studying so much about our magnificent land, now i was able to visit a part i had always dreamed of seeing. It was really happening. i love traveling, not only for the sights, but to meet the people and spend time with them, and learn about their life styles. The Lord has created us all different, yet alike in many ways. Especially, with a void in our hearts that only He can fill. Many a time i have been told, 'no one is a stranger to me.' The Lord created us all, and all so very special, and just love to meet and greet anyone the Lord puts in my path.

Mike was delighted to have us visit, and was excited about showing us around and introducing us to part of his family. Fred and i went for walks each day in the beautiful country, taking in the fresh air. Seems strange, when we think of New York, most of us think of the Big City and lights, traffic and people. Just like many think of California as Hollywood, Los Angeles, San Francisco, San Jose and the business of the Bay Area. This was not so, in upper state New York, like Northern California, it was country, peaceful and quiet.

Buffalo is not far from one of the many Wonders of the World, Niagara Falls. i had never been to see this wonder, the Lord had created for us humans to enjoy, but Fred had been there several times when he lived in Canada. He was excited about taking me and showing me the falls. Yes, they are amazing, something i will always treasure in my heart. Different from the Grand Canyon, Bryce, Zion, Yosemite, Yellowstone and the many wonders the Lord has created, yet awe inspiring.

We enjoyed spending time with Mike and listening to his World WarII stories. Yes, he's the one who actually gave the P.O.W.'S, he was to oversee in Germany, the knives or whatever, to make those wonderful woodcarvings i talked about earlier. He was the one who was in the **Battle of the Bulge**[18.] Fred and i spoke with him recently, to thank him for serving our Country. As i write this, Mike just turned 93 in May 2014.

On our trip home, we stayed in Arizona with Jeff, his wife and our little Laurel and Franz, which was a delight. Then Fred and i flew home to California. Upon returning, there were quite a few messages on the answering machine,; one in particular, was from Suzanne's sister. i immediately called her to hear that Suzanne had died. i was shocked, yet wanting to know when the service was going to be held and where. Her sister said they were unable to get a minister to do the service and the Lord led me to offer my services. Her sister accepted and with the Lord's help, prepared to speak at Suzanne's service. It was to be held the very next day. Which didn't give me much time, but the Lord provides, and we must trust Him. i was thankful to be home in time for her service.

Another dear friend and sister-in-Christ, Berni and i, went together to Suzanne's service. i remembered to take a pottery piece that Suzanne had made and was going to throw out, because she didn't like what she had done. It was of Jesus and the children, as the Bible teaches how the children went to Jesus in, **Luke 18:16 "... Let the children come to me, and do not hinder them, for the kingdom of God belongs to such as these..."** It was perfect, the Lord led me to use this as a visual when i spoke at Suzanne's service; she was much like a child, and this lovely piece she made, portrayed her life.

After the service, we went to the hall for the close and celebration of Suzanne's life. It was there we met some of her friends and family that neither Berni nor i knew. On the way home i shared with Berni how disappointed i was because we did not meet all the people she had told us about. Oh yes, some of the names were the same, but where was the doctor and his small daughter, the many characters she told us about? i came to

236

realize these must have been a wonderful world of fantasy of this dear sweet child of God. Oh, how i loved her and would miss her and her beautiful stories that were so captivating.

Recently i was going through the first Bible i studied from, and was surprised to find the many eulogies the Lord used me to speak. i'd like to share a few more of these special people, who touched my life and others, in so many ways. Ray, was a sweetheart, he had polio since he was a young boy, but worked three jobs at one time to support his dear wife and six lovely children. When we met he and his wife, he asked if our sons could help them on their small ranch. Franz, was the first to comply with weed whacking. Then our Jeff worked almost daily for Ray. One day, Jeff came home and said, " Mom, i think Ray just likes my company, i really don't do a lot for him and sometimes feel guilty taking any money." i was so thankful for Jeff's honesty, but encouraged him to continue helping Ray and if he paid him, then that was his way of showing appreciation.

Ray was very kind and generous with Jeff. At the time i was home schooling Jeff and he was invited to a Prom, which was unusual for a homeschooler. Of course we did not have a suit for him to attend the Prom, so in order to save money, Jeff asked Ray if he had a suit he could borrow. i have a great picture of Ray standing proudly in his workshop with Jeff beside him in Ray's suit.

Ray had a Portuguese ancestry as i have. At one point Berni was doing an ancestry research on Ray's Portuguese side of the family, and told me that part of his ancestry's last name was; Rose. i just knew it, he must be related to me, and i told her my grandmother on my father's side's, last name was Rose. She presented me with a picture of a couple, dated in the late 1800's or early 1900's, with the last name of Rose. i gave it to my mom and she did know who these people were. One day i will do more research, as the Lord permits. i realize that most of us are curious about our backgrounds, but we must face the fact, we are all related to Adam and Eve. And of course

237

their sin nature, they passed on to us. In the scope of all this, what really matters is our personal relationship to Jesus Christ.

Jeff went to the Prom, and called us at one or so in the morning, to tell us he had problems with the truck. We drove to meet him, called a tow truck and waited until three or so in the morning, before it came. Oh, the memories of the things we do for our wonderful children. Today, as i look back, i wish we could do this and many of these things, no matter how difficult it seemed at the time, all over again. Berni and i became very good friends. She would tell me she did not have a best friend, that many friends were her best friend, in different ways. i liked that and agreed. Today, i do not like to say i have one best friend, because each is like a best friend in a different way. Berni, and i had good times; we grew in our faith, each week we would meet at she and Ray's home, for a home cooked meal, Bible study, family videos and fellowship. Those times were so special and i miss them. Although, we attended different churches, we had a great love for our Lord Jesus and were able to agree not to disagree. She was also, part of the group of us gals who met for birthday celebrations. On one of my birthdays, i requested a 'Tea Party,' which Berni put together so beautifully. We had fun shopping and spending time together. i am not a shopper, per se, but we loved just being together. On one of our shopping trips, we were in the arts and crafts department, when i saw a sweatshirt that was made for Christmas, that said J O Y. Berni's middle name was Joy, and i had told her it stood for J esus, O thers' and Y ourself. She liked the sweatshirt so much, without my knowledge, went home and made one for me. i still have it and enjoy wearing it during the Christmas season and, each time, thinking of my dear friend, Berni. Once, we were in a Christian bookstore and i saw the picture that depicts the Trinity, The Son Jesus, wrapping his arms around the believer, as if to say; 'Welcome home', the Hands of God encircling the Son and believer, and finally the Dove; The Holy Spirit, over the top of the Son and believer. When my birthday arrived, Berni presented me with that lovely picture; it now hangs in our home, welcoming all. She was like that, just loving and giving.

The last time i saw Ray, was while he was lying on his bed holding his hand over his throat, having a difficult time breathing, yet speaking to me with the greatest effort. His words were sweet and soft, as he struggled to say, "You know us Portigees, we have to talk." i knew what he meant, he knew it, too; he was dying and that was his way of accepting the fact. But i didn't want him to die and told him he would be fine.

That very afternoon, as i was having lunch with a dear friend, another dear friend told me that she had received a call that Ray had passed on that day. i just couldn't believe it, and later as i was driving home, the full moon was out and i was talking to the Lord about Ray, and was he safe in His loving arms?

i didn't go directly home, i stopped to see Berni. There peering out the window was their beloved poodle Sammy, he was waiting for his masters arrival. That sweet little dog was Ray's sidekick, oh he loved Berni too, and she adored Sammy, but there was a special bonding between he and Ray. Sammy would sit on the top of the sofa for many months after, just staring out the window and waiting for Ray.

Berni, asked me to speak at Ray's service, as well. He lived an interesting life, being an announcer at the Fremont Dragstrip. He too, knew my half- brother; Leslie Joseph. i finally realized exactly what Ray meant when he made the comment about not being able to speak; his obituary read something like; with his song bird voice. He was a special man; i will always have fond memories of him.

Ray would tell me, how he remembered his mother praying, and maybe that is what he needed to do more, was pray, especially for his children. He loved his children and grandchildren. i remember visiting he and Berni, and coming in while he was on the phone with his children, just to see how they were doing, and to hear their voice. That left quite an impression on me, and to keep in practice the importance of communicating with your loved ones on a regular basis.

Jeff not only worked for Ray, but thought of him with love and inspiration. Jeff was now living in Arizona and came home for his wedding, to be held in Copperopolis. When he arrived, he said to us, "Why, couldn't Ray have hung in there until i came home?" He wanted him to be present at his wedding, which wasn't to be, it was not the Lord's plans. For the Bible tells us in **Psalm 139:16b " All the days ordained for me were written in Your book before one of them came to be."** Not long after our dear friend Ray passed, his wife Berni became very ill. Personally, i didn't think she would die so quickly. i guess i just didn't want to accept her illness and was in denial. She was one of my dearest, closest, friends and i just couldn't think of her being gone. We had so many good times together, but it was no longer to be as such. i remember receiving the regretted call from her son, that she too, had passed.

This time i asked if i could not only speak at her service, but wanted to include the children she and i ministered to over the years. The family lovingly agreed, and the children i could muster from our past Good News Club, and I, sang one of Berni's favorites; **Jesus Loves Me**.

i believe losing Berni was one of most difficult losses i suffered. But that was not to be the end, i would experience the loss of many other close friends and the closest was my mother.

The book of Ecclesiastes states it well;

"There is a time for everything,

and a season for every activity under heaven:

a time to be born and a time to die,

a time to plant and a time to uproot,

a time to kill and a time to heal,

a time to tear down and a time to build,

a time to weep and a time to laugh,

a time to mourn and a time to dance,

a time to scatter stones and a time to embrace and

a time to refrain,

a time to search and a time to give up,

a time to keep and a time to throw away,

a time to tear and a time to mend a time to be silent

and a time to speak

a time to love and a time to hate,

a time for war and a time for peace." Ecclesiastes 3:1-8.

Two more wonderful friends and neighbors come to mind as i write this section on 'Friends'. One was to go home to be with the Lord and his wife would move from the area. They were such a pair, i'd like to share some of their antics, of which i am confident they would appreciate, besides giving us the joy of laughter.

They both loved the Lord Jesus and were/are devout Christians. They were also from the Bay Area/Silicon Valley; we shared many fond memories of days gone by in that fertile valley i shared with you, the reader, early on in this book. They had a wonderful apricot tree in their yard in Sunnyvale, and would make jam and dried cots from it's fruit. Like us, and many others we have met here in the Gold Country, they too, grew tired of the many changes in the Bay Area, and desired a more peaceful life. It is my personal belief that the closer one lives to nature, the more one experiences the reality of God, our Creator, and want to draw closer to Him. Many, who have come to visit, share that same feeling with us while here. As a matter of fact, Joyce's words to me were; "I was coming up your drive-way to stay with you and Fred for a couple of days and i began to cry. The reason is; your home is like coming home for me." Another friend, Eva, who would come to visit said, " 'Each time we drove over the cattle guard, I immediately had feelings of peace and love that lasted until we drove back over the cattle guard upon leaving.' she went on, ' I used to think it was because there was

241

so much love in the Bodenmüller home. Now I know I was feeling the presence of God.' Yet another dear friend said, "Opening your home to us is so warm and peaceful. I can tell lots of prayer occurs in this home, there is a quiet, peace upon it." Andrea. Yes, we do spend quite a bit of time in prayer in and around our home, but it's never enough. The Word of God says; **"Pray continually." 1 Thessalonians 5:17.** It's true, the closer we draw to the Lord, the closer He draws to us. The Book of James says it better; **"Come near to God and He will come near to you." James 4:8a.** i am so very thankful the friends mentioned above felt the very presence of the Lord in our home, and pray, until He takes me home, it will be as such. Only the Lord knows how many other lives our home has touched and i am thankful to do His will. He has given me the gift of hospitality and i want to use it to the best of my ability for His glory; because, as the youngest, i wasn't able to do so. The Book of Romans says; **"Share with God's people who are in need. Practice hospitality." Romans 12:13. 1 Peter 4:9** says it this way; **"Offer hospitality to one another without grumbling."**

Opening our home to others, reminds me of the many excuses we can find, to not show hospitality to others. Such as: my home isn't clean enough, I don't have the proper food, others are better cooks than I, or I can't do it as well as so and so. i once heard, that an excuse is, just plain old, not wanting to do something, so we make excuses. But when we look at the above verses from the Bible, it seems the Lord is making it very clear to "Offer hospitality." Another verse that comes to mind is; **"I can do everything through Him, who gives me strength." Philippians 4:13.** It is my hope, to instill in all of us, the importance of 'offering hospitality.'

There i go again, off on my own tangent. Hopefully, i keep your interest and where am i going next. Let's see, oh yes, the couple i mentioned earlier from the Bay Area, purchased land not far from us and built a nice home. They were both originally from Europe and were very thankful to be in the United States and practice the freedoms they so dearly loved. Before meeting them, he told me he and his sons had driven past our ranch, on the way to theirs, when one of his sons, looking up at our home, said, "Wow, look at that home, they must be rich." The father corrected him and said, "They must be hard workers." Perspective, we see most things in different ways. The father's comment of course, was correct, hard workers. Fred and i both knew what hard work was, and what one could accomplish by working hard, and we passed that on to our sons as well. Interesting how each of us perceives things differently.

It wouldn't be long and this dear servant of Jesus, and his sons, would soon join us for dinners, and fellowship. Many times the father would stay for hours, and he and i would discuss theology. One of our favorite Pastors was; Dr. J. Vernon McGee, the very one i would listen to on the radio on my way to work, years prior. Eventually, we would meet the rest of his family, including his lovely wife who would send delicious homemade cookies and food along with her husband and sons. Her husband was afraid she was too much of 'blue blood' and would not enjoy the country life. She proved him wrong. She and i became the closest of friends once she moved here permanently. We still keep in contact, although she has moved into a retirement home, some distance from us. i am in hopes to visit her soon.

When he called her a 'blue blood', i did not understand the terminology, until she explained it to me. It seems, as she told me, she was raised in a very influential home; she was not even allowed to associate with children who were not of her caliber in society. When WWII broke-out, she and her mother had to flee to Germany for safety. They were placed in camps, until their denomination was able to send them to America. Her mother was a wonderful seamstress and made clothing for their denomination. The daughter, my dear friend, became a servant to the ones who brought them over to America. This was very humbling for both mother and daughter. In saying this, she learned we must all humble ourselves, as Jesus did on the cross. Not one of us is better than the other. As Billy Graham once said, " We must all stand naked before the Lord." She, like many of us, learned more about humility over the years.

We loved them both, their children and grandchildren; they became a big part of our lives. The father, we referred to as the 'absent minded professor.' He was very intelligent, yet, like the professor, was simple, loving and kind. Some of the stories that were shared of his mishaps were funny. He had a great sense of humor. i guess in some ways, he was like a male "Lucy". Please allow me to share some of the humorous antics that were his, and his alone. He and his wife had purchased a new screen door, which they had tied down on the roof of their car. They kept asking the people at the lumber store, where they purchased it, 'would it make it home on an hour drive without problems?' They were assured it would, but by the time they arrived from that long drive home, the door was nothing but a mangled mess. Another time, as they were coming home, the dear wife said she saw sparks flying beside their car and heard a terrible racket, and asked her husband to pull off the road to check it out. He reluctantly did so, finding the bumper had come loose, was bent, and part of it was driven into the front tire with the rest dragging on the ground causing sparks as they drove. Someone came by to offer a helping hand, and asked how far away they lived? The husband answered, "Just a few miles." It was more like eight, and he was going to drive home. The man who stopped, insisted on changing the tire, even though it was a tiny spare, it was better than driving with the bumper stuck in the tire. The kind man changed the tire, and our friends did make it home, safe and sound. As one of their sons said to his mother, "The angels have protected you all these years." i can relate to that, and want to remember to pray each and every time our car or truck leaves our driveway.

Another crazy episode of our dear "Lucy" friend was, the youth group was selling Christmas trees at our church and his wife wanted him to drive the six miles, or so, to purchase a tree. They both made the trek to town to purchase the tree, but they did not tie it down, and, as usual, left the tailgate of their truck down. Much to their dismay, when they reached home, and went to unload the tree, it was not in the truck. Her husband drove the road back, in search of their Christmas tree. i guess the Lord wanted to bless someone else with a tree for Christmas, because it was never to be found.

There was something about him that did not want to put the tailgate up, although we warned him many times to do so. As my mom and i were coming home one day, there on the road before us, lie pieces of sheet rock, and there ahead of us was our dear "Lucy" friend, with the tailgate down on his truck and pieces of sheet rock were falling out the back, as he dreamily drove along. When Fred arrived home he told me about the pieces of sheet rock along the road; i knew exactly what he was talking about. i am not sure if this was our "Lucy" friend's way of just not realizing what was happening, or his difficulty with hearing or whatever the case. He just brought us much joy and laughter; he himself laughed, too. As the Bible says in **Proverbs 17:22 "A cheerful heart is good medicine,…"**

i would love to tell you more of the crazy humorous things this dear "Lucy" man did, knowingly or unknowingly, but i will close with these, that the Lord has laid on my heart to share. We live in a world with so much serious stuff; it's good to reflect on the humor.

Most of us collect one thing or another. For me it is teapots, not that i cared about collecting anything for that matter, except perhaps Bibles. The teapot escapade just seemed to happen when my sisters got together some years ago, and purchased a lovely teapot for me, for my birthday. Other friends, caught wind of the gift, and knowing how much i like herbal teas, they got me teapots, i was on a roll. With teapots for my birthday, Christmas gifts and on it went, until i finally had such a collection, that Fred had to build two special shelves for all of them. Then it stopped; no one purchased another teapot for me. i was grateful, yet relieved, after all, one can only use so many teapots.

Once i received all these lovely treasures, i thought 'what am i going to do with all of them?' Well, the answer came when i received a lovely teacup and saucer from a dear friend, who went home to be with Jesus. A sweet note came with the teacup from her daughter-in-law and son, telling, how her grandmother gave her a teacup and saucer and thus began her collection. The note went on to say, the set was from her collection and i was one of the chosen ones who was a part of her life, and they wanted to present it to me in remembrance of her and to "drink from the Living Water," Christ. i was surprised to be thought of in this way, yet honored to be counted as a dear friend.

Wow, what a great idea, so, i have asked each special person who enters our home to choose one of the teapots, and at a certain time, i will present it to the one whose name is on the piece of paper in the tea pot. Hopefully, they will be blessed and remember me, and our times together as we shared a cup of tea. What a blessing!!!

The dear lady whose teacup and saucer i was blessed with, had a special place in my heart and life. She and her husband were both very devout believers in Christ, and were married for quite some time, and had not been blessed with children. There was a young boy, who they knew and watched, as he traversed their property to school each day. Sometime later, the young boy's mother was killed in a tragic auto accident, leaving several siblings and her husband. In those days, there was nowhere to place the children except the local jail yard, until someone would possibly adopt them. This couple decided, (i'm sure, with much prayer), to adopt, at least, the young boy. They took him in and raised him in a wonderful Christian environment.

When this young man grew up, he became the Superintendent of Schools, and was sworn in, in the very room of the courthouse where the couple had adopted him. i was there when he was sworn in, and he testified, (that very statement)recalling that, he was just a boy going through the adoption procedure. Right here in this room. Now here he was again, only now he was being sworn in, to serve the people.

The reason i attended the swearing in, was, he had asked our young son Jeffrey, (about six or seven at the time), and his little friend, Jimmy, to be ushers for this important event. Now, as i think back, i wonder, did he choose these two little boys, remembering, he too was a little boy when he appeared in that same court room? Many times we think these are coincidences, but i think not; i believe this is a God incidence, and our son was part of this blessing. Whether that was the case or not, there was one proud mother of a precious little boy, who was chosen to serve as his usher. There stood our sweet son, all dressed up with the warm hand knitted light blue sweater his aunt in Germany had made and sent him. She had also made a matching one for his brother Franz. But this was Jeffrey's special day to wear the sweater; beneath it was a white shirt, and special pants and shoes for the occasion. i can see him now, as i write, standing proudly, handing out the schedule to each person as they entered the room.

We had met the new Superintendent Jeff was serving, at the church (the father of this man) his father had started; his father was now a retired minister. He was a patriarch in the church. Every Sunday he would be at the entrance doors of the foyer, ready to reach out to whomever's hand he could reach, just to greet and welcome them. There he stood, not straight anymore, but hunched over from years of toil as a carpenter, gardener and just a hard worker. He'd reach out with those wonderful gnarled hands and a twinkle in his aging eyes, to say; "Glad you're here, and welcome!" Oh, to have men of such faith, and strength in our churches today. Just knowing you are welcome in the House of God, what a blessing.

His wife, whom i mentioned earlier, was an excellent cook and homemaker. And could she ever play the organ; i can just hear it now as we entered the sanctuary for Sunday morning service. Occasionally on Sunday's, we were treated to not only hear her playing, but her son joined in with the piano. What harmony, what wonder and beauty; the Lord had gifted these two lovely souls to share with the congregation.

We were regular attendees, and i am sure the son kept his watchful eye on our sons as they grew into adults. It was during this time of his observation, i am sure he selected our Jeffrey and his friend Jimmy, to serve in his swearing-in, at the courthouse.

My not growing up in the church and understanding all of the in's and out's of Christianity; this was quite an experience for me. It is one that i have, and will continue to cherish, over the years. There were so many wonderful brothers and sisters in Christ i grew to know and love. And it is all because of their commitment to the Lord Jesus Christ and to one another that changed their lives and mine. i must tell you, the reader, being a Christian is the most wonderful experience you will ever have in your life. But it is also, the most difficult challenge you will ever have in your life. Yes, we are set free in Christ, but as the book of Romans states, we are not free to do, as we like. **"What shall we say, then? Shall we go on sinning so that grace may increase? By no means! We died to sin; how can we live in it any longer? Or don't you know that all of us who were baptized into Christ Jesus were baptized into His death? We were therefore buried with Him through baptism into death in order that, just as Christ was raised from the dead through the glory of the Father, we too may live a new life." Romans 6:1-4.** Galatians goes on to say; **"I have been crucified with Christ and I no longer live but Christ lives in me. The life I live in the body I live by faith in the Son of God, who loved me and gave Himself for me." Galatians 2:20.** Hallelujah!!!

Jumping into the fun person i can sometimes be, i will share with you about a long time friend of Fred and i; his name is Henry. He and Fred met years ago, when Fred first arrived in America. They met at a German restaurant in San Francisco. The first time i met Henry, his wife and two children, was when they lived in Los Gatos, California. In their backyard grew one of the oldest, mightiest Oak Trees in California. Henry said to me, with a gleam in his eye and smile on his face, " I remember you, when you came to visit us and climbed the old Oak Tree." He was very impressed with this young American girl of twenty, like a tomboy climbing the Oak. Later when we celebrated his sixty-fifth birthday, he would be in for yet another surprise.

i decided it would be fun to pop out of a huge cardboard box, at his birthday celebration and dance the hula. i didn't tell Fred my plans, so toting the cardboard box was out. On the day of Henry's birthday, i went into the bathroom, slipped into my swimsuit and Hawaiian costume, while asking a surprised Fred to watch the door. He still didn't know what i was up to, until i handed him a tape with Hawaiian music and a radio to play it on.

It was a beautiful November day, so all the guests were asked to step outside on Henry's deck, because his home was too small to hold everyone. i thought, this is perfect, outside on the deck. Well, as i stepped out to do my performance, the skies opened up and it began to rain. So, everyone was invited to go inside his home. They had set-up a huge table to try and seat everyone. Then, i came in, Fred started the music and i began my performance, with only space enough in a corner. Suddenly, everyone began clapping and saying, "Up on the table, up on the table, so we can all see you perform." i hesitated, but there was no stopping this mainly German crowd, insisting i get on the table and dance the hula. Finally, i gave in, but boy oh, boy was it hot dancing up there. After, a few numbers, i managed to get down from the table, with an applause and surprised look from Henry. Fred was amazed, yet proud of his wife's courage. It was fun. i performed the hula again for a dear gal friend on her fiftieth birthday. i believe i put the hula outfit away for awhile and i use it when our granddaughter's come to visit.

This chapter was spent on friends and friendships, i know i have not even touched on the many friends the Lord has so graciously blessed us with, during our years of living in the Gold Country. My dear friends, those of you who are reading this book, if i have missed mentioning you, believe me, it was not intentional. All of you will always have a very special place in my heart. i once heard a wonderful speaker named Joann, years later her son would become like a son to us; this was another one of our Lord's orchestrations. In her speech she said; "We have many chambers or rooms in our hearts. In each chamber holds a friend, and then another friend comes along. The new friend does not remove the old friend, because they each have their own chamber in our heart." So, for each one of you dear friends, there is a chamber in my heart just for you and i Praise and thank the Lord for each and every one of you and the part the Lord has given you in my life.

With that my dear friends, i will close with a verse from Proverbs, which is one of my favorites. **"A friend loves at all times,..." Proverbs 17:17**. And yet another verse; **"A man of many companions may come to ruin, but there is a friend Who sticks closer than a brother." Proverbs 18:24.** Yes, the Lord Jesus is the best friend any of us could ever ask for, and to have a relationship with Him is of utmost importance.

Chapter Twenty-Four

"I am making everything new."
Revelation 21:5

It is time for our sons to move on.
Have I given them the roots of faith in
Jesus, and now, the wings to fly on their
own? The tables are turned—now i am
caring for my mother after her injury.
i am now the parent, she is the child.

Well, well, well, that last chapter was a long one, probably because friends are so important to me. Most of us have heard the saying; 'You can choose your friends but you can't choose your family.' As another dear friend once said to me; "The family we have on earth is not necessarily the one we will have in Heaven." mmm, there's something to ponder. To take it a step further Jesus said; **"Enter through the narrow gate. For wide is the gate and broad is the road that leads to destruction, and many enter through it. But small is the gate and narrow the road that leads to life, and only a few find it." Matthew 7:13-14.**

i liked the verse because it spoke to me that the Lord had new beginnings for me; this is what i would like to share in this chapter.

Once again, i had everything planned out in my mind, and was truly expecting this to all work out according to my thoughts and plans. The Lord reminded me again; **"For My thoughts are not your thoughts, neither are your ways My ways," declares the Lord. Isaiah 55:8.** He is in total control; we just think we are in control. Oh, yes i admit sometimes i take the reigns and think, 'Let's go this way, or do this or that.' It isn't long before i say, "O.k., Lord i'm sorry. Please take the reigns." And of course the ride is a lot smoother, yes there are some bumps, ruts along the road, and mud from the rain. But then i am reminded of my dear Jeanette's words, "Honey, you have to have the rain in order to have the rainbow."

First, allow me to share my expectations. Franz, being the oldest of our two sons, i thought for sure he would be the one to move out of the home first, then Jeffrey would follow suit and then Fred would retire and we would enjoy life with just the two of us.

Here is what really happened. Jeff was now in his senior year of high school, in a home school program. He liked it very much and i loved it, it was great for him, he was getting his work done and he would soon graduate. He had taken on a job at a nearby pizza parlor, as well as working part time for our dear friend i mentioned earlier; Ray. Fred and i were happy to have him work and it was part of the requirement of his home school curriculum. Jeff still had his Christian punk rock band, in which he was the drummer, and a very good one. He also played drums for the church during the worship on Sunday. He was one happy, delightful young man and felt so good about himself, his accomplishments and his schooling. There was only one difficulty, he met a young girl while working at the pizza parlor, and they began to date. He brought her home to meet Fred, Franz and i. Well, i won't go there, but the Lord told me to love her and pray for her, which i did, we even did a brief Bible study together. At one time he brought her home and told me he prayed with her to accept the Lord, and they wanted to burn her non-Christian books in our burn barrel, which they did.

Prior to Jeff's graduation i was invited to travel with the teachers and staff of the home school, to speak at an event as a parent, on my thoughts of home schooling. The event was held in Monterey, California. i was delighted to attend this event, not only to represent the school, students and staff, but was able to use the gift the Lord had given me to speak. i opened my speech with the words from Harriet Beacher Stowe, who said, "The child's first classroom is a mother's heart."[19] Was she ever right on target. That is exactly where all learning begins. With her statement, i thought of some of the wonderful mother's in the Bible like; sweet gentle, Mary the mother of Jesus, Jochebed, who bore and nursed Moses, and Hannah who bore and nursed Samuel, only to name a few. As i think about Mary and giving birth to our Lord Jesus in that cold damp, animal shelter, that wonderful smelly stable. How she placed him in the manger, a feeding trough for the animals; she and Joseph were so poor they had nothing to wrap their newborn son, except swaddling clothes, or rags. Our Pastor brought it to our attention that our Savior was born in a feeding trough, and that's where we go to feed on Him through His Word the Bible. **'Then Jesus declared, "I am the bread of life. He who comes to me will never go hungry, and he who believes in me will never be thirsty." John 6:35.**

Then, there was Jochebed and Hannah who bore their sons and fed them at their breasts until they were about two or three years of age, which was customary for Jewish women during that time. And as i mentioned earlier in my writing, how one Pastor pointed out the importance of teaching children the first three years of their lives. And these two Jewish women, i am sure, taught them about the God of Abraham, Isaac and Jacob, until they were ready to give them up, one to Pharaoh's daughter to raise and the other to the priest Eli.

i thought of my dear sweet innocent mother, who didn't teach me about Jesus, but she taught me the basics of life. Like eating properly, manners, respect, potty training, walking and talking and so much more. Sometimes i wonder if she ever wished she didn't teach me how to talk. (For those who know me, you know how i love to talk). But when i was younger i didn't talk much, i was very shy. Then again, i am thankful she taught me, because now the Lord can use my speaking for His glory. Sometimes it's like when Charlie Brown said to Lucy, "It's time to wrap it up;"[20] meaning her talking. And i must take heed, to wrap it up.

i was pleased with the speech i gave at the Home Schooling event, and felt privileged and blessed to be able to travel with this wonderful group from the Home School. My reward as a parent was not only the speaking, but also the time we shared, an all expense paid trip, with wonderful meals in a seafood restaurant on the wharf, a lovely place to stay for the night, and the trip home. What a blessing, one i will remember for years to come.

Before Jeff graduated from the Home School, my mom and i made a trip to Arizona to spend time with my sister, Barbara. As i mentioned earlier in my writing, my sisters Josephine and Frances had married young men who i knew, and lived in Alviso, as i did at the time. So both sisters moved from San Jose to Alviso once they married these handsome men. Now that they lived within walking or riding-my- bicycle-distance from me, i got to know them once again.

But Barbara had a roommate, lived in San Jose and then moved to Southern California, so i really never had the privilege of knowing her as well. Although, i did stay with her in the apartment in San Jose once, and then in Los Angeles on Wilshire Blvd; she and her roommate both worked, so spent little time with me. But i still have fond memories of staying with them.

Going to visit her in Arizona would be a treat for both mom, Barbara and i. Little did i realize, this trip would have an affect on Franz and Jeff's lives. But i know and believe; the Lord is ultimately in control of everything.

Mom, the brave soul that she was, and i boarded the plane in Sacramento via Phoenix, Arizona. We were so excited to meet Barbara at the airport in Phoenix. The drive to her home in Cave Creek, Arizona, was amazing, with all the cacti, some in bloom and of course their native Saguaro Tree, a cacti that grows as high as seventy feet. Her home was nestled high in the Sonoran Desert of Arizona, where it is much cooler than Phoenix. The beauty of the desert is indescribable; it is breath taking, especially in the evening as the sun sets in its wondrous hues of pinks, reds, violets and blues.

Other than traveling through Arizona to see the Grand Canyon and the London Bridge while in our motor home in years past, this would be my first real trip of seeing the beauty of Arizona, and my mom's very first trip to see the sights. And the sights we did see, Barbara was very gracious taking us many places during our stay. We all enjoyed this special time together and would cherish this time for many years to come. The area in which she lived was known for being part of the Old West, with it's many old saloons, small little towns and Mexican flair in some of the areas. Western/American Indian type stores surrounded the area, and still do today, with their western wear, boots, saddles, and an array of the artifacts from the past and present. Something that mom and i liked as well, and Fred, when he would visit at another time, would appreciate, because that was one of the reasons he came to America. He remembered watching all the Westerns at the movies in Germany and wanted to be a part of that era.

The food was outstanding with a different kind of Mexican flair than in California, and of course the western type food of beans, beef, or chuck wagon type food reminiscent of the Old West. The portions were much more than any of us could eat, so we either shared portions or took home whatever we couldn't eat, to enjoy later for dinner.

My sister, unlike me, is an early riser, and was up watering her plants and doing chores before i could open my eyes. We went for early morning walks, because the heat in Arizona is so dry and intense, doing so later in the day, would make it almost impossible to even function. It reminded me of when Fred and i traveled to Spain, and how the workers started before the crack of dawn, took a Siesta mid day, and then started up later at night when the sun was setting. As for the walks my sis and i took, they were so special as we walked and talked about our lives. We grew closer in our relationship and got to know and love each other so very much. Reminds me of the time i spend each day with the Lord in prayer or reading His Word the Bible, and growing in relationship with Him.

During this time, i came to know the sister i really never knew before; she is so loving, giving, understanding, accepting and not critical. i learned she, like me, has the gift of encouragement. What a blessing to have such an encouraging sister. The time we spent together was good for our mom as well. Barbara went out of her way to make this a special time for all of us, a time of forgiveness and bonding. On one of our trips, she took us to see Sedona, Arizona. Sedona is a very peaceful city, with its rich red soil and rock formations; i could envision John Wayne riding through that open country, that's where most of his Westerns were shot, in Arizona. We also visited a beautiful cathedral; it was a vision women had to build as part of the mountain. There it was, small, yet very interesting as it stood out as part of this mountain in all its grandeur.

We were going to drive on, showing mom the Grand Canyon, but she got very ill and was throwing up. So we decided we'd drive back to Barbara's home the next day. Mom had an upset stomach quite often, and we were to discover later on, that it was because she had H-pylori, that had been in her stomach for years. Poor Mama, and she had suffered for a long time not knowing the cause.

Before our stay would come to a close with Barbara, she and i were discussing our nephew, his life and how gifted and talented he was with drawing. She suggested we check out a graphic design school near Phoenix. We found the school was very impressive and perhaps ideal for our nephew. Wow, wrong!

While in Phoenix we met a lady who sounded much like Betty Boop.[21] Not quite believing what we were hearing, my sister turned to me and said, "Is she for real?" We had never met anyone quite like her; she was very interesting. We learned the Lord has made us all very different and special.

When i called home to talk with Fred and our sons, and told them about this graphic arts school, Jeff was very interested.

At Jeff's graduation, students had to speak at the ceremony sharing what home schooling meant to them. i sat in tears, and do the same today as i watch the video of the graduation, as to what Jeff had to say. He gave glory to the Lord Jesus and thanks to his mom who supported, prodded and kept him on track until he graduated. This was quite an accomplishment for both of us, we had tried almost everything in hopes of this wonderful, glorious day of his graduating from High School, and he did it!!!

We invited many friends and family to join us in the great celebration. Our pastor, and friends, and much to our dismay only a couple of family members joined us. But we were thankful for Jeff's accomplishment, and were excited to see where the Lord would allow him to go next. He still wanted to check out the graphic school in Arizona. With much thought and discussion, Fred and i decided we'd pay for his flight to Arizona and return home, allowing him see for himself, if this were for him. He was very excited when he returned home; Barbara had taken him to see the graphic art school. He liked the school, Arizona, and he and my sister, have artistic minds, and hit it off. We began making plans for Jeff to attend the school. But he had other plans, he was not going unless Danielle went with him, she too insisted on being with him. i told them, as a Christian, i did not approve of them living together. They respected my feelings and planned a small wedding at the church we attended, before leaving for Arizona.

It wasn't to end here, many things transpired before he would make the transition to Arizona. He was playing drums for the church we attended, and on Saturday nights he would take his girlfriend out on a date, and sometimes not return home. His excuse was, she lived close to the church and he felt it senseless to come home at night and then return to the same area in the morning. Fred and i did not agree with this at all. So, we laid down the law and said if he did it again, he was not to come home; he was to go out on his own, we would not allow this while he was living at home. The next Sunday morning, i found he was not in his room, i called his girlfriend's home and of course that is where he was spending the night. When we arrived at church, he was playing drums as usual. After the service i told him

257

to come home, pack his belongings and leave. This is something he had been wanting to do, but was caught by surprise, not believing his mom would go through with the action. He came home laughing as he packed his things, then drove off, with no job, no place to stay and a broken hearted mother. Within an hour he called; i was thinking he was calling to apologize and was relieved; not so, he had forgotten something and wanted to know if he could come home and get it; i said yes, of course.

Where he stayed, slept, ate and cared for himself, i do not know. But i did care, and cried and prayed before the Lord, for his safety, daily. i thought, "Is this what is called 'tough love'?" Well, it is, and i did not like it one bit, but knew i must stay strong. That was probably one of the toughest decisions i had ever made in my life; this was our son, and here i told him to leave the comforts of our home, and just go if he chose not to live by our standards. Fred backed me up all the way, but i was the tough one, just as i was with my Mama, when she and my father separated. This was even more difficult; this was our son i gave birth to, and loved dearly. One of my biggest faults is co-dependency; i work on that problem all the time. While attending an Al Anon meeting, not long before this episode, i asked what it meant to be co-dependent. One of the members said, "If you or I saw a man lying in a gutter, we would stop, put a blanket over him, ask him how we could help him, what can we do? If it were someone who wasn't co-dependent, that person would say as they passed by this man in the ditch, "Look at him, why doesn't he get up and take care of himself?"" That, my friend, is the difference. i know there is a fine line between compassion and co-dependency. i am still learning, but will tell you, most of my dear friends are battling the same battle, for 'It takes one to know one,' that's why we get along so well. Top that off with being a Christian, and just where do you draw the line? It takes courage, prayer, love, prayer, understanding, prayer, discernment and lots of prayer.

All the while, the days went by slowly for me, missing our son, his fun nature, laughter, love and caring spirit. We would see him every Sunday at church playing the drums.

One afternoon he called asking if could have the motor home that was given to him and his band. That is a story in and of itself. Friends of ours had an older motor home they were willing to contribute to a worthy cause, our son's band turned out to be the worthy cause. The motor home sat on our ranch needing repair work, which the fellows from the band could not afford. When Jeff asked to have it, of course we said 'Yes.' It wasn't ours anyway and would provide shelter for our son. Later that day his girlfriend drove him to pick-up the motor home. i handed him a couple of large garbage bags filled with things he would need to set-up house keeping. When he asked me what the filled bags were for, i told him i was keeping my promise of giving each son needed things for their first home. He took them with gratitude, and he and his girlfriend drove away. My mom was with me at the time and witnessed my strength, yet broken heart.

Jeff parked the motor home alongside the church we attended, so each Sunday, like Hannah from the Old Testament bringing a new outfit for her son, i would, without a word, leave fresh baked cookies or something for our son to show my love for him.

Winter came and along with it, pouring rain. One of those wet rainy days; Jeff called and asked if he could come home, he was getting soaked from all the holes in the roof of the motor home. i told him to come home, have dinner with us and we would talk it over.

He immediately accepted the invitation. After dinner, we told him what we expected of him as long as his feet were placed under our table. Mainly, it was respecting us, and our values, he agreed and held to his agreement.

Jeff still planned on going to the graphic art school in Arizona and would not give-up on first marrying Danielle, so she could go with him. i was thankful they chose to marry and not live together, but they were both so very young and neither had really experienced living on their own. With much dismay, we finally agreed. Prior to their marriage, Jeff was on his way to meet Danielle, when his car swerved, flipped, and landed on its side in grazing land. One of the metal fence stakes came through the driver's window between Jeff and the steering wheel. If he were not as thin as he was, the stake would have gone directly into his abdomen. When we went to see the damage to the car he was driving, i told him, "i could visualize the blood of Jesus all over it, protecting him." He said, "One thing i know for sure, this gives us more reason why we should get married." i was shocked.

The day came, and our Pastor performed a small wedding for Jeff and Danielle before their departure to Arizona. They would return in the fall and we would have a nice church wedding.

With tears in my eyes and a terrific pain in my heart, i helped them pack and get them ready for their trip to Arizona. As Fred, Franz and i were helping them pack, i over heard arguing; it was Jeff and his new bride. i went to them quickly, held their hands and began praying for them. The arguing ceased. When they left, i cried until their moving trailer was out of sight and cried and wept some more. My greatest consolation is that Jeff knew the Lord Jesus, and He would get them through, and my dear sister Barbara would also be there for them.

Not long after, i was having my quiet time in our nice deep claw foot tub, with bubbles and hot water surrounding my aching muscles. It seemed, since the boys were young, they would come into the bathroom, when i was taking my bath. i was thankful for the bubbles that covered me, while they proceeded to ask questions. Perhaps, they came when they knew mom couldn't get away, and i would listen. Well, in walked Franz; he wanted to discuss with me whether he should or shouldn't leave for Arizona as well, and dream his dream to attend flight school. My question to him was; "Is this what you want to do?" Of course his answer was yes, and now with his brother and new bride in Arizona, and my sister living there, he felt this was a great opportunity.

So, we checked into the funding at the flight school he decided to attend. Later we discovered, it was directly across the street from the one where the terrorist attended, who took down the Towers in New York. The one Franz chose was less expensive, offering almost the same type of education. Even so, it was very expensive. Had we known there were other options in becoming a pilot, other than the military, who had refused him due to his asthma, we would have gone that route. Believe me, we did our research before he made this decision.

Franz sold his first truck, he had purchased and worked so hard on with his Dad, Lowell and others to get up and running, to a friend, in order to help pay for flight school. For the rest of the tuition, he took out a loan. He transferred with U.P.S. to Arizona, which helped with his lively hood and part of his tuition. He lived with Jeff and Danielle in an apartment in Arizona and learned to live on his meager income as a loader.

Prior to his moving to Arizona, Jeff and Danielle settled in a small apartment in Tempe, Arizona. They found work at a theater and then finally were hired on, at the Phoenix Airport, loading and unloading baggage from the planes. It was a tough, backbreaking job in the tremendous heat of Arizona. But now Fred and i could fly from Sacramento to visit them, because they received passes for their parents to fly anywhere throughout the United States and Mexico; all we had to pay was the tax. What a blessing.

Before Franz left for Arizona, we had planned one more trip to Hawaii; Franz joined us on this last trip. We stayed at a resort in Maui. One afternoon, we were all walking down to the beach, and who should come walking toward us, but a friend we hadn't seen in years. We had lost contact with he and his wife, when they moved to Japan. The man immediately said, " My wife is down at the beach." When i spotted her on the beach sitting on a chair visiting with a friend, i got down and began talking to her, she answered back and then looked up at me and with great shock and said, "Gloria, it's you!!!" We had a great time of reminiscing and sharing our lives, especially since, she too, was a Christian, we had a lot to share. Since that time, we still keep in contact. It always ceases to amaze me how the Lord works in each and every one of our lives, as if we were the only one of us on earth. **Matthew 10:30 says it well; "And even the very hairs of your head are all numbered."** These are the very words of Jesus.

We had a joyous time, finally after all the stress of Jeff's marriage and Franz's soon departure, on this last visit to paradise. Little did i know we would be facing yet another stressful event. Once again we would have the rain that would bring the rainbow, this time it was my dear sweet mother.

One evening as we were resting, after a full day of warm sunshine, swimming snorkeling and enjoying the beauty of which the Lord made for us in Hawaii, a phone call came in from Arizona. It was Jeff and my sister Barbara, with great fear in their voices, they told us my mom was in an automobile accident, and had broken her neck. My mom was seventy-nine years old at the time, and had never had one broken bone in her little body. As a matter of fact she had never been to the hospital in all those years, except to give birth to one of her six children.

i had so many questions, and felt so helpless being so far away and not there to assist in any way. Questions like; 'Where did it happen? How did it happen? When did it happen? What hospital is she in? How bad is she?' i just wanted to be there, see her and comfort her through this terrible experience.

i too, needed comfort and a woman's understanding heart. That is where the love of the friend and sister-in-Christ, came into play. That is one reason the Lord had allowed Sandy and i to connect once again in Maui. What an awesome God we serve. My friend just sat and listened to me as i shared about my mom's injury; she too, knew my mom, and that made it more comforting.

i was thankful our vacation was almost over, and i was anxious to return home and see my mom. Although Jeff and Barbara re-assured me that mom was in good hands and would be o.k., i really never knew the extent of her injuries until i saw her at the hospital.

When we arrived home, we not only had jet lag, needed to unpack and do all the necessary things after a week vacation, the grapes needed to be harvested as well. Since, i thought mom would be o.k., i stayed home an extra day or two to help harvest the crop of grapes from our vineyard. That did not help with my wanting to see her. i had mixed feelings, knowing i had to help Fred with the crop, and yet wanting to see my mom. i know the Lord tells us; " **Do not be anxious about anything, but in everything, by prayer and petition, with thanksgiving, present your requests to God. And the peace of God, which transcends all understanding, will guard your hearts and your minds in Christ Jesus." Philippians 4:6-7.** i prayed and the Lord did give me the peace i needed to wait until i could see my mom. We are still in this flesh and sometimes it is not easy to 'let go and let God.'

Upon arriving at the hospital with my aunt Mary and sister Josephine, i witnessed mom lying in bed, her head wrapped in bandages. i went to her, spoke with her and loved her, as i shared Jeff's coming home and upcoming church wedding. She reassured me she was going to be there for his wedding. Prior to this injury, she and i had shopped for the wedding reception together. Mom loved her grandchildren and wanted to assist in any way she could, and did so, for this reception. It appeared she was doing fine, just this bandage around her head, it probably would be removed before the wedding, that was my thought. Then i heard my sister and aunt in a different part of the room discussing some sort of apparatus that sat on a table in mom's hospital room. The words i heard were not comforting, saying mom would not be able to attend the wedding because she was going to have this apparatus placed on her head. i walked over to see what they were looking at and discussing. It was then i realized, mom was not as good as she appeared, and that she was going to be placed in this 'Halo' apparatus, for a few months because the break in her neck was very severe.

i was to find out later from the physician who did the surgery for mom, if he hadn't been there to perform this delicate surgery she would have either been paralyzed or perished. What a shock, i was not prepared for this news. i drove what seemed to be a forever drive home with tears flowing down my cheeks, disappointment, a broken heart, and wondering what the end results would be for my Mama.

Fred and i made the next trip to visit mom and i continued to visit her until the doctors and staff called for a family meeting as to where mom was physically and mentally. This accident had taken a toll on her frail little body. Seemed not long before when i took her home to build her up, after she had malnutrition, now here she was once again, weighing less than a hundred pounds and couldn't eat. She had to be fed through a tube and then later through her stomach.

In the meantime Jeff and his wife were making plans to return to California for their church wedding celebration, they were not working for the airlines at the time, so my dear sister Barbara, in her kindness, love and generosity, not only paid for their round trip airfare, she joined them, and then stayed on, to visit mom in the hospital. She also helped me with the wedding plans, what a blessing. In the last minute, we arranged for all the food, drink and i prepared the wedding cake. Barbara was amazed at my giftedness.

She would tell me later, she never realized how intelligent and gifted i was and attempted anything and everything without fear. Well, there are a few things i would not attempt, one being, jumping into the swimming pool, there again that fear of water. But as the Word of God says," **Let another praise you, and not your own mouth, someone else, and not your own lips." Proverbs 27:2.**

i will always remember the kindness of my dear friend, Berni, who offered to prepare a pan of lasagna and said, " I will make a meatless one, because that is what your daughter-in-law prefers." That my friend, and what my sister did is an example of true Christianity. **"love… is not self-seeking,…" 1 Corinthians 13:5b** Sad to say, mom was not able to attend the wedding, the only two of my siblings who attended were Barbara, Frank and his family. i forgave the others, but the pain remained for awhile. We were thankful for the friends who came and supported us.

All of us children were present at the meeting for my mom except Barbara, who listened over the phone as we met. The staff went over our mother's development, and how she could not quite remember the names of the different seasons and other things. When we all left the meeting to discuss where mom should go after leaving the hospital, our brother Frank, knowing our sweet mother's simplicity, remarked, " Mom, didn't know some of the questions they asked her before the accident, that's just mom. " We appreciated his honesty and humor in this most difficult time, and laughed. Once again, remembering in **Ecclesiastes 3:4, " a time to weep and a time to laugh,…"** There would be plenty of time for weeping, now we laughed, and were thankful we still had our mom, simple or not.

After the meeting and our sibling discussion, we took mom aside and Frank asked her; "Mom, when they release you, where would you like to go? You can come home with me, where there are the four of us children and Bill's wife is a nurse. Or you can go home with gloria, what would you like to do, mom?" As i write, i have tears coming down my eyes, because of mom's choice. Yes, much to my surprise her words were, " I want to go home with gloria, she has more friends." It was settled, mom would go home with me once released from the hospital. i was thankful, Frank took the initiative to ask mom and allow her to make the decision.

Once the decision was made, the nurses took me to mom's hospital room and began to show me how i was to feed mom through her stomach. i watched the procedure and said, "i am not a nurse, i am afraid i will not do this properly and cause more injury to my mom. Please let me wait until she can eat and then release her."

Within a few days, my brother Frank called and said mom had been released from the hospital, and could i meet him at our aunt's. When i arrived at our aunt's he showed me how i had to feed mom, she could only drink liquids, which had to be thickened with a gelatin formula. Because she had not eaten in several weeks, she had to learn like a child, how to chew and swallow without choking. Those were tough times, because we lived at least twenty minutes from the hospital; i was in constant fear that mom might choke and could i get her help in time to save her. i know the verse very well, **"For God did not give us a spirit of timidity, but a spirit of power, of love and of self- discipline." 2 Timothy 1:7.** i remember telling our sons when they were young, "Fear knocked at the door, Faith answered, and there was no one there." But it is one thing to say it, know it, and then live it out. Amen.

Believe me i did a lot of praying as mom and i traveled those two and a half hours home. But then, the Lord had another blessing in store for us; her name is Jeanne. Jeanne is a wonderful, caring nurse and a dear friend, who was at that time in charge of nurses who would come to the home and help out the patient and caregiver. Well, within a few days, due to Jeanne, we had nurses, speech therapist and wonderful servants of God to help us. Because mom would not be able to take a shower or bath while wearing the 'halo', they came and showed me how to clean around the bolts of the halo, how to give her sponge baths, wash her hair with a washcloth and so forth. The speech therapist came mainly to teach mom how to swallow again. But she did even more.

On one occasion when she arrived, she detected i was not doing well, and asked me what was wrong. i poured my heart out to this dear lady, about how my mom was being very obstinate, which was unlike my sweet mother. i understood how difficult it must have been for her being in that 'halo' and all, but it was tough on me as well. Just getting up in the middle of the night caring for her, not getting sleep and feeling overwhelmed. Sometimes it can be tougher on the caregiver than the one being cared for. The therapist who was very understanding said, " I will have a talk with her." Then she went into mom's room, closed the door, when she came out, she said, " Your mom will be fine now, I told her she should be very thankful you and your husband have taken her in; she could be in a convalescent home instead." That made mom think, because her whole demeanor changed, and we did much better.

We not only had to have a local geriatric doctor to care for mom, but in the beginning, would travel once a week to San Jose to the specialist who did the neck surgery on mom. Mom also had **C- difficieal**, which is common for elderly folk to get, usually from their stay in the hospital. It is caused from bacteria that somehow get into the intestines and causes horrific diareahha, which is black and has a terrible odor. i was thankful we lived in the country, because each time i changed mom, i would run outside with her diaper in hand, head for the garbage can, and take a deep breath of fresh country air. i felt so sorry for my poor Mama. We went to her geriatric doctor and he prescribed an antibiotic, it stopped it while she was on the prescription. The moment she was off the prescription, the C- difficieal returned with a vengeance. i told the doctor and asked if he would mind if i tried another way besides the antibiotic, he agreed; he too was at loss.

In desperation i turned to the Internet and made contact with a pharmacist. As i look back i know the Lord orchestrated this whole adventure. The pharmacist was very helpful and recommended, of all things, the supplement Fred and i had been taking, but in larger doses, to add yogurt with all the live bacilli cultures, acidophilus and colustrum from the cow in capsule form. Within a week or so, the C- difficieal was gone; what a relief for both mom and i. PRAISE THE LORD!!!

Then there was the specialist in San Jose, where we made our once a week visit. Jeff was now working for the airlines, so he would call, find out what day mom's appointment was on, and make arrangements to have the same day off, in order to meet us and help me get mom to the doctor. Was i ever grateful for our wonderful, caring son! Mom and i would drive to San Jose, spend the night with my aunt, then in the morning, i would drive to San Jose Airport, retrieve our Jeff, who was flying in from Arizona. i did not tell mom where i was going, then when i arrived with Jeff, there was always many tears of joy shed as mom hugged, kissed and welcomed Jeff. Mom, loved all of her children and grandchildren, but there was a special bonding between she and Jeff i could not describe, until recently. i will share what the Lord showed me about that bonding, later in my writing.

The doctor's office was near Good Samaritan Hospital, where our Franz was born. A long time friend of ours lived very close to the hospital, and on one occasion i took Jeff and my mom to meet him. Actually, he was one of Fred's first German buddies, whom Fred met when he came to America; they had shared an apartment and many fun stories of life together. This made it even more special for him to meet one of Fred's sons, our Jeff.

After the doctor appointment, we would have lunch and then take Jeff to San Jose Airport. Imagine a young man taking his only day off to care for his mom and grandmother. i had not been to the airport in years, and could hardly believe my eyes at the size of this once one horse town airport. Amazing what the computer chip did to the area. Recently, i read that San Jose is the tenth largest city in the United States of America. As we drove to the airport, mom and i shared stories of the beauty of the area in the past, with all the fragrant orchards, dairies and peace and quiet. i am sure Jeff listened, taking it all in, of days gone by.

On one of these trips to San Jose and meeting Jeff, he told me what his graphic design instructor said, which was; "Jeff, I cannot believe you do not have a computer, being from the Northern part of California, where they

268

were first constructed." After he shared this with me, i told him we were going to go and look at computers. He found an iMac®²² laptop that fit the bill perfectly. The school preferred Mac's because they worked best for graphic design. I called Fred at his work, and he said, "How much is it? Go, and purchase it for him, we will pay for it with my first social security check." What a generous thoughtful father Jeff has, much like our heavenly Father. As it turned out, the cost of the iMac®²³ was the amount of Fred's first social security check. PRAISE THE LORD!!! Another blessing from the LORD!!!

After the purchase, I took Jeff to Cupertino, California, where the Apple®²⁴ Store was at the time. And i went on to explain how much the area had changed, from all the lovely apricot and fruit trees, their fragrant blossoms. The country roads i remembered as a child, the feed store on the corner of Highway 9/Saratoga-Sunnyvale Road and Stevens Creek Blvd. St. Joseph's church, where his dad and i got married, and of course, the beauty salon i managed in Saratoga.

He was not only thrilled to have his very own laptop, but to see where it all began in the Bay Area, Silicon Valley/Santa Clara Valley. Then, to hear his Mama's stories of days gone by, over a delicious lunch; this would be a day, he would not soon forget.

Mom and i returned home, and began the process of getting through this turbulent time. Her local doctor wanted to put her on Prozac for depression; i asked if we could do something natural instead. As we were driving along, after one of her doctor appointments, the Lord led me to tell mom, 'look at the beautiful clouds and the surrounding country.' She did and it lifted her spirits. Mom tried hard to overcome her depression. She didn't need Prozac or any mind-altering drug. My friends would tell me, "She is getting better and less depressed, just being with you, gloria jean."

We loved shelling walnuts, and our walnut tree produced a very large crop. Mom was thrilled, 'halo' and all, she had something to do, shell walnuts, and she did it with such fervor. The first year after mom's passing, we had a bumper crop of walnuts from that tree. i remarked, "Mama, are you talking with Jesus and asking Him to send me all these walnuts to shell?" It was fun recalling the joy mom and i would have shelling them together.

Mom loved and missed her gardening as well, so a dear friend brought her a large metal tub so she could at least plant flowers. We purchased some lovely plants, filled the tub with potting soil and manure, placed it on the deck within mom's reach so she could care for her plants. Was she ever thrilled, it put a smile on her precious aging face.

Which reminds me, my sister Barbara said our mom looked like Dean Martin, only she was a woman. She was right; every time i see a picture of Dean Martin i see my mom, same nose, dark Italian skin, and beautiful smile. Perhaps, it's my mother's Italian, coming into the Swiss part.

There were days i could hardly take the difficulties of caring for my precious mom, it was continuous and draining. At times i would run down our steep drive-way and literally cry out to the Lord saying, " Father, i cannot do this anymore." i would pray, call family and friends and soon the painful feeling of helplessness would pass.

My dear sister Barbara, flew in from Arizona to help care for our mom. My sister, Josephine and her husband, came once and spent the night, cared for mom, so Fred and i could go out for an evening. My brother Frank came and helped Fred cut firewood, so we could keep the house warmer during Mama's stay.

We attended church whenever we could, but it was difficult for mom, she got so tired carrying the extra weight of the 'halo'. Because of the 'halo' she could not pull anything over the top of her head, so i cut used sweatshirts like a cardigan, and they kept her nice and warm. Whenever i had to go grocery shopping or pick-up medicine for mom, i would call on one of our dear sweet neighbors to sit with mom. Much to our dismay, no one from the church we attended at the time, offered to sit with mom, not even for us to attend church. i have learned from this, where there is a need, we must try and fill it somehow and to forgive. As Jesus said, **"Father, forgive them, for they do not know what they are doing." Luke 23:34**

Chapter Twenty-Five

"For I know the plans that I have
for you; 'declares the Lord."
Jeremiah 29:11a

Caring for my mother is over for now.
It's time for my husband and i to begin again.
Miraculous healing in my body; the Lord has
other plans for my life. Our son and granddaughter come to live with
us. A new bonding for me.

The time had quickly arrived for Franz to leave and attend flight school in Arizona. We had a nice celebration before his departure. Much to his surprise, i presented him with a handmade king size quilt, i had been working on over the years. The squares were made from his baby clothes, soccer shirts, Boy Scouts, and friends and family made squares to fill in the rest to make it complete. It was in four sections, the top represented our church, the second was our home, third school, and the last sports and other activities. i also made one for Jeff, and presented it to him later, thinking he was going to leave after Franz. Franz was surprised and thankful. i had gotten the idea from a friend whose mother made a quilt for each of her daughters using their old dresses. Here's a little tip for you mother's, grandmother's, aunt's or friends, you can do this also with your loved ones old garments. Life itself is a quilt, and as long as we allow the Lord to put it together we will be blessed. **"Blessed are all who take refuge in Him."** **Psalm 2:12c.**

Franz was very excited to start his dream of flying. Now, that we could fly with the passes Jeff earned from working at the airlines, we took advantage of this great opportunity. Since my sister Barbara no longer lived in Arizona, we stayed with our children in their apartment during our visits. Barbara had met Franz when he arrived at the airport to attend school in

272

Arizona, and announced she and her hubby, Richard, were moving to Cyprus, in the Middle East. This was very disappointing for Franz, because he so wanted the opportunity to know her better. Franz took Fred and i to tour the flight school he attended, and then he took us up for a test flight. i forewarned him of how i get motion sickness and was immediately handed a bag for the purpose. It was a glorious unclouded day (not unusual for Arizona) as Franz listened to flight instructions that took us high above the Sonoran Desert and cacti. He really is an excellent pilot, and i had no need for the bag to prove it.

The flight school was good, but it did not fulfill the promises it had made to these young fledgling pilots. Not only did Franz sell his beloved 1946 truck to pay for part of the schooling, but he also had to take out a large loan to pay off the schooling, and was promised completion with that amount. It was not to be, and he was running out of money. One time he flew home using a pass from his brother. As he and i sat waiting for his return flight at the airport in Sacramento i handed him a check. He took it with great joy and surprise, i gave all that i could give and still it was not enough to complete his training, very disappointing for him and us.

Right after that visit, he arrived safely in Arizona and called to tell me that as the plane was taking off from Sacramento, the Lord showed him through the massive cloud formations, that this is what He wanted Franz to do, as far as being a pilot. That was confirmation for him to continue his flight training, no matter if the funding was there or not. i am sorry to say, he is still paying on the cost of the schooling and due to circumstances beyond his control, was unable to fly as a commercial pilot for large airlines. Oh, he did fulfill his dream, completed flight school, later he flew out of El Paso, Texas, and later California, a Lear Jet, in order to complete his hours.

My mom was still recuperating, and staying with us. She stayed with my brother and his wife when we made this trip to Arizona. Mom would soon be celebrating her eightieth birthday, and i wanted to have a big

273

family/friend gathering for the event. i was so thankful that all of my brothers and sisters and most of their siblings came to honor mom at this special time. It was not to end there; we siblings were to have a meeting as to where mom was going to remain. As far as my mom was concerned, she wanted to go back and live with my aunt, as she did prior to the accident. But my aunt would not have her, until, as she put it; "Your mom is one hundred per cent better." Well, being mom's caretaker, i knew mom was close to 100 per cent, but she was not there yet. All of us siblings and Fred went down to the barn during mom's celebration to discuss this matter. Much to my surprise my sister Barbara spoke up and said, " Fred is the only son-in-law, he and gloria are the only ones who opened their home to our mother, and i believe we brothers and sisters should each pay a fixed amount each month to them for caring for our mom." i said thank you, but that is not necessary." They all agreed, saying Barbara was right and each should contribute said amount.

Now, my dear reader, you must remember, mom was there for us in our younger growing up years, but she was distant, we came to realize as we grew older. Not her fault of course, because for her, it was a matter of survival and as one sibling said, "Mom loved us, but once we were eight or ten years of age, that was more than she could handle, as far as intelligence and understanding." i mention this because i want you, the reader, to know what loving, caring, forgiving siblings i have; they loved and forgave my mom and were more than willing to pay for her care.

Mom's desire to go back and live with my aunt was so strong she would do anything to go back. Yet, it wasn't to be, for a while. The day finally came when mom could have the 'halo' removed from her little body. She was so relieved. i can just see her now, with that miserable necessary apparatus attached to her little head and upper body, sleeping quietly on her back in her bed. It must have been so uncomfortable, not being able to turn from side to side, let alone sleep on her side. Mom never complained about the 'halo' or her sleeping condition. Then one evening, after she had the 'halo' removed, Fred and i were sitting in the living room, after getting mom settled in bed and resting for the night. Suddenly, there was a big crash and bang that came from mom's room. i jumped up quickly running to her room to find out what caused the crash. There lying on the floor was my mom writhing in pain. Poor little soul, she was so used to having the 'halo' she'd forgotten how to function without it. We took her to prompt care for X-rays and then another eleven miles to the hospital for a technician to read the X-rays. Sure enough mom, like our Franz when he was two, broke her collarbone from the sudden fall. Like our Franz, it couldn't be cast because it was a collarbone, and due to her age, it would take quite some time to heal. We then discovered she had osteoporosis, which probably was significant in her broken neck from the accident. Jokingly, my brother Frank would say, "Mom, always told us not to pull certain stunts or we might break our neck." Much to our surprise, she broke her neck. Sometimes the very words we speak come back at us. Once again, not to make fun of our mom, but to listen to what we say some times, we all need to look at ourselves and our comments, and sometimes laugh or think, before we speak.

Which reminds me of my mom telling me, "You are going to make yourself sick if you keep thinking about it." Or whatever the case might be. Years later, i now understand exactly what she meant, as i can just her words in a caring voice. She is right. The Bible says; **"The tongue has the power of life and death,..." Proverbs 18:21**. That, my friend, is very powerful. **James 3:5 & 6 say; "Likewise the tongue is a small part of the body, but it makes great boasts. Consider what a great forest is set on fire by a small spark. The tongue also is a fire, a world of evil among the parts of the body. ..."** Wow.

Mom finally healed from the fall, was able to function once again without the 'halo,' and soon returned to live with my aunt. In one way, i hated to see her leave, but in another, she was more than ready, to the point

275

she became very belligerent because she wanted to be with my aunt. Although it hurt, yet i understood. Healing and forgiveness had to take place in my life. As our Lord tells us in **Matthew 6:14 & 15 "For if you forgive men when they sin against you, your heavenly Father will also forgive you. But if you do not forgive men their sins, your Father will not forgive your sins."** That's a tough one to follow in this human body of ours, but with the power of the Holy Spirit, we can and must forgive. This is a never-ending battle with the flesh that i still deal with; i pray and then give it to Jesus. As my Jeanette would say, " Just lay it at the foot of the cross, honey." i have time and time again, and did so with my sweet Mama, as well.

As everything began to settle down and we started getting back to normal, (a setting on my dryer), i concentrated on my Beauty Salon business and was also hired to care for an elderly lady. i had worked part time in the Salon in our home, even while caring for my mom. A friend, who was helping with my mom, told me a home for the elderly was under construction in Angels Camp, and they needed a beautician. She suggested that i apply, before the facility was complete. i talked it over with Fred, brought it to the Lord in prayer, and we decided we would talk with the manager of this new facility. She showed us around the building, telling us where the Salon would exist. It was evident the building would take several months before it's completion. We were fine with that, and made an agreement with the manager to rent the space provided for the Salon. i was excited, a dream come true, my very own salon in town, with wonderful elderly people i could help make feel special in caring for their hair needs; another blessing from Lord.

In the meantime, Fred and i took advantage of traveling to Arizona every opportunity we got, since Jeff was able to give us airline passes. Jeff, called one evening to say; "Congratulations, Mom and Dad, you are going to be grandparents." We were excited, yet, concerned.

Upon thinking and praying for our children, we thought it best that they have a home we could invest in; they could make the payments and it would be less than the apartment and give them more room. Fred and i were both working, and once we found the home for them, we applied for the loan in our and Franz's name. The home was in a lovely area in Peoria, Arizona. It was a new development, so we were able to qualify Franz for this loan. The home was brand new; it had three bedrooms, two baths, a lovely kitchen, living room and nice fenced backyard. It was perfect for our children, and they had a home to call their own. On one of our visits, we noticed the walls had been textured and painted by our children; it tied in with the Arizona motif, looked great! We were thankful they were taking pride in this place they called home.

Not long after we helped them move into this lovely abode, our precious first grandchild made her appearance, yes my friend, finally the Lord blessed our family with a girl. Jeff and Danielle named her Laurel Shea. She was to become the delight of this Oma and Papa.

Now, that we had a little girl to visit and help care for, as well as our children, i would make many trips to Arizona. Fred and i considered retiring and moving to Arizona; we even looked in the surrounding areas for a home to purchase; we were serious. California gets hot in the summer, especially where we live, but not like Arizona. The heat is ongoing there, during the summer months, because it is the desert, thus making it almost impossible not to use the air conditioner day and night. There were many other factors, which caused us not to retire in Arizona. We are happy we didn't and enjoy our home here in California.

When Jeff worked on the tar mat at the airport, he had to keep well hydrated; otherwise he would experience heat stroke. On one particular visit, i had our Laurel Shea in a little baby seat, as i worked planting flowers in their backyard. After i put her down for a nap, i too felt exhausted and lie down as well. When Jeff arrived home, he noticed my inactivity and said,

"Mom, you must have had a heat stroke, you don't notice how hot the sun can be here and how it just dehydrates and exhausts you. Please lie down and rest." That's our caring son, he was right, the heat there just creeps up on a person, and before you know it, your exhausted, and having a heat stroke. With that in mind, we constantly had the air conditioner on day and night during the summer, and were not able to go out side for a walk, unless it was early in the morning or late in the evening; it was just unbearable for us. Fred and i both love the outdoors, and this just wasn't for us. To do Arizona justice, the winter's, spring and fall are gorgeous, but that summer heat is just not our cup of tea. Regardless of the heat, it did not stop us from going there to visit our children, and help out in any way we could.

While working for the airlines, Jeff was able to come across really great deals, and told us about one, a trip to Mexico. We chose to go to Puerto Vallarta. We stayed at a time-share there, and enjoyed it tremendously. The climate in Puerto Vallarta is much like Hawaii, because it is almost on the same longitude and latitude. We would go there for many years after, even when Jeff no longer worked for the airlines. We made some good friends there and still keep in contact with one. As traveling with the airlines got more and more difficult, the prices of the flight and stay, became so costly, we decided to cease our travels to this beautiful beach area we came to enjoy. Besides, once we would leave the comforts of the resort, go into the city and see the reality of the poor people, especially the children, it brought back painful memories for me. It was time for us to visit other places closer to home. Since i love the beach and ocean, Fred and i make a yearly trip to enjoy the beauty of the beaches near Pismo Beach, California. We find it very restful, peaceful, enjoyable, not too costly and not far to travel.

When Fred and i were unable to make the trip to Arizona, Jeff would hop a plane with our little Laurel Shea in tow, and fly home to see Dad and Mom. This was after the horrible happenings of 911, and the security became very strict at the airports. Jeff experienced this quite often, before he boarded the plane carrying our precious Laurel Shea strapped in a car seat. Yes, he was stopped many times, especially checking out what might be hidden under the baby's car seat. This made the trip more difficult and uncomfortable, but he kept coming, persistence like his Mama, i guess. Our car knew the trip to Sacramento Airport very well, as we would retrieve Jeff and his lovely bundle almost every weekend. We considered purchasing a used car and parking it at the airport just for them to drive back and forth. The airlines Jeff worked for decided to have smaller planes fly into Stockton Airport. What a relief for all of us, it was so much closer and the flight wasn't as packed, so there was less waiting. The airport reminded me of San Jose's, once small accommodating airport.

i recall our sweet son, Jeff, disembarking the plane looking like a pack mule. He carried Laurel Shea in her car seat, luggage over his shoulder, and a bigger car seat wrapped over his arm. It was then, that i decided we needed to purchase a car seat to keep in our car, just for Laurel Shea. But toting all this extra baggage didn't seem to bother Jeff, he never complained, he was determined to come home and bring his daughter with him.

As grandparents and parents, we were delighted to have them almost every weekend, giving us the opportunity to know Laurel Shea better, teach her about Jesus, the love for the country, and spend time with Jeff. Although, with each visit, Jeff was getting thinner and seemed very worried. We suspected something was terribly wrong, but never pried.

Flight school was going well for Franz, except that he did not know whether he would be able to complete his training, as he was running out of finances. He called and told us he was being sent to El Paso, Texas, where he would co-pilot a Lear Jet. This would give him opportunity to complete his flying hours and they would actually pay him a small salary. This was a great opportunity for Franz, but not for us. Because this meant Franz would be moving out of the home we helped him finance in Arizona, and Jeff and his wife could not pay Franz's share. They were just getting by, financially. Jeff had completed his requirements at graphic art school, and was hired at a furniture design studio in Scottsdale, Arizona. He would receive a small starting pay, as a graphic designer. We were proud of both of our son's accomplishments, but were left in dire straights, as far as the home was concerned. We were thankful, Fred was still working as a machinist and we were able to carry Franz's share for a while, but knew we would need to have someone rent the extra room in the home to help pay the mortgage.

Time went on and we received an e-mail from Jeff that he, his wife and our Laurel Shea, were moving to Southern California. Apparently Danielle was offered a job working for a friend. We were shocked, yet what could we do and what were we to do with the home in Arizona? Most of the furnishings were left behind, not to mention the extras we put into the home: fans, new washer and dryer (wish i had today), and much more. Fred and i made the trip to retrieve all the furnishings we could haul home. We stopped in Southern California on our way to Arizona, to visit Jeff and his little family. We met them, went out for dinner, stayed in a motel and then drove on to Arizona the next day.

Now that Jeff was no longer working for the airlines, he did not have flight privileges, so he would drive to visit us of course with our little bundle, Laurel Shea. On one of his drives home, he took the wrong turn-off, and ended up in Yosemite. And it was in the middle of the night. When he stopped to fill the car up with fuel, he discovered there was no money left on the debit card, he had no cash, no phone, what was he to do? There was a man, an angel i believe, who was filling his car with fuel at the same time. Jeff approached him and asked if he could borrow enough money for fuel to get him home to his parents. Once he was home, he told the man, my folks will send you the money that was borrowed. The man not only filled Jeff's tank, but told him have a safe drive to your folks. Jeff, thanked him, asked him for his address, the man just smiled and drove away, never to be heard of again.

Being the typical mother that i am, i waited up all night for the arrival of our dear children. Over the years of living out in the country, i learned to tune my ears to noises, especially a car coming up our driveway. This night was no different as i was keeping busy sewing, i listened intently for that car which was carrying our precious bundle. It was getting very late, and i just kept praying, listening and tried to keep my hands busy at the sewing machine. When suddenly, i heard that wonderful sound of an engine coming up our driveway. PRAISE THE LORD, it was our children. Jeff was relieved as i ran out the door to meet them, and Laurel Shea was half asleep, yet excited to see her Oma.

They slept well that night, awaking in the morning to share the glorious story of the Lord's providence over them. It was then Jeff finally opened up and shared what was troubling him. We listened, discussed and prayed for our son. He only stayed for a couple of days, then left for Southern California. This time with funds in his pocket for the exhausting long drive.

We kept in contact with Jeff, through e-mail. Soon the work for his wife ceased and they moved in with her aunt. When we conversed with Jeff over the phone, we sensed the discouragement in his voice, living with an aunt that was a blessing, yet he had no job, no car and was just devastated. Not working and being the good provider and protector, as God calls the man to be, and as his father was, really disturbed our son.

He and his wife, applied for a job once again with the airlines, but were unable to make the commute with no car or mode of transportation. Once they got the jobs, moved into an apartment, Fred and i drove down with a car for them to drive for commuting. We then took a flight home, using the passes Jeff received as part of his pay.

Once again, Jeff started flying back and forth on weekends to spend time with Fred and i, and of course bringing our Laurel Shea with him. We always kidded them saying, " She had probably flown more than any child at her young age." She loved coming to our home; one of her first words was 'pupbo', which meant puppy. We had a Yorkie named Beethoven, and he became the love of her little life. i purchased a stuffed puppy and slippers to match with puppy face and ears on them. Later she named the stuffed puppy Beethoven, and takes him with her everywhere she goes to this day. Oh, what memories for these precious children. Jeff taught her to call Fred; Papa and me; Oma. Now, all little children refer to us as Papa and Oma. i guess Jeff loved calling his Oma from Germany, Oma, and gave me the name; so why he didn't name Fred, Opa, is a wonder. Both Opa and Oma are German for grandpa and grandma, and Fred is the German. Works for us and we love being called Papa and Oma. Papa showed her the cows on the ranch and taught her to say; 'moo cow.' This was all new for Fred spending time with a girl, and a special little one like Laurel Shea.

Now that both Jeff and his wife had jobs and a sister to care for Laurel Shea while they worked, we felt relieved and got on with our lives as well. But as we all know, we must have the rain in order to have the beautiful rainbow. God's promise is shown as a reminder in the rainbow. **"And God said, "This is the sign of the covenant I am making between Me and you and every living creature with you, a covenant for all generations to come. I have set my rainbow in the clouds, and it will be the sign of the covenant between Me and the earth. Whenever I bring clouds over the earth and the rainbow appears in the clouds, I will remember My covenant between Me and you and all living creatures of every kind. Never again will the waters become a flood to destroy all life." Genesis 9:12-15.**

i continued working at the facility for the elderly, Fred was still working in Lodi and we were enjoying life and the blessings the Lord bestowed upon us. One day i came home from work only to find the downstairs of our home had flooded. This was not in the winter, and the smell from the water was awful. We realized a pipe that went into the septic tank had split, causing the septic to back-up into our downstairs.

Immediately, we called our homeowners insurance company, who quickly came with huge siphoning hoses and fans to remove the water and moisture downstairs. The smell from huge fans was intoxicating, so we opened windows and doors to help get rid of the odor. The insurance company replaced all the carpets, flooring and cabinets, and anything that was destroyed by the septic water. Finally, after a couple of weeks the smell subsided. This reminded me of the floods we experienced in San Jose and Alviso. i was no stranger to floods or smells.

Within a week or so of the flooding, i was making a return trip from dropping Jeff and Laurel Shea off at the airport, when Fred called me on my cell to ask me to pick him up after work. i was curious as to why he wanted me to pick him up, he had a truck, what was this all about, this was so unlike him. He went on to tell me his truck had been stolen from the parking space directly in front of the building where and while he was working. One of his co-workers came into the shop and asked Fred how he got to work; Fred replied i drove my truck. The co-worker replied, " Then where is it? It's not in the parking lot." Shocked, Fred went to check it out and sure enough, in broad daylight, his truck was stolen. It took the police a couple of days to find his truck parked somewhere in Sacramento, with the radio and the dashboard torn up. Fred's truck was just a small commuting vehicle with no special stereo or anything of the like. Once again our insurance company came to the rescue and covered to have it repaired.

Within a few weeks of that episode, Fred and i went out for dinner and i got food poisoning. If you have ever had food poisoning, you understand what i am talking about, the nausea, dry mouth, dry heaves, tremendous pain in the stomach, couldn't eat or drink anything including water; it would not stay down, the only thing that helped was sucking on ice. Well, the pain was so bad Fred took me to emergency at our local hospital. For some reason i was given an X-ray on my chest, i wondered why, but the Lord knew i needed that chest X-ray. The hospital called to check on me and said i should see my doctor to discuss the outcome of the X-ray. Not being a problem, i went to the doctor and he very quietly, yet positively said the X-ray showed i had lymphoma. Lymphoma, what does that mean? i am not a doctor and not familiar with certain terminology. He finally explained it was a form of cancer, and wanted me to have a P.E.T. scan to verify the findings of the X-ray. The only place we could go for such a test was in Lodi. We made the appointment and Fred took me, dropped me off at the technician where i sat in the waiting room. All that was offered for reading material was on cancer and its treatment. This was very frightening for me, i had gone in for food poisoning and now i was being diagnosed for cancer. Questions, questions were going through my mind like; i have eaten right most of my life, exercised, spent quiet time with the Lord, and have taken care of my body, this temple in which the Holy Spirit of God resides. What was happening? i was taken into a room in which was a huge tubular contraption, similar to the one my mom had gone through when she had her injury. i was given that lovely gown to replace my clothing, told to lie face up on the bed that was part of this machine. Ever so slowly every inch of my body was scanned. i felt the prayers of many of my friends and family. i tried to relax, and began to pray for our children, Fred, family, friends and just kept bringing my prayers for whoever the Lord brought to mind, to the Throne of Grace. Before i knew it, i was being removed from the tube. Taken aside and given the news right there and then, confirmation i had lymphoma.

When Fred arrived to pick me up, i was in a state of shock, i guess he was too, because he didn't seem to understand the realty of the diagnosis. Stressed, upset, and unbelieving, i began to attack him for his lack of understanding and concern, and yelled out; " Don't you understand, i have lymphoma!!!" Then i just sat there crying my eyes out, wondering 'what is happening, Lord?' Fred, just didn't know what to say or how to handle the situation; the hour drive home was very quiet. i went to work as usual the next day, still in shock. Then i was given a notice by the facility that was very discouraging. It was time for me to move on, my customers were very disappointed about my decision. i would miss them, but knew this was best for all concerned. i had come to love these dear souls and spent many wonderful hours with most of them.

At one time Fred and i had them at our home; we prepared lunch for them and they said it was one of the best outings they had since living in the facility. They became very dear to our hearts, but when the Lord directs us we must follow. i moved the Salon back into our home and had to start building my clientele all over again, the Lord blessed the business and still does today. **Jeremiah says; " For I know the plans I have for you," declares the Lord, " plans to prosper you and not to harm you, plans to give you hope and a future." Jeremiah 29:11.** i must trust Him.

We were still concerned about my diagnosis and what we should do next, we prayed and left it with the Lord. That's not to say we forgot or gave-up, no on the contrary. i hate the word 'worry' and use concern instead, but truthfully we were worried. Also, realizing what our Jeff was still going through, i believed in my heart he was coming home with Laurel Shea and we were to help him raise her.

One evening while taking my shower, i literally cried out to the Lord saying; " Father, i know that i will help our son raise Laurel Shea, please Father heal me from this lymphoma. " At a later date the Lord would give me **Psalm 66:16-20** which reads; **"Come and listen, all you who fear God; let me tell you what He has done for me. I cried out to Him with my mouth; His praise was on my tongue. If I had cherished sin in my heart, the Lord would not have listened; but God has surely listened and heard my voice in prayer. Praise be to God, who has not rejected my prayer or withheld His love from me!"** Once again, He was showing me to trust Him. Proverbs 3: 5-6 came to mind very strongly; **"Trust in the Lord with all your heart and lean not on your own understanding; in all your ways acknowledge Him, and He will make your paths straight."**

We had a dear Christian family that had once lived in Circle XX, and i remember when i first met the mother and daughter-in-law, they were more like mother and daughter. What a wonderful blessing they were to each other. They had seen the sign i had placed at our front entrance announcing a new Bible Study starting in our home. They came, sweet Tempe and her daughter-in-law Debbie, we became good friends and sisters-in-Christ. Not long after, Tempe was diagnosed with cancer.

The last time i had an experience with this dreaded disease was when our Franz was just a baby, and a dear friend and former customer, lie in the hospital given little hope of recovery. When she went to a convalescent home for her final days, she asked me to come and do her hair. When i arrived, she told me her hairdresser gloria was coming to fix her hair. When i told it was me, she replied; " Oh, listen to me, i didn't know it was you, gloria, of course." As she lie in that bed, frail, face withdrawn and her eyes looking bigger than normal, i held back the tears. Knowing she didn't even have the strength to get up and have her hair washed, i just took out my comb and nifty curling iron, and began working on the front of her hair; being thankful she had hair. That was the last time i saw her, and look forward to meeting her once again in heaven, because she too had given her heart and life to Jesus.

Well, i was at Bible study when Tempe called for the last time to give us her fair wells. One of the girls in the group with tears welling up in her eyes, said; " No, this can't be; my mom had cancer and she is fine, please don't give-up and leave us!" Tempe with her lovely sweet voice answered; "But you see i am ready to meet the Lord, i was diagnosed with cancer when i was pregnant with our twins. At that time i asked the Lord if He would allow me to live long enough to see them grown? And He did, my sons will graduate from High School in a few months. The Lord kept His promise to me. i am ready." With that, our call was finished and we prayed and thanked the Lord for Tempe.

The Lord had blessed Tempe and her husband with several children. The one that Debbie was married to was Dan. They stayed and lived in our area for a short time, then eventually moved to Oregon to raise a variety of berries. We always kept in contact throughout the years. When vacations came for them, they would make the trek to California to visit friends. We were thankful to be part of their excursion, and for their many visits. Each time they came, a new child had been added to their lovely family, whether biological or adopted, they were theirs. When they heard i had been diagnosed with lymphoma, they made the long tiresome trip from Oregon to visit me. Not only did they visit, but they entertained me. i had been blessed with the "Von Caldwell Family Children Singers." What a blessing it was to hear those lovely voices, all singing well blended together, just for me. What can i say except; PRAISE THE LORD!!!

When it was time for them to leave, i had such joy and peace in my heart and to think they did this for me. Oh yes, of course we closed in prayer giving glory to our Lord Who had sent them "... for such a time as this."

They continue to visit us from time to time. The last time they visited, they stayed at a time-share in Angels Camp. They spent most of their time with us, in our pool swimming, then making homemade ice cream and just enjoying each other's company; a little bit of heaven, i think so. Always at the end we would gather around in a big, and i mean big, circle and pray. Dan and Debbie have done a marvelous job in raising their children for the Lord.

One day a dear friend called and asked how i was doing, and then went on to recommend a thorax doctor. Why, i will never know, but once again we serve an awesome Lord and He knew. With great expectancy we made an appointment with this doctor. He didn't even examine me; he just listened as to what had already been done to me. Much to our surprise he said, "I believe you have Sarcoidosis, sometimes it shows up in X-rays and the P.E.T. scan as lymphoma.' he went on, ' I would like to do a biopsy, in

287

which i would make a small incision in your neck." Fred, and i just looked at each other in shock, this man was giving us hope. We decided i would have the biopsy.

On the day of the surgery, our Pastor Bill, my brother Frank, and of course my Fred, were there for me prior to going in for surgery. My brother drove from Redding to St. Joseph's Hospital in Stockton to be there for Fred and i. Upon entering this wonderful hospital, i was welcomed in the lobby by a huge statue of what we believe Jesus looks like, that was comforting to me. Thank the Lord we had health insurance at the time, but there was a huge co-payment we had to pay prior to the surgery. i was writing out the check for the co-pay, knowing full well we did not have enough funds at the time in the bank, but knowing with Fred's next paycheck we would have enough funds to back-up the check. The Lord provided even more: when i went to pay the co-pay, i was immediately directed into the room for surgery. 'What i thought, no co-pay?' i have the check in my old Bible waiting to write the amount for the co-pay. We were never asked for the co-pay and the doctor never sent us any more bills. A miracle, i believe so. He is my (our) Jehovah-jirah **"The Lord will provide." Refer to Genesis 22. Also, Philippians 4:19 " And my God will meet all your needs according to His glorious riches in Christ Jesus."**

After the surgery, and the diagnosis, my brother Frank and Pastor Bill went home. Fred stayed until i awoke and the surgeon came in to give me the results. i was still out of it, due to the anesthetic, and could hardly see or believe what the doctor told me. There he was, standing over my bed looking like a big blurry object as he announced, "I was correct, it is not lymphoma it is Sarcoidosis." Did i have lymphoma and the Lord healed me, or did i have Sarcoidosis all along? Only our Lord knows for sure. He is the great physician.

Relieved i reached out for Fred's hand for comfort. He too was exhausted for i had asked him to stay with me overnight after the surgery;

he had slept in a chair next to my bed, talk about commitment. When i finally awoke and we were on the road to our home, i cried out to the Lord with great thankfulness. He had healed me, but what was this Sarcoidosis, and what could i do to overcome it?

My answers came years later when Fred was in the hospital having prostate surgery. As the Lord would have it, the nurse who was taking care of Fred, we knew well. Next to Fred's room was a man who was crying out in horrible pain. i asked our nurse friend if i could go and pray with him, she said it was all right. It was then i discovered he too had Sarcoidosis, which does not just go away, it starts in the esophagus and increases as it travels down into the lungs, causing difficulty in breathing. As i discussed Sarcoidosis with our nurse, she explained its difficulties. All i could say to her was; "i had it as well, and the Lord healed me."

i knew this because right after my diagnosis, my primary doctor made an appointment for me to see a pulmonary specialist. This specialist had me blowing up balloons with deep breathing, and all kinds of tests in order to check my lung capacity. i wondered why he kept having me do these tests over and over again, he finally said with great frustration, "You have been misdiagnosed, you don't have Sarcoidosis." Immediately, i began telling him that is what the biopsy showed, and i had been praying, as well as many others, i also took mega doses of immune supplements. i also began to share my faith in Jesus the great healer, with him. He listened, but really didn't listen. As my dear friend Pam said, " It could have been the supplements that healed you, or the Lord just did it, doesn't matter; He healed you whatever the means." That is so true, we must pray and do as the Lord directs.

i just knew the Lord had healed me when i called upon Him while taking a shower weeks prior, knowing we were soon going to help Jeff with our Laurel Shea. By the way, the day He healed me was on June 27th., my dear friend and sister-in-Christ; Joyce's birthday. She said it was the best gift the Lord had given her, my healing. PRAISE THE LORD!!! Fred and i needed a break after all these happenings, so we made the trip to see Joyce in Santa Cruz, not long after the surgery to relax and celebrate.

The time of relaxation was not to last. When we returned home, i went to work at the facility for the last time with many tears in my customer's eyes and mine. Fred and Franz came and helped remove all of my equipment from the Salon, moving it back home. It would take time, but i would rebuild my cliental once again.

It was not to stop there. Fred came home very discouraged as he announced he had been laid off for the first time in his life. Wow, what were we to do? Fred's income had stopped, i had closed the Salon in town and with being self-employed, had no unemployment benefits. We applied for Fred's unemployment, but like everyone else it would take time and we had to wait. At the time we were still trying to build a business with a supplement company. Since Fred and i still had passes to fly, thanks to our Jeff; we decided to fly to a conference being held in Seattle, Washington, to help build our business. While there, a call came over my cell phone, it was a desperate voice crying out for help. It was the voice of our son Jeff telling of all his difficulties and could he come home until he could sort things out? Yes, of course, 'was he bringing our precious Laurel Shea as well?' He assured me he was; he would fly into Sacramento, so we left the conference early and would meet him there in Sacramento.

On the drive home, he poured out his painful heart to Fred and i. Thankfully, Laurel Shea was just two at the time, and did not really understand any of what was happening, although, she must have been very frightened.

When our sons left home, they each had a car of their own and other personal positions. Jeff came home without a car; he had left the one we gave him with his wife, so she could get back and forth to work. He quit his job with the airlines and was in search for one, while living with us.

During the Bible study i guided, i shared with the girls what was going on and asked for their prayers and work for Jeff. One of the dear ladies was having her home built and the contractor needed an assistant. i came home and told Jeff about the offer, i shall always remember he immediately retrieved a tape measure, handed it to his dad and said will you help me dad? Thankfully, Fred had the knowledge of carpentry; he sat down and shared with our son what he knew about the building trade.

The home that was being built was in our neighborhood, so Jeff could ride our a.t.v., to work, come home for lunch, spend time with Laurel Shea, return to work and come home after the days end. The room that was my dear mother's downstairs, now became Jeff and Laurel's. We were delighted to have him home and now with our Laurel Shea. i thanked the Lord again and again, for His healing my body and preparing my heart to help Jeff raise our Laurel Shea. As we get older, it is more difficult to have and care for little ones, i can't even imagine being ill as well.

Jeff, still wanted his marriage to be healed and he tried very hard to bring about that healing. He attended church with us and our Pastor Bill ministered to him. He made arrangements for Jeff and his wife to meet with him, even though she still lived in Southern California. At one point she flew to Sacramento where they all met and tried to work things out. He recommended that Jeff get a place of his own and have his wife come back. That of course, broke my heart due to the pain i witnessed in our son, but then the Lord wants to have relationships healed, this was not about me, it was about our children and their future.

Jeff was now working for a printing company and had more funds to be able to move out on his own. He also was able to purchase a vehicle. He moved out of our home with little Laurel Shea, with his wife to come and try to work things out with him. i remember the day, when they were to move in together, they came picked up Jeff and Laurels' last belongings and were going to leave. i was holding Laurel Shea in my arms as they were getting

291

things ready, she could feel the tension. i took her and placed her in her car seat in their car and she just sobbed and begged me to keep her and not let her go. That, my friend, broke my heart. Guess it brought back tears of my child hood, we may heal, but the memories are ever present.

Within a day or so, early in the morning i received a desperate phone call from Jeff while he was at work, could i please come and get Laurel Shea. i dropped everything and drove off to retrieve our little girl. There she stood next to her daddy with a bewildered look on her face, yet happy to see her Oma. Things just didn't work out for our children, so Jeff and little Laurel, moved back with Fred and i. Of course i was thrilled.

Prior to Jeff moving back home, Franz moved back for several months just biting at the bit to find a home of his own. Many of us parents, so it seems these days, have what i call swinging doors, children moving in and out. But with both of our sons staying at home, this was not going to be permanent, we had given them the roots and now they were using their wings to fly out of the nest. That bittersweet experience, knowing it is good for them to be on their own, yet wanting to hang on to them. As the writing on my mirror reminded me: To Let Go and Let God. Besides it is very healthy for our grown children to take on the responsibility of having a home of their own.

Franz was delighted when a friend he had worked for offered him a home on one of his father's ranches. The home was small but lovely; it sat on a three thousand acre ranch with a nice gravel road going to the house, it was surrounded by gorgeous year 'round pasture fed by a spring, very unusual for our area. There were horses kept on this wonderful green grass. Cows also were kept on the remainder of the land. Franz's main job was to make sure the pipes were changed in the meadow where the horses grazed, and once in awhile to round up cows that went astray. The ranch itself had many wonderful treasures including the blacksmith that housed all the tools for the smith, and wonder of wonders the Conestoga wagon the original owners traveled in, to reach California.

Many times Fred and i would have Sunday bar-b-q's with Franz; i even offered to trade homes with him. This home may have been small, but it offered so much, a walnut tree in the front yard, never ending spring water, beautiful old rose bushes, pomegranates, an array of old fashioned flowers and peace and quiet. We had that peace too, but it was different here amongst the green of the meadow that surrounded the home. It reminded me of the 'little house on the prairie.' Here i go again, one foot in the eighteen hundreds and the other on my computer, as i write, liking one, but loving the other.

Franz began dating different girls, and one named Lexie. We liked this young lady, she too was a country girl, a Christian, very giving, loving, well mannered, a gentle spirit and lovely. In the meantime we had purchased a used small motorboat to take out on the many lakes in Calaveras County. Franz helped his dad repair the boat, so he, Lexie, Jeff, Laurel, Fred and i would go boating on Saturday, or on Sunday after church. Lexie would stay over night with us, which i admired Franz for not taking her home with him to spend the night. She had her own room with us, which was a blessing. On one occasion, after coming home early from boating, Jeff was cleaning out the fish tank he had purchased for Laurel Shea, and i noticed Lexie was just sitting there conversing with Jeff as he cleaned the tank. Franz had gone home, and Lexie stayed with us to spend the night.

After cleaning the tank, Jeff asked if we would watch Laurel Shea, so he and Lexie could go and pick-up some fish for the tank, in Sonora. i said that was fine, thinking Lexie would take her own vehicle and head home since she lived in Sonora. It wasn't to be; she and Jeff drove off in Jeff's vehicle. Was this an official date, what was i to tell Franz, or was i to tell Franz? Early on i could see the interest Jeff had in Lexie and Lexie in Jeff, and had told Fred i thought the two wrong ones were dating; mother's intuition.

It should have been Jeff and Lexie. Jeff was divorced now, which was difficult for all of us. But life must go on, so i felt good about his dating again, but what about Franz?

i did call Franz, to fill him in on what just transpired, and ask if it was all right with him for Jeff to date Lexie? He assured me that he was good with the idea. Guess, later, as he thought it over, it really wasn't. But it was too late; Jeff and Lexie hit it off, and still love each other very much. Lexie was very good to Laurel Shea as well. So much so, when i was putting Laurel's clean clothes in her drawer, i noticed all these new clothes for her. i thought, 'where did all these lovely clothes come from?' Oh, i know, Lexie must have purchased them and lovingly placed them in Laurel's drawer without a single word. One weekend, as she was leaving, i asked her about the nice clothes, she just smiled, as she was walking out the door. i knew it was a gift she didn't want us to know about. As the Scripture says; **"But when you give to the needy, do not let your left hand know what your right hand is doing, so that your giving may be in secret. Then your Father, who sees what is done in secret, will reward you." Matthew 6: 3-4.** i believe at that very moment i felt a love for this precious girl, as never before. Not just because of her giving, but to whom she was giving, a child, and as many know i have great love and compassion for children. This kind gesture helped us too, as Fred was now receiving unemployment benefits and his social security and i was working on building the Salon.

Time went on, with Jeff's permission, we registered Laurel Shea in the same pre-school Franz and Jeff had attended at her age. She loved learning and being with other children. i also, was able to get a few children around her age to come to our home once a week for sharing, learning and playtime. One of the little girls, Emily, has become one of Laurel's dearest friends. i am so thankful, they keep in contact still today, although they live miles apart. But with all the new technology they are able to communicate with each other, what a blessing. The mother of the girl and i have kept in close contact as well.

While Laurel Shea was with us, she learned the basics that i talked about early on in this book, of how important it is to learn to potty train, walk, talk, eat properly, manners, and most of all about the saving grace of JESUS in her little heart and life. Laurel, like our sons, learned early on about Jesus, as we sat and read the children's Bible and prayed together. i remember when Laurel Shea started Kindergarten she said to me, "Oma, you mean there are children who don't know about God and Jesus?" Much to her disappointment, i told her, "Yes." This was most difficult for her to understand. When i worked in the Salon, Fred cared for our Laurel Shea. This was also a great time for her Papa to work with her and teach her, and sit with her, read and watch edifying videos or D.V.D.'s. This was all new to him, he had never had the opportunity to do these things with our sons, because he worked so far away, leaving early in the morning and returning home in time for dinner in the evening.

During the time Fred was unemployed, he felt pain in his wrists ('risks' as he calls them), Laurel and i like to tease him about his 'risks.' He just smiles and says, "Don't full with father (fatter) nature." Anyway, as it turned out, he had carpel tunnel in his 'risks' caused from cranking handles for many years at the machine shop. He had surgery for the carpel tunnel, and of course was unable to work, so applied for disability insurance. That was a blessing, it was more income than unemployment; we were surviving much better. Soon, that was depleted and we were faced with Fred having to find a job as a machinist, which was difficult as he was now in his late sixties. Not many want to hire an elderly person. We took this to the Lord in prayer and He answered abundantly more than we could think or ask. As **Ephesians 3:20-21 states; " Now to Him who is able to do immeasurably more than all we ask or imagine, according to His power that is at work**

within us, to Him be glory in the church and in Christ Jesus throughout all generations, for ever and ever! Amen."

My was that verse ever true, not only did Fred have a job as a machinist, but the machine shop was about six miles down the road from where we lived. Was this a miracle yes, indeed! To add more to this blessing, the shop Fred had previously worked in Lodi, was now sending the work to this shop for Fred to do. The owner really liked and appreciated Fred's work, and gave him a raise within in a week or so.

Once again, as life would have it, things began to change in the machine shop as well. Fred, came home one day to announce the shop had been sold, and the man who purchased it, was one of the men Fred had to fire at the shop he was foreman in, in Lodi. His fear was this man would not keep him as an employee. The exact opposite was to occur. The new owner told Fred one of the reasons he was purchasing the shop was because Fred was under their employ. He told Fred and i both, when he worked with Fred in Lodi, he loved watching and learning from Fred. He went on to say, he had never seen a machinist like Fred, whose work was incomprehensible; he was very impressed with Fred's work as a machinist. It was an honor to have Fred under his employ. We were delighted, as was his new boss. The Lord truly works in mysterious ways.

Chapter Twenty-Six

"... weeping may remain for a night,
but joy comes in the morning." Psalm 30:5

Time for our son and granddaughter to move on with their lives.
Letting go once again, it's not easy.

In the meantime, Jeff was biting at the bit to move out, so he and Laurel Shea could have a home and life of their own. Of course, as parents, we were very concerned. Lexie's parents had a rental on their ranch they offered Jeff to rent. He was so excited, checked it out, and on a rainy day, rented a truck to begin the moving process. This was too much for us; we would not only miss Jeff, but had become so attached to Laurel Shea. For me personally, i felt probably the same pain as Hannah, dedicating her little Samuel to the Lord's service, and of the mother of Moses. How did these godly women do it? These children were the one's they gave birth to. Surely, Hannah saw her son each year when she brought him a little tunic, she had probably made. She presented it to him when they went to the dedication each year. Then, what about Moses' mother, did she ever see her son again after Pharaohs' daughter raised him in the Palace? i did not give birth to Laurel, yet there was a bonding between us. How would this transition affect us, and our love for Laurel. Everything was so sudden, done with such haste.

The house they rented was at least an hour drive for us. When they first moved there, Laurel told me she saw the horses on the ranch. Then told me, in her small, little way, she was figuring in her mind how she would ride one of them to visit her Papa and Oma. She too, missed us. She continued to attend the preschool, and i kept involved helping out once a week and then taking her home. Praise the Lord, this was working out, and i would not have the pain of separation, as Hannah and Moses' mother must have experienced. None-the-less, it wasn't the same. Perhaps, this was more difficult for me, because she was the daughter i never had, i was older, she left at such a young age, and then maybe i was secretly and unknowingly, living my childhood through her. i have searched my heart to understand, but only the Lord knows for sure.

As with most things in life, and as the Word of God says, **"For our light and momentary troubles are achieving for us an eternal glory that far out weighs them all. So we fix our eyes not on what is seen, but on what is unseen. For what is seen is temporary, but what is unseen is eternal." 2 Corinthians 4:17-18.** Our life went on, the Salon business was building up once again, and Fred enjoyed his new job and didn't miss the long daily commute. We kept in contact with our children and Fred and i were actually beginning to relax a little and enjoy each other's company. Were we finally experiencing "The Empty Nest Syndrome?" If so, this was pretty good. We planned short trips here and there, one of which we will not long forget, or maybe we would like to forget.

It happened this way, i loved hot tubs and going to natural hot springs. We had been to the one in Fred's hometown in Germany, which was wonderful. So i decided i would check on the computer to find one in our area. Sure enough, there was one near Lake Tahoe. Fred is not fond of hot tubs, because we were in a man made one at Lake Tahoe years prior, and he felt like he was having a heart attack. We had been in it for far too long, and not realizing it at the time, of course felt the side affects. This would take some convincing for him to go with me to this natural one in Tahoe. He finally conceded.

Upon arriving at the place, we came to a huge two story white home where we paid the fees to use the facilities. We then got on our swim wear and trudged up a hill to try out the first natural spring, which was made into a swimming pool. We went into the dressing room to change, and then were going into this warm refreshing pool. As we were entering the pool, we both opened our eyes with such a surprise it must have startled the ones in the pool. Much to our amazement, they were all stark naked. Oh my goodness, what had i done? Was this a nudist colony? The advertisement on the web page didn't say anything about it being a nudist colony. We were in such a state of shock that we couldn't help but stare, which didn't help matters. We decided to try out some of the other bathing areas in the facility; it became more and more difficult and uncomfortable. Not long after, we left for home, never to return.

Joyce also had a second home in Tahoe, which she and her husband generously let us use. Jeff let us take Laurel Shea a couple of times to spend the weekend at their home in Tahoe. Laurel loved going down to the lake with us, delightfully playing in the sand, water and meeting other children. On one of those trips, Fred had just had prostate surgery and was wearing that awful catheter. Somehow it got infected and became very painful, and we spent most of the night at the hospital. Laurel Shea was with us, and was a very good sport about it; she was praying for her Papa as he lay in the hospital bed.

i had always wanted to go on a sleigh ride, so for my sixtieth birthday, Joyce took me to their home in Tahoe, so i could go on a sleigh ride. We stayed in her lovely home in Tahoe, cooked our own meals, read and enjoyed sharing our faith in Jesus.

At the end of a long day, we headed for a warm bed, a good nights sleep and looking forward to the sleigh ride the next day. When we awoke the next morning, it was snowing, so we bundled up after breakfast and drove to the sleigh for the long awaited ride i had always dreamed of taking. Guess we didn't bundle up enough, because it was mighty cold, even with the warm woolen blankets they had given us to cover ourselves. i wondered how people prior to the automobile survived; wow do we have it made these days. i was just thinking of a school teacher back in the eighteen hundred's, hitching the sleigh, bundling up, placing a hot brick under her feet for warmth for the long trip ahead; only to arrive at a one room school with just

299

a pot belly stove, where she had to gather wood to start the fire, before the children arrived for school.

Needless to say, this one ride was enough for me. i'm too much of a California girl, like a lizard, needs the warmth of the sun. We returned to Joyce's home, read, relaxed, shared and stayed inside enjoying the warmth of this lovely home nestled in the pine trees of Tahoe.

After a restful nights sleep, we woke up to snowflakes flowing gracefully down from heaven. Soon after, the flakes were increasing in number, and the snow began to pile up around our wonderful warm abode. For some reason i went into the garage to retrieve something from the car; Joyce followed behind. As she was coming out the door that led into the garage, i said, "Don't let the door...." it was too late; it closed behind her; that was the end of my message. As the door closed it locked shut. There we stood in the icy cold of the garage, which wasn't so bad, but we were in our pajamas and i in my house slippers; thankfully Joyce had on her Ugg boots. But how were we going to get back into the house? There was a side door in the garage, which led to a side gate, but by now the snow was piled so high against the gate making it almost impossible to open. Guess we both were on an adreline high, because we shoved and pushed until the gate opened. Saying a quick prayer that the front door would be unlocked, i ran out into the snow, hoping a neighbor wouldn't see me, finally coming to the front door. Yes Lord, You are faithful, the door was unlocked and opened with no problem.

Our fun had just begun, i told Joyce i thought we should be going back home. She has so much faith and replied, " Oh, don't worry, we'll be o.k., and get out safely." i having been in snow several times before, and many of them not good experiences, was very concerned about getting out and home. Remember, you the reader, are dealing with two crazy California girls. Soon our cell phones were ringing, husbands and friends calling and telling us the storm was getting worse and we should leave and head for home. Soon the power was out and we had no communication, just our loved ones calling every so often checking to see if we had left yet.

We began packing, getting ready to leave. The snow kept coming, more and more of the beautiful white flakes and it was getting deep, and if we didn't leave soon, we too, would be in deep, (trouble that is). Finally, getting everything loaded, i turned to Joyce who wasn't used to driving in the snow and said, "Now, as we go down your steep drive way and road, act as though there was an egg between your foot and the gas pedal." She did so, and we safely were on the road to home. We did not have snow chains, so we prayed the snow tires would suffice as we traveled down those mountainous roads. Joyce did much better than I; her confidence and faith were amazing. We sang songs as we drove along on the snow-covered roads, finally coming to black pavement, a welcoming sight.

It was getting late and darkness was beginning to surround us as we were taking a different route home; we prayed once again, this time so as to not get lost.

In the meantime, Fred had invited a number of friends to celebrate my birthday with our usual Bon Fire (Barn Fire). We knew all about it, and hoped we would make it home in time to join in on "my celebration." A funny thought occurred to me, if we didn't arrive in time everyone would celebrate without the Birthday girl, which was fine with me, i just wanted to get home safely.

That we did, as we drove up our steep driveway we could see the flames of the huge Bon Fire Fred had built in my honor. Everyone was glad to see us, and our prayers were answered. We were tired, yet excited to be home and celebrate with great food, family, friends, a nice warm fire, dancing in the barn and no snow. Yeah!!!

301

Chapter Twenty-Seven

"El Roi: The God Who Sees"
When, if Ever, Does the Pain Cease?

The difficulty of letting go and letting God.
"With the Lord all things are possible."

Although, i kept busy in the Salon, gardening, Bible Study, caring for Fred, our ranch, and home, there was still a big piece of my heart missing in the name of, Laurel Shea. i had grown to love this little girl, and believed, as my sister Barbara said, " i was living my childhood that i never had, through Laurel Shea." i knew this was not good. But i kept remembering the time when she and Jeff were living with us. For instance, she loved Winnie the Pooh.[25] We decided we would call our ranch "The Twenty Acre Wood", with all the characters from that story: Pooh, lived in the pump house on the ranch; in the tree she could find owl or "Owl Up" is what she called him; along with gopher, who lived in a well shaft that we could call down into and hear our echo; she thinking it was really gopher. What an exciting, loving adventure it was for her. We flew kites, skipped rocks in the pond, and fed the cows, pigs and chickens, gathering their eggs at the days end. Then there was Oma's beloved vegetable garden. We had so much fun digging in the soil; she had her own little set of gardening tools our dear friend Robin purchased for her. There was planting and, of course, reaping the harvest of our labor. Oh yes, the fun time she and Emily had making mud pies, looking like two little mud pies when Emily's daddy came to take them home. i must mention one of Oma's all time favorites: baking, fresh cookies, cakes, pies, bread, cinnamon rolls and whatever we wished, as long as we had the supplies on hand. Yes, i did most of this with our sons as well, but for some reason this was different. Was it because she was the little girl i had always wanted or was it because i was getting older and appreciating life and relationships more?

We have dear friends in the Valley whom i shared the ministry of Bible Study: Ray and Louella. They have become very good friends as well as our dear brother and sister in Christ. While we were caring for our Laurel Shea, Louella presented her with a tea set for a child. It was darling, so little and lovely. How Laurel and i would love to have tea parties with this little set. Her daddy would put on a silly hat along with Laurel and, they too, would have a tea party. The set was something i wished i had as a child. What a blessing to have such wonderful caring friends as Ray and Louella.

They also have an almond orchard and are very generous in sharing fresh almonds with us. We in turn brought them fresh eggs and range free beef. We took Laurel with us to have lunch and spend time with our dear friends Ray and Louella, and to pick apples from their huge trees for us, and our cows. The almonds were on the ground ready to be harvested. But today, unlike my experience of picking fruit by hand, they now have harvesting machines that shake, pick, sweep the orchards, load them on trucks, all ready to haul to the packer. The machines had not come yet, so i asked if Laurel Shea could pick some to take home. They gave her a little bucket for the small crop she picked. It was a good experience for her and for her Papa too, because he didn't realize the almond could be picked off the ground still in it's outer shell, then shelled from the inner and outer shell and eaten, delicious raw almonds.

During lunch, Ray presented Laurel Shea with a freezer bag full of shelled almonds. Papa, who loves almonds said, "Oh, look what Ray has given us." Ray corrected him saying, "No, those are for Laurel." Papa Fred bent his head in disappointment. Laurel was delighted to have such a wonderful gift; she would share them with her Papa as well.

On our trip home i was showing, our now three year old, Laurel how to take the outer light green shell off the almond, explaining when we

303

arrived home, we would remove the light brown shell, because it was too messy to remove it in the truck. So, we sat in the back seat of the truck removing the outer shell, as Papa drove us home. Suddenly, Laurel began singing in her precious sweet little voice; "Amen, amen, amen, amen." as she was shelling the almonds, she thought they were called "amens," short "a." It shouldn't have surprised me; we were bringing her up in a Christian home and why not "Amens" instead of almonds? Never the less, it was adorable and we will always cherish this time of harvesting "Amens." Which reminds me, why do we call them almonds and salmon: 'samon?' Actually, most almond growers do call them 'amons,' short "a." Whatever, it's like the song, " ' You say tomato and i say tomato.' Let's Call the Whole Thing Off.' "

That is one reason i titled this chapter: El Roi: The God Who Sees. Yes, the Lord God sees it all, knows all, and comes in, to embrace and comfort us during these trying times. He was, and is, always there for us. Then again the Scripture that comes to mind, and one of my favorites is; **2 Corinthians 1: 3-5**, referring to the God of all comfort, who comforts us, so we in turn, can comfort others, with the same comfort we receive from Him. Meaning, if we never experience a situation, then how can we truly understand and comfort someone who is going through any particular experience? How much easier it is to understand and comfort if we've gone through the same type of pain. This is one reason i believe the Lord allows us to go through the sufferings, trials, tribulations we experience: so we can comfort others. i know the Lord will use this experience i had, for His glory, and for me to comfort others as He has comforted me.

It wasn't long and Laurel Shea started Kindergarten; she loved school. i had helped in the pre-school she had attended in Angels Camp, so made arrangements to help once a week in her Kindergarten class, too. This was a little more difficult; because it was an hour drive to the school she attended, whereas before, i drove only twenty minutes. But i wanted to participate in her learning, so decided to proceed with the idea. After school, i was able to take her out for ice cream and do some shopping, then take her to her home. This worked great, up until she was in the forth grade in school; we both looked forward to these special times together. Not only was i helping in the classroom, but also i became good friends with one of the secretaries and remain so to this day.

The secretary's name is Cindy. She, her dear mom, and her dear sweet grandmother, became my customers. What a blessing that was; here they were three generations, twenty years apart, and all would come together to have their hair done. It was interesting how the Lord made each one. Cindy's grandmother's hair, had the most beautiful waves and was so easy to shape, she even told her granddaughter that only once before, had someone been able to cut her hair the way i did. i'd been told before, that i knew just how to cut wavy hair. i must admit it is a gift from the Lord, i really wasn't taught in Cosmetology school, except not to cut into the wave. Then there was mom, who had perfectly straight, wiry hair that was almost impossible for me to give her a perm, but we managed. Then there was my dear Cindy, who had lovely blonde hair she would have me cut and donate for cancer patients. i was so blessed to meet these ladies and serve them in this marvelous way. After we were finished, Fred helped me prepare a lovely lunch for all of us. Our lunch usually consisted of fresh lettuce from our green house, and a lovely quiche made with our fresh eggs, bacon and fresh veggies. What a delight and fun time we had sharing stories at the table, after we thanked the Lord for His many blessings.

i enjoyed helping at the school as i had done when our sons were young. The children and i had the pleasure of getting to know each other as we would gather around the lunch table and i listened and visited with them. i had begun writing Christian books for children, and would get many ideas from these little ones.

The main reason i began to write is because of our Laurel Shea, and all that she had already experienced as a young child. Divorce affects everyone, especially children. i believe that is why Jesus, after speaking of divorce in chapter nineteen of Matthew, when he finishes at verse twelve, he concludes with the children, and said, **"Let the children come to me, and do not hinder them, for the kingdom of heaven belongs to such as these."** When He had placed His hands on them, He went on from there. **Matthew 19:14-15**. It seems to me, He was telling us it is the children who suffer such a dramatic time when parents divorce. i believe that is why so many children blame themselves and take on the burden that was not meant for them to bear. When Jesus placed His hands on them, He showed how much He cared and loved children.

i learned, during my time with these little ones, the fears and anxieties they were experiencing with their parents divorced or perhaps living with someone else, that too, brings on heart ache for all involved. That is not how our Lord meant life to be, as such. None-the-less, life must go on and we must accept it, make the best for everyone concerned. For me, being with these children gave me opportunity to listen and offer to pray for them. One such boy loved sharing with me and frequently asked me to pray for him and his situation. He asked me at one time if i would pray for his dad who wouldn't stop smoking; this troubled the boy, knowing how it could affect his dad's and other's health. i prayed. The next week the boy came to me very excited sharing how his dad had quit smoking. The next week, he told me he had attended church with his grandmother and was looking forward to going again. There were many such stories as these, which I will always treasure in my heart. The reason i went to the school was to bring Laurel Shea her lunch and spend this important time, mainly with her. She loved and enjoyed my coming, but i noticed in time, she would eat and then run off to play with the children. Leaving me with other children at the lunch table. At first this troubled me, then i realized she felt good about my coming, secure in the freedom to spend fun time with her friends. This gave me opportunity to spend time with the children who needed love, prayer and just a listening ear.

i then went to her classroom and helped out in any way i could. i recall many times taking the opportunity, whenever possible, to share the Gospel with these little ones through love and kindness. On one occasion, it was St. Patrick's Day and the teacher was teaching the children about leprechauns, of all things. She was really into this and excitedly came to the back of the classroom and said to me; "Isn't this fun, they believe in what i am teaching them about leprechauns?" The door opened wide for me to speak as i said, " They really believe you, don't they?" She replied, "Oh, yes." i then said, "May i share with the children about the real story of St. Patrick?" She directed me to some books including encyclopedias in her classroom, where i could find more information if i needed it. i thanked her and then went to research these books on St. Patrick, as well as leprechauns. To my astonishment, there it was in the very books she had on the shelf, the falsehood of leprechauns. i was thankful for the truthfulness of St. Patrick that i also found in those books. And very grateful, the teacher was going to allow me to share, the following week, the truth about St. Patrick. Perhaps, she had not known the truth about St. Patrick.

After sharing St. Patrick's story with the children, i took it upon myself to tell them, that as a Christian, i believe in the Trinity. Then i took a green sheet of construction paper, made a three-leaf clover, and explained what we believed: The Father, The Son and The Holy Spirit. St. Patrick was in Ireland, which is covered with green pastures. He was being held as a captive and it is believed he probably took a green clover and explained the Trinity in the same way to the pagans who lived there at the time. Thus, God the Father, Jesus the Son and the Holy Spirit are one. The clover has three leaves, but one stem; just as God is One, yet Three. What a joy and pleasure it was that the teacher allowed me to share, and these little ones were so attentive. i am thankful for the many times the teacher allowed me to share with the children.

Working with these children, the teachers, and being involved in Laurel Shea's life, helped to ease much of the pain i was experiencing. It's wonderful to realize we can all grow deeper in our faith when we have these painful times, or just the opposite, we can become bitter and angry. Just as sand can be an irritant to an oyster and it becomes a beautiful pearl, or a caterpillar becomes a lovely butterfly, so it is with life's experience, pressure and pain; when we give it to the Lord, it can become something beautiful and we become stronger in our faith and become more like Jesus.

A pastor once told me, as i was sharing different concerns, "gloria, do not become bitter in your pain." He was right and it all begins with forgiveness, because if we do not forgive, we become angry which turns into bitterness.

Ephesians 4:30a-32 says it well; **"Do not grieve the Holy Spirit of God... Let all bitterness and wrath and anger and clamor and slander be put away from you, along with malice. Be kind to one another, tender-hearted, forgiving each other, just as God in Christ also has forgiven you."**

Don't you just love the Word of God? First, He tells us what not to do, then, He tells us how to respond and tells us what good to do to replace the evil.

Chapter Twenty-Eight

"Jehovah-shammah: The Lord Is There"

Realizing i can no longer care for my sweet mother

During this time, my mother had a fall and was hospitalized. From the hospital she went into a skilled nursing facility. Fred and i went to visit her in these facilities in San Jose, then i would travel by myself, spend time with Mom, do her hair and then spend the rest of the time with my Aunt Mary, Mom's sister.

The day came when Mom was released from the skilled nursing facility and went to live with her sister, Mary. Both were now in their seventies, and it was becoming more and more difficult for Aunt Mary to care for herself, let alone my Mom. i made arrangements to interview a couple of people to care for Mom, while she lived with Aunt Mary. My sister Fran, her husband Don, my brother Frank, Fred and i, met at our Aunt's to meet the caretakers. It was not to be; the caretakers never showed for their interview. This was a blessing, a powerful indication they would probably not show up to care for Mom. What next?

With most plans, we hope and pray for something, and then something else transpires unexpectedly. In this case, i was thankful for some things that i did not know, concerning the pain and hurt my brother and sister experienced from our past. Wow, what an eye opener! i was not the only one who was affected by the experiences we had as children. i will always thank the Lord for hearing the truth from their lips.

Remember, as i shared before the harmful situations, especially in our homes? We walk around situations as if an elephant were in the middle of the room and do not discuss matters that may be troubling us. Now, these many years later, the truth was unveiled. Praise the Lord!!! The end result was healing.

Back to the drawing board, what shall we do now for someone to care for Mama? i had offered once again for her to come live with Fred and I; she wanted to either stay with Aunt Mary or be placed in a convalescent home near my aunt. The search was on to find one close to my aunt. i believe it was my brother Frank, who found one within driving distance from my aunt, perfect. We got Mama all settled in to her new home. Later i made a trip to San Jose to take Mama and my aunt out for the day. Since Mama and my aunt both loved flowers, i took them to the beautiful Rose Garden in San Jose. Much to my surprise, they told me their brother, my uncle Joseph, was a gardener for the city of San Jose and part of his job was to care for the roses in the Rose Garden. Was it any wonder he too had a special gift for caring for plants and neatness in caring for them? He had already passed on, so i was unable to learn more about plants from him; oh, the opportunities we miss in life because we do not converse and build relationships.

As i pushed Mama in her wheel chair, through the array of sweet smelling, delicate, remarkable beauty of each rose, the Lord created, she was her usual self. She wanted to just take a small cutting from each of the roses she loved most. She had a green thumb as i mentioned before, and had started most of her gorgeous plants from cuttings. She once told me, with a sly grin, "The ones you snitch do the best."

We then drove to 24th Street, where her parents raised Mama, my aunt and their four brothers. There was the home Mama had always told me about; it seemed much smaller than the way she explained it to me. Yes, it had a basement where my grandmother did the laundry, most likely by hand. Mom once told me, grandma was carrying a large tub of hot water from her kitchen to the basement to do laundry and slipped, spilling hot water all over herself. Mom also told me it was in the cellar where the salami, cheese and homemade wine were kept. She went on to tell me how my grandfather put a lock on the door to keep my grandmother out of the cellar, away from the wine. The lock didn't keep grandma from taking an ax to the lock breaking it, so she could have her beloved wine. When my grandfather came home from work and found my grandmother, probably drunk, he began to beat her for breaking into the cellar and getting polluted, (as Mama, said). That was when my mom came between my grandparents to stop him from beating grandma. Mom said her father never laid a hand on her mother again, after she stopped him.

Mom loved plants, trees and flowers of every kind, but she did not like Palm Trees. And she made no bones about telling anyone who would listen, whenever she saw these tall trees. She would say, "They are worthless, they don't even give a person shade. What are they good for?" As we parked in front of their old home, there in the front yard stood a very tall lonely Palm Tree. i asked my mom, "Mama, was that tree there when you lived in this home?" She answered, "Yes, that worthless thing." i questioned her no more and we drove off.

Upon arriving at the convalescent home, my sweet Mama cried and didn't want to even get out of the car. Finally, with much coaxing we were able to get her into the home, with promises of making other arrangements. i drove home broken hearted, praying for guidance.

The next day my brother Bill visited Mama and called me saying, "Mom, is crying and wants you to come and get her and take her home with you." Fred and i decided that is what we must do, so i made plans to drive back and pick-up my sweet Mama. i first drove to San Jose Airport to pick-up my sister Barbara who flew in from Mexico, where she was now living. She had offered to help me get Mama settled in our home and help out for a brief time.

We drove back to Aunt Mary's to pack Mama's little possessions; i shall never forget all her earthly belongings fit in a large garbage bag. After dinner we sat at the table and had a discussion with our Aunt Mary, it was one in which i will always keep within my heart. Our aunt said, as she looked at the bag containing Mama's things, "This is all your mother had, not much." Barbara's response was perfect, as she answered, "Maybe, Mama had it right." i added, " Yes, you are right Barbara, the Bible says; **'Naked we come into the world, and naked we depart.'" Job 1:21** paraphrased. Then, Barbara asked our aunt, "Where are you with the Lord?" Our aunt quickly responded, "Ask, Gloria, she knows." shocked at her remark i said, "i don't know anyone's heart, only the Lord knows." Not long after our aunt made some unkind remarks about someone close to us, i said to her, "If you know Jesus, He wants you to forgive that person, you must forgive." She was silent.

The next day, Barbara and i went to pick-up a very grateful, teary-eyed precious soul: our Mama. i shall not forget, i had given her a picture of what we believe Jesus looks like, and handed it to Mama as we were leaving the home. She took, kissed it, made the sign of the cross as i witnessed the gratefulness in her little heart. Then i knew Mama believed and new Him as her own, as she would have stated.

i was thankful for Mama's patience, as we stopped on our two and 1/2 hour drive, to pick- up adult diapers and other needed items. When i got to the car, where she and Barbara sat waiting for me, i handed Mama a beautiful plant with an arrangement of her beloved potted flowers of all sorts. She thanked me with tears of joy.

When we arrived home, Fred and Jeff met us. As i mentioned before, there was a special bonding between Mama and Jeff. He made the trip to be there when his grandma arrived; he was so delighted to see his Grandma, and she him. He helped her up the stairs into the room where she would be staying. After she rested, we all sat out on our deck and visited, making plans for the next day's trip to Redding. Brother Bill's daughter was getting married in a couple of days and we, with my entire family, would attend. This also would give us the opportunity to discuss with all of my siblings after the wedding, our plans for our Mother. The day before the wedding we all went to brother Frank's home for a family gathering and bar-b-q. Mom, seemed to being doing fine, until it was bedtime. She was crying most of the night, for the nurse to come and rub her burning feet. i was the nurse. It was then we realized Mama had dementia. Frank heard her crying out as well, and would come running down the stairs to assist me. He finally said, "Gloria, you can't do this, it will wear you out. We need to do something else." He was right; i hadn't gotten hardly any sleep and was not very polite the next day. None-the-less, i got Mama all dressed and ready for the wedding of her sweet granddaughter, Candace.

The wedding was lovely and was held outside in Bill and Deannie's garden. They had done a lot of preparation for this lovely event. When it came time to seat Mama, several of her caring grandsons escorted her to her seat, with such love and respect. i have a picture of them all running to help their sweet Grandmother, who looked lovely in her favorite color green flower print dress. They stood beside her while the ceremony proceeded.

When the vows were said, and everyone was seated, waiting to help themselves to the light desserts for refreshment, Mama must have been really hungry, because she called to me and said, "Gloria, bring me something to eat." i told her there were different kinds of desserts, she replied, "No, i want to eat something solid." i told her we had already eaten before the wedding. She didn't remember; i realized the dementia was getting worse. She wouldn't quit; she must have been hungry, or thought she was, or just confused. Bless her. She then grabbed my brother Bill and said, "i am hungry." Bill tried to explain, there were desserts, but no, she didn't want desserts. He left and brought her a plate of solid food, as she called it.

The next day, i was still out of sorts, as i had not slept much due to Mama's constant crying all night long. It wasn't her fault; she did have neuropathy, and felt a burning sensation in her feet, although, they were ice cold to the touch. In the morning once again, tired and grumpy as i was, i managed to get myself, and Mom ready for the day. The entire family was invited to go to Bill and Deannie's home for a nice meal

Once we arrived, Barbara announced she was not going to stay with me for a while as planned and help care for Mama. She had decided to return home to Mexico. Perhaps she could see Mama needed to go into a convalescent home. i didn't understand, was tired, and this upset me, because i so wanted to take Mama home with me and was looking forward to Barbara's help. i just don't remember exactly what transpired that day.

Perhaps, all my siblings realized Mama needed more care than i could give her. It was me who didn't want to give-up; i had promised Mama and myself, when i was just a child that i would take care of Mama in her aging years. i watched her care for my grandmother, her mother, and felt it was my duty to care for my Mama. i was probably on the biggest river in the world: 'Denial' (the Nile). i wanted to believe i could care for Mama, and just needed that brief time for my sister to help me.

Somehow, someway, we got into a big family argument, which left me crying with remorse that i could not take Mama home. My sister Fran, came to my defense and said, "Can't you see? Gloria is so tired from caring for Mama the last couple of nights, give her a break!" i felt relieved with her kind words of caring. But those words also brought me to the realization: i could not care for Mama any longer. She had to go into a home, not just any home, but one where they understood dementia and could give her the loving care she needed. That was a tough one for me to swallow, but i knew i had to let go once again.

My dear sister, Barbara, did stay on with the rest of the family, as she and Bill searched for the right home to place Mama in, in Redding. That was another issue for me, i knew Mama didn't like Redding, but this is where she was, and the Lord must have wanted her there for a reason. That reason and many more were to be shown in a short period of time.

In the meantime, Fred and i left for home, me crying and disappointed, yet grateful. i still hadn't relinquished Mama to the Lord. There would be times, my sister Fran and i would discuss, via the phone, ideas of what to do for Mama. Soon, Barbara and Bill found a nice convalescent home for Mama, a residence where they thoroughly understood dementia. i was so thankful to both Barbara and Bill. As i write this and think about the whole situation, my dear sister Barbara, knowing the strong, bull headed, persistent person i am, told me she could not stay and was returning home to Mexico. Only then, would i realize i couldn't care for Mama without help. Thank you Barbara, Josephine, Frances, Frank and Bill, for your caring heart, not only for Mama, but, for your determined, persistent sister, me.

Now, that Mama was in a nice facility in Redding, Fred and i would make monthly trips to visit and spend time with her. The first time we visited, i was heart broken, because she had a monitor placed around her ankle. The monitor was to help the staff know where Mama was, since her dementia became so severe, she could walk off in a moment; they would not know without the monitor. i understood, but for me, it was like some sort of imprisonment, which it was not, it just seemed that way to me, her daughter.

Fran had decorated the room in a very welcoming fashion, and continued to do so, as long as Mama was in the facility. Even at Christmas time, Fran made sure Mama's room was decorated to celebrate the birth of Jesus. i added pictures of Mama's family, children, grandchildren, placing them on a large white poster board for Mama to enjoy.

Each time we visited, her dementia was more and more apparent. But the Lord sustained me, and with His grace and mercy, got me through those trying times. The last time we visited, i brought her a small c.d. player with c.d.'s of her favorite singers: Dean Martin, Perry Coma, the one's of her era, that she could listen to, with earphones. She loved it and would listen as she drifted off to sleep. We were taking her to the lunchroom on that last visit, and she looked down at my pink cowgirl boots and remarked, "I sure like 'them' boots." i thanked her as we escorted her to the lunchroom. As she was eating her lunch, she turned to me and said, " Are you taking me home?" i replied, "Who, am i?" She didn't say a word, because she didn't know who i was. i then said, "Why would you want to go home with me, you don't even know who i am?' Then i said, "i'm gloria." She continued eating, asking once again, "Are you taking me home?" i said, "Who am i?" She replied, "gloria." i said, "That's because i told you who i am." Seems cruel, but i just wanted to make these moments fun and special, no harm meant, just love and laughter.

We knew how much she loved the sunshine; she was always so brown and never used sun block. Her darkened skin gave evidence of her love for the outdoors, her flowers and warm sunshine. We learned the rays of the sun gave her the much-needed vitamin D, "the sunshine vitamin" she called it, which also helped prevent memory loss in years past. While there, we pushed her in the wheelchair to absorb the sun she so loved.

Later she showed me her painted fingernails, which Mama seldom did, paint her nails. i said, "They look nice Mama, who did them for you?" She replied, "My daughter, Frances." i knew then, for sure, even though i was the one in the past who cared for her and still wanted to do so, she didn't really know who i was.

The miracle, and one of the reasons Mama was there in Redding, was not only for the care she received, but, she had four of her sibling children and grandchildren living close enough to visit her on a regular basis. That was so much more than Fred and i could do for Mama. But the main reason, i believe, was to have closure with my sister, Frances. Yes, she is the one who painted Mama's nails, and Mama remembered her taking care of her and being there for her. Oh yes, the others were there too, but Frances and Mama needed this time, and closure. i will always thank the Lord for allowing this to happen for my sister and Mama. PRAISE THE LORD!!!

That last time we saw Mama, i took her to Frank's home in order to give her a permanent and style her hair, which takes at least two hours. After i had finished, she kept asking us to take her home. We tried to explain to her that she was at Frank's home with us, she didn't understand. She kept insisting we take her home. This was difficult for us, because we wanted her to stay and visit with us; truthfully we wanted our Mama back. She had now conceded that the facility and the familiarity of it was now her home. It was hard for us to swallow, but this is the reality of dementia.

This was also a time of healing and family gatherings for me, which i loved. Each time we went to visit Mama in Redding, one of us siblings (brother and sister-in-laws too) was having a birthday. What was so special, was, we would all go to a nice restaurant for dinner and who's birthday it was we were celebrating, the other couples would pay for the dinner of that birthday couple or person. Then we would gather at one of the sibling's home for dessert, fun, reminiscing and laughter. Those were days i will long cherish. As an added reward, Mama's wish and prayer was coming true, her children were together, sharing love and laughter.

Mama hadn't been in the facility long, when i received that most dreaded tearful phone call from my brother Frank, that Mama had passed. It is interesting to note, a week to the day, before she passed, after Fred had left for work, a little music box in our room, played just a couple of notes. It was just a couple of notes, to get my attention, enough for me to get up and move. i immediately called the facility where Mama resided, to ask how she was doing. They responded, she was just having breakfast.

The strange thing about this music box was, it was given to me, by some people in Switzerland; it was on the trip with Mama, me, my sister Josephine, Aunt Mary, and Franz. One day, as we were all sitting out on our friend's patio where we were staying, overlooking the beauty of Lake Major in Switzerland, i pulled the string on the music box. My Mama not noticing, said, "Oh, here comes the ice cream man." The sound of the music was just like the sound of the ice cream man's truck in California Mama had remembered as a child. i laughed, and said, "No, Mama, it's the music box, i just pulled the string." She just smiled.

That to me, my friend, was a delightful sound, when the music box played those few notes a week before Mama's passing. i believe the Lord sent an angel to pull the string on the music box, to get my attention because it instantly reminded me of Mama. It was used to send me a message of comfort. That music box has not gone off since, except when our grandson comes to visit and loves to pull the string to listen to the sound of the ice cream man coming.

My heart was heavy over the loss of my dear sweet Mama, for years a day wouldn't go by without my remembering my Mama. In year's prior, she had also given me a plant called a Hoya, which produces clusters of pink flowers. When they first come out, they look like little wax stars, then they open up and look and feel like little velvet stars. i have that Hoya plant hanging in the kitchen between two windows. The plant had never bloomed, until a year after Mama went home to be with Jesus. That February, a year later, after Mama's entering the presence of heaven, the plant bloomed for the very first time. For me it was a gift from Mama, and as much as to say, "Remember me, I'm watching over you." Perhaps, i'm wrong, but i like to think as such.

i do know the year after she passed, we had an abundance of walnuts from our tree. i told Fred, "i think Mama is talking with Jesus, and asking Him to bless us with walnuts." You see, Mama and i loved to crack and shell walnuts during the winter months, for baking throughout the year. We both loved walnuts, and memories of picking them in Silicon Valley/Santa Clara Valley.

Chapter Twenty-Nine

"Jehovah-Shalom: The Lord Is Peace"

My mother's final days on earth. The loss of my sweet mother; she is finally at total peace, resting in the gentle arms of Jesus. Her final reward for her service unto Him.

"Peace I leave you; My peace I give you. I do not give to you as the world gives. Do not let your hearts be troubled and do not be afraid. " John 14:27. Yes, at last Mama was at peace resting in the arms of Jesus.

Prior to Mama's going to the facility in Redding, i was going through her things, getting them ready to send to my brother, Frank. Each and every scrap of paper, so it seemed, that Mama had in her purse, was written the names of all of us children in birth order. i believed, we were the ones she lived for in this life, and she prayed for us continually. Oh, she loved all of her grandchildren, in-laws and many others as well, but her children had a special place in her heart. i believe her prayers over the years helped get us through the many difficulties we faced in life. Her love and prayers for us, was the glue that kept us children together. She would always tell me, " No matter what happens, you kids stick together." Thank you, Mama. It is my hope and prayer that she is looking down from heaven and continues to pray for all of us, as we stick together. Her prayers have been and continue to be answered, as we siblings all get along.

i am thankful Frank had been helping Mama set aside money every month to help pay for her funeral. In the end, there was very little to pay, but as it was, she was our Mama and we all gladly chipped in. Once again, her prayers were being answered, bringing us all together to help pay for her service. Frank did most of the work behind the scenes, to have Mama's remains brought back to San Jose, for the burial. We knew she would be buried with our father; that was her desire. Frank had Mama's remains placed in her favorite color, green, casket. It was lovely arrayed with a spray of gorgeous pink carnations. i had hoped all my siblings would agree and allow me to give Mama's eulogy, which they did; i was grateful and honored to share about Mama's life. i had contacted all Mama's children and grandchildren to give me their take on Mama. This made for an interesting celebration of her life. Fred and i went in search of background music to play at the service. The Lord provided, and led us to a music store in San Jose, where we found Nat King Cole's c.d., which had most of Mama's favorite tunes: The Autumn Leaves, Wondering Rose and many more. When i was young, she sang most of these songs as she went about her daily chores. As sweet as Mama was, i am sorry to say she couldn't carry a tune in a bucket, but what a blessing it was, just to hear her sing. i guess we children got our music ability from our Papa, since he could play the harmonica and accordion by ear. But i realized as i listened to these wonderful songs, i too am a romantic, just like Mama. :)

Someone once told me, "Blessed is the grave that it rains upon, on the day of their burial." Well, it not only rained, but there was a downpour, with thunder, lightening and more rain. My brother-in-law Don told me, "As you were speaking, the sun shone directly just for a moment on Mama's casket, it was amazing." As if the Lord was telling us, Mama was o.k.

Prior to the service, my dear brother Bill said to me, "We siblings have been discussing your speaking today, if it becomes too difficult, just let me know and i will step in for you." i thanked him, and reassured him, i would do fine. The Lord is my help and i knew He would get me through. Besides, speaking was the gift He had given me, and i love it. **Philippians 4:13 states, "I can do all things through Him who gives me strength."**

For Mama's service, i wore the pink cowgirl boots Mama had commented on while she was in the facility, with a red cowgirl hat and red scarf around my neck that had hearts and the words, Jesus, written on it, along with a blouse, pink jacket and jeans. It was simple, like my Mama. Because Mama liked Roy Rogers and Dale Evans so much, i had Happy Trails played at the end of the ceremony. During the service, i started with how Mama's life would carry on through each one of us siblings life, with the love of flowers, fun, laughter, caring and so forth; the qualities of our Mama. Then i shared the comments her grandchildren had made about their grandmother. Some of which were, from Robbie, "My children learned to cuss, whenever they heard grandma rooting for her favorite sports team." Another said, "She would overcook something or whatever, and say, 'Don't tell your dad or mom; Grandmother's secrets.'" She loved sending Andes chocolate mints in the mail to her grandchildren, a favorite of hers, as well. Sarah and Candace especially liked them. i had purchased some, and as Mama would have done, pitched them out to all who were present saying as Mama would say, "Here, catch, have some!" "... **remember the words of the Lord Jesus, that He Himself said, "It is more blessed to give than to receive." Acts 20:35b**. Then of course i shared Scripture, from my Bible.

Many came to me at the end of the service and told me what a nice job i did in Mama's honor. i will always remember my nephew Brent coming up and staring at the casket after the service, then turning and just embracing me. And then his Dad, my brother Frank, removing four angels from the corners of the casket he had placed there, one for each one of us sisters. The angels reminded us always of Mama's name; Angelina, which in Italian means, Angel or God's messenger; that was our sweet Mama. And the cross that sat on top of the casket, he presented to our brother Bill. Sometime before, i had given Mama an angel and Frank told me that would be his angel to remind him of Mama. That's my thoughtful brother, Frank, always thinking of others before himself, like Mama.

Holding our Laurel Shea's little hand as we left the cemetery, she looked up at me with those beautiful green eyes of hers, and said, "Oma, where is my Uhr Oma?," meaning where is my great grandmother? i glanced down at her sweet little face and with great confidence said, "The angels are carrying her to heaven." Little did i know at the time i was quoting Scripture.

Please allow me to share how the Lord would show this to me as i was writing "Our" Christian children's book entitled: Heaven. There it was in **Luke 16:22-24, which reads; "The time came when the beggar died and the angels carried him to Abraham's side. The rich man also died and was buried."**

Does this mean that only the poor go to heaven and not the rich? Not necessarily, although Jesus did say to His disciples, **"I tell you the truth, it is hard for a rich man to enter the kingdom of heaven. Again I tell you, it is easier for a camel to go through the eye of a needle than for a rich man to enter the kingdom of God." Matthew 19:23-24.** How many times had i read that passage in Luke over the years, and did not see it, until an inquisitive, innocent child asked me, and then it was confirmed when i did the research for "Our" book: Heaven. Thank You, Holy Spirit, for revealing it to me, in Your time, as i shared with our Laurel Shea. After Mama's service and celebration of her life, we went home to relax. Well, i guess my family was right, i held up very well for the service, but as soon as i got home, i became very ill. So very weak, tired and just completely exhausted. i didn't realize just planning, speaking and being the encourager, that God gifted me to be, could be so wearing. Mostly, the reality of my mom not being here on earth really struck me hard. Mom was the first one i called when i had a problem or difficulty, knowing somehow, she would take it to the Lord in her own special way. Although, i knew she couldn't solve the problem, it was comforting just knowing she was there to listen. Oh, i know she had dementia toward the end of her life, but she was still here.

Once again, i began to question; did she really know Jesus? Is she really in heaven? One time i called my dear sister-in-Christ, Pam, just to share my concern, and have some relief and reassurance. She listened and responded, "Your Mom never rejected Jesus, and so she's with Him in Heaven." Those words, somehow gave me the peace and belief i needed and reassurance that Mama was indeed with Jesus. And i too, will see her again, she will greet me with open arms when i go HOME.

Chapter Thirty

"El Shaddai: The All Sufficient One"

Coming to the realization that the Lord has gifted me in so many ways. What is it He wants me to do with these gifts? A new gift to use for His glory and honor: writing and speaking for Him.

Many times the Lord will have us do something for Him that we least expect, or think we can ever accomplish. For me it was writing; it happened like this; Mama, Joyce and i were at The Nutcracker Ballet performance in San Jose. During the break i turned to Joyce and said, "The Lord has blessed me with so many gifts, and i just am not sure what He wants me to do" She replied, "What is it you want to do?" Without hesitation i replied, " i want to speak for the Lord." She then said, " Well, you should write a book and then that way, when you speak you can have your book for purchase, to follow-up with your speech." i turned to her, shocked and said, " Are you kidding, me write a book? What are you crazy?" Thankfullly, she is such a good understanding friend, who took no offense.

The opportunity to write a book was in the way of our Laurel Shea, as i explained earlier, realizing how difficult life can be for children, and me included. As i wrote "Our" first book, **Angels All Around Me,** it was then the Lord opened my eyes and heart to see what He saw in me. i looked back over my life thinking about the affect teachers had on me and my writing and speaking. For the speaking, it was definitely my eighth grade teacher Mr. Hayes, who gave me the confidence to speak, choosing me over others to speak at the graduation ceremony of eighth graders, i was in the seventh, at the time. i learned later on, that public speaking is the number one most dreaded encounter for almost all humans. Not for me, this was my gift, i later discovered from the Lord. i love speaking in public, i am in my element when i speak. Yes, i know i have the gift of gab and as Charlie Brown25 told Lucy, when she wouldn't stop talking, "Wrap it up." Yet, many others like to talk, but not speak in public.

Another gift the Lord had given me was writing, as i look back at my high school English teacher, Mrs. Gillette. She's the one, i shared with you, the reader, earlier about how my brother Bill (ten years younger than i) came to me and asked if i remembered her? He went on to say, i was a hard act to follow because of the thousands of students she had taught all those years later, she remembered me as one of her top students. Wow!!! Then of course i remembered writing a weekly article for the San Jose Mercury News. Hmmm, had i had this precious gift all along and never realized it? Was it because i didn't believe in myself, and this gift from the Lord? Probably. As you, the reader, may recall, i never received much encouragement while attending school, Mama was just trying to survive and my father was too much into himself and indulging in drinking. My words to parents are to encourage those little ones, take away or limit the electronics and get involved in their little lives.

Well, not only was i writing these wonderful little treasures for children, but i discovered i could do the illustrations as well. Many a time, i would sit and pray and ask the Lord to show me and work through my hands. He was faithful, and answered many of those prayers. At one of my speaking engagements, after the mother of a little girl purchased one of "Our" books, the child looked at the book and said, " Mommy, look she draws just like i do. "What a lovely compliment from a child. In Matthew, Jesus states; **"Yes," replied Jesus, "have you never read," 'From the lips of children and infants You have ordained praise'?" Matthew 21:16b.**

Within a two year period and with the help of the Lord and with Fred's cooperation and support, i was able to write and illustrate seven Christ centered books for children. i had taken several writers classes, attended numerous writers conferences, and after a period of time, writing and studying, i received a certification from Long Ridge Writers Group in Connecticut. i was on the way, or so i thought.

Now, that the work was done, how was i going to get these little books published? i had an offer from a publisher, and took the information to our wonderful Christian attorney, Steve. He looked over the offer, called and asked me if i would like what i had done changed? i told him, "No, i want it printed the way the Lord had given it to me." He then said, "Then, you will need to self-publish." i hesitated and said, "Fred does not want me to do that, it's too much work." i then asked him, "What his fee would be for doing this work?" His answer was remarkable, "Self-publish." i turned to Fred and told him, Fred agreed, what a sweet price to pay.

i found a printer who would print "Our" books according to the amount we wanted them printed. Guess, you the reader, wonder where the "Our" comes in to the picture? Well, we were a team, the Lord, Fred and i. And since we had the Lord of the universe as a partner, we capitalize the "O".

The first book printed was, **Angels All Around Me**; that one i dedicated to Laurel Shea; it was for her and all children. i cannot describe the first time i held the first copy of the book in the palms of my hands and read it. The feeling is absolutely amazing; here was a book i illustrated and wrote, now it is published and in print. It still ceases to amaze me that i did it, of course with the Lord's help, Fred and many others encouragement.

The next step was to get these little treasures into the hands of children throughout the world. That is when the thought came to me, from the Lord to contact churches that would allow me to speak and share "Our" books. The first year, i had so many bookings it was a blessing.

Since some children and adults learn in different ways, i decided to have c.d.'s included with each book. But we needed songs, children to sing them, an accompanist, and a way to record them. The Lord provided everything. As He states in **Philippians 4:19 "And my God will meet all**

your needs according to His glorious riches in Christ Jesus." Our granddaughter Laurel Shea, her friend Alyse, Kelly, Emily and i were the singers, Lois accompanied us with the Autoharp and my dear sister-in-the Lord, Norma, recorded us. What a blessing. Although, for the first book, our friend, Marge accompanied us on the piano, later, it was Lois on the Autoharp.

As time and technology would have it, we needed to put the books on e-book, have a web page set-up, and business cards made. With little funding, how were we to accomplish this? Once again the Lord provided, in the name of a dear Christian brother, Joe. He not only set-up the wonderful web page, he somehow connected an account with Pay Pal, and was able to get the books on e-book. It still amazes me how he did it. Now, that is a gift from the Lord, and Joe used it to bless "Our" ministry. As for the business cards, i mentioned, my dear daughter-in-Christ; Andrea set those up for "Us." She used the angel i had drawn on the front of the Angel book for the cards; she was another gifted soul using what the Lord had given her for "Our" ministry.

Printing of the books was "Our" greatest expense, and we wanted to have these little books be more cost effective. We were at a book signing and the Lord would have us meet a dear Christian lady who published small books like "Ours," but her prices were much lower than "Ours". She told me of an online company who would print them; it didn't matter if it were one or a hundred, the cost was the same, very reasonable.

i contacted the company and they were very helpful in getting "Our" books set-up for printing. We had one printed as a copy and then decided to go with them. Also, when printing and publishing with them, they in turn, contacted Amazon, so now the books are available through Amazon. And just recently, much to my surprise, i received a small royalty check from Amazon for the e-books. The Lord keeps working behind the scenes as i continue to write, what a blessing!

i spoke for a couple of years at different churches and had book signings after each speaking engagement. Fred had now finally retired at age seventy-five and loved escorting me to these speaking engagements. When he was unable to attend, my Tonto or sidekick, Lois, would attend with me. On one occasion, Lois and i sat in the car and were about to pray, when i turned to Lois and said, "i forgot my speech." She reassured me i would do fine. Which i did, it was one of the best speeches the Lord would have me give. i started out with, "Ladies i am sorry, i forgot my notes today, so all you have is me, but most important, the Bible and the Holy Spirit." Of course, all three were ever present, God the Father, Christ the Son and the Holy Spirit. How could i go wrong? The ladies loved what the Lord had given me to say and almost everyone purchased books. PRAISE THE LORD!!!

i recall the first time i was asked to speak at a Christian luncheon. It happened like this: a dear Christian Brother called me one evening and told me this group of Christians was having a luncheon the next day at a restaurant and he had just discovered the speaker was unable to attend. He immediately thought of me, and asked if i would speak at the luncheon. Shocked about even being asked to speak, i told him i had to talk it over with Fred and of course pray about it. He said, he needed an answer that evening, which i could understand. i got off the phone, turned to Fred and shared what had just transpired. He said, "What are you going to tell him?" i said, "i am going into our bedroom and pray." My dear Christian friend, Jeanette, had given me a picture of Jesus standing at the door and knocking, representing the verse in **Revelation. "Here I am! I stand at the door and knock. If anyone hears my voice and opens the door, I will come in and eat with him, and he with Me." Revelation 3:20.** Many children, including Fred and I, have knelt by our bedside with that picture hanging overhead, as a reminder that He hears our every prayer.

i spent a little time praying with the door of room closed behind me. When i got up and went into the kitchen, Fred again asked, "What are you going to do?" i said, "The Lord led me to accept the invitation, but what i will speak about i don't know."

The next day i arrived at the church and joined the group for lunch; although, i did not have much of an appetite. When the meal was complete, i was introduced and spoke before the group. i do not remember what i spoke on, rest assured it was the Words the Holy Spirit had given me. The group i spoke to was very charismatic, Holy Spirit filled and i know prayed for me.

After i spoke, the man who had invited me to speak thanked me. It was then i shared with him, what was going on with me. He was thankful to hear my words, that i was having terrible stomach pains all week long, prior to his asking me to speak. With such pain, i didn't think i could speak, let alone join them for a meal. i believe as i was obedient to the Lord's calling me to speak, He healed me as they were praying for healing and other prayer requests. i am truly blessed.

Prior to Lois coming on board, the children and i sang the song **Angels Among Us**26 by: Becky Hobbs27 and Don Goodman28, at the Bret Hart Theater in Angels Camp. The very gifted Steve Hall29 accompanied us on the piano. i also spoke about angels, and then Steve Hall presented an amazing concert in conclusion. This was an evening we would not soon forget; what an honor to have this wonderful, gifted, caring man, accompany us. We became friends with he and his lovely wife Robin. Steve has since gone home to be with Jesus, and i am sure playing beautiful music for Him and others. As for me, i will hold those fond memories in my heart.

As i was writing and illustrating "Our" Christian children's books, i listened to his relaxing music, along with his son Daniel, when they played together. On one occasion when i was ordering c.d.'s directly from Steve, i said, "Guess what i am listening to as i write?" He immediately answered, "'Steve Hall.' 'Right,'" i said. Now, as i am writing this book, once again, i'm listenening to his beautiful comforting music in the background. Just a note of how the Lord works, my dear friend Lynne, had given me, the then tape recording of Steve Hall, called; **Angels Among Us**. The Lord was already working on my writing "Our," Angels book, without my realizing.

Chapter Thirty-One

"Jehovah-jireh:
The Lord will provide"

Welcoming children into our
family. Daughters-in-love (law).

During the time of sharing the Word of God and "Our" books with others, the Lord was also working on our little family. Franz introduced us to Jennifer, and soon after they were engaged. i remember her telling me one evening as i was preparing dinner, her mom had asked her if she had met me yet, and what did she think of me? i was surprised, yet pleased with her reply. She said she told her mom, "She (me) talks to Jesus as though He were her best friend." Wow, what a blessing; i just pray everyone who comes into my path, sees the very presence of Jesus in my life, because He is my life. That's not to say, i am perfect, believe me i am far from being perfect, that is why i need the ONLY PERFECT ONE, JESUS.

Once again as a mother, i had to let go and let God. By the way, that is written on our bathroom mirror; Let Go and Let God. Every so often, Fred looks at me and points to it, just to remind me. He is so right. i know i say that Jesus is my life, but when i was raising our sons, and later on, they were my life, or i should say, my life revolved around them. With that in mind, it is difficult to let go and let God. But in time, i have learned and sometimes am still learning the difficulty of letting go. Franz and Jennifer had a large wedding at Jennifer's Christian church in Sonora. i remember Jennifer on her special day, she was so radiant. Unlike me, she must have been planning this special occasion since she was a child. She reminded me of a princess who had found her prince, and this was the day she had dreamed about for years, marrying her prince.

It was probably one of the hottest June days we have ever had in our area in years, well over 110 F. The day before the wedding, Fred was not feeling well, as a matter of fact, he was so ill, the doctor wanted to hospitalize him. Because he was the father of the groom, he talked the doctor out of it, and asked him to just give him some strong antibiotics. i felt sorry for him running a fever, hot as it was, and wearing the "monkey suit" as he called it. As we were leaving the ceremony, Fred went to the restroom and practically tore off the "monkey suit;" he was relieved to put on the cooler clothing he had brought.

Then there was our Laurel Shea, who was the flower girl with her little arm in a pink cast. She was now in Kindergarten and had broken her arm not only once, but twice within a short period of time. None-the-less, she looked adorable as she approached the area where Franz and Jennifer were to say their vows. The wedding was held outdoors on the lawn area of the church. i was thrilled to have all of my siblings and their spouses, except Barbara, our Aunt Mary, and our niece Sarah and her husband Jordon, attend the ceremony. The words that stuck in my mind that the Pastor said to Franz and Jennifer were: 'Remember when you marry, you are marrying not only your partner but their family as well, and all of these people here. It starts with you two, extends to each of your families, the church and community. We are not alone in this matrimony.' i totally agree with him, we not only marry the individual, but their family. Oh yes, i believe in the verse in **Genesis 2:24 "the two become one flesh."** But i also believe the verse in **Ephesians 6:2 that states, "Honor your father and mother."** We must take the Word of God as a whole and not just in part.

After their honeymoon, they settled in the lovely little house on the ranch where Franz was living. Not long afterwards, they purchased a home in Angels Camp. Since then, they have purchased a home in the country, in Sonora. And the Lord has blessed them with three sons; Steven Joseph the oldest and a few years later twin boys; Kasey and Ryan. Ryan has the reddish hair like his daddy did when he was born, taking after their Papa Fred. All three boys have beautiful blue eyes, like their mom. We are thankful they live within an hour driving distance from us. We love spending time with our grandchildren. Steven Joseph usually comes to our home on Friday after school to spend the night with us. We love making home made pizza, cookies and have fun popping popcorn in the air popper without the lid. i have taught him about planting seeds, caring for flowers, gathering eggs from the chickens and other chores. He loves learning, and it is a joy for Fred and i to teach him.

As i said, the Lord was working on our little family; Jeff had proposed to Lexie. They had a lovely wedding in Pismo Beach with the Pacific Ocean splashing against the coast in the background. Lexie is our very organized daughter-in-love, and did a great job planning this special occasion with our son Jeff. They are a lovely couple.

Once again, our Laurel Shea was a flower girl, who looked lovely in her red velvet dress. Jeff, had purchased a ring for her as well; it made her feel so special. The Pastor performed a wonderful Christian ceremony. It was fun to see Jeff, the groom and all the men who were part of the wedding party, dressed with white shirts, ties, black dress pants and cool flips flops (as they are called today); we called them thongs years ago. My, how words and meanings change. It made sense, ocean wedding, men wearing flip flops, including our new daughter-in- law's cowboy dad; he honored his daughter by wearing them, as well.

Jeff and Lexie left for their honeymoon and Fred and i excitedly took Laurel Shea home with us. She would spend part of the time with us and part with our daughter-in-law's parents; her new grandparents.

When Jeff and Lexie gave birth to a little girl, Aubrey, they were considering what to give her as a middle name. Laurel and i rooted for the name, Joy. i had taught Laurel early on; **J** is for **Jesus**, **O** is for **others** and **Y** is for **you**. We loved that, and she would repeat it often, and would soon live it.

We were so thankful when they decided to call this new precious girl, Aubrey Joy. Laurel and i jumped for joy. As the book of Nehemiah says; **"Do not grieve, for the joy of the Lord is your strength." Nehemiah 8:10c.** Now, at last, Laurel had a little sister to love. As Lexie was carrying Aubrey Joy in her tummy, it fascinated me the different things she did, to welcome the baby and to have Laurel part of that welcoming. For instance, about a month prior to giving birth, Lexie made a huge paper chain and placed it in Laurel's room. Each day before the baby was due, Laurel removed one link to the chain. As the days got closer to her arrival, Laurel would say, "She is coming soon."

When we arrived at the hospital to greet this new little member of our family, Fred held her in his arms and Jeff lovingly pulled back her little blanket to expose her tiny feet. He pointed out to his dad that her two first toes were webbed like his, Franz's and of course his dad. Fred was proud to see his inheritance carried on to Aubrey Joy. She too, like her daddy, uncle and Fred, now with confidence says; "I'm a good swimmer because my toes are stuck together, like a duck." A good swimmer she is for sure.

Chapter Thirty-Two

"Jehovah-shalom: The Lord is Peace"

**Our son's accomplishment. We're so proud
of him; he overcomes all obstacles. The Lord
is with him and blesses him, beyond measure. PRAISE HIM!!!**

i had chosen to name our oldest son, Franz Joseph. Franz was Fred's middle name, his uncle's name and my brother's name is Frank and my maiden name was Joseph. Besides Franz being a German name, it sounded good with Bodenmüller. i remember my family saying where did you come up with the name Jeffrey, it doesn't sound German. i told them Fred had chosen to name our second son, Jeffrey John. His name means, "God's peace." As i write this i just discovered it is Germanic for: "Divine Peace." Wow, it is German after all. Fred didn't know at the time what Jeffrey meant; it's amazing how our Lord orchestrates everything in our lives, and for us to recognize His mighty hand at work.

As much as we love our Jeffrey, he was anything but peace while growing up in our home. Franz was the compliant one, where Jeffrey was not defiant, but rather hard headed, like his mother, yes, me. But as the years have gone on, he does bring God's peace to our family.

i recall a dear Christian sister describing one of her sons to a group of us ladies. She said she had one son who would drive her crazy and just about when she had, had enough, he would come in give her a hug, bring her flowers he had picked, or some other kind deed. Was she talking about our Jeffrey? No, it was her son. What was a mother to do with such a determined yet loving child? Love them back, as the Lord loves us with unconditional love.

It was late in the afternoon when the call came, "Mom, I just had the most exhilarating experience I ever had in my life." As he went on explaining this wonderful experience, i could hardly get a word in, unusual for me. Finally, i said, "Where were you and tell me again, what happened?" It was our Jeff, and for him to be so excited was exciting for this mother as well. i thought of the years, he didn't seem interested in anything and would tell me over and over again, "I don't care." i kept saying you must care about something. His answer was always, "I don't care." Can you imagine how painful this was for anyone to hear, especially a mother who cared so much for her children?

Today his call is different. Jeff's dear friend, Jason, invited him to attend a media highlight on the California Highway Patrol at the Academy in Sacramento. Jeff went and loved every aspect of the Academy. He even worked out with some of the cadets, and in completion of his visit, as he put it, "Mom, you should have seen the spread of food they put out for us and the cadets." He was captivated by the whole experience and wanted to become a C.H.P. officer.

Some time later, when i awoke in the morning this thought came to mind, ' Is it any wonder he wanted to be a 'peace' officer.' He was living up to his name; Jeffrey/Peace. What an amazing Lord we serve; a God incidence? Yes, i believe so.

His long enduring trek began soon after filling out the application. Fred and i went with him for that first exam, which took about four to five hours; held in Sacramento. The next test was just as long and tiring and was being held else where; Fred would travel with him, sit in the truck and just wait. One morning Fred said he was not going to go with Jeff for the next exam; just then the phone rang, and i asked Fred if he would go with him for moral support. Immediately, and without hesitation, Fred quickly changed clothing and was off with his son; this time to Fresno. i called later to check on Fred, he was fine, except he had decided to go for a walk and got lost and couldn't find the truck. Finally, he got directions and found it; that's Fred and directions. But, he was learning what his Mother called Gedult or patience.

Time and again she would say to him, "Du, Siegfried hast keine Gedult." Translated, "You, Siegfried have no patience."

There were many more exams for Jeff, and with it came patience for Fred. The Lord is always working on us; we are the diamonds in the rough and He is constantly chiseling to perfect us into that beautiful diamond, His Son Jesus. **"We proclaim Him, admonishing and teaching everyone with all wisdom, so that we may present everyone perfect in Christ." Colossians 1:28.**

The testing for Jeff went on for approximately a year, and then there were thorough investigations on his life and so forth. It seemed never ending, but he kept going on for the prize. Just as Paul says, **"Do you not know that in a race all the runners run, but only one gets the prize? Run in such a way as to get the prize." 1 Corinthians 9:24.** Jeff was indeed running in such a way as to get the prize, receiving the, much desired, invitation to attend and complete the C.H.P. Academy.

Early November, prior to Jeff's thirty-second birthday, the coveted invitation came from the C.H.P. What an excited young man we had, something was finally working for him. But it was not to be. A few years prior, Jeff's lung had collapsed for no known reason; seemed it affected some seven thousand young men about Jeff's age in the United States. Fred and i remember that occurrence well. It was a hot July day, Fred's birthday to be exact, when Jeff called us from the hospital and asked us to come. Lexie and the girls had spent most of the time with him and needed a break. We filled in, waiting patiently with Jeff for the doctor to release him.

Now, it was happening again, his lung collapsed, the week prior to his accepting the invitation. What was happening? Was the Lord telling him, "No, this is not what I want for you, my son." We were all questioning, and would the C.H.P. extend the invitation? Would his lung collapse again? Oh, so many questions and so little time for his fulfilling the commitment he made to go to the Academy. All those hours he spent in preparation, all the testing, the investigations on his life, was it all for naught?

He was hesitant about saying anything, but knew he must tell the truth and ask if he could re apply? They graciously understood and told him, he could probably attend the following January. An excited, yet fearful young man accepted the invitation. Thinking, what if this happens again? What if I am in the Academy and the strenuous workouts have an affect on my lung? Will I be able to handle the stress, always thinking what if my lung collapses again? There it was that little, yet powerful, word: "if". Once again we were all learning to trust the Lord. **Proverbs 3: 5-6.**

Jeff, went into the Academy the following January. We all spent much time in prayer and fasting for him to accomplish this tough task that was set before him. We are ever so thankful for the special, wonderful young lady he has in Lexie. She was there for him, all the way, from getting his uniforms clean to shaving his head almost bald. Yet, she lived out on the ranch with two little girls to care for. Her parents had moved to Oregon and she managed, handling broken water pipes, chasing bulls out of where they shouldn't be, at one time she and the girls walked about two miles to their home on a bumpy dirt road. She did it, she managed, just like our ancestors of old who came over in covered wagons, caring for their families and supporting their husbands. Yes, she is a rarity today, and we are proud to call her our daughter-in-love.

For Jeff it was tough as well, especially with his learning difficulty, and the everpresent fear of a collapsed lung. He told us there was a Marine in his class who told him, the Academy was tougher than the Marines. i can't begin to tell you, the reader, how difficult this was for him and the other cadets. But many had done it before, so he too, could accomplish his mission. It was probably the toughest experience Jeff had ever had, but so good for him. i remember when he first got accepted and came home to show Fred and i a picture what his quarters looked like, neat and tidy. i said, "Well, not

338

far from how you were raised, with neatness and organization." i spent many a restless, sleepless night praying, waking, reading Scripture, praying and giving our son and the situation to the Lord, while he was undergoing the Academy.

Chapter Thirty-Three

"Jehovah-raah: The Lord My Shepherd"

The blood of a lamb saves my life from a rattlesnake bite. The Gospel becomes a reality to me. He is not finished with me yet.

It was June first and Jeff was to graduate in July. He was still at the Academy when we had Lexie, her mom, Laurel and Aubrey, over for a bar-b-q and swim to celebrate Laurel Shea's eleventh birthday. Although we missed Jeff, we had a lovely time with family. The next day Laurel left to spend a couple of weeks with her biological mother. i mention that, because what happened the following day i was not going to tell our Laurel, until she returned home.

June second two thousand twelve, the day after Laurel Shea's birthday, i was walking up from our barn when i stopped to thank the Lord that in all the years we had lived on our ranch, i had never gotten bitten by a rattlesnake. As with Job, satan must have heard my prayer as well, because what happened next was incredible. i went into our vegetable garden to harvest onions. i pulled the onions and then set them down behind a retaining wall, previous to what happened next is important and how the Lord cares for us.

Years prior, while working in the garden, i was drinking from an open container, when a bee, who was enjoying my drink as well, i didn't see, took a sip and was immediately stung on my tongue. This experience took me to the E.R., because my tongue began to swell and my trachea was closing up. The doctors and nurses took great care and resolved the problem. It wasn't until later that evening, while guiding a Bible study, the Lord completely healed me with a soup the hostess was serving; it loosened my

340

tongue so i could speak and guide the Bible study. The Lord had allowed this to happen so i would not panic for what was going to transpire on the second of June.

i went to retrieve the onions behind the retaining wall and felt a terrible sting on my right thumb, i turned to Fred, who thankfully was working in the garden with me, and said, "Oh no, i just got stung by a bee again." i was in the same area as before, when i was stung by the bee. i quickly looked at my thumb and saw blood coming out of two holes; it was then i shouted, "Fred, i just got bit by a rattlesnake!!!" The pain was like the bee sting, but about a million times more intense. Fred came quickly and told me to run to the house and wash it real good. Fred had taken C.P.R. and knew exactly what i should do. But, he too panicked; i should not have run, because it caused the blood to circulate faster and go to my heart. He killed the snake and then ran to get ice for me to help alleviate the pain. It seemed like forever, for him to come with the ice, get the car started, and take me to the E.R. In reality, he made it to the hospital in fifteen minutes, which would usually take twenty to twenty five minutes.

By the time we reached our mailboxes two miles away, my whole body went numb and i shook from the excruciating pain. All i could do was hold the ice on the bite and sing songs unto the Lord. i managed to call my dear friend and sister-in-Christ, Denise, to ask her to pray and have others do the same. Fred, was so concerned and kept telling me, calm down you will be all right. i said, "i am, i am singing unto the Lord; He is in charge."

i was taken in immediately at the hospital, and given the anti venom. Later we were to discover that this was the only hospital, of the three in our area, that had the anti venom. i was taken immediately to the intensive care unit, and was kept there for two days. i had no idea the extent of the bite, until i was released. Because the snake that bit me was a baby, it had injected all it's venom into my body. Amazing, a creature as small as that could damage or even kill someone or something. Now, i understand why the nurses gave me so much attention, for fear of losing me.

Many friends and family came to visit and the phone kept ringing, finally the nurses said, "No, more calls, she must rest." i was thankful to be cared for and loved. The next day was June third our Franz's birthday, and as i spoke with him, i said, "Thirty thirty-six years ago today, i was in the hospital giving birth to you and now i'm in the hospital fighting for my life." i believe the Lord allowed this to happen between Franz and Laurel's birthday, lest i forget.

It is interesting to note what i discovered about the anti venom. The venom is milked from a rattlesnake, injected into a lamb, and then taken from the lamb and given to the patient. This reminded me of the verse in John, "The next day John saw Jesus coming toward him and said, **"Look, the Lamb of God, who takes away the sin of the world!" John 1:29a.** i wondered, did this lamb have to suffer and die for me, just as Jesus did so many years ago on the cross for me (us)? The Gospel became very real to me. i am listening to The Old Rugged Cross being sung, as i write, a constant reminder. Praise the Lord for what He has done for me, and not only me, but all who accept Him as Lord and Savior.

Lexie and Aubrey were returning from visiting Jeff at the Academy in Sacramento, and took the time to stop at the hospital to visit me. i was thrilled to have such a loving caring daughter (in-love) and granddaughter, visit me. Little Aubrey was a little bit afraid, as she saw me lying in that bed with a swollen arm and hand, hooked up to all those tubes. Being that the Lord has gifted me with love for children, i soon made her visit fun, taking a glove and blowing it up, making a silly chicken out of it, and then telling her to draw a picture for me on the white board. She loves drawing, so this was fun. i can still hear her little giggles as she and her mommy shared this precious time with Oma.

The Lord sustained me, as i was still in pain and not myself, due to the snakebite and the anti venom. But the Lord got me through this special time with our Aubrey Joy and her Mommie, to share my love (His love) and take away the fear for our little one, seeing me with the swollen arm and hooked up to the i.v. and all.

The next day was Sunday, and i asked Fred to bring my Bible for me to read. When he arrived, our dear brother- in-Christ, Tom and his wife Denise, my dear sister-in-Christ, were there visiting me. Tom was studying to become a Chaplain, so i asked him if he would serve us Communion. He went to the nurses and asked if he could have some crackers and juice. He then took my Bible and we celebrated the Lord's Supper together. Being in intensive care, i was only allowed so many visitors at a time, and as we were about to have Communion, i asked others who were there, to come in and join us. Tom gave a lovely blessing as he served us all communion; what a witness to the staff; to those who received Communion, and a great opportunity for him to serve our Lord in such a marvelous way.

The next day, our wonderful, caring Dr. Randall Smart, came to see me after Dr. Peterson, who was the charge doctor that day. Later, as i was healing, i went to see Dr. Smart, and he smiled and just told me i was his 'Hero,' after such an incident with the rattlesnake. He went on to say, that a man had been bitten about the same time i was; he was treating him, but he wasn't doing very well. i told him, many had been praying for me, and that i had alternative treatment by my Sara, and others caring hands. i was also thankful Fred got me safely to the hospital that had the anti venom, and i received good treatment, at the Mark Twain St. Joseph's Hospital.

i was told by the medical staff there, that my arm and hand would turn black and blue, but they did not; my hand was terribly swollen, and my fingers looked like sausages ready for the frying pan. My treatment and days of rest were about to begin; getting bit by a rattlesnake is not like what we see in the western movies. In the western movies, the hero or heroin, gets bit by that rattler, makes a cut by the bite, sucks the poison out, ties it off with a kerchief and off they ride into the sunset. Not so today; we are told not to make any cuts, but get the patient to the hospital immediately.

As Fred and i were leaving the hospital, i turned to him and said, "i just realized, it could have been just one of us driving away today." With a bite such as i got, if Fred had not gotten me to the hospital in time and they didn't have the anti venom, i would probably not be writing this story. PRAISE THE LORD for HIS omnipresent, love and omniscient care, for HIS children.

When we arrived home, the love and care did not stop at the hospital. i am ever so thankful for the many friends, neighbors and brothers and sisters- in- Christ, who came to visit. Most of all Fred, not being a cook, was thankful, because they brought meals. As one neighbor said, "We were coming to visit and bring something, but there was an endless line of cars coming daily, so we waited until it let up."

i am sorry to say, the church we were attending and serving at the time, were not here for us. i forgave them; **as Jesus said, "Father, forgive them, for they do not know what they are doing." Luke 23:34.** On the positive side, Fred came to realize what a tremendous ministry i had outside the church walls, with all the people coming, calling and sending cards.

One thing i will always remember, that sits well in my spirit, my brother Bill called me while i was in the hospital. He then said, Jeff had told him; "If something happened to my Mom, i would leave the Academy and come home." That hit me hard, the love he has for his Mama. If he were to have left the Academy, he would not be able to return, unless he started from the very beginning. He was willing to make that sacrifice for me. What can i say, but thank the Lord for a wonderful, caring son. i guess i did my homework and raised him right.

My dear friend and sister-in-Christ, Paula, cried over the phone when she heard what had happened to me; she understood the danger of a rattlesnake bite, because she knew, first hand, of someone getting bitten. She insisted on driving from her home in San Jose, come to our home, and help in any way she could. She came, took me for my follow-up visit with Dr. Smart, then took Fred and i out for lunch, and was going to purchase a lovely dessert at the bakery, but decided not to purchase it. i tired easily, so we went home. Upon arriving home, there was a note from a friend and neighbor, on the kitchen counter stating our dinner was in the refrigerator.

Later, Paula opened the refrigerator to retrieve the prepared meal; she noticed the dessert and just looked at me and said, "You called your friend and asked her to make this, right?" i looked and there, before my eyes, was the very dessert Paula longed for, from the bakery, but the one she held in her hands, was much bigger, fresher and homemade. i told her, "No, i didn't call my friend, i didn't even know she was bringing dinner for us. But the Lord knew, and told her to make this for you, Paula, for your love and taking the time to be here for us." She just smiled, shook her head in disbelief. i said, "Sister, stick around you will witness many more miracles like this." It was true; the Lord kept bringing and supplying all our needs. Another dear sister-in-Christ, Charlotte, sent me wonderful essential oils for healing my swollen hand.

i was working on this book before I'd gotten bitten by the rattlesnake, and was wondering how i would be able to write again. Even today, i still have numbness and discomfort in my thumb, especially during cold weather. Once again, the Lord would meet my need. Our dear friends, and brother and sisters-in-Christ, Carl, Judy, Sara and Mary were there to help. Sara, as i mentioned before, gave me alternative treatment, and Judy brought delicious meals; she and Carl prayed and gave me alternative medicine. Mary, their youngest, and i, have a special bond, and she, too, likes to write. Once she learned i had most of my story written down in long hand, she offered to type it up for me. What a blessing; i soon took advantage of

345

her generous offer. So it was my Mary, who listened to me over the phone, as i dictated my story as she typed away.

i will forever be grateful to her and her lovely family for their love, care, prayers and support. i have learned that the family we have on earth will not necessarily be the family we were born into. As **Jesus says in Matthew 19:29 "And everyone who has left houses or brothers or sisters or father or mother or children or fields for My sake will receive a a hundred times as much and will inherit eternal life."** Wow!!!

Chapter Thirty-Four

"Adonai: The Lord"

The graduation. It is not over yet.

Fred and i had always wanted to go Sacramento just to spend some time with Jeff during one of his free evenings while at the C.H.P. Academy. So, we decided to make the trip. As we neared Sacramento, the traffic got heavier and heavier, being in the country, we were not used to this traffic, and it made me very nervous. We finally connected with Jeff, and took him to a huge place for pizza and beer. Although i was glad we made the trip and it was nice visiting with our son and giving him a break from the norm, the restaurant was very cold, compared to being in the intense summer heat outside. The thought occurred to me, i'm becoming a cold-blooded creature like the snake that bit me. i then realized i could not only not stand being cold, i could not handle the noise level or being around a crowd. Is that why the traffic made me so nervous as well? What was going on with me? i loved crowds, enjoying and visiting with people, but this was overwhelming. i learned later on, that the snake bite affected my nervous system, and that is why i felt uncomfortable.

We thoroughly enjoyed our visit with Jeff, and were very proud of his accomplishments. Yet, we were thankful to return home for the peace and quiet.

July finally arrived and Jeff had completed the most strenuous Academy, and was preparing for graduation. Proud parents, wife, daughters, his brother and family, Lexie's parents, my brother and wife, Jason and other friends, were there to honor Jeff's accomplishment. On the day prior to graduation, he proudly escorted us around the campus of the C.H.P.

Academy, showing us the room he bunked in those many months, the classrooms where he and his fellow cadets studied, introducing us to some of his fellow cadets, others, and officers, as we walked around the campus. Coming to the area displaying all the cadets' names from years past written on huge golden plaques. There in the center of the room, was the newest plaque, displayed beautifully on a tripod. Written on it were the names of the cadets of this class, and there it was, our son's name; Jeffrey Bodenmuller; a sign of his accomplishment that will remain at the Academy in Sacramento. We were a very proud Dad and Mom to see his name engraved on that plaque.

i have chosen **Adonai: Lord**, for this chapter, meaning: He is my Lord, He is my Master, He is my life, I am His. It is always a Christian parent's wish to have their children and grandchildren, make Jesus, their Adonai: Lord, personal Savior. From his early years as a child, Jeff, like Franz, knew, loved and served the Lord. But we all, one day, need to come to Him and know Him as our personal Lord and Savior, to make Him Lord of our lives. i believe this is what happened to Jeff, with the many trials and tribulations he had gone through in his life, the academy topped them all. He depended on the Lord, his **Adonai**. Sure the love and prayers of all of us helped tremendously, but the Lord is the One Who got Jeff through it all. As the song goes, **"I've learned to trust in Jesus."** It was true, he really came out of the academy, not only as an officer, but a soldier for Jesus Christ; ready to fight His battles.

At one point i asked Jeff, "Why do you want to be a C.H.P. Officer?" His answer to me, i shall not forget, was; "Because that is how i can serve God by protecting others." While he was in the Academy, he sent me an e-mail with a story of a man who came and spoke to the Cadets about the shepherd and the sheep. It was an amazing story and reminded me of the Great Shepherd: Jesus, and, we are the sheep of His pasture. **Psalm 95:7 says; "For He is our God, and we are the people of His pasture, the flock**

348

under His care." That verse has given me great confidence knowing where our son was heading, and also knowing the Lord would go before and with him.

Hebrews 13:5 says; "Keep your lives free from the love of money and be content with what you have, because God said,

"Never will I leave you;

never will I forsake you."

Our Lexie made all the arrangements for our overnight stay at a motel not far from the Academy. She is an amazing young lady, and continues to be so, to this day. We are blessed to have her as part of our family. How she managed to do this, as well as get the girls (our granddaughter's) and everything ready for Jeff's special day, and then to top it off, getting packed and ready to move to Garberville, where Jeff would be stationed, was beyond me. But that's our Lexie.

That evening after settling in our rooms we went, caravan style, out for dinner. It was a huge restaurant somewhere in Sacramento, where we all sat around an immense table. Once again, i realized i could not take the noise and commotion; talked it over with Fred, and we were to leave early. Retiring to our room, i was hoping and praying i could attend the graduation ceremony and get over being around so many people. That rattlesnake bite really had an affect on my nervous system as never before.

The next morning i dressed and got ready, thanking the Lord i was able to attend the ceremony. It seemed to drag on, but we were grateful to be there for our son and his family. When his name and commission were announced i was already near the stage to take his picture. If you have never been to a C.H.P. graduation, i highly recommend it. It is one of the most organized, outstanding performances, given by these young Cadets, you will ever witness. The formation, the obedience, the command, the marching, everything, is done to perfection. What an awesome experience.

After each Cadet has been commissioned, they march in formation to receive their well-deserved badge. We all stood in awe, as once again, the young Cadets marched outside, to their assigned position, to receive their badge. Our Lexie was honored to pin the badge on our Jeff's uniform. The whole event brought tears of joy, pride, and a sense of wonder for what this held for our son.

A couple of days after the ceremony, reluctantly, we helped pack and load their belongings to take to their new home, way up in Northern California, close to the Oregon border. Frustrated, i was unable to help very much, due to my swollen hand, so i spent time with the children. A blessing.

After the loading was complete, we all went out for pizza. Lexie's parents not only paid the bill, but also used their cattle trailer, truck, and car to help move 'our' children's belongings to Garberville.

Chapter Thirty-Five
**Jesus said, "Let the little children come
to me, and do not hinder them, for the
kingdom of God belongs to such as these."
Matthew 19:14**

The gift of a child for her beloved father.

On one occasion, when Laurel Shea and i had our special time after
school on Friday, she made a discovery at one of the gift shops. It was two
figures, a police officer with his German Shepherd. Laurel and her family had
a beautiful German Shepherd they got as a pup from our dear friend, Sue,
who raises German Shepherd's. This reminded Laurel of their German
Shepherd, and since her daddy was studying to become a police officer, she
decided this would be the perfect gift for him upon graduation. Of course the
item was very expensive, so i told Laurel she could earn it for her daddy by
doing things for Papa and i. i had already decided we were going to purchase
it and put her hard earned money in her bank account.

Not knowing for sure, until the very end of the academy, as to
whether Jeff would graduate, i put off the purchase of the figurine for a
while. It was much too long, and not trusting the Lord, was the truth in the
matter. When i decided to make the purchase, the item was no longer in the
store. i called other stores, searched on the internet, but could not find the
exact item Laurel so desired for her daddy. Then one day, as our Lord would
have it, i stopped in a little gift store in Angels Camp. Much to my surprise
and amazement, there it sat on a shelf in the store, and it was on sale. i
quickly made the purchase, later telling Laurel how the Lord heard our
prayers and provided. She was delighted.

On the night at the pizza parlor, after getting Jeff and his family
loaded for their move, i asked Jeff to stand in front of everyone, because

351

Laurel had something very special to give him. Was he ever surprised, as she handed him this treasure, and i went on to explain to him and all who were present, how the Lord answered our prayers.

As i write this and think back about the times Laurel and i shared on those special bond-building afternoons, i get teary eyed. i would miss those times, and also the time of working in her classroom with the children. Also, I would miss my dear friend Cindy, the school secretary, whom i came to love as a sister. Things for me would change with the move our children were making, but the Lord would fill my time with new adventures.

That first year was most difficult; i had set aside every Friday to spend with Laurel, and the children at the school. It took a while, before i would venture to Sonora to shop; the memories were too painful. i knew i must have closure and it finally came one afternoon at the golf course with Fred and some dear friends. i pushed myself to go down the very road, nearing the school Laurel had last attended. i had won a raffle at her school for a round of golf for four. This was a perfect closure, i was able to look at everything from a different perspective and gave it all to the Lord.

Now Franz and his family live in Sonora, Fred and i try at least once a week to pick- up our Steven Joseph from school, Franz and Jen's oldest son. We love spending the time with him and usually take him home with us to spend the night. Once again the Lord has filled the void.

That doesn't mean i do not miss Laurel Shea and our special times together, now we have special memories. i miss our Aubrey Joy, as well. They have since moved from Fortuna to Anderson, California. As our Lord would have it, He moved them close to my brothers and sisters, aunts, uncles, and cousins. i can't tell you, the reader, what a blessing this is for Jeff, Lexie and our granddaughters, to live close to family, family they hardly knew. It is also closer to Lexie's parents who now live in Oregon. The Lord indeed does provide.

Laurel, like her daddy, has difficulty in learning. Since their move to Anderson, she and Aubrey attend a Charter school, that my niece Barbara Jean helped start. The school has been a blessing for Laurel's learning, and Aubrey likes it too. No matter what the situation, the Lord undertakes and provides over and above all that we ask or think. **"Now to Him who is able to do immeasurably more than all we ask or imagine, according to His power that is at work within us, to Him be glory in the church and in Christ Jesus throughout all generations, for ever and ever! Amen." Ephesians 3:20-**

Chapter Thirty-Six

"Elohim: The Creator"

**Closure with family in Europe.
My last visit with loved ones.
Meeting new family members
from my mother's side.**

Please allow me to take you back to the time when Franz graduated from High School. The year was nineteen ninety-six. When Fred's cousins visited us and we traveled with the motor homes, they told Franz they would send him a round trip ticket to Germany for his graduation. They kept this awesome generous promise.

i decided i would like to go as well, and invited my mom, aunt and sister to go with us. Jeff would stay with my brothers and their families during this time, which was a blessing, in that Bill would minister to him and they would bond. Since that time, Jeff and his family are bonding with my brother Frank. The Lord is so good.

As we were making plans and arrangements for this long trip, we received a phone call that Fred's sweet mother had gone home to be with Jesus. Before her passing, we were told she had Alzheimer's, could no longer live alone, and was placed in a home. Also, due to the expense of the home, we were asked by his brother to send funds to keep her in the home. Fred being the caring son, father, that she taught him to be, without hesitation met her needs.

During this time our relationship was suffering and i thought this time away would be good for our marriage, a time to think. Sometimes, absence makes the heart grow fonder.

Fred called his cousins to make arrangements for my mom, aunt, sister, Franz and i to be picked up at the airport in Zurich, Switzerland. That was quite an undertaking, because they drive smaller cars than we do in America; this was a very kind gesture for them to pick us up at the airport. We all stayed at the cousin's large home in Germany, which was quite generous on their part.

Prior to leaving America, i was able to contact cousins from my mom's side, who lived in Switzerland. When i wrote the letter in English, i said i hoped someone could understand English, as i didn't speak Italian. Sure enough, a cousin answered, her name is Monica; i still keep in contact with her today. She was so excited about our coming, and said to me, "You are very persistent, don't ever stop." i am thankful that is one of the gifts the Lord has given me, persistence. My sister once told me, "Jeff, is persistent, just like his Mom." i have learned many things in being persistent, one being you'll never know until you try. Throughout my life i have done many things, including being a Cosmetologist, guiding children and adults to live for the Lord, baking, cooking, healthy living, cake decorating, gardening, sewing, crocheting, painting, and now writing. Some may call it stubbornness; i choose to call it, determination or persistence. Some things i do well, others not so well, but i do try my best as the Lord blesses me. i believe every accomplishment begins with the decision to try.

We stayed in Germany for about a week with these most generous, loving, kind souls. Then we rented a car and drove over the Guttard Pass into Switzerland to stay with friends, who live in a lovely two-story home, high in the Alps, overlooking Lake Major. Their home was in the Ticino Canton of Switzerland, the same area my grandparent's and my Uncle Slim came from. This was convenient, because we had a wonderful place to stay as we visited cousins in Switzerland. The trip over the Alps was overwhelming with the majestic mountains surrounding us, as we made the steep treacherous climb and decent. It was just as i remembered it when Fred and i had made the trip years prior. This time would be different as we were to meet family. We stopped along the way, to use the restroom. My aunt came running out and saying, "Gloria, i think this bathroom is for men." She had made the discovery i had made in the past, with the toilet hole in the middle of what appeared to be a shower. i reassured her that this is what public bathrooms were like in many parts of Europe.

Franz stayed with the cousins in Germany and took the train later on, to meet us in Switzerland. That was a great experience for Franz, as he was the shy one of our two sons, and not speaking any of the European languages is always challenge for travelers. He did very well, and was happy to see us once again.

The friends we stayed with in Switzerland were like family, very loving and hospitable. They gave us our own quarters for our stay with them, including, sleeping, bath, kitchen and a wonderful balcony overlooking the gorgeous blue of Lake Major. It was on that balcony, Mama had thought she had heard the ice cream man's music; it was a story i shared earlier. Here, we would make many more fond memories.

Within a short time, we made arrangements to meet our distant cousins. The two first cousins of my Mama and my aunt, were the ones who were like my Uncle's in America, total opposite of each other. The one dressed in his bibbed over halls, drove up riding in his American built tractor, the other, his brother, arrived well dressed, slim and trim and willing to show us the village of Biasca.

One of the first things he showed us was the church, which was built prior to the bubonic plague and was a hospital for those who later had the affliction. It wasn't until years later, when the whitewashed walls were uncovered; the village people would see the well-preserved paintings on the walls of Christ and others of the Christian faith. The church itself was built upon a huge stone or rock, reminding me of the **"wise man who built his house upon a rock." Refer to Matthew 7:24b**. As we looked at this magnificent church from the outside, the foundation was firm and well built. But as the structure went up, i noticed the change in the care and building of it, reminding me of how we too do the same, many times, in our walk with the Lord. That is, putting Him last instead of first.

There was another smaller church he showed us, and told us that in the winter, it would be buried in snow, with only the steeple showing. As a matter of fact, that is how the church was discovered; that it even existed. A pilot was flying over the area in the winter, and noticed something peaking out of the snow; after digging it out, there it was, a lovely little church. Behind the church was evidence of the Roman road that led over the Alps into Germany and traveling as far north as England. This was such an amazing story of the history in Europe, and there we stood, to see the facts.

One evening, as we were about to enjoy a typical Swiss Italian meal at a local restaurant, i asked if we could pray before we ate? One of the cousins said, "You're just like the Guidotti's: religious." That was amazing to me; i was grateful, upon hearing about being known for our faith. Although i know i am not religious; i have a relationship with Jesus. Religion is man's way to God, we do thus and such; having a relationship is God's way to man; as Jesus hung on the cross with outstretched hands and said, **"It is finished."** **John 19:30b**

This same cousin began to tell us of the Swiss Chalet that was in the family for years, and how it took five hours of hiking to get to it. "One time," he went on to say, "I had forgotten the tobacco for my father's pipe and my father had me go all the way back down the mountain to retrieve his tobacco. A lesson I would not forget." The more active cousin said he could make the ascent to the chalet in less than two hours. His brother said he could do it in less, with a helicopter to drop him off. They were a pair.

Wasn't long and our trip would soon be over, Franz would stay on with the cousins in Germany for another month or so, the rest of us would fly back to California. Once we were back home and settled, the cousins took Franz to visit France. i decided to call Franz, who was now in France. As i thought about the call, i wondered how i would tell the one who answered the phone, "i would like to speak to my son Franz," although i know this is France. In telling you this now, you can pronounce our son's name as the French pronounce it, France, with a short a.

i am very thankful we made that trip, especially so Mama and my aunt could finally meet family. They were impressed with all the beauty that was to behold, all that the Lord had created for us to enjoy. He surely is our Elohim our Creator.

That was the last trip i made to Europe, and i hope to go again one day, taking Laurel Shea with me as i have promised. i enjoyed being with Fred's family, but missed not seeing Mutti. A couple of the cousins presented me with some special items that belonged to Mutti, like her prayer book with a picture of Fred's father she kept inside, her rosary, other little books about being a good Haus Frau, and so much more, and her watch. These are all treasures i will pass on to our children one day. She too, like my Mama, had very little, but it doesn't matter, we have such a treasure in heaven that awaits us, those who have accepted Jesus as our Lord and Savior. i look forward to the day to meet her once again in Glory, because of Jesus' sacrificial death for us.

One other person, we did see, and i hope to see in Glory as well, was Tante Fine. We were able to travel to Fred's hometown of Saulgau, to visit her and other friends. She and i had a special bonding. She, like me, loved to cook, bake and had a lovely garden, flowers and vegetables. Her hands were rough from the many years of toiling, but she never complained, as difficult as life was for her. As we were getting ready to depart, i told her i would visit her again. As i looked at her beautiful weathered face, tears welled up in her sky blue eyes, as i said in German, "You, don't think i will see you again?" She only nodded a reluctant 'yes.' She was right, not many years later we received a letter from Fred's brother saying she had passed.

i was most grateful for all the years i had corresponded with Mutti in German, because during this trip i was able to communicate in German.

The Lord had truly blessed me, in that i had not forgotten. The sad thing i learned from the cousins while visiting, was, they wanted to know, why did i stop writing to Mutti? They told me, before going into the home care residence, she would watch and wait daily, looking for a letter from America from me. i was very saddened to hear this news, and told them; i was told she had severe Alzheimers Disease. And she would not have even remembered me. It was not true, according to them. How was i to know, living so far away? This too, i had to put in my Creator's loving hands. Mama, and my aunt would soon no longer be with us. And so it was, the end of our trip to see not only family, but all the beauty of Elohim, our Creator.

Chapter Thirty-Seven

"Jehovah-tsidkenu: The Lord Our Righteousnes"

Our purpose as Christians.
Sharing my faith; the Gospel.

"It's no use. We will continue with our own plans; each of us will follow the stubbornness of his evil heart." Jeremiah 18:12. That was pretty much what Fred and i decided; "We can do this, we can stay on the ranch, we've done it for 36 years and we can continue." We were fooling ourselves in believing we could do it; meeting the everyday challenges that faced us, getting enough firewood for the winter (those five cords of wood we cut, split, stacked and used for fuel to heat our 3,600 square foot home and Salon,) raising beef cattle, mending fences, keeping a large garden, canning and preserving, and then there was the draught and wells to contend with, a large swimming pool, a vineyard to prune and maintain, chickens, with never ending weed whacking and always a rattlesnake where we would least expect it. And of course, continuing on with my Beauty Salon, that is what helped bring in the needed extra income. Now, with my writing and the Lord laying it on my heart, to share my story with the world. All of this, along with church involvement and our love for entertaining, we wondered, where did our grandchildren and children fit in to the equation?

Not too mention we were living on our social security and everything was going up in price. Oh sure, we got that little increase each year, but it didn't keep up with the ever increasing economy. Having the Beauty Salon in our home did help with the little extras we had, but i was getting tired as well, and it was difficult to keep up with the trends. When i started many moons prior, we had what we called 'Bread and butter customers.' They were the ones who came for weekly appointments; that was our "Bread and butter," we could count on them providing for our needs, but not so today, it's once a month for color, cut, and when money got tight for some of them, it was once every six weeks. Then there were the permanent waves, every three months, but fewer and fewer people were getting them. i always wondered why we called them "permanent" when we knew they only lasted a few months. Before retiring, as i was doing her daughters hair, one of my long time customers asked," gloria, how long have you been doing this?" My quick reply was," Don't ask." It had been quite a few years, fifty to be exact from start to finish.

It was time for Fred and i to stop with the stubbornness and move on; so we put our home on the market. Oh, we had it on the market the previous year, but it didn't work out. So we thought, 'let's try again.'

While our home was on the market we continued on as usual with all the work set before us. i continued writing as well. Then an opportunity came up for me to attend a Christian Writers Conference, but knew we could not afford for me to attend.

My dear friend and sister-in-Christ, Joyce, arrived laden with gifts and to visit us for a few days. i told her about the Writers Conference, and how i would love to attend but knew we couldn't manage my attending. She then said, "I have some funds, and i would like to send you to the conference." Shocked, but not surprised, because i know my Joyce is a very giving person.

She then said, "Let's check it out on the web," which we did, and when she went home she continued to get me all setup to attend the conference. This was a no, no for Joyce, normally she didn't usually follow-through. Once again, i was shocked at how quickly she got on this project. i told her, i think we finally found her nitch, in helping others with certain projects. She was adamant about my attending this conference and was bound and determined to see it through, until i was in my room at the conference grounds and ready to learn, see, and do what the Lord had for me.

This whole process not only blessed me, but it blessed Joyce to get the job done. Although, she insisted on funding the conference for me to attend, i thought, discussed and prayed about it. Then i shared with Joyce that I felt I should give others the opportunity to have a part in this and be blessed in this adventure. She agreed, so we came up with a letter to send out to all who i thought might like to participate. The responses were amazing! As the funding came through, Joyce made the arrangements at the conference grounds, and sent the funds to them. Within a short period of time the total amount was paid. i want to stop right here, and personally thank all who contributed and believed in what the Lord had for me, in writing for Him. Thank you.

As for me, the work had just begun to prepare for the conference. i was sent all the classes that were being offered, and what was expected of me prior to the conference. The only problem was, most of the information was sent to Joyce instead of me. As i discussed this with my faithful friend, Joyce, she decided she would make the 3 and 1/2 hour trip to our home, to go over the format of the conference with me.

When she arrived, we worked diligently for hours getting everything in order. There was a main class to choose, along with classes that would enhance the chosen class, we went over all the information, praying and making decisions along the way. And copies and more copies that had to be downloaded from the website and placed in a binder.

i remember it was a very wet rainy day as we worked hard on what was needed for the conference. Then it happened, the printer broke down. We had only one choice and that was to purchase a new printer, because we still had numerous copies to make. We drove to Jackson, about forty-five minutes away, to purchase the printer. It was nice to have a break, after working all day.

When we arrived at the store, i immediately sought the Lord's direction as to which copier He would have us to buy. Both, Fred and Joyce suggested different ones, but the Lord kept directing me to the one He wanted me to purchase. i just love it when He gives us clear direction. Yes, it was the perfect one for what we were going to do, and when the sales clerk finished the transaction, we paid way less than we had expected. PRAISE THE LORD!!!

We went home, prepared a nice dinner and proceeded to finish our work. We hadn't finished, and much to my surprise, Joyce said she was leaving early the next morning. She would keep in contact with me, to see how things were coming along and then take me to the conference grounds when i arrived in April.

i felt overwhelmed with all that had to be accomplished before the conference. As it turned out, i was doing much more than was required. Upon arrival at the conference grounds i was told all that was needed from my book was the first twenty or so, pages. For some reason, i misunderstood, and thought the whole book was required for review.

The day the conference was to begin, i drove to Joyce's home, rested and then i followed her to the conference grounds. It was comforting to have her go with me and help me get settled into my room. The first thing i did was to lose the keys to my room! i stopped, prayed, looked down and there they were, Praise the Lord.

i had made prior arrangements to have "Our" Christian children's books placed with other books for sale at the conference. Joyce helped me carry the books into the bookstore. i was very pleased that some of "Our" books sold, because there were so many books for sale.

Soon it was time for Joyce to depart and i was on my own, i knew no one at the conference and felt lost at first. Not long afterwards, i had such a sense of peace about being on the grounds of Mt. Hermon, an appropriate name for such a majestic place nestled in the Redwoods of California. As you may recall, Fred and i had our first home only twenty or so minutes from Mt. Hermon, amongst the Redwoods. So this atmosphere was very familiar to me; it was like going home to visit.

The first session i attended, our spiritual, Godly leader challenged each of us with; "You are here to work on your book or for whatever reason, but i want you to go back to your room and ask the Lord why He has sent you here?" That was very touching for me and i did just as he asked.

As i sat in my room and looked out the window, there stood at least three or more of those beautiful creations of the Lord, reaching mightily to the sky. i was able to get a glimpse of the blue sky above the top of those Redwood branches. No i was alone, but not lonely, because the Creator of the Universe was ever present during this whole conference. It all began in that room, as i prayed and sought the Lord and His purpose for my being at the conference.

The next day brought it to culmination; His reason for my being there was to be with Him and to be who i am in Him. This is probably one of the largest Christian Writers Conferences held in the United States and i was surrounded by hundreds of authors, would-be-authors, writers, speakers, agents, publishers, and yet i felt i was alone with the Lord Jesus. i felt His ever presence as i walked hand in hand with Him on the conference grounds.

Please allow me to try and explain this wonderful experience. As a writer/author, i sit at my computer typing my thoughts, oh yes i pray before each time i sit down to type. But none-the-less, i am virtually alone with my thoughts, prayers and computer in front of me. It can be very deep, and lonesome at times, even with the Lord's presence. i believe it is especially difficult for those of us who write non-fiction, particularly about our lives; because many areas have not been dealt with in years, so there are tears, laughter, and joy, as i am working through the past.

In my case as i wrote this book, i developed high blood pressure, pain in my shoulders and back from sitting at the computer for hours on end.

i finally realized i needed to take a break while writing, just to go for a walk on our ranch and cry out to the Lord, which really helped relieve some of the pressure.

Also, i am not a sit down person (as most of my friends would testify), so it is more difficult to sit for long periods of time for me; i'd rather be socializing and learning from others. Well, with that in mind, the Lord used my gift of boldness to talk with the agents, publishers, speakers and so forth, at the conference with no holding back. And with the Lord walking right beside me, i had no problem. He was so wonderful to me, as i went through the schedule, planning out whom He wanted me to speak with or which class He wanted me to attend, He made it very clear to in front of me, and i would make my appeal to them right then and there.

Because there were so many fewer agents, publishers and speakers than writers/authors, i was to learn in the classes i took, that we were to approach these people in certain ways, and work with them to set-up an audience with them. Oops, i goofed; i had already made my approach before learning all this information. But for me, as i mentioned before, it was a joy to just go up to them and set-up meetings etc. i was not the shy little girl from Silicon Valley/ Santa Clara Valley, anymore; the Lord was beside me and i knew what i must do in the short time i was at the conference.

The first night i was there, i sat with a lovely couple from Texas. The wife pointed out an elderly man in the room and went on to say, he wrote Dale Evans memoirs. That did it for me, after dinner i walked up to him, introduced myself and asked him about his writing Dale Evans memoirs. He said, yes he had written them for her. i then pointed to the pink cowgirl boots i was wearing and said, "i always admired her as a child, and i wasn't a Christian then, but i knew she and Roy Rogers had something i wanted. One of the reasons i wear these boots is because they remind me of her." It wasn't long and i had set up a meeting with this wonderful talented man, for another day during the conference.

The meeting with him lasted quite awhile, we spoke mainly about his life and his marriage to his wife of over fifty years. He did share with me a little about writing Dale Evans memoirs. He presented the memoirs to me just as i remembered; they were very kind, loving people. i had concluded from reading about them in the past, they had experienced some very trying times. And i knew their only hope was in Jesus.

Roy Rogers and Dale Evans were well known celebrities of cowboys, cowgirls and westerns. Roy was known as "The King of the Cowboys." They were one of Hollywood's best-loved married couples. They were on national television and made live appearances throughout the United States.

When our sons were young, i purchased a video from one of Roger's television shows. As Roy Rogers came riding out on his horse, Trigger, he had the horse rear up on it's hind legs, then Roy Rogers dismounted, took off his cowboy hat, bowed his head and prayed. Our sons turned to me in surprise and said, "Mom, did he always do that?" i had forgotten, but enjoyed that part of the video as well.

As i remember them, they were a couple that youngsters could look up to, with great admiration. They portrayed a very healthy, lifestyle. i sometimes wish our sons, and especially the children of today, could have the same opportunity of having some one like these people to admire and want to portray.

My next interview was with an agent from Arizona. He was a very likable person and easy to talk to. Once again, i had made the appointment with him prior to knowing how to get an interview. Then again, the Lord was with me and guided me directly to this man. He sat and spoke with me only briefly, but during that time he gave me some good information that i will definitely use in my writing.

i was able to take classes from both of these men, and learned so much more in the classes they presented.

As i noted previously, i had my partial manuscript done and it was submitted prior to my arrival, to the publisher/agents, Joyce and i both thought would fit what i needed. We were both in hopes either or both of these would consider publishing my memoirs. Upon the second or third day of the conference, those of us who had submitted our work could pick it up and set-up an appointment, if desired with the agent/publisher.

While waiting for the results of the submissions, i carried on with the Lord walking beside me in my classes, meeting other authors, agents, speakers and potential writers. My roommate had not yet arrived, and i was looking forward to meeting her. On the second day of the conference i was pleased to meet my roommate, a very loving caring Christian sister; Ann. Ann was from Ohio, but was familiar with California. She and her husband had co-authored two books, of which she generously presented me with both of them.

We hit it off well and had a great time together; except for one problem, but the Lord helped us get through it. He helped me, especially, to accept and love. In her kindness and generosity, she had the whole set of c.d.'s from the conference, sent to our home as a gift. i will always treasure our time together, and her giving spirit. She will remain a friend forever, because we will share eternity together.

Ann, like me, had submitted her work to an agent or publisher. We both awaited the results of our submissions. Upon receiving the results, even though an offer wasn't made for publishing, i rejoiced at their comments on my writing. Now, keep in mind, these are very professional people, who work for well-known publishing companies, so their positive comments gave me hope. One said, i was a good writer and the other agreed. What a blessing.

As for my dear sister, she was not too pleased with the results of her submissions. So, i held her hand and we prayed. She and i did a lot of praying together or for one another, during the conference. As for the submissions, each person has a different perspective on one's writings and gives different comments. i have read the books Ann and her hubby wrote and enjoyed reading them. To each their own perspective.

Another dear sister-in-Christ i met was Jing; she was originally from China and had a great testimony to share. We became fast friends. i asked her if she would join me in speaking at different churches; she just smiled. i really meant it and intend on hooking up with her real soon. i keep in contact with both of these dear ladies and PRAISE THE LORD, HE brought us together.

When the conference concluded, i packed, prayed, said good bye to many wonderful people i had spent time with, at this special place, set in the peace and quiet of Santa Cruz Mountains. It was difficult for me to depart, not knowing if i would ever see or meet these dear ones again, and to leave this place of restoring my spirit and soul for those several days.

One comment i heard a fellow writer say was, "What we have learned and done here in the short time of four or five days, is equal to ten years of writing experience for a writer." He was correct; we learned so much in such a short time, how was i ever going to be able to retain all the information? Aha, the wonderful cd's my sister Ann had given me and of course the Holy Spirit bringing it to mind. Thank you, Lord.

i drove to my dear friend Joyce's home, to relax, share and contemplate on what had just transpired. i was thankful Joyce lived only fifteen or twenty minutes away, so i wouldn't have to make the three and a half hour trek home.

Joyce and i laughed and shared during my brief stay. i had the joy of sharing some of my adventures with her sweet daughter Merissa, who is like a niece to me. i just love her and enjoy our times of sharing.

After a lovely dinner that Joyce prepared, we went for a walk overlooking the great Pacific Ocean and sandy beaches. Joyce and her husband Gary are blessed to live in Santa Cruz, within walking distance of the ocean. As we walked along, Joyce and i had a great visit and talked about her limping. Since she and i are the best of friends, i was able to share my concerns and make her promise me she would have it looked into. Tears welled up in her lovely eyes as she shared her pain in walking and accepting my care and thoughtfulness. She did follow-up, had hip surgery, and is doing fantastic. She has always been there for me, this time i felt i could be there for her. The only problem is, i was not able to be there for her physically when she had surgery and recovery, due to health challenges i was having at the same time; which i will share in my next chapter.

i left Joyce's home the next day, excited to get home and share with Fred and others, my wonderful experience at Mt. Hermon and the Christian Writers Conference. My words to you, the reader, if you ever consider writing, i would highly recommend your attending the conference.

Prior to attending the conference, Joyce came once again to our home and helped me put on a luncheon for all who supported "Our" ministry. About twenty or so joined in this time of fellowship. A wonderful group of musicians came and played for us while we enjoyed lunch. Our dear friend and brother-in-Christ, Thomas, who had not long before became a Chaplain, and my sister-in-Christ his wife, Denise, came as well. Thomas anointed me with oil and prayed for "Our" ministry. At the end, one candle was lit, it was used to light our brother or sister's candle that was next to us and we all sang in unison. It was a day i shall remember with all the love and support of Christian brothers and sisters.

Before leaving Joyce's home, my sister-in-Christ Paula, called to invite me for breakfast. i was to meet her at a restaurant in San Jose, and, as it turned out, it was the same restaurant, and one of the last restaurants, where my Mama and i enjoyed a lunch in San Jose, together. This too, of course, brought back memories as i drove into the parking lot; i remembered my Mama's words years before. "Your Aunt will be well taken care of when she gets older, she has paid up for a home. What will happen to me? Will i be thrown into some ditch and left?" i knew what she meant because my aunt had been paying into a retirement home. i quickly answered Mama and said, "Mom, i will take care of you. As a little girl, i remember you took care of your mother and i made a promise to myself then, that i would take care of you." With that, she did not say another word and we went into the restaurant to have our meal.

Paula was already at the restaurant awaiting my arrival. We had a full breakfast, i was so excited sharing about the writer's conference; i didn't eat much, so i took the rest of my meal with me. Paula, had many concerns on her heart: one was, her son had just lost his job and how she wanted to help him, but it would be difficult for her. He was an apprentice machinist. Oh my! Fred was a retired machinist and had some great tools, a wooden chest, and roll-about we were trying to sell. What a great opportunity for this young man getting started. Most of Fred's tools were made in Germany, Switzerland and the United States, unheard of today. As i shared this with Paula and suggested he apply where Fred worked, she was overjoyed. She asked me to ask Fred how much he wanted for the tools, i called him and he made her a great offer. She replied, "Sold. But i will have to pay in installments." We were all blessed; she bought the needed tools for her son and we finally sold them. What a blessing. We thanked the Lord as we prayed together in the restaurant and especially for the job He had in store for her son.

We were standing outside the restaurant saying our good byes, i was facing Paula and the sun was shining brightly behind her. Suddenly she just started crying and saying to me, "There is a Light all around you, gloria. It is so hard to explain, it is as though you are shining and i can hardly look at you, it is so bright." She said she thought she had her sunglasses on that gave a glow or some sort of reflection, but realized she didn't have any sunglasses on, at the time.

This was amazing to me, i just stood there in peace and quiet and said, "Don't forget, i just had a mountain top experience, perhaps that is what you are witnessing." She said, "i don't know what it is, but i have never seen anything like it before." With tears in her eyes and peace in her heart and mine, we said our good byes. It was not to end there.

We departed ways, and i drove to the area in South San Jose where i was born and raised. Tennant Avenue was difficult to find, as i shared in the first chapters of this book, it is now Silicon Valley Road. Once i found that, it became the old Tennant Avenue i once knew. It still amazes me today, with all the new homes built in that area, that the ranch house of the rancher we worked for, still stood standing, with the huge barn beside it. Of course i took pictures and share them in this book. i just know the Lord allowed this to remain the same because He knew i would write this book about Silicon Valley, one day.

Fred was thankful to have me home once again after almost a week. The poor man, i wouldn't quit talking and sharing. Didn't matter that we spoke nightly over the phone while i was at the conference, i just wanted him included in almost every experience i had during and after the conference.

That's when, i decided to get into the Word of God, the Bible, to search what Paula saw while we stood in that parking lot outside the restaurant. The Light that Paula had witnessed, reminded me of the Light i saw around our bed many years prior, just before Fred invited Jesus into his heart. **John 8:12 says; When Jesus spoke again to the people, He said, "I am the Light of the world. Whoever follows Me will never walk in darkness, but will have the Light of life."** This verse reminded me also of what i just experienced, as i walked through the Writers Conference with Jesus walking right beside me. PRAISE HIM!!!

Paula called and shared a verse with me as well; she said that is exactly what she saw that day in the parking lot. A verse that came to me about what Paula saw is: **"Those who are wise will shine like the brightness of the heavens, and those who lead many to righteousness, like the stars for ever and ever." Daniel 12:3** Dear one's, that is not my righteousness, but the righteousness that comes through Jesus Christ, my Lord and Savior. What a blessing to walk and talk with the God of this universe, what a gift!

Chapter Thirty-Eight

"Jehovah-nissi: The Lord My Banner"

The Lord my banner. The sale/the move.

At the beginning of the previous chapter i shared with you, the reader, about putting our ranch on the market.

The Christian Writers Conference i had just returned from was held in April. We had put our home on the market just previous to my attending the conference. Perhaps, an offer was to come soon, so there was a lot going on, trying to gather as much information as i could about the conference, working on "Our" book, getting back to work in the Salon in our home, start looking for a new home, and begin the purging process. Fred and i had to consider many things, after all we had resided in our home for thirty six years, raised our sons, held Bible studies, youth groups, Good News Clubs, had barn fires, celebrated birthdays, holidays, enjoyed the pool, entertained and ministered to numerous folks, planting and gardening, cutting and hauling firewood, raised animals and so on. We also, had made friends with quite of few of the neighbors, but many of them had moved on or passed away.

i guess the most difficult part was the purging after all those years. What do we take, what do we donate, sell, or toss? One of my dear friends had said, "gloria, you have been good at purging over the years." That was a plus. She was right, as i mentioned earlier in this book, our Franz once said, "Mom, the poor children dress better than us, because you give everything away." He has a good sense of humor, yet, was partially correct. My giving probably comes from not having much as a child, now was an opportunity to give and bless others.

While purging, we had no idea as to where we were going, how large the home was going to be, that the Lord would provide for us. Or were we to purchase a motor home to reside in, until we were in a home? All this affected what we were supposed to keep, dispose of, or pass on.

The day arrived, in a short period of time, when an offer was made on our ranch. Our dear and long time friend, Hank was visiting us from Wisconsin on one occasion, when the potential buyers came. Hank, who had been in real estate at one point in his life, gave us some pointers to make our home more welcoming. When he heard me share with the potential buyers our love for the ranch, Hank went on to say, that i was the one who sold them the home, by my kind, honest words. We enjoyed our visit with Hank, i can just visualize he and Fred now, sitting out on the huge Redwood deck, which overlooked the grand Sierra's. There they sat with a glass of wine or brandy, and a cigar sharing old memories and enjoying each other's company.

Hank, having attended Multnomah School of the Bible in years past, is now a very devout loving Christian man. He spends a good amount of time reading and studying the Word of God, daily. With that in mind, we had a lot to share with our brother-in-Christ.

After Hank left, Fred and i made a trip to visit our children in Redding. It was there, that our son Jeff found the home the Lord wanted us to have, located in Valley Springs, California. Fred, had wanted to move to this area, but i dug my stubborn heels into the ground, because i wanted to live either in Angels Camp or Murphy's, California.

Then one evening, when i couldn't sleep, the Lord directed me to checkout the Valley Springs area. Much to my surprise there were lovely homes, most of them sitting on half acres, with little or no upkeep, and they were within our price range. The next day, i shared with Fred what the Lord directed me to do, and showed him pictures on the Internet, of the possibilities. We decided to call our realtor, so she could take us to see some of these finds. Of course there was the one our Jeff had shown us; the minute we walked up the stairs and into the home, we knew this was the one the Lord had for us.

Anyone, who has sold a home, knows about the final papers being signed and the monies being transferred, etc. etc. Well, it was the same for us, as we waited patiently and sometimes not so patiently. In the meantime, there were well meaning people who kept asking if we had sold and where are you moving, when are you moving? Finally, our answer would be, "When the money is in our hand."

Meanwhile, many decisions had to be made, one being, should i continue working as a cosmetologist or was it time to close Shop? Fred answered that question one day, as we were driving along, he calmly said, "You are not going to do hair anymore." i was shocked, we weren't even discussing the subject, his comment came out of no where, but he was firm and meant it. i was somewhat relieved, but did i really want to retire, what was i to tell my customers? What were they to do after all the years i cared for them? They weren't just customers, many of them were friends. We shared our lives, our families, tears, hurts, pain, love, joy, and most of all our relationship with Jesus. i would miss them and my work.

i knew Fred was right and i must move on to other things; this book was one, our children and grandchildren, another, also, our new home, church, family, friends and Fred and my relationship. He had been retired for a few years, while i continued working, and we rather enjoyed each other's space. This would be different, constant companionship, even different when we were first married.

i am here to tell you, dear reader, sure it is tough at times, but the good far outweighs the bad. We enjoy each other immensely, sharing God's Word; the Bible, Bible study, church, talking, sharing, walking, swimming, golfing, cooking, planning, watching good old westerns, and shows like the Walton's, Andy Griffith and more. When i want time alone, i go on the computer, work on my writing, keep in contact with friends and keep informed about happenings in the world. We are enjoying life more and more until the Lord takes us home.

There i go again, getting ahead of myself. Back to selling our ranch and moving. Once we decided on the home the Lord and our Jeff led us to, it was time to make an offer, since our home was in Escrow. i made many calls to my dear sister Barbara, she had been in real estate, so i called to asked her for advice. She really helped Fred and i a lot, in making the offer for our new home. i will always be grateful for her good, sound advice.

Finally, all the paperwork had been done for our ranch and our new home. It was so involved, i would rather not go there, just be grateful we were moving on. We had to be out of our 3,600 square foot home, plus 460 square foot cellar, a 1,200 square foot barn, outer buildings, a huge swimming pool and garden, in one week. It was summer and hot, as i sweat, packing all those boxes my dear friend Denise, collected for us. Oh, yes many friends had offered to help, but i being the stubborn one, thought i could do it all on my own. Finally, when the last day arrived, my dear friend Lynne offered to come and help, i was so relieved and thankful for her help. Keep in mind, we had lived in this home for thirty-six years, i was that much older and had forgotten how tough it was to move. i read somewhere, that moving and divorce run very close in giving the most stress. i would discover later, how true it was, as far as moving was concerned.

My siblings and their spouses offered to come and help us with the move. What a blessing. They all live in Redding, California so for some it was a four, or more, hour drive one-way. Both of our son's and their wives also came to help with the move. Two dear precious couples and wonderful friends were there to help as well. Most of our friends who wanted to help were either ill or not available. We decided the Lord would have whom He wanted there, to help. Besides, sometimes too many helpers can be too complicated.

376

Once my job of packing, and Fred's job of delivering furniture to the thrift stores or wherever, was done, it was time for the actual moving. Our family arrived early on the day of the move; Jeff and Fred had already gotten the truck to haul our belongings, the night before, so it was ready to be packed. Many hands helped with the moving, but it took someone special to pack the truck just right, and that someone was our brother-in-law; Don. He had a lot of experience packing furniture, which he learned as a young man, helping his father with their furniture- auction business.

Somehow, i managed to prepare a honey-baked ham, a pot of chili, French bread and cookies for dessert. That was a relief to all who helped, there was no time to stop and go to a restaurant. We stopped, held hands and thanked the Lord for His provisions, and after everyone ate, the moving continued. i spent time with our grandson, Steven Joseph, while everything was being moved into our new home. Our daughter's-in-love unpacked, and set-up the kitchen for me. i just stayed out of the way, prayed and enjoyed the time with Steven.

At one point i came into the kitchen, and there on the counter lay a picture in a frame face down. i picked it up and thought, wonder why this picture is here, the only one that appeared in such a manner? As i turned it over, i knew why; there it was, a picture of my Mama, taken forty or so years prior. i just stood there in awe as i stared at my precious Mama, and then realized she had always been there for me in our moves, trials, joys, and here she was again. For me it was confirmation, that she was with us and happy for us, that we had made this move for a better life in our later years. My sister-in-love, Deannie, confirmed my thoughts when she said, "Your, Mom would be happy for you moving here."

The move was finally complete and our family left for home, tired and worn out; all except my brother Bill, who was having some medical problems during our move and was taken to the local hospital, during our move. His wife, Deannie, came the next day to retrieve him. Thankfully she is a very kind, Christian nurse and could understand the medical terminology.

The doctors had kept Bill for more tests, so Deannie and he, were able to stay with us. We were thankful to have them, along with Jeff, Lexie and the girls, as our first official guests.

Soon after everyone departed, Fred and i began the unpacking. Within a short period of time i went into complete exhaustion. i went to our doctor; he ran numerous blood tests and so forth on me. Everything came out normal (a setting on the dryer), but his conclusion was, fatigue-malaise. i needed rest and lots of it. i was completely exhausted from the top of my head to the tip of my toes; just can't explain. Now, as i look back, could this be what brought on what i will share in the next chapter? Perhaps.

Chapter Thirty-Nine

"Jehovah-rapha: The Lord Who Heals"

Healing.

The move was complete on June 15, 2014. Interesting that we had moved to the ranch in June 1978, i remember celebrating Franz's second birthday on June third, outside our trailer, in the hot California sun. Our new neighbors surrounded him and our dear Kiyoko baked a birthday cake for him.

This time it was different. Now it was just Fred, i, and our little Yorkie Biscuit, celebrating the newness of our home.

Our new home is situated over-looking the opposite side of Mt. Ararat in Calaveras County. We had lived directly over on the other side of the mountain, and at night we can still see the red lights blinking, now from this side. A young man and i were discussing how amazing it was that the Lord would place us directly here, as we peered at the mountain. The thought came to me, 'that the Lord had something new for us here on the other side of the mountain.' And 'something new' He does have for us, as i will explain later in the chapter.

Figuratively speaking, on the other side of the mountain, we were at the bottom, climbing and climbing to reach the top and over to the other side. Truly, we did have many trials and tribulations on the other side of that mountain, and it was as if the Lord were allowing us to reach the very top, ever so slowly, and now on this side, He had the new for us.

We really like our new home; it is almost everything we had on our ranch, just smaller. For example, our kitchen sink, which faces that mountain, that reminds me of new things, has a large kitchen sink, just like i had on the ranch. Above the cabinets, there is room enough for not only my collection of teapots, but for other kitchen collectibles, too. Our bathroom has double sinks, just like on the ranch. We have a small swimming pool; our Laurel Shea calls it a jellybean pool, due to its shape. It is much smaller than the one on the ranch, so is easier for Fred to maintain. Under the whole length of our home is a basement, much like what we had on the   ranch, a great place for storage. Our home sits on one-half acre instead of twenty acres, and it is all fenced. There is so much more, our Lord didn't miss a detail when He blessed us with this home.

i am most grateful for being close to my new doctor, post office, grocery store, thrift stores and many fine restaurants, the golf course and the peace and quiet of Hogan Dam. All are within five to ten minutes away, amazing!!! As my dear friend Joyce, said to me when she and her hubby visited, not long after we moved in, "I will no longer be concerned about you and Fred. I loved your home on the twenty acres, but I was always concerned about the distance you lived from everything, especially now as you are both getting older." That loving, caring statement brought tears to our aging eyes.

We had a lot of company and caring family and friends who came to visit us. On one occasion as i stood at the kitchen sink doing dishes, Fred came and said, "Come stand on our deck and look into the night sky." As we peered up into the heavens above, there were beautiful amazing fireworks, and it wasn't the forth of July. i quickly ran to our swimming pool where our granddaughters were swimming and shouting, "Oma, look at all the fireworks!"

When it was all over, the traffic passing our home just kept coming. i told Fred "We have not seen this much in the thirty some years we have lived in Calaveras County." We discovered that this firework show takes place every year prior to the forth of July. Believe me, in the coming years, we will invite family and friends for a bar-b-q and swim on that particular day, and watch from the comfort of our home; This was yet another blessing.

We were almost settled in our new abode, when we decided it was time to take a trip to our friends in Nevada; we had kept promising to visit them. We had a lovely time with them, but the day before we left from our visit i became very tired again. Prior to our trip, i knew i wasn't quite up to par, but thought getting away would be good to relax and enjoy.

The morning we were to leave, i could hardly drag myself out of bed; it was so unlike me. We prayed with our dear friends and made the descent over Highway 88, toward home. As we drove over the mountain pass, my ears hurt so badly, and i couldn't get them to pop, to relieve the pressure. They finally popped once we reached the bottom of the mountain.

i was still tired and needed lots of rest once we reached our home. Several days later, as Fred and i were enjoying a lovely dinner out in our patio, everything was going around, around. i pushed myself, just to make it to the bathroom, but the spinning continued to get worse. Up came all of my dinner and then some. i was so weak i fell to the floor and just wept. The spinning wouldn't stop. Fred was able to get me up and practically drag me into our bed. i lie there for several hours, getting more and more dizzy and dehydrated. i kept begging Fred to take me to the E.R. The poor man thought i would get better, and prayed for me.

i could not take the discomfort anymore; i couldn't keep water down and told him, he just had to take me to the hospital. i felt so sorry for him, here we were in a new home, with no landline phone, only the cell, which he didn't know how to use. Keep in mind, Fred is going to be eighty years old next year, and sometimes things are just moving too fast for him to keep up with.

What he decided to do was to run out in the middle of our street and flag someone down to help him get me in the car and to the hospital. All i could remember is a big man, (an angel), help Fred carry me and place me in the backseat of the car. The ride was terrible, but i was once again grateful we were not living on the ranch and having to drive windy roads to get to the hospital.

The diagnosis was severe vertigo. i have since learned so very much about vertigo, and believe one reason the Lord has allowed me to experience this malady, is to understand and help others. Once again, I think of **2 Corinthians 1:3-5**. Different ones have asked how i was doing? i reply, "How can i explain to someone who has never had it, how i feel? Not to offend anyone." i went on, " For example, i have never gone through a divorce, thank the Lord, but the one who has, can better understand."

i learned there are different types of vertigo, and i have been told by a specialist, the one i have, is caused probably by a virus, which causes the imbalance in the inner ear. And it will take time and exercise for it to be healed. As of this writing it is now going on eight months, having vertigo. When anyone mentions going on a cruise, i tell them, "No, thank you, i have been on a cruise for quite awhile now and want to get off the boat."

Actually, having vertigo is like going on a merry-go round or whip at an amusement park. When you get off, it feels as though you are still on the ride. As i told one of my friends, when she asked me how i felt. I said, "that on my left side i'm not as good as on my right side." She said, "Then lean to the right and you will always be right." The reason i feel the spinning sensation more on my left side is because my inner ear on the left side has not healed yet, after almost eight months. i asked the specialist if anyone has healed one hundred per cent, and he replied, "Yes, in time, and with exercise, sometimes it takes a year."

At times i become very depressed, because it is like being in prison in your own body. To resolve this, i pray, read Scripture, get involved with fellow believers, loved ones, keep busy and take a nap. i know that resting my body is very important. During the first few weeks, Fred kept telling me i was losing weight. i responded, "Yes, of course, because you don't cook, what am i supposed to do?" i couldn't cook because i could not keep my balance and was afraid i would burn myself. So, i began calling friends and people at our new church, asking them if they could just provide a meal or two a week. It was amazing, how our friends, and now, new church family responded to my call. That led me to take pictures of these dear souls, and put their pictures in a scrapbook. Doing this gave me something to do each day. i then began working on a cookbook with some of my recipes and others, for our Laurel Shea. This would be an amazing gift for her, as i usually do not measure when i cook. Different people, who have sampled my cooking, would ask for the recipes. i will gladly give them, but i only guess at the measurements.

Working on these two projects gave me hope for each new day i awaken with vertigo. Most importantly, i got into the Word of the Lord more and more intensely. i have always spent each day in the Bible; i could probably count on one hand, how i had missed one day over the last forty some years, since i became a Christian. This was different; i drew even closer and more dependent upon the Lord. As Pastor Bill said, at one time when he came to visit, "I had been thinking about **Psalm 23 verse 2, "He maketh me to lie down in green pastures...."** After he said that, it finally dawned on me, 'yes' **"HE MAKETH ME TO LIE DOWN..."** It wasn't of my choosing to have this vertigo, but with it, i was learning how the Lord is in control of my life, i just think i am. Once i realized that, it was easier to accept that HE allowed this to happen to me, in order to draw me closer to HIM, be more dependent on HIM, and to totally trust HIM. Not only HIM, but Fred, as well; i had to rely on Fred to help me shower, help dress me, drive me places i needed to go, and much more. This lesson also helped Fred not to be so dependent upon me, to fend for himself, to help with laundry and other household chores, that are taken for granted. Oh, yes since his retirement, he had been helping me more, but now he really had to step up to the plate.

i was reading a wonderful book at the time, about gifts. This book helped me so much, i decided after my time with the Lord to write down, every day, in a journal the different gifts, to be thankful for, that HE had given me that day. This was such a blessing, not only thanking HIM, but yet another project to keep me busy and to keep my eyes on HIM.

i had journaled in the past, and realized this was important to do once again, as i could look back, not only at the way our Lord provides, but to see HIS almighty hand in everything. The journaling also helped me getting back to finishing this book.

i was finding it very difficult to work on the book using the computer and transcribing from the handwritten page to the computer screen. Along with this, i kept giving myself more and more reasons not to write. Until my dear precious friend Joan, who checked on me regularly, called and asked if i had been working on the book. i told her my concerns, and mostly excuses, then added, "Would you like to hold me accountable for writing and finishing my book?" She agreed, and it was her texting, calling and words of encouragement, that has gotten me to finish this manuscript. Thank you, Joan and thank the Lord, for sending her to me. In the process, i set a date and decided to have it published by spring of 2015. That meant, i had to ask my dear Mary, to edit it by February or March. Then, i needed to get all the pictures scanned, have the footnotes in place, the chapters and everything aligned. There was so much more to do, and the Lord kept closing the doors, i knew it was not to be published by spring of 2015. In reality, it is more like the Fall of 2015. i was putting my trust in me and not HIM, and now have welcomed HIS timing, not mine. i am still that diamond in the rough, HE is still chiseling to make me into HIS perfect stone. That will not happen until i am in heaven with HIM. Thanks be to the Lord.

Chapter Forty

**"In the beginning God created
the heavens and the earth." Genesis 1:1
"In the beginning was the Word, and the
Word was with God, and the Word was
God." John 1:1**

Committing my work to the Lord;
writing and speaking for Him

What or Who can i attribute my life? There is only One person can i attribute my life to: Jesus Christ and His Word, the Bible. Please allow me to share, in closing this book, how much reading, studying and putting into action, His Word, the Bible, has and will continue to have in my life.

Where shall i begin? At the beginning, as this chapter states **"In the beginning God..." Genesis 1:1**. i just heard a pastor say, "We must read the manufacturers Manuel in order to know how to operate the product, and the Lord wants us to read His Word to know how to live." He made us; He is our manufacturer, knows all about us and wants to teach us how to live for Him, and know how to live, is found in His Book, His Word, the Bible. Just read Psalm 139 if you really want to understand who you are and how the Lord made you. Before Fred became a Christian, he referred to the machinist Manuel as his bible. That troubled me because i knew, as a Christian; there is only one Bible. For the Word of God says; **"All Scripture is God-breathed and is useful for teaching, rebuking, correcting and training in righteousness, so that the man of God may be thoroughly equipped for every good work." 2Timothy 3:16-17.** But in making that statement, he showed me the importance of the machinist Manuel for him to refer to, as he worked as a machinist. Aha, that is true with God's Word, too, but even more so, because we are talking about us, His creation. As a Cosmetologist i refer

385

to my Manuel's, as they teach me how and why. So it is with God's Holy Word, the Bible.

When Fred became a Christian, and now as he is retired, we read and study God's Word every day together, and we witness the changes He has made in our lives. i as a Christian, cannot express to you enough, the importance of reading and studying the Bible every day; it is food for your soul. Before Fred and i read the Word together, i would have my quiet time with the Lord and His Word. We eat, drink and exercise our bodies, but our soul needs this nourishment as well, and the only way we get it is through His Word, the Bible. i challenge you, the reader, today, to pick-up the Bible and begin reading it for five minutes, then ten minutes and increase the time spent in His Word each day. Please, do pray, before you begin your reading for the day, asking the Holy Spirit to show you what He wants you to learn, for that day. Then read, study, pray, and meditate on the Word. i guarantee you, you will have a hunger for His Word as never before; there will be a change in you, that will ignite others, and they will desire what you have, and so it will grow and we may witness a changed world; changed for the better.

i shared earlier in this book, about the first Bible study i attended and how the Lord came into my heart and life, and changed me. He lay upon my heart, these words from **Psalm 51:10-13 "Create in me a pure heart, O God, and renew a steadfast spirit within me. Do not cast me from Your presence or take Your Holy Spirit from me. Restore to me the joy of your salvation and grant me a willing spirit, to sustain me. Then I will teach transgressors Your ways, and sinners will turn back to You."** i knew He was telling me to begin a Bible study in our home in Circle XX, Angels Camp, California.

My dear sister-in-Christ, Sue, who was a co-coordinator with a wonderful ministry, guided the first Bible study I started in my home. Not knowing many people, i just started inviting people i'd meet, to come join us; from that study many came to know the saving grace of Jesus Christ, right there in our living room. i keep in contact with some of them. One, among many, is my dear sister Beth, whom i have seen the Lord change into a beautiful butterfly, to fly for Him. In and through this Bible study, the cookie exchange i held at Christmas, and the Live Nativity the children did in our barn each year, touched many hearts and lives for Jesus.

i became the strange lady 'up on the hill,' to those who did not know me, or care to know the One i serve, Jesus. Oh yes, i was persecuted for my faith, but kept doing as the Lord had called me to do, share the Gospel. As i shared my hurt and pain of not being accepted with our Pastor at the time, he said, "Well, what do you expect, many of these people moved here for the peace and quiet, and then along comes the evangelist." The first time i was called the evangelist was by my dear sister Barbara; she is so wise and could see long before i, the gift the Lord had given me. It is a joy and a pleasure to be an evangelist for the King of Kings and Lord of Lords, to Him be praise, honor and glory!!! He has chosen me, even me. Back to these wonderful Bible studies, and the changed lives for Jesus. During one of our lessons, our guide Sue, had arrangements for the next week of our Bible lesson, and told me i was now capable to guide the study. Not i, said, "Jonah." i did not think i was capable of guiding the Bible study. i loved that this ministry called us guides and not teachers, because the Word of God says in **James 3:1 "Not many of you should presume to be teachers, my brothers, because you know that we who teach will be judged more strictly."**

The next week, i found myself guiding the Bible study, and loving what the Lord had given me to do. It wasn't before too long, that i too, became a guide and would guide many Bible studies. i not only would witness lives changed before my very eyes, but am thankful to say, many of the ones who attended became like family. They were the ones who would be there for me, when Fred or i got sick, needed help, needed support, prayers or love. Many of them are family through the blood of Jesus. As my dear sister, Joyce said, "Remember, when we get to heaven, that the family that joins us there, will not necessarily be the family we were born into on earth."

Please allow me to share some of the experiences i enjoyed in teaching these Bible studies. At one point, there were at least three or four African American ladies who joined our group; what a blessing they were to our group of ladies. At one of the ladies homes, where we were having our lesson, someone asked the hostess about a plant in her home. She replied, holding up her white finger, "I don't know, as i have a black thumb, when it comes to plants." Without hesitation one of the African American ladies held up her black thumb, and said, "That's funny, i have a black thumb, too." What a great sense of humor.

One of the ladies in our group invited Fred, our sons and i, over for dinner. There were quite a few of us who gathered that evening, and our eldest son said, "Mom, we are the only white people here." i said, "i know, isn't it nice we were invited?" The food was good too, grits, hog jowl, collard greens and all kinds of spicy, cajun treats. Their Pastor had joined us as well. As he was leaving i overheard the guests say, "Get the jug out, brother, he's gone now." i just laughed. That's funny, who are we trying to kid, the Lord sees all. The people there were all so kind and loving to us, we felt so much at home and welcome.

One of these dear sisters' husband had passed, (as they say) and she called to ask if i would help her with the service. Thinking she meant helping with the food, setting up or serving, i said i would. Little did i know she wanted me to give her husband's eulogy, which i did do. i do recall her saying, "You are good at this, and i want you to do it for me." Wow, there must have been something, these dear ones who would ask me to give the eulogy, recognized in me, that i didn't realize; i had the gift of speaking.

Yes, we studied the Bible, but we had fun, too. As my dear sister-in-Christ, Diana said, "Trust the Lord and have fun." She and her hubby, Larry were not part of our group, because they lived so far away, otherwise they too, would have joined us. But i have to say, they both have such a great sense of humor, which makes their marriage special and life as well.

During one of the Bible studies, we would take turns once a month, to learn something new. Each girl in turn would teach us a craft, or whatever, the Lord wanted them to share. This reminded me of the days of Little House on the Prairie, where women sewed, cooked, helped with child birth, canning, and just being there for each other. We miss out on so much of that today. i have a couple of young mothers i enjoy mentoring, and they in turn teach me; that's my Andrea and Robin.

The Word of God, the Bible comes to life each time you read it. Because it is the living Word of God, you cannot read it like a book, you must pray, read, study and apply what it says every day. Our Pastor Bill said, "It is the living Word." Another dear friend and brother-in-Christ; Ross said, "There is a red thread running through the Bible from the book of Genesis through to Revelation, the red thread is Jesus." Revelation says it clearly, **"I am the Alpha and the Omega, the Beginning and the End, the First and the Last." Revelation 22:13.** Jesus is the central point of the Bible.

Please allow me to give you, the reader, an overview of the Scriptures as i understand them; **In Genesis; Jesus is the Seed of the woman, Exodus; He is the Passover Lamb. Leviticus; He is the Sacrifice. Numbers; He is the Rock struck. Deuteronomy; He is the teacher. Joshua; He is Captain of the Lord's hosts. Judges; He is our Deliverer. Ruth; The Kinsman Redeemer. Kings; The Promised King. Nehemiah; He is bringing back the nation of Israel. Ester; He is our rescuer. Job; He is the suffering servant. Psalms; He is the One to look up to God for redemption. Proverbs; He is the One to wise up to God's teaching. Ecclesiastes; He is the ultimate goal: heaven. Song of Solomon; We are His Bride, (the church) He is Our Groom: Jesus and His Church. Prophets; He is the coming Messiah. The Gospels; He came to save the lost. Acts; Christ's resurrection, the Church, Holy Spirit comes. Epistles;**

Christ the Head of the Church. Revelation; Christ will come again in glory!!!

He is the red thread, my friend; that Ross told me about, that runs from Genesis to Revelation. **"For he Word of God is living and active and sharper than any two edged sword, cutting down to the bone and marrow...." Hebrews 4:12a.**

Along with what i have shared in this book, i have witnessed first hand of how the Lord Jesus has worked and continues to work in my life and other's lives. In many of these circumstances He has used His angels to help, protect and give us messages direct from the Father's throne of grace. He has brought people into my life to serve Him, by using the gifts He has given me. Many tell me i have the gift of evangelism. i sometimes wonder is it the gift of evangelism, or is it the gift of witnessing and telling others about Jesus as He commands all believers in Him to do? **Matthew 28: 19-20 "Go into all the world and preach the Gospel ....** that my friend is the Gospel. Sometimes we may think, "But Lord who am i, just one person to reach so many?" Aha, how about the twelve disciples, i often think, if it weren't for them sacrificing their very lives, would we who have accepted Jesus into our heart and lives, would we have known? The Lord can use the most insignificant person, at just the right time to share the Gospel. We have a hurting world, in which there seems to be no hope. i once heard a person can live without food for a certain period of time, without water for a time, but not without hope. We believers, must give the world hope, and that hope i have found in Jesus Christ, my Lord and Savior. Recently, i was sharing with one of my elderly customers, the love of Jesus. She was asking me about heaven and reincarnation. First i told her, the Bible does not speak of reincarnation, but eternal life when you invite Jesus Christ into your heart and life and live for Him. She was surprised that reincarnation wasn't even in the Bible. Later she was telling me how much her son loved her. The Lord led me to say, "You, are telling me how much your son loves you." Jesus loves you more and died for your sins and mine. He paid the price on Calvary's cross for you, (the reader) and me to receive. Romans says, **"That if you confess with your mouth, Jesus is Lord," and believe in your heart that God raised Him from the dead, you will be saved." Romans 10:9**

Another dear soul, whose hair i had done, i asked if she had invited Jesus in her heart? She wanted to first know about a baby, who had died at birth. Someone had told her the baby went to hell. "Was that true?" she said, "and if so, i do not want any part of God." i immediately consoled her and said, "i believe this little baby is with Jesus." With that i confirmed my belief with Scripture, when King David's baby son died; **2 Samuel 12:23 says; "But now he had died; why should I fast? Can I bring him back again? I will go to him, but he will not return to me."**

After i shared and explained that verse to her, and then i shared what Jesus did for us, she then said to me, "I am ready to invite Jesus into my heart." We said the sinners prayer together. i then brought her a little witnessing tool for her to sign, because she was legally blind; i showed her where to sign. i kept that pamphlet in my Bible as a reminder to pray and to continue to teach her the love of God.

It is amazing to me, when people are hurting, Christian or non-Christian, they know who to call. The first time i received such a call was a neighbor had cut herself badly, while using a chain saw. For some reason, she knew to call me and ask for prayer. Another dear friend called to say her grandmother was dying in the hospital and would i go see her and pray for her? Also, the Lord will have us just where He wants us, when he wants us. In another instance, not knowing what had happened to my friend the previous night, the Lord led me to visit her the next morning. She asked me, "What are you doing here?" She really needed someone and prayer, because her teen aged daughter had run away from home. i didn't know, but the Lord knew, and used me at that particular time. **"...because those who are led by the Spirit of God are sons of God." Romans 8:14.**

Recently, i received a call from out of state, (the number and state appeared on my phone). The male voice asked if i were gloria, i replied, "Yes, but who are you?" He said he was my cousin. i had not heard from him in over twenty years. As our conversation went on, of course i asked him where he was in his faith. We had a long discussion. He also shared with me and thanked me for speaking at his father's (my uncle's) funeral. Apparently, he must have remembered some of the things i said, and then went on to tell me of a health challenge he faced. In closing i told him i loved him and Jesus loved him.

When our conversation was over, i called my siblings to tell them of his call, my sister, Josephine remarked, "He knew the right person to call." i hesitated, thought about what she said, and gave thanks to the Lord for using me. i do remember as i spoke at this uncle's funeral, i shared about ants and how would
we communicate with them? i said to the people there; this is the story i told my uncle, while visiting him. He told me, "We just die, go to the grave and the maggots eat what's left." i said, "Uncle, do you see those ants crawling on the ground? If you wanted to communicate with them, how would you, you are so much bigger than they?" He didn't answer. So, i said, "You would become an ant, right?" He agreed. Then i said, "Well, that's exactly what God did, He became a man; Jesus. In that way He could communicate with us and show the love of God and then die for us." My Uncle was very quiet and just listened. i pray this is the message my cousin and others heard that day.

There were many such God incidences where the Lord wanted to use me; it is not our ability, but our availability He wants and needs. i am thankful He has continued to use me in my life and in "Our" Salon at home. It was such a great opportunity to share the love of Jesus openly with my customers. Many of them have grown in their faith over the years, as i have as well. Fellowship with other believers is so important, as is attending worship service. We are like a log that is part of the fire, when we are removed from fellowship and worship, we become like the log that was removed from the fire, it dies out. So it is with us, we die out and become worldly. **Jesus said, "They are not of the world, even as I am not of it."** **John 17:16**

If you have never invited Jesus into your heart and life, i want to give you the opportunity to do so right here and now. Don't put it off, it is the most important decision you will ever make in your life, and the choice is yours. The Bible says, **"He who has the Son has life; he who does not have the Son of God does not have life." 1 John 5:12.**

That, my friend, is very clear. Will you choose life today? It's very simple, yet profound.

Let me explain; let's say you have committed a grievous crime and the judge sentences you to prison for life. Your brother, sister or friend steps up to the judge and says, "I will pay for their crime, sentence me." My friend, here is one that is innocent of the crime, but is willing to pay the penalty. That is exactly what Jesus did; He paid the penalty in full, for our sins. All we have to do is accept His free gift of eternal life and live for Him. Yes, He paid a high price for us, but He is giving it free to all who believe and receive that gift. **Jesus answered, "I am the way, the truth and the life. No one come to the Father except through Me." John 14:6.**

Once we accept Jesus as our Lord and Savior, the Holy Spirit comes to dwell within us, and we become One with Christ. It's a package deal, God the Father, Christ the Son and the Holy Spirit.

Reminds me of a story about a man who decided to take the ship across the deep blue sea, to the land he always wanted to go to; America. He paid his fees to board the ship, climbed aboard and nestled himself in a corner of the great ship. There he sat, slept and ate the meager bit of food for his long journey. Just a day before anchoring in the United States, he once again pulled out his little bit of food he had left, and began to eat. Someone came by and asked what he was doing, he explained. The reply, to him was,

"Come with me," as the dear fellow passenger led him to a banquet room. There to this poor traveler's amazement, was a long table arrayed with all kinds of delicacies. The man who led him to the table said, "You see, sir, this comes with your passage fee." The fellow just stood in a state of awe, realizing what he had missed out on, during all those days of travel.

So, it is with us, once we accept Jesus as Lord and Savior we get the full package deal. The whole enchilada, as some would say. Oh, yes there are gifts of the Holy Spirit, and they come more and more as we seek the Lord and His will for us. He develops them in us, to better serve Him in edifying the church. That is why we must stay in His Word daily, get involved in a Bible Study, and attend a Bible believing church fellowship.

1 Corinthians 12:28 and Romans 12: 6-8 name the gifts of the Holy Spirit.

In conclusion; **Revelation 3:19-20 says; "Those whom I love I rebuke and discipline. So be earnest and repent. Here I am! I stand at the door and knock. If anyone hears my voice and opens the door, I will come in and eat with him, and he with me."**

Is He standing at the door of your heart and asking if He can come in and be your Lord and Savior? If so, don't hesitate; ask Him to come in right here and now. It will be the greatest decision you have ever made in your lifetime. Don't put it off, do it now!

Chapter Forty-One

"I commit my work to You, Lord, knowing You will establish it."
Proverbs 16:3

May it always be, that i love the work i do, and be able to do the work i love.

As i come near to the conclusion of "Our" book, i would like to share some insights with you, my friend. First, i feel as if i know each and every one of you who is reading this book; that is why i call you friend. There is another friend, who is closer than a brother, and my hope and prayer is that you will come to know Him; He is the truest, most faithful, caring, loving, always there friend, you will ever have in your life.

My friend, you have noticed i use the small 'i' in writing this book, and have been told it is improper English. That being the case, i apologize for offending my native tongue. The reason i choose to write it as such: 'i', is because i wanted you, my friend, to see the importance of Jesus in my life; for my life is not about me, it is about Him, who created me, to be the person i am. i thank Him and praise Him for the life He has given me, the parents He chose for me, the family He allowed me to be part of, the pain, the suffering, the good, the bad, and life in general. i do not regret the life He has given me, but want to share it with you, my friend.

i have said over and over again, when this book is published, my prayer is, that if it changes the heart and mind of one individual, and that person comes into the saving grace of Jesus Christ, then i have accomplished what the Lord has given me to do. Praise Him!!!

i also want to share with you, i am not a writer. Oh yes, the Lord has allowed me to write, illustrate and publish seven Christian Children's Books, which has been an honor.

But to write this book has been a real challenge. As i look back, the Children's Books were a cinch to write, because that is where my heart is, with children.

In writing this book, if it had not been for my prayer and support team and the Lord's almighty hand upon me, i probably would not have finished the task He set before me. It has been difficult, in that i had to face the truth and be bold and naked before my readers. As a fellow author, who had just completed a book she and her son had co- authored, said, "Let's write a fiction the next time, it is much easier." When the Lord directed me to write this book, there were many times i questioned Him, "Are You sure, Father, You want me to write this book?" Then came the difficult part of putting pen to paper.

Psalm 45:1 says;

"My heart is stirred by a noble theme
as I recite my verses for the King;
my tongue is the pen of a skillful writer."

Once i got it down on paper, then i had to transfer it to the wonderful computer my dear Mama blessed me with, then came the rattlesnake bite which deterred me from writing. But as the Lord would have it, He sent my Mary, to help me complete the manuscript. When I finally was able to type it on my own, came the excuses. Next came surgery at our wonderful Stanford Hospital. Then came the opportunity to attend the Christian Writer's Conference and Joyce's encouragement to attend. Not so, then came the sale of our ranch, settling in our new home, and now vertigo.

The Lord had His hand on me, and sent my beloved Prayer and Support Team. Then came the editing and reliving all that i had written, again. Because i am not a sedentary person, you might have guessed, sitting at the computer and typing, played havoc with my health. i learned to write and then take a nice walk on our ranch, breathing in the fresh air and enjoying the beauty of the Sierra Foothills surrounding us, and just meditating on God's Word. Praying, releasing, and giving it all to Him, it was a time of renewal and cleansing. He tells us in His Word He is our comforter, counselor, **John 14 and Isaiah 51:12**.

As for His healing hand on my health, He gave me a vision at a prayer meeting He had directed me to start for His glory. While at the prayer meeting, i asked for prayer for a sister-in-Christ, who was having some pain and also for the health problem i was experiencing. As the dear ones laid their hands on me and prayed for healing, it was then, the Lord gave me the vision. With eyes closed and accepting their prayers for me, i envisioned the blood of Jesus washing over my body and cleansing me with healing. "Healing in his wings." my sister Lynne, reminded me of the verse. The complete verse, which i love, especially the part about "calves leaping from the stall", is: **"But for you who revere my name, the sun of righteousness will rise with healing in its wings. And you will go out and leap like calves released from the stall." Malachi 4:2.** i can just imagine little calves leaping and jumping as they are released out in the pasture. As a matter of fact i have witnessed them doing just that, what freedom and joy. What an awesome thought and such peace, that we can give it all to the One who created us, and then move on to whatever He has for us.

i can say with all truthfulness, that He has been my Ebenezer. It is interesting how the Lord works without our sometimes realizing it. We had sung a song at church, something about Ebenezer. During our time of fellowship after church, i asked Pastor Bill what the song about Ebenezer meant. He knew and wanted to share the verse that talked about Ebenezer. We searched the Scripture and found the verse. That verse was meant for me, and for writing this book. It states; **"Thus the Lord has helped me." 1Samuel 7:2.** As many times as i have read the Bible, i do not remember this verse, but that is just like our Lord, He will give us the verse or whatever we need at the time we need it. Once again, here is a reminder that the Bible is the living Word of God.

Recently i read the following:

'Good things come to those who believe.

Better things come to those who are patient.

The best things come to those who don't give-up.

i Praise the Lord He hasn't given up on me or anyone for that matter. And He most definitely has not given up on me to complete this book. With all the challenges, struggles, roadblocks or whatever the evil one has put in my path, not to complete the task, the Lord has been my Ebenezer.

Chapter Forty-Two

"Lord, You have been our dwelling place throughout all generations." Psalm 90:1

"He is my help in ages past..." I know He holds the future.

"Jesus Love me This i Know"

Do you my friend, know the origin of that children's song: "Jesus Loves Me This I Know?" i once heard about it's origin on a Christian radio station. By the way, i want to share the importance of listening to a Christian radio broadcast. My dear sister-in-Christ, Rachel, would listen to Christian radio in her home daily. i was very impressed, and like her, i continue to listen each and every day, either at home or in our car; it is a blessing to hear the Word of God over radio.

Going back to the song, it seems it was written prior to the Great Depression, by two, once very wealthy, sisters, as a poem. It caught on quickly and musical notes were added; thus we have this precious song; Jesus Love Me This I Know. It is so true; He loves us all, red and yellow, black and white, we are precious in His sight. That's another lovely song for His children. If anything comes across to you my friend in this book, the main thing is, for you to become His child. i pray you have made the decision to become His child. Refer to **John 1:12**. The choice is yours. Remember, God has no grandchildren.

As i write this final chapter of "Our" book, i want to share a little bit about my beginnings in Santa Clara Valley/Silicon Valley, where my life began those many years ago.

What was, and is Silicon Valley? Sixty plus years ago it was a beautiful rich garden, probably much like the Garden of Eden we read about in Scripture, with wonderful fresh tree ripened fruit and garden fresh vegetables. Fruit trees of apricots, prunes, cherries, pears, walnuts, and almonds were in abundance. Dark rich soil to grow a variety of farm fresh vegetables. It was known throughout the world as the land of fruits and nuts, the food basket of the world.

Today, it is known for the world of technology, due to the discovery of the computer chip. There, in Silicon Valley, came the inventions that led to radio, television, computers and modern technology. It is truly a different world than what it stood for in the past.

Just as with many things in life, my beloved Santa Clara Valley/Silicon Valley has changed and continues to change, for me, and many who grew up and knew it as it was, with all the fragrant blossoms in the springtime, to the luscious tree ripened fruit in the summer. Now it is the center of technology for the entire world. And to think i grew up in this world-renowned place, amazing!!! Who would know, but the Lord.

This change i do not choose to live with, as many do, for a better life. Oh, i realize people move there in hopes of making more money and for some, to seek a fortune. It is one of the most sought after places in the world. But the Bible says, **"What good is it for a man to gain the whole world, yet forfeit his soul?" Mark 8:36**. That's not for me, as the Word says, **"But as for me and my house we will serve the Lord." Joshua 14:15c.**

i instead, choose to enter a place that will never change: heaven, our final home for those who have invited Jesus Christ into their hearts and life. What is heaven like? It has a river flowing from the throne of God, trees bearing fruit, streets paved with transparent gold, no tears, no sorrow, peace beyond measure. There is life forever and ever, in the presence of God, Jesus and the Holy Spirit, the angels, and our loved ones, who have gone before us. What a wonderful, magnificent life. There's so much more, i tried to capture some of it in "Our" Heaven book. You can check it out on "Our" website: christianbooks4children.com, if you are interested. What will you choose my friend? The choice is yours: Jesus paid the penalty for our sins. Will it be life forever in heaven, or death and eternal damnation?

Johann Sebastian Bach, who began his work by writing, "JJ"---Jesu, "Jesus, help me"---on his manuscript. That is the universal prayer for all writers. At the end of a piece he would write three letters---- S.D.G. or Soli Deo gloria, which means "To the glory of God." i have prayed each time i worked on this book. Jesus did help me. i re-affirm with Johann Sebastian Bach, as i conclude this book; **"To the glory of God."**

Interesting, i have concluded "Our" book with my name, gloria; **"TO THE GLORY OF GOD."** A German composer wrote the words. My husband, Siegfried, is German, yet not a composer. Is the Lord's mighty hand on "Our" book? A definite **YES! "TO THE GLORY OF GOD." IN JESUS NAME, AMEN.**

Conclusion

Some of you have asked what has happened to my five siblings. i will share a little about them and their lives. First, i want to say, the Lord has kept us together these many years, and part of the reason, as i shared in the book is, our loving Mother. As ewe may recall after her death, when i was getting her few things in order, i found in her purse little pieces of paper. On each piece of paper, was written in order, (us), her five children. i believe she used those notes as a constant reminder to pray for her children, we and all of her family were her life. She would tell me time and time again, "No, matter what happens you children, stick together." With that in mind, here goes with my siblings.

My oldest sister, Josephine has been married to her hubby for over fifty years now. They have two sons and one daughter, and all are married. The oldest son and wife have a son and daughter, in Southern California. Their second son and wife, have one son. Their daughter and husband have two sons and one daughter. They all reside in Redding, California. The second son resides in the Bay Area. My sister and hubby own and operate a welding business, and are very involved in their children's lives, church and community. They are very devout Christians and are dear to Fred and my heart.

My second sister, Barbara Ann, and her hubby Richard, recently moved to the Oregon Coast. They have been married over thirty years and have a little puppy. Barbara is retired from being an entertainer and nail tech. She is very gifted with her hands in decorating; like our Mama, loves plants. She has had some health issues in which she knows the Lord has healed her. We PRAISE AND THANK HIM FOR HIS HEALING TOUCH ON BARBARA. She is my prayer warrior. Her hubby works with designing golf courses, as a result, they have lived in areas like, Arizona, the Orient, Cyprus, in the Middle East, Panama, Mexico and Canada, to name a few. They too, are very dear to our hearts, and we love spending time with them.

My third sister, Frances Jean (same middle name as mine), and her hubby, Don, have been married over fifty years. They are retired from the carpeting business and have a lovely home in Redding, California. Frances has a great love for flowers and plants, like our Mama, and her home shows her love. She and Don must spend many wonderful hours caring for what the Lord has blessed them with. They know and see through these plants, the love Jesus has for them. They have a married son, and with his wife, together, have five children. He has another son, married and they have two children. So my sister is a great grandmother. (Doesn't seem possible). They have a daughter, who is very loving and cherishes them. They all reside in Redding. We love them all very much as well.

My brother, Frank, is the oldest of mom's two sons. He and his former wife have two sons and one daughter. Mama would tell me in her later years, "Of all my children, i never thought Frank would be here for me." He has a wonderful heart of compassion and love, and knows Jesus loves him. Frank is a licensed building contractor, and, as i mentioned before, he is more than a contractor. The Lord has gifted him in design and know-how, and he has such an appreciation for his work. His work is outstanding. He has taught his sons the trade as well. Frank loves to fish, motorcycle ride, has a hot rod that he just finished revamping; it looks great. He is much like our father, who was fascinated with engines and working on them. Frank too, is like mom in his love for plants. His home in Redding is an array of his artistic work in and around the home, adorned with plants. His oldest son is married with three sons. His second son works most of the time, with Frank. His daughter is an expert esthetician, married and she and her hubby have a son and daughter.

My youngest brother, Bill or William (named after our father), has been married to Deannie for over thirty years. Bill recently retired from teaching for many years. He was more than a teacher; he took many of his students under his wing (in their home), and mentored them, spiritually and physically. He and Deannie have a great love for the Lord and serving Him. They both love sports, particularly running and competing in races. Bill is a great athlete, as i mentioned before, he earned a scholarship to Sacramento State University for running. Bill and Deannie spend a great deal of time in the Bible and have taught many Bible Studies. Deannie is an outstanding nurse. They have two married daughters, and they, along with their son-in-laws, love the Lord, and each has been blessed with a girl and a boy. Since, we had no daughters, i think of them as the daughters we never had. Bill i believe, thinks of our son, Jeff, as the son he never had. The oldest daughter is also a licensed Cosmetologist. i remember asking her, "Why she chose Cosmetology?" Her answer was, "When i was little, Auntie gloria, don't ewe remember as i watched ewe doing hair in your styling chair, i said, 'Someday, i am going to do that.'" That touched my heart. The Lord has blessed her with a good, understanding Christian man. The younger daughter is a teacher, like her Dad. Her hubby is a good God-fearing man as well.

Our family is truly blessed by God the Father, the Holy Spirit and Jesus Christ our Lord and Savior. We love our new home and our church family, "Glory Bound Fellowship," and Pastor Dennis and Susie Baskin.

The Story Goes On

It was a typical hot, humid summer in 1936, when she almost bled to death giving birth to her first born. He was a handsome son, with reddish hair like his paternal grandfather, which would be a hindrance, as he grew older. Having reddish hair was very rare for a boy, let alone brothers, growing up in war torn Germany. But it made them both strong and great defenders, which would pay off later in life. The war was just beginning on their Country, and they had to be tough. Then, at ages two and one, their father would be hospitalized for a year. He had been a gifted wood carver. Now Mom or Mutti, had to work during his hospitalization, in order to feed, clothe and house she and her small sons...

To be continued. Look for this new book about Fred next year. Aufwiedersehen!

Notes

Chapter 2 page 23

1. "This is one of the most fertile of the many small valleys of the coast;..."
John Muir. Old and New 1872-1893. Re-walking John Muir's 1868 trip from
San Francisco to Yosemite: Trans-California Ramble 11 Santa Clara Valley.
Rambles of a Botanist 1872.

Chapter 10 page 78

2. Apple® Inc. Technology Company Apple® Inc. is an American
multinational company headquartered in Cupertino, California that designs,
develops, and sells consumer software, online service, and personal
computers. Wikipedia

Chapter 10 page 84

3. Stonecroft Ministries
Stonecroft.org-- Reaching women with the Gospel where they are, as they
are.

Chapter 11 page 89

4. From Wikipedia, the free encyclopedia **"Tear down this wall!"** was the
challenge issued by United States President Ronald Reagan to Soviet Union
leader Mikhail Gorbachev to destroy the Berlin Wall, in a speech at the
Brandenburg Gate near the Berlin Wall on June 12, 1987, commemorating

the 750th anniversary of Berlin.[1][2] Reagan challenged Gorbachev, who was then the General Secretary of the Communist Party of the Soviet Union, to tear it down as an emblem of Gorbachev's desire to increase freedom in the Eastern Bloc through *glasnost*

("transparency") and *perestroika* ("restructuring").

Chapter 12 page 110

5. Quotable quote C.S. Lewis "Isn't it funny how day by day nothing changes, but when you look back, everything is different..."

— C.S. Lewis

Chapter 12 page 113

6.   The Doobie Brothers are an American rock band. The group has sold more than 40 million albums worldwide throughout their career. The band has been active in five decades, with their biggest success occurring in the 1970s. Wikipedia

Chapter 16 page 132

7. Calaveras Telephone Company

Family owned and operated Calaveras Telephone Company has pursued a path

of providing customers with innovative service since 1895 when 16- year-old

James A. Tower using barbed wire fencing, strung the first telephone line

for what was to become the Calaveras Telephone Company.

In 1899, Mr. Tower personally negotiated with Alexander Graham Bell to get equipment and a connection agreement with Bell's Pacific Telephone Company

that connected Calaveras customers' telephones with the rest of the world.

Chapter 21 page 144,144/167

8, 9 and 10. Dare to Discipline   by James Dobson, P.H.D. James C. Dobson, Ph.D., is founder and chairman emeritus of Focus on the Family, a non-profit, multimedia organization with a global reach. As founder, Dr. Dobson's vision and philosophical perspectives shaped Focus on the Family at its inception and supplied the impetus for its outreach for the first three decades of its existence. Even though a new generation of leadership now bears responsibility for carrying out the ministry's mission, Dr. Dobson's influence remains significant.

Chapter 21 page 175

11. See You at the Pole (SYATP) is an annual gathering of Christian students at a flagpole in front of their local school for prayer, scripture-reading and worship, during the early morning before school starts. The American SYATP events occur on the 23 of September at 7:00 A.M. while gathering around a school flag pole. The events began in 1990 in the United States, where public schools cannot sponsor prayers and some Christians see public schools as hostile to Christian students. It has grown by word of mouth, announcements at youth rallies and churches, and the Internet. It is now an international event.

12. From Wikipedia the free encyclopedia

Suzanna Wesley

Susanna Wesley (20 January 1669 – 23 July 1742), born **Susanna Annesley**, was the daughter of Dr. Samuel Annesley and Mary White, and the mother of John and Charles Wesley.

"...although she never preached a sermon or published a book or founded a church, (she) is known as the Mother of Methodism. Why? Because two of her sons, John Wesley and Charles Wesley, as children consciously or unconsciously will, applied the example and teachings and circumstances of their home life."

Chapter 21 page 178

13.   Arnold Schwarzenegger Former Governor of California **Arnold Alois Schwarzenegger is an Austrian-American actor, model, producer, director, activist, businessman, investor, writer, philanthropist, former professional bodybuilder, and politician. Wikipedia**

Chapter 22 page 189

14. ProudtoBeAnAmerican **Artist:** Lee Greenwood
Album: American Patriot Released: 1992 **Lyrics: And I gladly stand up next to you / And defend her still today / 'Cause there ain't no doubt I love this land / God bless the U.S.A**

 Chapter 22 page 189,189

15 and 16. Attempted shooting of President Ronald Reagan

.Attempted assassination of Ronald Reagan - Wikipedia, the ...

https://en.wikipedia.org/.../Attempted_assassination_of_**Ronald**...

Wikipedia

Chapter 23 page 230

17. It's a Wonderful Life It's a Wonderful Life - Wikipedia, the free

encyclopedia

https://en.wikipedia.org/wiki/**It's_a_Wonderful_Life** Wikipedia**It's a**

Wonderful Life is a 1946 American Christmas fantasy comedy-drama film

produced and directed by Frank Capra, based on the short story "The

Greatest ... Donna Reed - Frank Capra - George Bailey - Henry Travers

Chapter 23 page 236

18. The Battle of the Bulge **The Battle of the Bulge (16 December 1944 –**

25 January 1945) was a major German offensive campaign launched

through the densely forested Ardennes region of Wallonia in Belgium,

France, and Luxembourg on the Western Front toward the end of

World War II in Europe. Battle of the Bulge - Wikipedia, the free

encyclopedia https://en.wikipedia.org/wiki/**Battle_of_the_Bulge**Wikipedia

Chapter 24 page 252

19. Harriet Beecher Stowe Harriet Beecher Stowe's Life

https://www.harrietbeecherstowecenter.org/... Harriet Beecher Stowe

House Life of **Harriet Beecher Stowe**, best selling author of the anti-slavery novel Uncle Tom's Cabin.

Chapter 24 page 253

20. Charles Monroe Schulz, nicknamed Sparky, was an American cartoonist, best known for the comic strip Peanuts. Wikipedia

Chapter 24 page 256

21. Betty BoopCartoon character Betty Boop is an animated cartoon character created by Max Fleischer, with help from animators including Grim Natwick. Wikipedia

Chapter 24 page 269,269,269

22, 23 and 24 Apple® Store Retail-store company
The Apple® Retail Store is a chain of retail stores owned and operated by Apple® Inc.,dealing in computers and consumer electronics. Wikipedia

25792001R00239

Made in the USA
San Bernardino, CA
12 November 2015